W9-DDI-229

SOLIDWORKS® 2010

NO EXPERIENCE REQUIRED™

SOLIDWORKS® 2010
NO EXPERIENCE REQUIRED™

Alex Ruiz
with Gabi Jack

WILEY

Wiley Publishing, Inc.

Senior Acquisitions Editor: Willem Knibbe
Development Editor: Susan Herman
Technical Editor: Ricky Jordan
Production Editor: Angela Smith
Copy Editor: Kim Wimpsett
Editorial Manager: Pete Gaughan
Production Manager: Tim Tate
Vice President and Executive Group Publisher: Richard Swadley
Vice President and Publisher: Neil Edde
Book Designer: Franz Baumhackl
Compositor: James D. Kramer, Happenstance Type-O-Rama
Proofreader: Publication Services
Indexer: Ted Laux
Project Coordinator, Cover: Lynsey Stanford
Cover Designer: Ryan Sneed
Cover Image: Alex Ruiz

Copyright © 2010 by Wiley Publishing, Inc., Indianapolis, Indiana

Published simultaneously in Canada

ISBN: 978-0-470-50543-4

No part of this publication may be reproduced, stored in a retrieval system, or transmitted in any form or by any means, electronic, mechanical, photocopying, recording, scanning or otherwise, except as permitted under Sections 107 or 108 of the 1976 United States Copyright Act, without either the prior written permission of the Publisher, or authorization through payment of the appropriate per-copy fee to the Copyright Clearance Center, 222 Rosewood Drive, Danvers, MA 01923, (978) 750-8400, fax (978) 646-8600. Requests to the Publisher for permission should be addressed to the Permissions Department, John Wiley & Sons, Inc., 111 River Street, Hoboken, NJ 07030, (201) 748-6011, fax (201) 748-6008, or online at http://www.wiley.com/go/permissions.

Limit of Liability/Disclaimer of Warranty: The publisher and the author make no representations or warranties with respect to the accuracy or completeness of the contents of this work and specifically disclaim all warranties, including without limitation warranties of fitness for a particular purpose. No warranty may be created or extended by sales or pro-motional materials. The advice and strategies contained herein may not be suitable for every situation. This work is sold with the understanding that the publisher is not engaged in rendering legal, accounting, or other professional services. If professional assistance is required, the services of a competent professional person should be sought. Neither the pub-lisher nor the author shall be liable for damages arising herefrom. The fact that an organization or Web site is referred to in this work as a citation and/or a potential source of further information does not mean that the author or the publisher endorses the information the organization or Web site may provide or recommendations it may make. Further, readers should be aware that Internet Web sites listed in this work may have changed or disappeared between when this work was written and when it is read.

For general information on our other products and services or to obtain technical support, please contact our Customer Care Department within the U.S. at (877) 762-2974, outside the U.S. at (317) 572-3993 or fax (317) 572-4002.

Wiley also publishes its books in a variety of electronic formats. Some content that appears in print may not be available in electronic books.

Library of Congress Cataloging-in-Publication Data

Ruiz, Alex, 1974-
 SolidWorks 2010 : no experience required / Alex Ruiz. — 1st ed.
   p. cm.
 ISBN-13: 978-0-470-50543-4 (cloth)
 ISBN-10: 0-470-50543-5 (cloth)
 1. Computer graphics. 2. Engineering graphics. 3. SolidWorks. 4. Computer-aided design. I. Title.
 T385.R855 2010
 620'.00420285536—dc22
                              2009052155

TRADEMARKS: Wiley, the Wiley logo, and the Sybex logo are trademarks or registered trademarks of John Wiley & Sons, Inc. and/or its affiliates, in the United States and other countries, and may not be used without written permission. SolidWorks is a registered trademark of Dassault Systemes SolidWorks Corporation. All other trademarks are the property of their respec-tive owners. Wiley Publishing, Inc., is not associated with any product or vendor mentioned in this book.

10 9 8 7 6 5 4 3 2 1

Dear Reader,

Thank you for choosing *SolidWorks 2010: No Experience Required*. This book is part of a family of premium-quality Sybex books, all of which are written by outstanding authors who combine practical experience with a gift for teaching.

Sybex was founded in 1976. More than 30 years later, we're still committed to producing consistently exceptional books. With each of our titles, we're working hard to set a new standard for the industry. From the paper we print on, to the authors we work with, our goal is to bring you the best books available.

I hope you see all that reflected in these pages. I'd be very interested to hear your comments and get your feedback on how we're doing. Feel free to let me know what you think about this or any other Sybex book by sending me an email at nedde@wiley.com. If you think you've found a technical error in this book, please visit **http://sybex.custhelp.com**. Customer feedback is critical to our efforts at Sybex.

Best regards,

Neil Edde
Vice President and Publisher
Sybex, an Imprint of Wiley

To my wife Griselda and my children,
Orion, Ian, Venus, and Maya.
—Alex R. Ruiz

Acknowledgments

I am forever grateful to all those who contributed to the publication of this book. It all started with a fellow blogger, Donnie Gladfelter (the CAD Geek), introducing me to Lynn Haller. Lynn would eventually become my agent, and she helped me work with acquisitions editor Willem Knibbe. Willem was the driving force behind this book, and without his hard work and encouragement, you would not be reading this now.

My good friend and fellow SolidWorks blogger, Ricky Jordan, served as the technical editor. With his advanced knowledge of SolidWorks, Ricky ensured that every step of the tutorial was the best possible way to complete the project. Susan Herman served as the developmental editor, and she kept track of all my submissions and updates. Without her, the book would not have progressed as well as it did. Angela Smith was the senior production editor, and she and her team helped with the language and syntax. With their help, I sound smarter than I actually am in real life. Gabi Jack, another SolidWorks blogger and someone who has become a good friend over the years, helped me immensely when I fell behind schedule. She came into the project and helped write a few of the chapters. Without her, I don't know what would have happened to this project.

I am also very appreciative of the help and support of the amazing people at SolidWorks, including Matthew West and Nancy Buchino. Everybody at SolidWorks was more than helpful, and they all went out of their way to provide me with all the support I needed in writing this book. I cannot mention SolidWorks without a tip of the hat to the amazing SolidWorks community of users and bloggers. The community was always quick to give their opinions and share their expertise whenever I became stuck on a problem.

I would also like to thank my close friend and boss, Matthew Wixey. Without his support and understanding, I would have never had the time to write this book. Most bosses would not have been so flexible, and I am grateful.

I also want to thank the rest of the team at Wiley. Everybody has worked so hard to get this book to print, and I am humbled to be supported by such a team. I look forward to working with everybody again on future updates of this book.

Finally, I want to thank you, the reader. I hope you find this book not only educational but also enjoyable. I hope you have as much fun using this book as I had writing it.

—Alex R. Ruiz

About the Authors

Alex R. Ruiz is a Certified SolidWorks Professional (CSWP) and engineering manager for a leading medical device manufacturer. He designs new products and trains and supports more than 100 SolidWorks users. Alex has close ties to the development team and is very well known in the SolidWorks community as the SolidWorks Geek, which is the name of his blog (**www.TheSWGeek.com**).

  Gabi Jack is a Certified SolidWorks Professional and mechanical engineer who maintains a popular blog about solid modeling, design, and engineering (**www.GabiJack.com**).

Contents at a Glance

CONTENTS

CHAPTER 6   Creating a Subassembly   233

CHAPTER 7   Creating a Simple Assembly Drawing   263

CHAPTER 17   **Creating Simple, Stunning Renderings**   **545**

FOREWORD

Do you really want to read a Foreword? Really? If I were you, I'd be skipping to the chapter on creating impressive looking surfaces, but since you're here, I've got something really important to say to you. You are living in an amazing time. Way more amazing than the last "amazing time" someone told you about. This is the year you are learning SolidWorks. There's a lot to be said about taking that on, but I'll whittle it down to this: You're in for a ride.

When people go about learning a 3D modeling application like SolidWorks there's a hesitation that simmers in the idea that there's just way too much to learn. It's true. There is too much to learn—in one day. However, just as languages have a set of commonly used words, so too does SolidWorks have a set of commonly used features. Features which, after a week of practicing using this book, will give you all the abilities needed to introduce SolidWorks to your team, verify a design, get a better job, or create a new idea. I imagine one of those abilities is going to be very important for you over the coming years. What's even more important is how you start gaining those abilities.

You could have started modeling 3D geometry 15 years ago when SolidWorks first came on the scene. You actually may have, but don't kick yourself if you didn't. Over those past 15 years, developing products in 3D has changed immensely. SolidWorks has been a big part of making that happen. I've seen the program gain an enormous feature set that has expanded from basic modeling features to complex assembly and surface design with added functionality for rich simulation and motion analysis. It is a program that spans an increasing number of industries and disciplines. With all of that it truly becomes a program which, in the right hands, would turn a capable person like yourself into a modeling genius. That's the potential you have starting right now. Plus, you're not alone. I've seen the user base grow to become one of the largest in the mechanical design communities in the world. People from around the world interact daily within online resources spanning video tutorials and model data across a growing number of web sites, blogs, and forums. If you want to model it in SolidWorks, there's likely someone out there doing it.

So, you probably get the idea that there's a lot of information out there about SolidWorks. It can get distracting and overwhelming. So, I want to give you a challenge. Focus intently on this book for a week with all the passion you can muster. Write in the margins, highlight the text, and apply each topic to what you design. This is it where it gets real. This is where you start to not only learn more about how to master SolidWorks, but also how to apply what you can do with SolidWorks daily to expanding your career. Many times the only thing missing is the right book. I'm convinced this book, is that book. So now, you have a great program, a great book, and a challenge to complete. You won't be disappointed.

—Josh Mings
  SolidSmack.com

INTRODUCTION

Whether you are a new user of SolidWorks or a professional who wants to improve your skills, this book was written for you. Learning any software can be difficult at times. You launch the software for the first time, and you feel overwhelmed, not knowing how to even start a new document. In 3D CAD programs, it can be especially difficult. Many times a whole new vocabulary and a whole new creative environment are introduced.

In this book, you will learn how to use the software—it covers everything from what you see when you open SolidWorks for the first time to 3D solid modeling and to how to create high-resolution renderings of the desk-top lamp that you will create by following the examples. With plain-English step-by-step tutorials, you will create 3D parts, assemblies, and drawings. Not only will you learn how to create models and drawings, but you will be introduced to some of the reasons why certain techniques are used and how to put them to use in your daily job.

As with previous releases, SolidWorks 2010 has introduced many new tools and commands to make your daily life easier. You will be introduced to the new tools in parts, assemblies, and drawings, including the new mouse gesture support, the changes to reference planes, the Dimension Palette in drawings, and many more. You will also learn how to create various templates and how to customize your workspace, all meant to increase your productivity. Although many of the more advanced modeling techniques are not covered in this book, any level of user will still be able to find something new about the software.

At the end of it all, you'll use the model of the lamp to create photorealistic renderings using the newly updated PhotoView 360. In 2010, PhotoView 360 was updated with even more tools to create renderings rivaling that of PhotoWorks. With new ways of controlling scenes, support for background images and custom environments, and new camera effects, you can create images that bring your models to life. As with all the chapters in the book, you will learn how to create your own images with step-by-step tutorials.

What You Will Learn in This Book

Each chapter was written to gradually introduce new tools and concepts as the design progresses. Each subsequent chapter will describe progressively more advanced techniques. Specifically, the book is structured as follows:

Chapter 1 describes the SolidWorks user interface, including the menus and toolbars, the CommandManager, the FeatureManager design tree. You'll also learn about ways to improve productivity with shortcut keys and mouse gestures.

In **Chapter 2**, you will learn the basics of using SolidWorks, including the various document types, how they relate to each other, and how parts, assemblies, and drawings are created.

In **Chapter 3**, you will create your first 3D model of the lamp base. You will learn how to create a fully defined sketch and how to use it to create extrusions that form the model.

In **Chapter 4**, using the model created in Chapter 3, you will create a 2D drawing suitable for manufacturing using a variety of drawing methods, including importing annotations from the model, using the Dimension Palette to tolerance a dimension, and creating various drawing view types.

Chapter 5 will demonstrate how to create the shaft for the lamp base by using a revolved feature.

Chapter 6 will continue to explore the revolve command to create a washer and washer cover for the lamp shade. Then, after creating the two models, you will learn how to create your first assembly, and you will be introduced to assembly mates.

In **Chapter 7**, using the assembly created in Chapter 6, you will create an assembly drawing and learn the basics of how to use a bill of materials (BOM).

In **Chapter 8**, you will learn even more modeling techniques, including how to create a swept feature, add reference planes, and use mirrored features. You will even learn how to create a modeled thread on the part.

Chapter 9 will show you how to create in-context models within a subassembly when you create the lamp's shade. More assembly mates will then be demonstrated when you create multiple configurations to define the shade's positions.

Chapter 10 will demonstrate some of the methods used to modify existing SolidWorks documents using a variety of techniques.

In **Chapters 11** and **12**, you will put everything together to create the top-level assembly of the desk lamp. After creating the assembly, you will learn how to add a BOM to the environment as well as create an exploded view of the top-level assembly to see how it all goes together.

Chapter 13 will show you how to create the final drawing for the desk lamp project and some additional drawing techniques meant to increase productivity.

In **Chapter 14**, you will learn various techniques for sharing your model and drawings with other users, manufactures, vendors, and sales teams.

Chapters 15 and **16** will describe the process for creating your own templates in SolidWorks.

Chapter 17 will introduce you to PhotoView 360 and will show you how to create photorealistic renderings of the desk lamp using new enhancements in the rendering software.

At the end of the book is a glossary of terms that are used in the book and that are related to SolidWorks and mechanical design, followed by an index.

Files on the Website

A few exercises in this book require additional files such as templates, tables, and some models not created in the exercise. The entire project including each part, assembly, and drawing is also available for download. You can download the accompanying files from this book's page on Sybex's website at **www.sybex.com/go/solidworks2010ner**. Click the Downloads button on that page to access the files. You can also find the same files as well as additional content, forums, and more examples at **www.swner.com**.

How to Contact the Author

I welcome feedback from you about this book or about books you'd like to see from me in the future. You can reach me by writing to **alexruiz@theswgeek.com**. For more information about my work, please visit my website at **www.theswgeek.com**.

Sybex strives to keep you supplied with the latest tools and information you need for your work. Please check its website at **www.sybex.com**, where we'll post additional content and updates that supplement this book if the need arises. Enter SolidWorks in the Search box (or type the book's ISBN—9780470505434), and click Go to get to the book's update page.

CHAPTER 1

Becoming Familiar with SolidWorks

- ▶ Start SolidWorks
- ▶ Navigate the SolidWorks Interface
- ▶ Use the CommandManager
- ▶ Use and Customize the Menus
- ▶ Use Toolbars
- ▶ Use the Keyboard
- ▶ Use the Mouse

SolidWorks 2010 is one of the most popular 3D mechanical computer-aided design (CAD) packages on the market today. Since its introduction in 1995, SolidWorks has become a favorite design tool for many of today's engineers, mechanical designers, and industrial designers. In part because of its easy-to-learn graphical user interface and powerful set of tools, SolidWorks is used by many top companies worldwide to design, engineer, and document their products in a variety of fields.

At the core of SolidWorks is the ability to create parametric 3D solid geometry that is then used to create drawings, manufacturing instructions, instruction manuals, animations, full-color renderings, and other types of documentation. Regardless of the complexity of the item being created, the creation process is easy and follows the same basic steps. First a *sketch* is created that is turned into a *base feature*. The base feature is then further refined by adding features that add or remove material from the base feature. Individual *part models* can then be used to build *assemblies* that represent the final design. After creating the 3D part or assembly models, *drawings* are made to document the design and manufacturing process.

Learning a new CAD package can be a daunting task. In addition to the new terminology, first-time users may feel a bit overwhelmed with a new user interface, toolbars, and commands. In this chapter, you will spend some time launching SolidWorks for the first time, becoming familiar with the SolidWorks interface, and working with the CommandManager.

Start SolidWorks

Before installing and running SolidWorks for the first time, ensure that you meet the recommended minimum system requirements. SolidWorks currently supports the following operating systems:

▶ Windows 7 (32-bit) Professional, Ultimate or Enterprise Edition.

▶ Windows 7 (64-bit) Professional, Ultimate or Enterprise Edition.

▶ Windows Vista (64-bit) Ultimate, Business, or Enterprise edition, SP0 or newer

▶ Windows Vista (32-bit) Ultimate, Business, or Enterprise edition, SP0 or newer

▶ Windows XP Professional (32-bit), SP2 or newer

▶ Windows XP Professional (64-bit)

And here are the random-access memory (RAM) requirements:

Minimum 1GB RAM when parts contain fewer than 200 features and assemblies contain fewer than 1,000 components

Recommended 2GB RAM or more when parts contain more than 200 features and assemblies contain more than 1,000 components

Once you have verified that your computer is able to support SolidWorks and it is installed onto your system, you can launch it by selecting Start ➢ Programs ➢ SolidWorks 2010 ➢ SolidWorks 2010 SPX.X ➢ SolidWorks 2010.

 N O T E All images in this book are from SolidWorks running on Windows 7. You might notice a slight difference if you are using another version of windows such as Windows XP.

SolidWorks License Agreement

The first time you launch SolidWorks, you will be presented with the SolidWorks License Agreement. You must accept the license agreement in order to use SolidWorks. After reading the license, click Accept to continue. If for some reason you do not accept the terms of the license agreement, clicking Do Not Accept will exit SolidWorks.

Help and Workflow Customization

After accepting the SolidWorks License Agreement, you will then be presented with the Welcome To SolidWorks window. This screen allows you to customize the appearance of dynamic help as well as the workflow. You will see this only the first time you launch SolidWorks on your computer, but you can make changes to the options anytime you want in the SolidWorks Options window.

Three options are available in the Help Customization section of the screen. Each option will provide the user with a different level of dynamic help, so consider your needs when making your selection.

I Am A New User. Show Quick Tips To Help Me Get Started. This option will provide you with pop-up messages that appear while working in different modes of SolidWorks.

I Am New To This Version Of SolidWorks. Show Me Interactive What's New Help. Experienced SolidWorks users will find this option helpful when they are working in a new version of SolidWorks. When this option is selected, a question-mark icon will be displayed on new menu items and new and changed PropertyManagers and will link to the corresponding sections of the What's New manual. The topics in the What's New manual will then provide more information about the new or updated functionality since the previous release.

Do Not Show Me Any Dynamic Help.   For more experienced users, this option will not provide you with any pop-ups or links to the What's New manual while working in SolidWorks.

 N O T E As you become more familiar with working in SolidWorks, you may decide to disable the Quick Tips. You can disable them by selecting Help ➣ Quick Tips or by clicking the question-mark icon in the status bar. After becoming familiar with the updates made to the new release of SolidWorks, you can disable the display of the link by selecting Help ➣ Interactive What's New.

The *Workflow Customization* section of the Welcome To SolidWorks window allows you to hide and display tools, links, and menus items based on your usage of SolidWorks. You can select one, two, all, or none of the following categories:

▶ Machine Design

▶ Mold Design

▶ Consumer Product Design

When you select an option in the Workflow Customization section of the window, the following changes will occur in your part document environment:

Machine Design   The Machine Design Overview, Machine Design Tutorials, and SolidWorks SimulationXpress links will be displayed on the SolidWorks Resources tab of the task pane. Sheet Metal and Weldments tabs will be added to the CommandManager. The Molds menu item will be hidden in the Insert menu. Draft Analysis, Undercut Detection, and Deviation Analysis will also be hidden in the Tools menu.

Mold Design   The Mold Design Overview, Mold Design Tutorials, and Import File links will be displayed on the SolidWorks Resource tab of the task pane. Surfaces and Molds tabs will be added to the CommandManager. The Weldments menu item will be hidden in the Insert menu.

Consumer Product Design   A Consumer Product Tutorials link will be displayed on the SolidWorks Resources tab of the task pane. The Surfaces tab will be added to the CommandManager. The Weldments menu item will be hidden in the Insert menu. The Undercut Detection menu item will be hidden in the Tools menu.

N O T E You can adjust your workflow customization at any time while in a part file by selecting Tools ➤ Customize and select the Options tab. In the Work flow Customization section, select or deselect the appropriate options.

For the sake of the project being demonstrated in this book, in the Welcome To SolidWorks window select the following:

1. In the Help Customization section, select Do Not Show Me Any Dynamic Help.

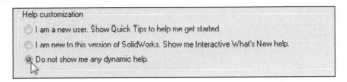

2. In the Work flow Customization section, select Consumer Product Design, Machine Design, and Mold Design.

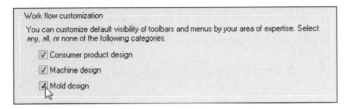

3. Click OK.

Navigate the SolidWorks Interface

Before using SolidWorks, you should become familiar with the layout of the user interface. Each of the three *document types* in SolidWorks (parts, assemblies, and drawings) has the same basic interface with a few minor differences. To start, we will examine the common elements of the three document types. Figure 1.1 shows the SolidWorks interface when you have a part model open.

Graphics Area

The place where all the action takes place in SolidWorks is the *graphics area*. Here you will be modeling your parts, putting together your assemblies, and creating your drawings. You will be exploring this area in a lot more detail in Chapter 2, "Learning the Basics," when we cover the three document types in more detail.

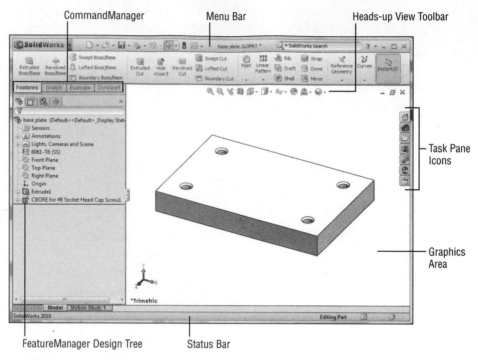

FIGURE 1.1 SolidWorks 2010 user interface

Heads-up View Toolbar

At the top of the graphics area is the *Heads-up View toolbar*. This transparent toolbar is always available at the top of your graphics area, giving you quick and easy access to the tools necessary to manipulate your views. Icons that display a small downward-pointing arrow provide you with more tools in a flyout, as shown in Figure 1.2.

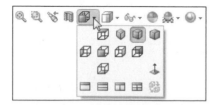

FIGURE 1.2 Flyout menu showing additional tools

As you become more comfortable in SolidWorks, you may discover that the tools available on the Heads-up View toolbar may not be what you use most often. The view tools shown by default are not the only tools that are available for the toolbar. To customize the Heads-up View toolbar, do the following:

1. Right-click any of the buttons shown in the Heads-up View toolbar, and select Customize from near the bottom of the menu.

2. Select the Commands tab at the top of the Customize window.

3. In the Categories section of the window, locate your desired tool set. For this example, select Standard Views in the Categories section. The tools included in the selected category will be displayed in the Buttons section, as shown in Figure 1.3.

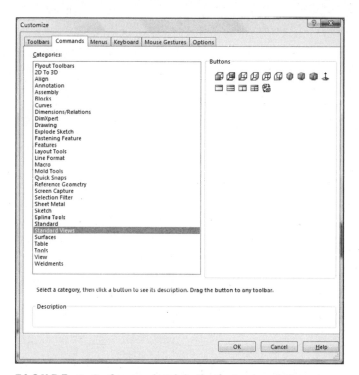

FIGURE 1.3 Commands tab in the Customize window

4. Drag the desired button in the Customize window to the top of the Heads-up View toolbar. When the mouse pointer changes to include a green plus, drop the button there.

N O T E The Heads-up View toolbar can be hidden in SolidWorks 2010. To hide the toolbar, right-click any button in the toolbar, and deselect View (Heads-Up) in the menu.

Status Bar

Along the bottom of the SolidWorks interface is the *status bar*. As the name suggests, the status bar will give you information about the actions you are performing in SolidWorks. The status bar can be turned off in the View menu, but we strongly recommend leaving it on since it can prove to be extremely useful while you work. Here are some examples of the information that you can find in the status bar:

▶ As you hover over a tool, the status bar will often provide you with a better description than what the tooltips will normally provide (see Figure 1.4). When you become familiar with the icons for the various tools in SolidWorks, you will require this information less often.

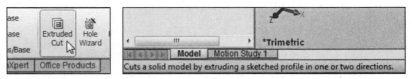

FIGURE 1.4 Additional tool information displayed in the status bar

▶ Selecting on an edge, point, or any combination of these will display basic measurements for quick reference, as shown in Figure 1.5. This should not replace the Measure tool, but it can be extremely helpful when you are just looking for a quick idea of the distance between two edges.

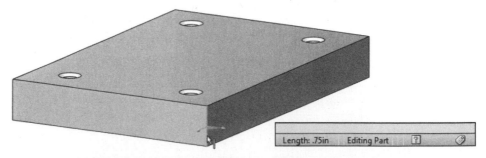

FIGURE 1.5 Quick way to show measurements in the status bar

▶ As you work in a sketch, the coordinates for your mouse pointer location will be displayed as well as the status of your sketch. The sketch status will be displayed as Fully Defined, Over Defined, Under Defined,

No Solution Found, or Invalid Solution Found. We will be covering what each of these means later when we start working sketches.

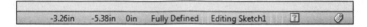

Task Pane

On the right side of the graphics area is the *task pane*. The task pane is a set of windows that provides a number of resources in one location. Normally, the task pane is hidden, and the tab icons are the only thing visible in the graphics area. This is probably the best option since real estate in your graphics area is very valuable. However, if you prefer to have the task pane always open, you can do the following:

1. Click any of the task pane tab icons.

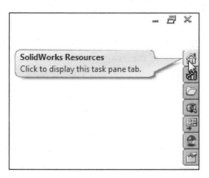

2. On the top right of the task pane, click the pushpin icon to "pin open" the task pane (see Figure 1.6).

3. The graphics will adjust to make room for the task pane, and it will remain open even as you click elsewhere in SolidWorks.

4. To set the task pane to autohide once again, click the pushpin icon.

FIGURE 1.6 Pinning the task pane open and hiding it again

In addition to be being docked on the right side of the graphics area, the task pane can also be floated. This is especially useful if you are working with dual monitors. We often find it is helpful to float the task pane onto a second monitor and pin it open. To float your task pane, do the following:

1. Click any task pane tab icon to open the task pane.

2. Drag the title bar away from the right side of the graphics area.

3. Release the left mouse button.

4. To redock the task pane, click and hold the title bar of the task pane with the left mouse button, and drag the task pane back to the right side of the screen. The task pane will snap back into place when the correct position is reached.

Now we'll take you through all the parts of the task pane.

 T I P   Double-clicking the title bar of the task pane when it is docked will return it to its previously floated position, and double-clicking the title bar while the task pane is floating will return it to its docked position.

SolidWorks Resources

 The *SolidWorks Resources tab* of the task pane gives you quick access to common tasks such as creating a new document, opening an existing document, and using online tutorials. Additionally, users can get to the SolidWorks customer portal, user forums, workflow-specific tutorials, manufacturers' websites, and even view the Tip of the Day. Often, the SolidWorks Resources tab is overlooked by users, which is a shame because it gives you access to a wealth of information in one place. Figure 1.7 shows the entire SolidWorks Resources tab.

Design Library

 The *Design Library tab* usually points to a location on the local PC that is used to store common reusable items such as parts, assemblies, and sketches. Documents that are located in the Design Library can easily be added to the active document by dragging and dropping. Figure 1.8 shows the Design Library tab of the task pane with the menu options collapsed.

FIGURE 1.7 SolidWorks Resources tab of task pane

FIGURE 1.8 Design Library tab of task pane

File Explorer

The *File Explorer tab* gives you access to your files on your local PC and network just like Windows Explorer, as shown in Figure 1.9.

FIGURE 1.9 File Explorer tab of task pane

You can adjust the folders shown in the File Explorer on the System Options tab, as described in the following steps:

1. Click the Options button in the menu bar.

2. On the Systems Options tab, select File Explorer.

3. Select the folders you want to be displayed in the File Explorer tab.

4. Deselect the folders that you want to be hidden in the File Explorer tab.

5. Click OK to accept your changes.

Search

 Searches that are performed in the *Search Assistant* in the menu bar are displayed on the *Search tab*. Searches performed in SolidWorks are faster than most search engines because the searching is done on indexed files, and SolidWorks does not have to go digging through your PC to find a file. When SolidWorks was installed, the Windows Desktop Search was also installed to create the index of your files. This index should have been created after installation; if not, it will be created the first time you do a search.

From within SolidWorks, you can quickly search for files by a full-text search, advanced search, keywords, or retrieval of all types of documents. One of the most common searches you will perform will probably be a keyword search. To perform a keyword search, do the following:

1. Click in the SolidWorks search tool on the menu bar.

2. Type the text or keywords for your search criteria.

3. Press Enter.

All the files that match your search criteria will be displayed in the Search tab of the task pane, as demonstrated in Figure 1.10. If the search returns more files than what can be displayed on one screen of the Search tab, you can navigate through the results.

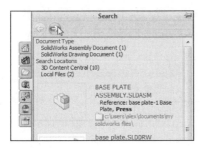

FIGURE 1.10 Search tab of task pane

4. To move to the next screen, click the blue right-pointing arrow, or click Next at the bottom of the Search tab (see Figure 1.11).

5. To return to a previous screen, click the blue left-pointing arrow.

6. To jump to a specific page, select the page number at the bottom of the tab.

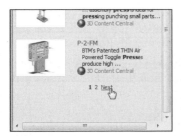

FIGURE 1.11 Scrolling through search results in task pane

View Palette

The *View Palette tab* contains images of standard views, section views, annotation views, and flat patterns that can be dragged into a drawing, as shown in

Figure 1.12. The View Palette tab displays available drawing views when you create a drawing from a part or assembly, browse to a document from the View Palette tab, or select a document in the list of open documents from the View Palette tab.

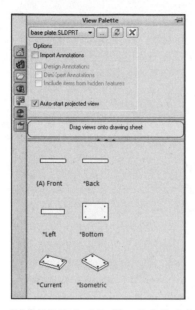

FIGURE 1.12 View Palette tab of task pane

Appearances/Scenes

 The *Appearances/Scenes tab* contains appearances that you can add to your models without actually adding the physical properties of the selected material to your part, as shown in Figure 1.13. By dragging from the Appearances tab, you can drop the material likeness onto your models to give them the look of metal, plastic, glass, and other material types. In Scenes, you can also change the environment in your models with different backgrounds and lighting schemes. We will be covering appearances and scenes in later chapters.

Custom Properties

 The *Custom Properties tab*, shown in Figure 1.14, provides you with a quick way to input custom properties for the active document. Before the Custom Properties tab can be used to update the properties for your documents, the property page must be built, usually by an administrator. We will be covering custom properties for parts, assemblies, and drawings in later chapters.

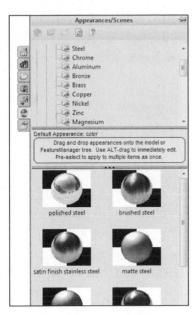

FIGURE 1.13 Appearances/Scenes tab in the task pane

FIGURE 1.14 Custom Properties tab in the task pane

Menu Bar

At the top of the screen is the ribbon-style menu bar, shown in Figure 1.15. The menu bar provides quick access to the most common actions including creating, opening, saving, and printing documents.

If you are familiar with previous versions of SolidWorks, you may notice the lack of pull-down menus. Not to worry, they are still there for the times you need them.

If you hover over the SolidWorks logo on the left side of the menu bar, the menu items will fly out. Nearly all SolidWorks commands are available in these pull-down menus, but some menus and menu items will only be available depending on the active document type.

FIGURE 1.15 SolidWorks menu bar

CommandManager

The *CommandManager* by default is located below the menu bar and is a context-sensitive toolbar, as shown in Figure 1.16. *Context-sensitive* means that the toolbar will update based on the toolbar you want to utilize and will be also updated based on the active document type. We will be discussing the CommandManager in more detail in the upcoming "Use the CommandManager" section.

FIGURE 1.16 CommandManager

FeatureManager Design Tree

To the left of the graphics area you will find the *FeatureManager design tree*, shown in Figure 1.17. The FeatureManager acts as a time machine, of sorts, by providing you with an outline view of the history of the construction of a part or assembly. You can use it to view the various sheets and views in a drawing. We will be spending some time on the FeatureManager design tree in later chapters.

Toolbars

Just like in all Windows-based programs, toolbars contain most of the tools available in SolidWorks. Each toolbar is named for the functions of the tools that are contained such as surfacing, mates, sketch tools, and so on. Figure 1.18 shows an example toolbar. Toolbars can be floated anywhere within the SolidWorks border or docked to the sides. Even though there are many toolbars at your disposal, we will be showing you a technique that virtually eliminates the need for toolbars in SolidWorks by using the CommandManager, shortcut bars, mouse gestures, menus, and in-context toolbars.

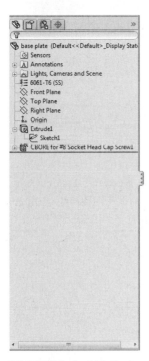

FIGURE 1.17 FeatureManager design tree

FIGURE 1.18 A SolidWorks toolbar

Use the CommandManager

The CommandManager was introduced in SolidWorks 2004 to mixed reviews. Since then, the CommandManager has evolved into the powerful tool you see today. The CommandManager plays a central role in the creation of SolidWorks documents by dynamically updating the tools based on the toolbar you are accessing. Depending on the document type you are editing, the tabs shown below the CommandManager will display the toolbars that are related. For example, when you are working in a part document, the CommandManager will display the Features, Sketch, Evaluate, and DimXpert tabs by default. However, when you are working in a drawing, the CommandManager will display only the View Layout, Annotation, Sketch, and Evaluate tabs.

Using the CommandManager couldn't be any easier. Instead of hunting down a particular toolbar, simply click the tab that corresponds to the set of tools you require, and click the desired tool. In some cases, the CommandManager will attempt to eliminate the number of clicks required by activating the tab that corresponds with the environment you are working in.

Access the CommandManager

If you find yourself sitting at an installation of SolidWorks that has the CommandManager turned off, don't try to fumble your way through; turn it back on. You can turn the CommandManager on using one of the following two techniques:

▶ Right-click the menu bar, and select CommandManager from the very top of the menu, as shown in Figure 1.19.

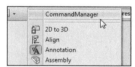

FIGURE 1.19 Accessing CommandManager from the menu bar

▶ Hover or click the SolidWorks logo on the left side of the menu bar to make the Tools menu visible; then select Tools ➢ Customize ➢ Enable CommandManager.

Float and Dock the CommandManager

Prior to SolidWorks 2009, the CommandManager wasn't able to be moved from below the menu bar but now it can be floated or even docked on a different side of the SolidWorks window. Here's how:

1. With the mouse, select the CommandManager with the left mouse button where no tool is present and drag the CommandManager from its original location down to the graphics area (See Figure 1.20).

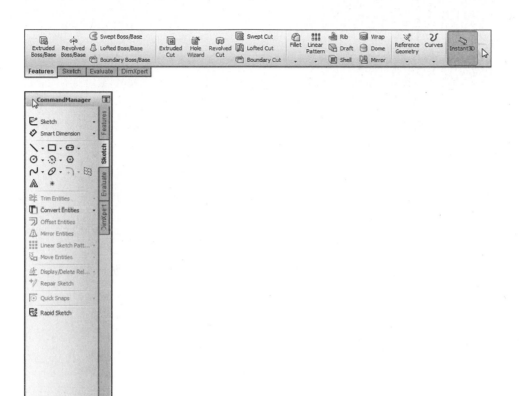

FIGURE 1.20 Floating and docking the CommandManager

   TIP Double-clicking the CommandManager when it is docked will make it float. Double-clicking the CommandManager when it is floating will return it to its last docked position.

2. If you release the mouse button while the CommandManager is in the middle of the SolidWorks window, it will "float" where placed. This can be extremely useful if you prefer to have the CommandManager close to your working area.

3. If you click the Auto Collapse button on the upper-left corner of the CommandManager, the buttons will disappear when it loses focus. A small box with the title will be the only thing showing.

4. To show the buttons available in the CommandManager once again, simply move the mouse pointer over the title of the CommandManager once again.

If you prefer, you can also dock the CommandManager on one side of the SolidWorks window by following these steps:

1. Select the title bar of the CommandManager, if floating, or select the docked CommandManager.

2. Drag the CommandManager over to one of the three available docking icons, as shown in Figure 1.21.

FIGURE 1.21 Docking the CommandManager to one side of the SolidWorks window

3. With the mouse pointer over the docking icon, release the left mouse button. The CommandManager will now be docked on the side of the window selected.

Hide Text in the CommandManager

When you begin to become familiar with the graphical icons of the tool buttons, you will no longer need the assistance of the text shown in the CommandManager. Hiding the text on the CommandManager will give you more space in your SolidWorks window for working in the graphics area. To hide the text on the CommandManager, do the following:

1. Right-click any spot on the CommandManager.

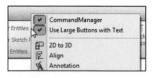

2. In the menu, deselect the Use Large Buttons With Text option.

3. The CommandManager will change to the smaller, less intrusive version.

Customize the CommandManager

The CommandManager, by default, has most of the toolbars and tools that you would require for your daily usage of SolidWorks. If you select the workflow options that apply to how you intend on using SolidWorks, additional toolbars will be available to you. However, as you begin using SolidWorks and start exploring more tools, you may discover that there are toolbars or tools that you tend to use more often, and therefore you'll want to add them to the CommandManager.

Add Tabs to the CommandManager

The first and quickest modification you can make to the CommandManager is adding tabs. Say, for instance, you find yourself using more surfacing tools, and you think it would be great to have these tools available in the CommandManager. Here is what you do:

1. Right-click any of the tabs in the CommandManager, and you will see all the currently available tabs that can be added, as shown in Figure 1.22. The items shown that have a check mark are currently in the CommandManager, and you can add the items without a check mark.

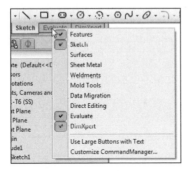

FIGURE 1.22 Adding tabs to the CommandManager

2. To add an item to the CommandManager, click an item in the list that does not have a check mark. The item will now have a check mark and be added to the CommandManager.

3. To remove an item from the CommandManager, click an item with a check mark. The check mark will disappear, and the tab will be removed from the CommandManager.

Add Existing Toolbars to the CommandManager

There may be instances where you want to add a tab that is not listed in the right-click menu. No worries, you can add any toolbar that is available in SolidWorks to the CommandManager. Here's how:

1. Right-click any of the tabs on the CommandManager.

2. Select Customize CommandManager from the menu.

3. To the right of the tabs displayed in the CommandManager, click the New Tab button.

4. Select an available toolbar listed in the menu. The new tab will be added to the CommandManager, as shown in Figure 1.23 (Quick Snaps).

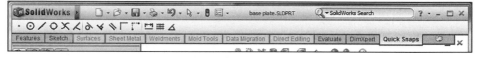

FIGURE 1.23 A new tab added to the CommandManager

The new tab will be available only in the document type you are currently editing. For instance, if you added a new tab while in a part document, the new tab will not be shown while editing a drawing or assembly.

It is possible to make the new tab available in the other document types while still customizing CommandManager by following these steps:

1. Right-click the newly created tab.

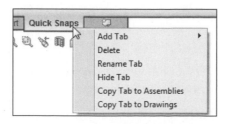

2. Select either Copy Tab To Drawings or Copy Tab To Assemblies.

 N O T E If you are adding a new tab to a drawing or an assembly, the option to copy the newly created tab to parts will also be available.

3. Once you are finished making modifications to the CommandManager, click OK in the Customize window, shown in Figure 1.24.

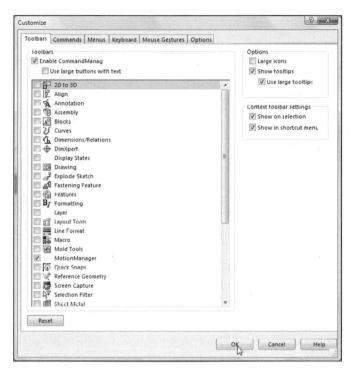

FIGURE 1.24 Customize window

Create a Custom Tab

One of our favorite features of the CommandManager is the ability to create a *custom tab* that can be used to create a group of some of your favorite tools. This can prove to be especially useful if you have a set of common tasks and you want to minimize the number of mouse clicks when selecting tabs. The first thing you will need to do is create a new empty tab on the CommandManager:

1. Enter the customize mode for the CommandManager as discussed in the previous section, and click the New Tab button.

2. On the very top of the menu, select Empty Tab. The New Tab name
will be highlighted.

3. Enter the name of the new tab.

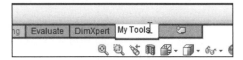

4. Add the desired buttons as described in the next section.

5. Once your new tab is finished, click OK in the Customize window.

 N O T E   By default, newly created tabs exist only in the document environment in which they were created. If you want to have the new tab available
in all environments, then use the Copy Tab To command discussed earlier.

Add and Remove Tools in Tabs

Adding tools to the CommandManager tabs is one of the great advantages of
using the CommandManager. SolidWorks, for the most part, did a good job of
anticipating which tools will be used most often in various environments, but
you may find that there some changes you would like to make. In this example,
you will add the Split tool to the Features tab:

1. Enter the customize mode for the CommandManager, and in the
Customize window, select the Commands tab.

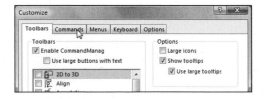

2. Make sure the tab that will contain the new tool button is active in
the CommandManager. If it is not already active, click the Features
tab in the CommandManager.

3. On the left side in the Commands tab, the Categories window contains all the tool sets available in SolidWorks. The category name will correspond to the function that the tool set will apply to. For example, you'll find the Extruded Boss/Base tool in the Features category. Click the Features category, and the available tool buttons will be displayed on the right.

4. Locate the Split tool in the Buttons section. If you are not sure which tool is which, briefly hover your mouse pointer above each tool in the Buttons section until the tooltip is displayed, as shown in Figure 1.25.

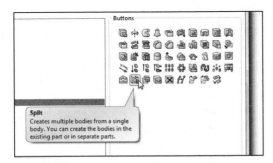

FIGURE 1.25 Selecting a button to add

5. Drag the Split button directly onto the CommandManager. When the tool can be added, the mouse pointer will change to include a green plus sign.

6. Release the left mouse button, and the tool will be added to the CommandManager.

Removing tools from the CommandManager is even easier. Here's how:

1. While still in the customize mode, select the tool in the CommandManager you want to remove with the left mouse button.

2. Drag it off the toolbar. When the mouse pointer changes to include a red X, release the left mouse button, and the tool will be removed.

Use and Customize the Menus

In SolidWorks 2008, the user interface was improved with the addition of a ribbon-style menu bar. The ribbon-style menu helps free up more space on your screen for other functions by automatically hiding when not in use. In the menus, you will be able to find nearly every tool available for each document type in SolidWorks in one of the following six menus: File, Edit, View, Tools, Window, and Help. To view the menus in SolidWorks, do the following:

1. Move your mouse pointer over or click the SolidWorks logo on the left side of the menu bar.

2. To hide the menus once again, move the mouse away from the menu bar.

If you prefer to have the menu bar available at all times, you can "pin" it open by doing the following:

1. Click or mouse over the SolidWorks logo on the left side of the menu bar.

2. When the menu list is visible, click the pushpin icon on the far right of the menu. The menu will remain open at all times.

3. To hide the menu, click the pushpin again.

As with most areas of SolidWorks, the menus are completely customizable to match your needs. Items listed on the main menus can be hidden or shown for each document type. If you hide a menu item in one document type, such as a drawing, it will still be available in another document type as long as it is normally visible in that document type. To customize a menu, follow these steps:

1. Click or mouse over the SolidWorks logo on the left side of the menu bar. Hover over the menu that you intend to customize.

2. Select Customize Menu at the very bottom of the menu. Check boxes appear next to each menu item.

3. Clear the check box next to items to hide them. Select the check box next to an item to show it in the menu, as shown in Figure 1.26.

FIGURE 1.26 Adding a menu Item

4. Once you are finished customizing the menu, press Enter or click outside the menu.

Even though SolidWorks gives you the ability to remove menu items, we strongly recommend that you keep all the menu items visible, especially while you are still learning. Once you become more familiar with using SolidWorks, you may decide that it would be best to hide some items, but we personally keep all items visible in the menus.

Use Toolbars

In the past, toolbars played a major role in using SolidWorks; however, with the CommandManager, shortcut bars, and mouse gestures, your reliance on the toolbars will be minimal. Even with the CommandManager, context menus, keyboard shortcuts, and shortcut bars, there will be times that toolbars will be helpful especially when you require a set of tools that you do not use very often. The toolbars in SolidWorks contain most of the tools and add-in products. Each toolbar is named to match a specific task such as Features, Drawing, and Layer.

Hide/Show Toolbars

By default, all the toolbars in SolidWorks are hidden, and even though there are a couple of toolbars that can be activated by keyboard shortcuts, the rest of the toolbars must be activated manually. To show a particular toolbar, you can do one of the following:

▶ Right-click in the menu bar or on the CommandManager. A toolbar menu appears. Select a toolbar listed in the menu to show it; deselect the check box next to the toolbars you want to hide.

▶ Mouse over or click the SolidWorks logo on the right side of the menu bar. The File, Edit, View, Insert, Tools, Window, and Help menus are now visible. Select Tools ➢ Customize ➢ Toolbars and click in the checkbox next to the names of the toolbars you wish to show; clear the checkbox next to the toolbars you wish to hide.

Rather than going through the long process of hiding visible toolbars, you can quickly and easily close floating tool bars by following these steps:

1. If the toolbar is docked, double-click the toolbar to return it to its last floating position.

2. To close a floating toolbar, click the red X in the top right corner of the toolbar.

Access the Shortcut Bar

We have mentioned a few times already how the *shortcut bar* nearly eliminates the need for menu items and toolbars. In SolidWorks 2008, the shortcut bar was introduced, and it has quickly become a favorite of many SolidWorks users, including us. Each environment in SolidWorks has its own version of the shortcut bar. Each one has a layout that presents you with the most commonly used tools in the environment you are working in near your current mouse pointer position. Unlike the other toolbars available in SolidWorks, the shortcut bar is not activated by using the procedures described in the previous section. To show the shortcut bar, press S on your keyboard while working in a part, sketch, drawing, or assembly. Make sure that you do not have anything selected when you press S. These are the four versions of the shortcut bar for each environment:

Part shortcut bar

Assembly shortcut bar

Drawing shortcut bar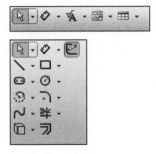

Sketch shortcut bar

Customizing a Shortcut Bar

To fully free yourself of using bars, you may find it necessary to customize your shortcut bars to add the tools you will need most often. You can customize each of the four shortcut bars using the same process:

1. In the graphics area, while in one of the four environments that use shortcut bars, press S on your keyboard. The shortcut bar appears.

2. Right-click anywhere inside the shortcut bar, and select Customize (see Figure 1.27).

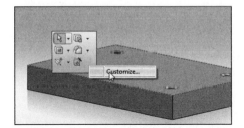

FIGURE 1.27 Customizing a shortcut bar

3. To add a tool to the shortcut bar, ensure that the Commands tab is activated in the Customize window.

4. Select the category that contains the desired tool set. Tool sets appear as icons in the Buttons section.

5. Select a command in the Buttons section of the Customize window with the left mouse button.

6. While still holding the left mouse button, drag the command onto the shortcut bar. When the mouse pointer changes to include a green plus sign, release the left mouse button (see Figure 1.28).

FIGURE 1.28 Selecting commands to add to a shortcut bar

7. Click OK in the Customize window to exit the customize mode.

There is still more you can do to customize the shortcut bar. For one, you can reorder the buttons on the bar. Here's how:

1. In the graphics area, while in one of the four environments that use shortcut bars, press S on your keyboard.

2. Right-click anywhere inside the shortcut bar, and select Customize.

3. Select a button in the shortcut bar with your left mouse button. While holding the left mouse button, drag the selected button to its desired location. Release the left mouse button.

4. Click OK in the Customize window to exit the customize mode.

As the number of buttons on your shortcut bar grows, you may reach the point where you want to resize the bar. You can also do that while you are in the customize mode:

1. In the graphics area, while in one of the four environments that use shortcut bars, press S on your keyboard.

2. Right-click anywhere inside the shortcut bar, and select Customize.

3. Move your mouse pointer over one of the four edges of the bar. The mouse pointer will change to a dual direction arrow.

4. Press and hold the left mouse button, and drag to resize the toolbar.

5. Click OK in the Customize window to exit the customize mode.

Access the Context Toolbars

In addition to the shortcut bar, the *context toolbars* provide you with quick access to the most frequently used commands while in a part, assembly, or sketch. When you select items in the graphics area or in the FeatureManager design tree, a context toolbar will be displayed above the mouse pointer. Select the command in the toolbar to continue (see Figure 1.29).

FIGURE 1.29 Using a context toolbar

Although we do not recommend it, you can turn off the context menu in SolidWorks. Here's how:

1. While in a part, assembly, or drawing, click or hover over the SolidWorks logo on the menu bar. Select Tools ➤ Customize.

2. On the Toolbars tab, there two options for the Context Toolbars in the Context Toolbar Settings section.

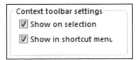

3. Deselecting the Show On Selection option hides the Context Toolbar when you select an item with the left mouse button.

4. Deselecting the Show On Shortcut Menu option hides the Context Toolbar when you select an item with the right-mouse button.

Use the Keyboard

In addition to using the CommandManager, Menus, and Toolbars; many SolidWorks users take advantage of the keyboard shortcuts available in SolidWorks. Keyboard shortcuts are great to quickly access your most commonly used tools and can be a real time saver. After learning the most common keyboard shortcuts and creating your own, you will be well on your way to becoming a SolidWorks master.

Use Default Shortcuts

Out of the box, SolidWorks comes with over 40 pre-programmed shortcut keys that in most cases will be more than enough for your daily SolidWorks usage. Shortcut keys can be either single keys or a combination of keys that are pressed simultaneously. Rather than go over every keyboard shortcut that is available, we want to just introduce you to the most used shortcuts that will give you a good start.

The following are keyboard shortcuts that are standard among most Windows based applications and can prove to be very handy in your arsenal. Shortcuts that begin with Ctrl+ are activated by holding down the Ctrl key on your keyboard and pressing the letter or number that follows. The same goes for shortcuts that involve the Shift key or Ctrl+Shift.

TABLE 1.1   Standard Windows OS Keyboard Shortcuts

Shortcut	Command	Description
Ctrl+N	New	Creates a new document
Ctrl+O	Open	Opens an existing document
Ctrl+W	Close	Closes the active document
Ctrl+S	Save	Saves the current document
Ctrl+P	Print	Prints the current document
Ctrl+Z	Undo	Undoes the last action

(Continued)

TABLE 1.1 Standard Windows OS Keyboard Shortcuts *(Continued)*

Shortcut	Command	Description
Ctrl+Y	Redo	Redoes the last undo or repeats the last action
Ctrl+X	Cut	Cuts selection to the system clipboard
Ctrl+C	Copy	Copies selection to the system clipboard
Ctrl+V	Paste	Copies selection from the system clipboard into the active document
Ctrl+Tab	Browse Open Documents	Switches between open documents in SolidWorks
Alt+Tab	Switch Applications	Switches between open applications in Windows

In addition to the shortcut keys that are available in all Windows based applications; SolidWorks has a large set of shortcuts that are used. Table 1.2 lists some of the most commonly used keyboard shortcuts available:

TABLE 1.2 Commonly Used Keyboard Shortcuts in SolidWorks

Shortcut	Command	Description
R	Recent Documents	Allows you to quickly browse the most recent documents opened in SolidWorks
F	Zoom To Fit	Zooms to fit the view of the model or drawing
Shift+Z	Zoom In	Zooms in by one step
Z	Zoom Out	Zooms out by one step
L	Line	Initiates the line tool for sketching

(Continued)

TABLE 1.2 Commonly Used Keyboard Shortcuts in SolidWorks *(Continued)*

Shortcut	Command	Description
G	Magnifying Glass	Displays a magnifying glass for viewing details in the document
S	Shortcut Bar	Initiates the Shortcut Bar
Alt+→	Spin Right	Spins the model right in relation to the viewing plane
Alt+←	Spin Left	Spins the model left in relation to the viewing plane
Enter	Repeat Last	Repeats the last command used
Ctrl+B	Rebuild	Rebuilds new or changed features in the model
Ctrl+Q	Forced Rebuild	Rebuilds all features in the model
Ctrl+R	Redraw	Redraws the screen

Add and Change Shortcut Keys

The keyboard shortcuts shown in the last section are a mere fraction of those that are available in SolidWorks out of the box. However, as you begin to use shortcut keys, you may discover that the shortcuts available do not fully suit your needs. Almost all of the commands in SolidWorks can be assigned to a shortcut; the only limit is how many shortcuts you can remember. As you begin to assign shortcuts to the various commands, you may be tempted to go overboard but in my opinion it is best to start out slow by assigning only a few new shortcuts or changing only a couple of default shortcuts. At the time you are creating shortcuts you may think that it would be very helpful to assign a shortcut to every command but in my experience, unless you consciously think about using the shortcuts every time you use SolidWorks, the shortcuts you thought would be a great idea will quickly be forgotten. We personally do not use very many shortcut keys other the ones listed in Table 1.2 but We have made a few modifications of our own.

In the following example, we will show you how to create a new shortcut. The following is one of the first shortcut assignments we perform on every installation of SolidWorks we use and this is purely a personal preference. If you are familiar with web applications, such as Mozilla Firefox or Microsoft Internet Explorer, you are probably familiar with the F5 key. In many Windows Applications, this is used to refresh the application with any updated information. we have found that many times, we want to press F5 while in SolidWorks to rebuild the model we are currently working on instead of using Ctrl+B or Ctrl+Q. To assign a shortcut to an existing SolidWorks command, do the following:

1. Right-click in the SolidWorks window border or on the CommandManager.

2. Select Customize... from near the bottom of the menu.

3. Select the Keyboard tab in the Customize window.

4. Type the name of the command that you wish to assign a shortcut to in the Search For field. For this example, Rebuild is added to this field. All the commands shown in the window will be filtered out except for the commands that match what is typed in the Search For field. See Figure 1.30.

5. Click on the row that corresponds to the command that you wish to assign a shortcut to. In the description section of the window, an explanation of the command tool will be provided.

6. If the command already has a shortcut assigned to it, the currently assigned shortcut can be removed by pressing Backspace on your keyboard or the new shortcut can be in addition to the existing separated with a comma. If no shortcut is assigned, select the field and move on to the next step.

7. Press the key or key combination that will be the new shortcut for the selected command. If the shortcut is to contain any key other than a letter or number, press the actual key rather than type the name of the key. For example, since we are assigning the key F5 to the rebuild, press the function key F5.

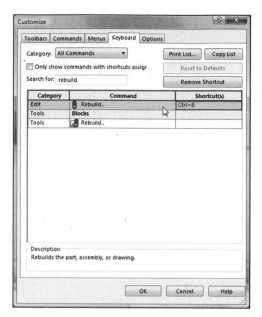

FIGURE 1.30 Assigning a Keyboard Shortcut to a Command

8. If the shortcut being assigned is already being used by another command, SolidWorks will prompt you with a message box asking if you wish to reassign the shortcut to the new command. If you are sure that you wish to change the shortcut, select Yes; otherwise select No.

9. Once the shortcut has been assigned, click OK to close the customize window.

Print Keyboard Shortcuts

With over 40 keyboard shortcuts and any additions you have made, you may find it incredibly difficult to remember all the combinations. Luckily, SolidWorks makes it easy for you to print out a list of shortcut keys that you can reference later. The following will print out the entire list of commands in SolidWorks along with any shortcuts that have been assigned:

1. Right-click in the SolidWorks window border or on the CommandManager.

2. Select Customize... from near the bottom of the menu.

3. Select the Keyboard tab in the Customize window.

4. Click the Print List... button in the upper left area of the customize window.

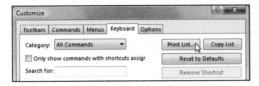

5. Select your printer and press OK. The entire command list will be sent to your printer.

 T I P   Instead of printing the entire command list, press the Copy List button to copy to the clipboard. You can then paste the list into a text editor or spreadsheet program that you can edit.

Use Accelerator Keys

Accelerator keys provide the user with another way to initiate commands in SolidWorks without the need to use the mouse. Nearly every menu item and dialog box can be accessed with the use of accelerator keys by pressing Alt on your keyboard and the letter that corresponds to the command. Unlike keyboard shortcuts, accelerator keys cannot be customized. However, as you become comfortable with the sequence of keystrokes, you may find your productivity increased. At the end of the day, we are all looking for ways to improve our overall productivity, right?

Here is an example of one of our favorite usages of the accelerator keys:

1. Press the Alt key on your keyboard. The menu bar will be displayed at the top of your SolidWorks screen but with a minor difference. One letter in each of the menu headers will be underlined.

2. The underlined letter corresponds with the key you must press to expand the menu list. To expand the File menu, press F on your keyboard, as shown in Figure 1.31.

3. Notice that the menu items also have letters that are underlined. For example, the menu item Properties has the *i* underlined. If you press *i*, the Properties window will open, since this is the only menu item that has an *i* underlined.

4. If there are multiple menu items that share the same letter underlined, such as Reload and Find References, which both have the *r* underlined,

pressing the letter multiple times will cycle through the menu items. When the desired menu item is highlighted, press Enter to initiate the command.

FIGURE 1.31 Using accelerator keys to access menu items

Use the Mouse

Probably one of the first things you learned when you first sat down at a computer was how to move the mouse around and click things. The mouse is one of the most important inventions in the past century because it allows even the most novice user to interact with a PC with little or no training.

Up to this point, you have been using the mouse to primarily select commands, options, and menus, but in SolidWorks the mouse plays a central role in nearly everything you may need to do. Not only is the mouse used to press buttons, select commands, and move toolbars, it's used to perform the following tasks and more:

▶ Select entities in the graphics area

▶ Select commands

▶ Manipulate views

▶ Display options for a selection

▶ Create sketches

▶ Create extrusions and cuts in models

▶ Move and rotate components in assemblies

More than likely, you are using a standard two-button mouse with a scroll wheel. Each of the two buttons and the scroll wheel has a variety of functions while working in SolidWorks, and we will be covering each of them in more detail throughout the entire book; however, there are some basic functions you should be familiar with before continuing.

The next few sections are easier to learn if you follow along using the part named ExampleSketch.SLDPRT, which can be downloaded from http://sybex.com/go/SolidWorks-2010-no-experience-required or www.swner.com. Once downloaded, you can open the part by selecting Open from the menu bar; then browse to the folder that contains the part. Click Open in the window, and the part will be displayed in the graphics area.

N O T E If you are using a mouse that has more than two buttons, normally the extra buttons can be programmed for particular functions in SolidWorks. Consult the manufacturer's documentation on how to use the mouse.

Select with the Mouse

When not being used to select menu items, buttons, and commands, the left mouse button is often used to select items in the FeatureManager design tree, entities in a sketch, features and faces on a model, models in an assembly, and items in a drawing. In parts, drawings, and assemblies, you need to be in the Select mode in order to be able to select any items.

Many times you'll find that you need to select multiple objects on-screen in a sketch, model, drawing, or assembly; with the mouse, you can "window" around the multiple entities that you want to select. We have found in the past that there are a large number of people who do not realize that the direction in which you drag the window affects the selection of objects.

Individual Entities

To select individual entities, do the following:

1. If you are not in the Select mode, click the Select button in the Standard toolbar.

2. Move the mouse pointer over an item in a sketch, model, assembly, or drawing.

3. Press the left mouse button and release. The item will be selected, as shown in Figure 1.32.

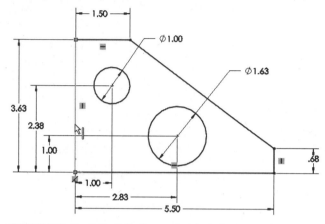

FIGURE 1.32 Selecting a sketch entity

4. If you select a second item, the first item will no longer be selected.

5. If you need to select multiple items, press and hold the Ctrl key while selecting the items.

Clicking a selected item while still holding the Ctrl key will remove the item from the selection set.

 T I P   You can use the Invert Selection tool to select all the other similar items in the document and release the originally selected items.

Box and Cross Selection

Two types of selection windows can be used in SolidWorks to select multiple entities: box and cross selection. Both of these selection types will select everything that is completely inside the window, but the cross-selection type will also select everything that crosses the box boundary line. It will help you in your usage of SolidWorks if you become familiar with the two selection types and begin to recognize the visual cues. Open any model, and play around with the two selection types, as follows:

1. Click anywhere in the graphics area with the left mouse button.

2. Hold the left mouse button down while you drag from right to left. This is the cross-selection window (see Figure 1.33). The color inside of the box is green, and the boundary line is dashed. Everything that falls within this box and crosses the dashed line will be selected.

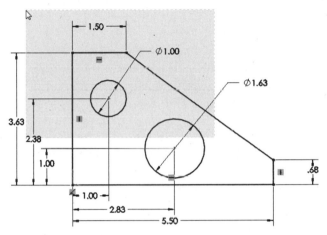

FIGURE 1.33 Cross selection using the mouse

3. While still holding the left mouse button, drag the mouse from left to right. This is the box-selection window (see Figure 1.34). You can see how the two selection types differ in their visual cues. The box selection window appears blue inside the box, and the boundary line is no longer dashed. For an entity to be selected, it must be fully inside the box.

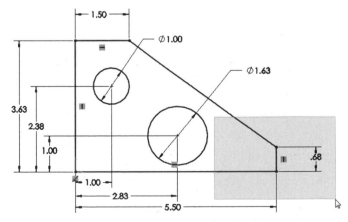

FIGURE 1.34 Box selection using the mouse

Use the Right Mouse Button

Up to this point, we have been using the right mouse button to select toolbars and customize the CommandManager, but those are not the only tricks it knows. The right mouse button in most Windows programs is used to access commands quickly and easily, and SolidWorks takes it a step further. The mouse button can be used in two completely different ways to select the commands you will most likely need in any situation. You'll take a look at both here.

Shortcut Menus

In an earlier section, we mentioned that the context toolbar can be hidden when viewing a shortcut menu. A *shortcut menu* is different from a shortcut bar; as you may remember, a shortcut bar is activated by pressing S on your keyboard while you are working in a sketch, part, assembly, or drawing. A shortcut menu is activated by the right mouse button when the mouse pointer is over an item in the graphics area or FeatureManager design tree. The shortcut menus give you quick access to some of the most commonly used tools and commands and are broken up into groups of related menu items that are shown with section headings that define the group.

To use a shortcut menu do the following:

1. In a sketch, part, assembly, or drawing, right-click an item in the graphics area or the FeatureManager design tree.

 T I P   Selecting the blank area of the graphics area of a part or assembly will display selection methods, view commands, and recent commands in the shortcut menu.

---

2. To show the entire menu, click the chevron at the bottom of the menu, and it will be expanded to its full length.

3. Select a menu item with the left mouse button (see Figure 1.35).

As with most menus in SolidWorks, it is possible to customize the shortcut menus to hide or show menu items, as follows:

1. In a sketch, part, assembly, or drawing, right-click an item in the graphics area or in the FeatureManager design tree.

2. Select Customize Menu.

3. Click an empty box next to the menu item you want to be shown. The empty box will be updated to include a check mark (see Figure 1.36).

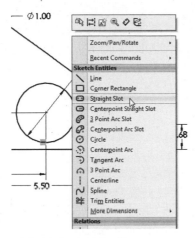

FIGURE 1.35 Shortcut menu available with right mouse button

4. To hide a menu item, select the box with the check mark, and it will become an empty box.

FIGURE 1.36 Customizing a shortcut menu

5. Once you are finished making adjustments to your shortcut menu, click outside the menu to exit it or press Enter.

N O T E   To restore all your menus to the system defaults, select Tools ➢ Customize then select Reset To Default in the Menu Customization section of the Options tab.

Mouse Gestures

The right mouse button can also be used in assemblies to move and rotate components; see Chapter 7.

As if the CommandManager, Shortcut Bars, Context Toolbars, and accelerator keys didn't make selecting commands quick and easy enough, SolidWorks 2010 introduces another way to design faster. *Mouse Gestures* are a quick and easy way to select commands without needing to select anything on the keyboard or even without moving the mouse away from what you are doing. At first you may not think about using mouse gestures but after getting used to them you will never want to give them up.

Just like with the Shortcut Bars, Mouse Gestures can be used in all four environments: Parts, Drawings, Assemblies, and Sketches. Mouse Gestures use what are called *guides* to give you access to eight different commands that are selected by merely moving your mouse. Give it a try and see how easy it is to select a command with Mouse Gestures:

1. While still editing the example sketch from the last sections, press and hold the right mouse button.

2. While still holding the right mouse button, slowly move the mouse in any direction. A wheel, or guide, will be displayed with eight different commands. See Figure 1.37. As you move in one of eight directions, while remaining within the inner circle of the guide, a different command will be selected.

FIGURE 1.37 Commands to select with Mouse Gestures

3. To select a command, move the mouse pointer to the highlighted command on the guide. The guide will disappear and the command will become active.

As we said in the very beginning, it may be difficult to remember the layout but as you become accustomed to the button layout you will be able to select a command often without even looking.

Manipulate Views with the Mouse

Although the Heads-up View Toolbar, the View Menu, and the Shortcut Menu provide you access to the tools needed to manipulate your views in the graphics area; the scroll wheel on your mouse is often a quicker way to go. The scroll wheel, or middle mouse button, gives you the ability to rotate, pan, and zoom in and out in the graphics area. If you are new to CAD, that last sentence may be a surprise to you. Yes indeed, the scroll wheel that is most often used to quickly scroll through documents is also a button. Give it a try, instead of spinning the wheel, push down directly on the scroll wheel. Now let's put that button to work for us by learning how to rotate the sketch we have opened.

To rotate the view with the middle mouse button in a part or an assembly:

1. With the mouse pointer in the Graphics Area, press and hold down the wheel.

2. Move the mouse around while still holding the wheel to rotate the view. The mouse pointer will change to the rotate view icon. See Figure 1.38.

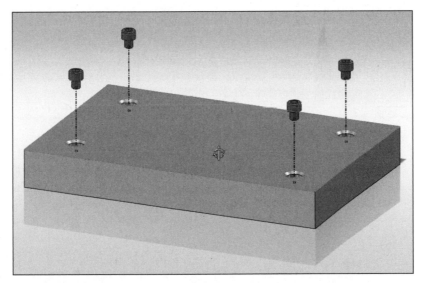

FIGURE 1.38 Rotating the view using the middle mouse button

You can also rotate the view around a vertex, edge or face in a part or assembly. In this example, we want to rotate the view in relation to the surface of a model. You will need to download the part named Base Plate.SLDPRT from the companion site before doing the following steps:

1. Using the Open button in the menu bar, open the model for the base plate.

2. Select a face of the model by pressing and releasing the scroll wheel with the mouse pointer on the face.
   The mouse pointer will change to show that the rotate view is limited.

3. Press and hold down the wheel.

4. Move the mouse around while still holding the wheel to rotate the view in relation to the face.

To zoom in and out using the scroll wheel in a part, assembly, or drawing, do the following:

1. In a part, assembly, or drawing, spin the wheel forward to zoom out in relation to the position of your mouse pointer.

2. Spin the wheel back to zoom in around your mouse pointer.

3. Move the mouse pointer outside the graphics area. For example, move the mouse pointer to the menu bar.

4. Spin the wheel forward and back to zoom in and out around the center of the graphics area.

In addition to rotating the view and zooming in and out, the scroll wheel can also be used to pan in a part, assembly, or drawing. To pan using the scroll wheel in a part or assembly, do the following:

1. In a part or assembly, press and hold the Ctrl key on your keyboard.

2. Press and hold the scroll wheel.

3. Move your mouse around to pan the view in relation to the viewing plane. The mouse pointer will change to show that you are in pan mode.

 T I P   In a drawing, the Ctrl key does not need to be held while holding the scroll wheel to pan since the view of a drawing cannot be rotated.

Are You Experienced?

Now You Can...

- ☑ Recognize the elements of the SolidWorks user interface

- ☑ Use and customize the CommandManager

- ☑ Use the ribbon-style menu bar

- ☑ Use and customize toolbars including shortcut bars

- ☑ Save time by utilizing keyboard shortcuts

- ☑ Select and manipulate views using the mouse

CHAPTER 2

Learning the Basics

▶ Explore the Document Structure

▶ Explore the Anatomy of a Part

▶ Use Assemblies

▶ Tell the Story with Drawings

N ow that you are familiar with the basic user interface of SolidWorks, it is time to explore the three environments in SolidWorks: parts, drawings, and assemblies. Learning the differences between the three and knowing how they relate to each other is important when using SolidWorks. Each mode is important in product design. In SolidWorks, the three document types are differentiated by the file type extension, which follows the dot (.) in the filename. The three document types are as follows:

SolidWorks part file	`*.sldprt`
SolidWorks assembly file	`*.sldasm`
SolidWorks drawing file	`*.slddrw`

In this chapter, we'll demonstrate the three different file types with a prebuilt assembly. You can download the assembly, as well as the parts and drawing, from the companion site to this book at **www.sybex.com/go/solidworks2010ner.com** or from **www.swner.com**.

Explore the Document Structure

The term document structure can refer to many things, but in this instance we're referring to the relationships between SolidWorks documents. In SolidWorks, certain documents cannot work without other documents. For example, a part can exist on its own with no outside dependencies, but its drawing will fail if you delete the part. In addition, any assemblies that reference the part will also be affected. In SolidWorks, files such as parts that are referenced by other files, such as assemblies and drawings, are called referenced documents.

The key to documents in SolidWorks is the bidirectional associativity of most of the documents. As changes are made to a model, such as dimensional changes, the drawing is updated. Also, changes made to the drawing, such as updates to tables and in some cases dimensions, are reflected in the referenced models.

Figure 2.1 illustrates the most basic document structure: one drawing with a single part file being referenced. This relationship between the part and drawing allows for changes made to the part to be reflected in the drawing and, in some cases, changes made to the drawing to be reflected in the part.

Figure 2.2 introduces an assembly into the mix. The assembly shown has its own drawing that documents the assembly instructions, and the two part files each have their own drawings to document the manufacturing process for the parts.

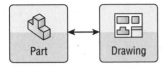

FIGURE 2.1 Single part with drawing

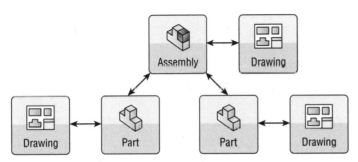

FIGURE 2.2 Basic assembly

Figure 2.3 takes the assembly to the next level; the top-level assembly consists of a subassembly as well as a part file. Once again, notice that the top-level assembly, as well as the subassembly and part models, has its own drawing.

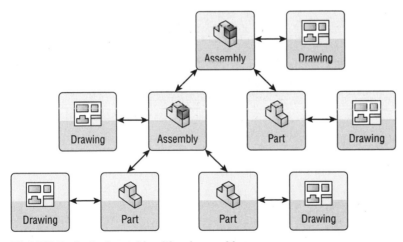

FIGURE 2.3 Assembly with subassembly

These three examples are the most basic representation of the document structure that you will likely encounter in your usage of SolidWorks. These examples are *scalable*, in that the basic concepts shown will work in most cases even in the largest of assemblies.

Explore the Anatomy of a Part

Part models are probably the most common of the three document types you will be using in SolidWorks, so it only makes sense to begin by examining a part model. In this section, you will learn what a part is and how the interface differs from that of a drawing or assembly.

A *part* created in SolidWorks is a 3D parametric solid model usually consisting of a base feature created from a sketch. The base feature is then refined with features that will remove or add material to the base feature. We mentioned that the base feature is usually created with a sketch because, as you become more proficient in SolidWorks, parts can be derived from other geometry, but that will be discussed later in this book.

It is often easier, when learning how to use SolidWorks, to examine models created by others. Before continuing in this section, you will need to open the part model that you downloaded in the previous chapter. The steps are as follows:

1. On the menu bar, click the Open button.

2. In the Open window, navigate to the folder that contains the files you downloaded from the website. Locate the file named Base Plate.SLDPRT, as shown in Figure 2.4.

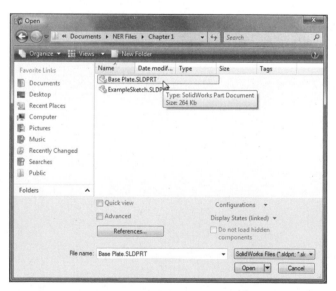

FIGURE 2.4 Opening an example part model

3. Select the Base Plate file, and click Open.

Graphics Area

Now that you have the Base Plate part model open, the first thing anybody notices is the graphics area. As we mentioned in Chapter 1, the graphics area is where all the magic happens in SolidWorks, so you need to feel comfortable in this area. If you read the previous chapter, you should have a good feel for how to zoom, rotate, and pan the Base Plate part model. However, in parts and assemblies, there is another way to manipulate the view of the part model in the graphics area.

You can also open a part by double-clicking the file in Windows Explorer or dragging and dropping it in the SolidWorks window.

Reference Triad

In SolidWorks 2009, the reference triad was introduced, giving users the ability to change among the standard views of a model. The reference triad is located in the lower-left corner of the graphics area, and it is used to display the orientation as you rotate a model by showing the location of the x-, y-, and x-axes in relation to the model being shown.

If the reference triad is not visible in the graphics area, it needs to be turned on in System Options. Here's how to do it:

1. On the menu bar, click the Options button.

2. On the System Options tab, select Display/Selection.

3. In the options list near the bottom of the window, select Display Reference Triad.

4. Click OK, and the reference triad will now appear in the graphics area.

Not only does the reference triad orient you as you rotate your model, it can also be used to quickly switch between the six primary views in your model: Top, Bottom, Front, Back, Left, Right. Obviously, SolidWorks cannot possibly know what the top of your part is or which side is the left side. Instead, the six views are based on the X,Y,Z directions of the model environment. Positive Y corresponds to the Top view, Positive X corresponds to the Left Side view, and Positive Z corresponds to the Front view.

ORIENTING PARTS TO THE REFERENCE TRIAD

This scheme refers only to the model's environment and does not take into consideration how the model was created. There may be times that the author of the model did not follow this scheme when creating the model. For example, the top of the model may not match the Top setting of the environment, but this can be easily avoided by considering the orientation of your part prior to creating your first sketch. In this book, we will make every attempt to preserve the integrity of the part orientation as we model.

Here are a few tricks that you can use to amaze your friends using the reference triad:

1. With the Base Plate part open, click the red arrow of the reference triad, shown with an X (see Figure 2.5). Regardless of the previous part orientation, the model will rotate to make the Right view normal to the screen. Once the part orientation changes, the new named view will be shown below the reference triad.

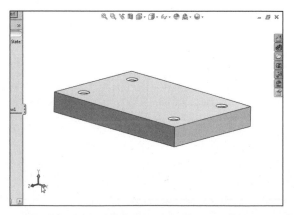

FIGURE 2.5 Rotating a model to the Right view using the reference triad

2. Now that the Right view is being shown in the graphics area, you can flip the view around to show the left side of the part. Click the center of the reference triad, and the view will rotate around to the left side of the model, as in Figure 2.6. This can be done on any of the three axes on the reference triad; for example, if the Front view is the active view in the graphics area, clicking the center of the reference triad will flip the view around to the Back view.

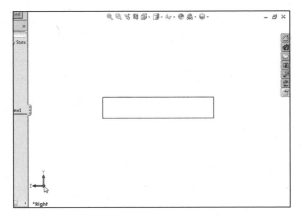

FIGURE 2.6 Rotating a model to the Left view using the reference triad

3. Not only can the reference triad be used to switch between the named views, but it can also be used to rotate the view around a selected axis. With the Left view of the part shown, you can rotate the view to show the Bottom view of the part by rotating the view 90° around the z-axis. If the part is in one of the six named views, it will still be in a named view after rotating 90°. If it is not in a named view, it will only rotate 90° around the selected axis. To rotate the view, hold the Shift key on your keyboard, and select the blue arrow of the reference triad shown with a Z (see Figure 2.7). The model will now rotate 90° around the z-axis and display the bottom of the part.

4. You can also rotate 90° around an axis in the opposite direction. Hold down Ctrl+Shift on your keyboard, and select the z-axis again. The model will rotate to its previous view.

5. The model can also be rotated about a selected axis by a predefined increment. Hold the Alt key on your keyboard, and select the z-axis of the reference triad once again. The model will now be incrementally rotated by a degree value set by the arrow key increment in System Options. See Figure 2.8.

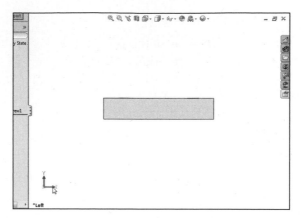

FIGURE 2.7 Rotating around a select axis on the reference triad while holding Shift

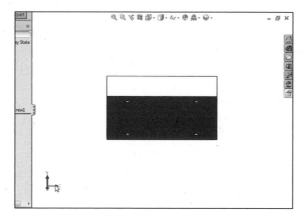

FIGURE 2.8 Rotating a model incrementally around a selected axis

TIP You can modify the increment that the model will rotate around the axis when holding the Alt key by adjusting the value in Tools ≻ Options ≻ System Options ≻ View ≻ Arrow Keys.

6. Lastly, the model can also be rotated in the opposite direction by the same increment. Press Alt+Ctrl and select the Z axis again. The model will rotate in the opposite direction.

Origin

The reference triad shows you the direction of the x-, y-, and z-axes of the part model but not the origin of these axes. The origin of the modeling environment is located at 0,0,0, and every point in 3D space is described in relation to the origin. If you select any point on a model, the X,Y,Z location will be displayed in the status bar, as described in Chapter 1.

If the origin is not shown in your model, it can easily be turned on in the Heads-up View toolbar by doing the following:

1. On the Heads-up View toolbar at the top of the graphics area, click the Hide/Show Items flyout.

2. In the flyout, click the View Origins button.

3. The origin of the modeling environment will now be displayed, as in Figure 2.9.

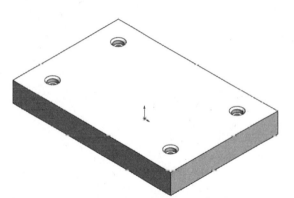

FIGURE 2.9 A part model showing the origin

FeatureManager Design Tree

The FeatureManager design tree plays a central role in parametric feature-based solid modeling. Most parts and assemblies modeled in SolidWorks are feature based. This means that a model is made up of features, such as bosses and cuts, to form a part or assembly. The FeatureManager design tree gives you access to the features and allows you to make changes to previously created features to update the overall model geometry. This is referred to as parametric modeling because the model is modified by changing its parameters.

In the previous chapter, we mentioned that the FeatureManager design tree is a time machine of sorts, since you can go back to a previous time in the model and make a change. You can even change the order that you created features and delete features altogether. Before we get into that, though, we think it is time to give you a proper introduction to the FeatureManager design tree. Figure 2.10 shows the FeatureManager design tree for the Base Plate part model.

FIGURE 2.10 FeatureManager

Filter

At the very top of the FeatureManager design tree is the filter bar, which will filter out everything that does not match the string being typed.

The FeatureManager design tree can be filtered by the following:

- ▶ Feature names
- ▶ Types of features
- ▶ Sketches
- ▶ Folder
- ▶ Mates
- ▶ Tags

The ability to filter the FeatureManager design tree is extremely helpful when you have a model with many features and you are looking for a specific feature or feature type. When you are finished filtering the FeatureManager design tree, clicking the X will clear the field, and your tree will return to normal.

N O T E   The filter function in the FeatureManager design tree acts the same in assemblies, but it also filters out components in both the tree and the graphics area.

Sensors

Below the filter bar and the model name in the FeatureManager design tree is the Sensors folder. Sensors are used to monitor certain parameters in your part or assembly such as mass properties, measurements, interference detection, and simulation data. As the values of the sensors deviate from the specified limits, an alert will be displayed.

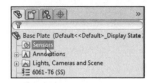

Annotations

Directly below the Sensors folder is the Annotations folder. In part files, annotations act like dimensions that can be placed directly onto the part model to satisfy the requirements of ASME Y14.41-2001. Placing dimensions and annotations directly onto the model eliminates the need to create paper drawings.

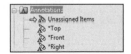

Material

Depending on what you are planning to do with the part model, you may find it necessary to apply a material. In some cases, it may not be necessary to apply a material to a part, but if you are planning to perform a simulation, obtain mass properties, or reference the material using custom properties, it will be necessary to apply a material to a part. When a material is applied to a part, the material is displayed in the FeatureManager design tree.

You can find more information regarding the various ASME standards referenced in this book on the American Society of Mechanical Engineers website at www.asme.org.

Planes

By default, every part and assembly has three planes when you create a new part: the front plane, the top plane, and the right plane. These three planes intersect at the origin in the part environment. The planes that are shown in the FeatureManager by default can be renamed and hidden, but they cannot be deleted.

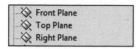

The planes that are shown in the FeatureManager can be seen in the graphics area, as shown in Figure 2.11, if the plane is set to Visible.

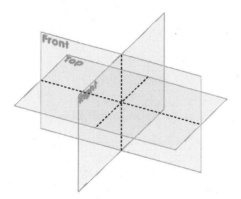

FIGURE 2.11 Planes in graphics area

You can see the planes in the graphics area by making them visible in the FeatureManager. To hide or show a plane, do the following:

1. In the FeatureManager, select the plane to be shown in the graphics area.

2. In the context toolbar, select Show to display the plane. When the plane is set to Show, the icon in the FeatureManager will be shown as a solid yellow color.

3. To hide the plane, select the plane again, and select Hide from the context toolbar.

N O T E If the plane does not appear in the graphics area after selecting Show in the context toolbar, the visibility of all planes in the graphics
area may be set to Hidden. To show planes in the graphics area, select View
Planes in the Hide/Show Items flyout on the Heads-up View toolbar.

Origin

The origin shown in the FeatureManager design tree represents the origin of the
graphics area. If the origin is not visible in the graphics area, you can select the
origin in the FeatureManager design tree, and 0,0,0 will be highlighted in the
graphics area.

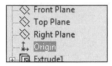

Features

We have reached the most important part of the FeatureManager design tree,
the tree. The features listed in the tree are the steps taken to create the base
plate model. Since the example is a really simple part model, there are only a
couple of features that were used to create the part. However, in some of the
more complex models, it is not unheard of to have a feature tree with hundreds
of features.

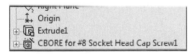

The first feature in the tree is the *base feature*. This is usually created using
a sketch or series of sketches that is then extruded, revolved, swept, or lofted.
The icon shown denotes the feature type that was used to create the feature. For
this example, the base feature of the Base Plate was created using Extruded Base/
Boss. The text next to the icon is the name of the feature that was automatically
generated on creation. The name consists of the feature type followed by a number that is sequentially incremented every time a similar feature is created.

 T I P You can rename features in the FeatureManager design tree by
slowly clicking the feature name twice and entering the new name when the
old one is highlighted.

Selecting a feature in the feature tree will highlight it in the graphics area. This is because the FeatureManager design tree and the graphics area are dynamically linked. Selecting features, sketches, drawing views, and construction geometry in either the FeatureManager design tree or the graphics area will highlight it in the other. Let's give it shot:

1. In the FeatureManager design tree, click the feature named Extrude1.

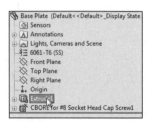

2. The entire part in the graphics area will be highlighted, except for the four screw holes because they were created with separate features, as shown in Figure 2.12.

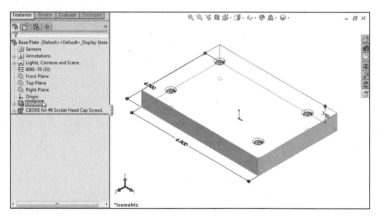

FIGURE 2.12 Using FeatureManager design tree to highlight features in the graphics area

3. What if you had hundreds of features listed in the FeatureManager design tree and you were not exactly sure where the one you wanted was listed? If you select the feature in the graphics area, it will be highlighted in the tree. Select one of the screw holes in the graphics area.

4. The counterbored hole feature that was created using the Hole Wizard will be highlighted in the FeatureManager design tree, as shown in Figure 2.13.

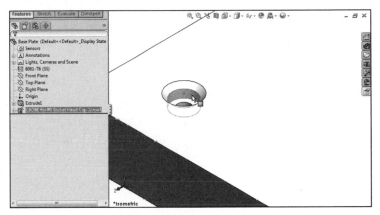

FIGURE 2.13 Selecting a feature in the graphics area to find it on the FeatureManager design tree

Now that you know how to determine which feature listed in the FeatureManager design tree relates to the actual feature on the part model, what can you do with that information? Well, one of the things you can do is see the *sketch* that was used to create the feature. Sketches are normally 2D open or closed profiles that are used to create extrusions, cuts, revolves, sweeps, and lofts. In Chapter 3, "Creating Your First Part," you will dig deeper into creating sketches. For now, follow these steps to view a sketch:

1. In the FeatureManager design tree, click the small plus in front of the icon for the Extrude1 feature.

2. The sketch that was used to create the Extrude1 feature will now be shown below the feature. This sketch is named Sketch1 since it was the first sketch that was created in this part.

3. At this point in the book, we won't cover how to open and modify the sketch, but it is possible to just view the sketch in relation to the part model and even see the dimensions that were used to fully define the sketch. Select Sketch1 in the FeatureManager design tree with a single click.

4. The sketch will now appear in the graphics area, as shown in Figure 2.14.

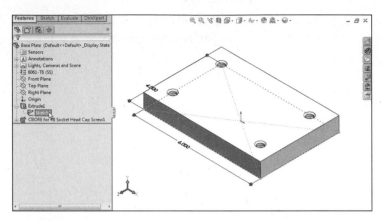

FIGURE 2.14 Viewing a sketch that makes up a feature

 N O T E   The dimensions that were used to define the sketch will be shown with a single click only when Instant3D is enabled. Instant3D can be turned on by selecting the Instant3D button on the Features tab in the CommandManager. If you do not want to enable Instant3D, the dimensions for the sketch can still be shown by double-clicking the sketch.

Rollback Bar

To extend the time machine metaphor even further, the rollback bar allows you step back in time and see the individual steps that were performed to create a model. The rollback bar is a line below the features in the FeatureManager design tree that can be dragged up or down in the feature tree. Any features that exist below the rollback bar act as if they have not been created yet. To get a better understanding of the concept, it is probably better to try it for yourself:

    1. In the Base Plate part model, move the mouse pointer directly above the line that is below the feature tree. When the mouse pointer changes to show a hand, press and hold the left mouse button.

2. While still holding the left mouse button, drag the **rollback bar** above the counterbored hole feature, and release the mouse.

With the rollback bar above the counterbored hole feature, the holes are removed from the plate, as shown in Figure 2.15. This is because, based on the placement of the rollback bar, they haven't been created yet.

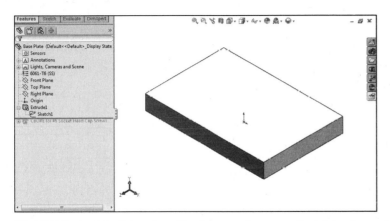

FIGURE 2.15 Using the rollback bar to view an earlier state of a part

One advantage to being able to step back in your feature tree is that it is possible to insert new features above features that have already been created. Later in this book, we will be working more with changing the order of features in the FeatureManager design tree. So, for the time being, return the rollback bar to its original position below the feature tree by dragging it back down.

Display Pane

The display pane is an extension of the FeatureManager design tree that provides you with a quick view of the display settings that are applied to the individual features, entire part, and bodies. The display pane is available in parts, assemblies, and drawings, but changes to the display pane can be applied only in parts and assemblies.

1. To show the display pane, click the chevron on the top-right of the FeatureManager design tree.

2. The display pane will appear to the right of the FeatureManager design tree.

The display pane is broken down into four columns, as shown in Figure 2.16. Each column is described next.

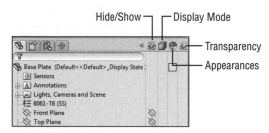

F I G U R E   2 . 1 6   Display pane columns

 Hide/Show   In the Hide/Show Column, some items in the FeatureManager display tree can have their visibility status changed, including solid bodies, planes, and sketches. Figure 2.17 shows an example of changing the visibility of a sketch. The actual features, such as extrusions and sweeps, cannot be hidden individually.

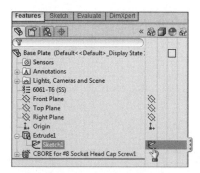

F I G U R E   2 . 1 7   Showing sketch in display pane

 Display Mode   In part files, the Display Mode column applies only to solid bodies and is used to display and change whether the solid body is shown with one of these settings: Wireframe, Hidden Lines Visible, Hidden Lines Removed, Shaded With Edges, or Shaded. Figure 2.18 shows changing the display mode of the solid body for the Base Plate model. Setting the display state this way will override the display state settings in the Heads-up View toolbar. To allow the state to be specified by the Heads-up View toolbar, set the state to Default Display in the FeatureManager.

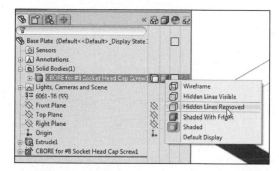

FIGURE 2.18 Changing the display mode in the display pane

Appearances   *Appearances* are used to add the look of certain materials to the entire part, body, or individual features. Items in the FeatureManager design tree that have an appearance applied to them will show a color block that reflects the color of the appearance. If there is no block shown in the Appearances column, then there has not been an appearance applied to the feature. Figure 2.19 shows that a matte aluminum has been applied to the Base Plate solid body. Later in the book, we will show you how to apply appearances to parts, bodies, and features.

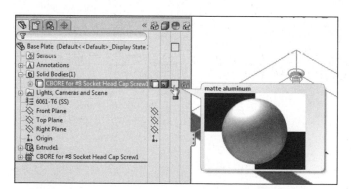

FIGURE 2.19 Appearances in the display pane

Transparency   Parts, bodies, and features can be made to be *transparent*, giving a glass appearance that allows you to view internal features or features or bodies that might otherwise be obscured. Items in the FeatureManager design tree that have been made transparent will show an icon to represent that the item is transparent. Figure 2.20 shows that the Extrude1 feature has been changed to be transparent. Applying transparencies to features and parts will be discussed later in the book.

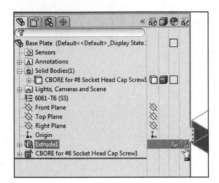

FIGURE 2.20 Changing transparency in the display pane

Hidden Tree Items

There are a number of tree items that you currently do not see in the Base Plate part. This is because they are set to be automatically hidden unless they are being used within the model. For example, the Equations folder is not visible in the FeatureManager design tree unless equations are being used in the model. You can adjust the visibility of tree items to always be hidden, visible, or automatic. Here is how to do it:

1. Right-click while the mouse pointer is anywhere inside the FeatureManager design tree including on any item in the tree. In the right-click menu, select Hide/Show Tree Items (Figure 2.21).

FIGURE 2.21 Selecting Hide/Show Tree Items

2. In the System Options window, click the down arrow next to the tree item for which you want to adjust its visibility (Figure 2.22).

FIGURE 2.22 Adjusting the visibility of tree items

The Automatic setting means items will display in the design tree only if they exist. For instance, if the tree item is set to Automatic and it is not shown in the FeatureManager design tree, then it does not currently have any items to be displayed.

3. Sometimes it is helpful to turn on the visibility of some folders or even turn off tree items that you do not use often, such as the sensors. If you want to hide the Sensors folder, select Hide in the drop-down menu. Click OK to close the System Options tab.

The Sensors tree item will now be invisible in the FeatureManager design tree.

N O T E For the sake of the examples shown earlier in this chapter, the Solid Bodies folder was set to Show when the part was created. Normally this folder is set to Automatic in the Hide/Show Tree Items and would not be visible when only one solid body is present in the model.

PropertyManager

Above the FeatureManager design tree are additional tabs that display more managers, each of which has its own set of tasks. The tab next to the FeatureManager design tree is the PropertyManager tab. The *PropertyManager* is where values are entered or changed when initiating commands or selecting entities in the graphics area. Instead of selecting the PropertyManager tab, it will automatically be displayed when you select an entity or initiate a command. Figure 2.23 shows the PropertyManager when a dimension is selected in the graphics area. Each command and entity has its own PropertyManager, and you will be learning about them individually as you begin to build the lamp project later in the book.

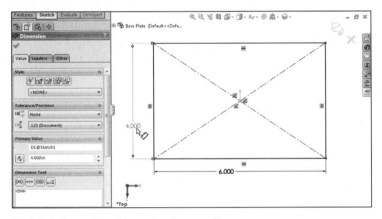

FIGURE 2.23 Dimension PropertyManager

ConfigurationManager

Next to the PropertyManager tab is the *ConfigurationManager*. The ConfigurationManager is used to create, select, and view configurations in parts and assemblies. Configurations are variations of a part or assembly such as dimensional differences of features within the same part. A good example would be a tube that can be produced with different diameters or lengths using only one part file. We will be going more into configurations in Chapter 9, "Modeling Parts Inside a Subassembly."

DimXpertManager

The *DimXpertManager* provides access to the tools necessary for applying dimensions and tolerances to the actual 3D model instead of using drawings. ASME Y14.41 and ISO 16792:2006 are both standards that allow for the annotation of

3D geometry to be used in lieu of paper drawings. We will not be covering using DimXpertManager in this book, but we encourage you to look into it once you become proficient at using SolidWorks.

Use Assemblies

An assembly is a collection of parts, features, and subassemblies that are mated together to create the end product. In SolidWorks, there are two approaches in creating assemblies: top-down and bottom-up.

The *top-down design* approach to creating an assembly means that parts are created in context to the assembly that will dynamically update as referenced geometry in the assembly is updated. The benefit of using the top-down approach is that as referenced parts are updated, the changes are propagated to the other parts in the same assembly. The drawback to creating top-down assemblies is that changes to one part can cause errors in other parts in some cases.

The *bottom-up design* approach to creating an assembly means that the parts are made independently and assembled together in the assembly using mates. Changes made to the individual parts will not affect other parts in the assembly. The advantage to the bottom-up approach is that changes to one part will not cause errors in other parts, except for the occasional mate error in the assembly. The drawback to the bottom-up approach is that each individual part will need to revised independently as the design progresses, and this leaves open the chance of missing an important change in another component of the assembly.

 N O T E Both the top-down and bottom-up assembly techniques have their own pros and cons; however, learning and using both will dramatically affect your efficiency in SolidWorks, and you will be using both approaches in subsequent chapters once you begin building the lamp project.

Before moving on the following sections, you need to open the assembly files that you should have downloaded from the companion website by doing the following:

1. If you have not done so already, close the part model used in the previous sections by clicking the Close icon located in the upper-right corner of the graphics area.

2. To open the Base Plate assembly, click the Open button located on the toolbar.

3. In the Open window, navigate to the folder that contains the files that you downloaded from the companion website, and select the file named Base Plate Assembly.SLDASM.

4. Click Open.

FeatureManager Design Tree in Assemblies

The FeatureManager design tree in an assembly has many of the same elements as in a part file, including sensors, annotations, planes, and the origin. The primary difference between the FeatureManager for parts and the FeatureManager for assemblies is that instead of just features listed, the tree displays components, subassemblies, and assembly-level features such as holes and cuts.

The FeatureManager design tree for an assembly displays the top-level components and subassemblies that make up the assembly. The icons shown in the FeatureManager reflect the type of component or feature used in the assembly. The features that make up a component in the assembly or the components in a subassembly can be viewed and modified from the FeatureManager design tree.

Display Pane

The display pane in assemblies is very similar to the display pane in part models, as shown in Figure 2.24. Changes applied to the parts in the display pane are applied only at the assembly level and do not propagate to the part level.

FIGURE 2.24 Display pane in an assembly

Hide/Show   In assemblies, each component can be hidden or shown via the display pane. Once hidden, the component can be selected once again to be shown.

Display Mode   Components and component solid bodies can have their display mode adjusted in the display pane to either Wireframe, Hidden Lines Visible, Hidden Lines Removed, Shaded With Edges, Shaded, or Default Display.

Appearances   Applying an appearance at the assembly level allows you to add color, texture, or a RealView material to a part, superseding any appearance that was added at the part level. Figure 2.25 shows how the Base Plate in the assembly has a different color applied at the assembly level than what was added at the part level. The lower-right triangle represents the color of the part at the part level, and the upper-left triangle shows the color applied in the assembly.

Adjusting the Display Mode setting of individual components will come in handy when you create display states, which are described in later chapters.

FIGURE 2.25 Appearances of components in display pane

Transparency   As in part models, components in an assembly can be made to be transparent, giving a glass appearance that allows you to view internal features or features or parts that might otherwise be obscured. Components in the FeatureManager design tree that have been made transparent will show an icon to represent that the item is transparent.

Mates

At the very bottom of the FeatureManager design tree in assemblies, as shown in Figure 2.26, is the Mates folder. This is where you will find the mates that were used to create the assembly. In Chapter 6, "Creating a Subassembly," you will be introduced to using the various mates available in SolidWorks.

```
Mates
  Concentric1 (Base Plate<1>,SHCS 8-32 UNC x 0.75<1>)
  Concentric2 (Base Plate<1>,SHCS 8-32 UNC x 0.75<3>)
  Concentric3 (Base Plate<1>,SHCS 8-32 UNC x 0.75<2>)
  Concentric4 (Base Plate<1>,SHCS 8-32 UNC x 0.75<6>)
  Coincident1 (Base Plate<1>,SHCS 8-32 UNC x 0.75<2>)
  Coincident2 (Base Plate<1>,SHCS 8-32 UNC x 0.75<6>)
  Coincident3 (Base Plate<1>,SHCS 8-32 UNC x 0.75<3>)
  Coincident4 (Base Plate<1>,SHCS 8-32 UNC x 0.75<1>)
```

FIGURE 2.26 Mates in an assembly

Tell a Story with Drawings

The drawing environment shares many of the same elements with parts and assemblies. Just like with parts and assemblies, the drawing environment uses the graphics area, FeatureManager, display pane, and PropertyManager, but they do act a little differently.

Graphics Area

The graphics area of a drawing is a 2D plane that represents a sheet of paper that is always normal to the screen. Unlike the graphics area in a part or assembly, the view cannot be rotated. In fact, the Rotate tool is not even available while you are editing a drawing except in drawing views, but we will get to that later.

Later in this book, you will be taking a closer look at creating drawings, so here we'll give you a quick overview of the different areas that make up a drawing.

Sheet Format

Back in the day of drawing boards and T squares, drafters would often use vellum sheets preprinted with title blocks. This would save the drafter valuable time that would otherwise be used drawing the title block every time they created a drawing. In SolidWorks, when creating a new drawing, the sheet format contains the title block associated with the selected drawing template. This is one reason why the drawing template and sheet format are often confused. Figure 2.27 shows the sheet format that can be seen when editing the sheet of a drawing.

> **NOTE**   A sheet format contains items that are part of the drawing sheet, but a drawing template can contain the sheet format, revision table, tables, notes, predefined drawings views, and so on.

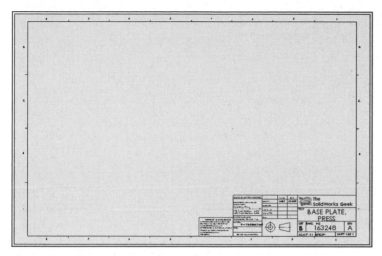

FIGURE 2.27 Drawing sheet format

Most organizations will have a variety of sheet formats they will use based on the sheet size and differences in title blocks. As you are creating a drawing, you can easily switch between sheet formats in the sheet properties. This is often the case when you are creating a drawing for a particular sheet size and you later discover that you need a larger or smaller sheet. Later in the book, we'll show how to switch between sheet formats.

Drawing Views

Drawing views act like windows that show a 2D view of your part or assembly. These views are linked to the part or assembly that was used to create them, allowing the view to update as the geometry is changed. A drawing view can show one of the orthographic projections or isometric views of your part. Drawing views can be moved in relation to a projected view or be made to move independently anywhere in the drawing, including off the drawing sheet altogether. Drawing views can also be set to any scale, but it is good practice to have the view scale be based on the sheet scale. Figure 2.28 shows the isometric view of the base plate.

Annotations

The term annotations is an all-encompassing term that includes dimensions, notes, tables, balloons, and so on. Figure 2.29 shows some annotations that have been applied to a drawing view. Some annotations can be inserted automatically when creating drawing views, but others are added manually to the drawing. Each of the annotations types will be explained in more detail in future chapters.

An annotation is anything used to better tell the story of the drawing that the drawing views by themselves cannot do.

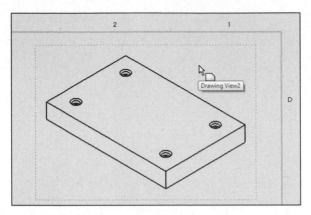

FIGURE 2.28 Drawing view in a drawing

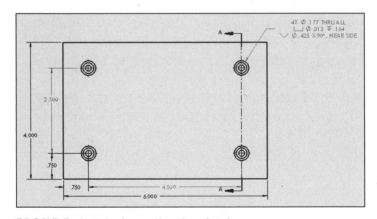

FIGURE 2.29 Annotations in a drawing

Sheet Tabs

If you have ever created drawings, then you would know that it is often difficult to fit all the necessary information into one sheet of a drawing. Luckily with SolidWorks, it is not necessary to create a different drawing for each drawing sheet. Using tabs, a single drawing can have multiple sheets easily accessible at the bottom of the graphics area. By clicking the sheet tabs, as shown in Figure 2.30, you can easily switch between each drawing and even add and remove sheets. If you hover your mouse pointer over a sheet tab, you will be presented with a preview of the sheet. This can be a good time-saver if you have many sheets, since you will not need to activate each sheet to find the one you want.

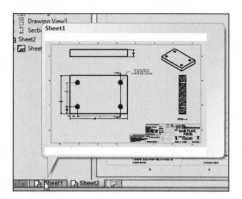

FIGURE 2.30 Multiple sheet tabs in a drawing

FeatureManager Design Tree

The FeatureManager design tree for the drawing environment is similar to what you find in parts and assemblies, except that instead of parts or features being shown, it shows a list of items on the drawing. In addition to displaying blocks and annotations on the drawing, the FeatureManager design tree shows the drawing sheets. The sheets that exist in a drawing are shown with an icon and the sheet name.

Figure 2.31 shows how expanding the sheet in the FeatureManager will display the sheet format and drawing views contained therein. As you expand the drawing views, the referenced models will be displayed.

If the drawing view is a *generated view*, like a detail or section view, expanding the view in the FeatureManager will display additional information such as the section line or detail circle. Figure 2.32 shows how a generated view, in this case a section view, contains the file references as well as the section line.

The display pane in a drawing differs from that of parts and assemblies in that changes cannot be applied to the display pane. The display pane will display the type of view that is being used in the drawing and the display mode for each view, as shown in Figure 2.33. To be honest, you won't need to view the display pane in your drawings unless you quickly want to view the display mode that is used on all your views.

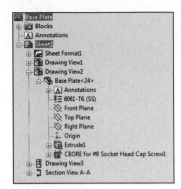

FIGURE 2.31 Drawing views and references in FeatureManager

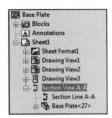

FIGURE 2.32 Generated views in FeatureManager

FIGURE 2.33 Drawing display pane

PropertyManager

The PropertyManager in the drawing environment will be heavily used during the drawing creation process. Nearly every aspect of creating a drawing relies on the PropertyManager, although in ➢ SolidWorks 2010 the reliance on the PropertyManager when specifying dimension parameters has been relieved with the introduction of the dimension palette. To access the PropertyManager, there is no need to select the tab; instead, select any entity in the drawing area. In the PropertyManager, you will be able to view or modify the properties for the item you selected. Figure 2.34 shows the PropertyManager when a section line is selected in the drawing.

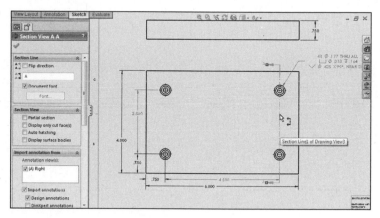

FIGURE 2.34 PropertyManager in a drawing

Are You Experienced?

Now you can...

- ☑ **Open various documents in SolidWorks**

- ☑ **Use the reference triad to change views**

- ☑ **Show/hide the origin in parts and assemblies**

- ☑ **Use the rollback bar in parts**

- ☑ **Hide/show the display pane**

- ☑ **Recognize the various elements of the FeatureManager design tree**

- ☑ **Recognize the differences and similarities between parts, drawings, and assemblies**

CHAPTER 3

THE SKILLS FOR SUCCESS

SolidWorks

Creating Your First Part

- ▶ Save the Model

- ▶ Set the Document Properties

- ▶ Create a Base Extrusion

- ▶ Add an Extruded Cut

- ▶ Add Boss Extrusions

- ▶ Core Out the Part

- ▶ Add Fillets and Chamfers

Now that you have spent some time going over the user interface of SolidWorks and have explored the different document types, you can begin creating your first project. For the rest of this book, you will be modeling and creating drawings for a banker's desk lamp. You will find that your first project is something familiar so you are not overwhelmed by the model itself. The project you are creating is just the basic parts and assemblies that make up the lamp minus the wiring and electronics that would complete the lamp.

The first step that you will take toward creating your desk lamp is creating a new part document. SolidWorks comes with its own set of *document templates* that you will be using throughout the book. If your organization has already modified these templates to suit their own needs, you will still be able to follow the examples provided in this book with little or no variation. To create a new part document, do the following:

1. Click the New button located on the menu bar at the top of the SolidWorks window.

2. The New SolidWorks Documents window, by default, offers three SolidWorks document types: part, assembly, and drawing. Click Part, and click OK.

   An empty part file will open in SolidWorks.

Save the Model

Before moving on to creating your model, this is a good time to save the model, which will allow you to name the part file. The first time you save a part, assembly, or drawing, you will be prompted to select the location and name of the file that will be created. Once the file is named, you will not be prompted again, and you can save the changes any time you want without adding extra time to the process.

To save the file and specify its location and filename, do the following:

1. Click the Save button located in the menu bar, or select File ➢ Save from the menu.

2. The Save As window will allow you to specify the location on your hard drive or the network location that you intend for the file to be saved. Find the folder that you want to store the file in, and enter the name of the file to be created. For this model enter the name **Base, Lamp** in the File Name field, and click the Save button.

Set the Document Properties

Document properties are options that are document specific including detailing, DimXpert, dimensions, units, line styles, and image quality. Once you set the document properties, you will not change them, unless you need to update them later during the design process. Changes are applied only to the current active document. If you make changes to the property of a particular part document, that change will not be reflected in other part documents.

 N O T E Document properties are applied only to the selected document. If you want changes to be applied to all future generations of a document, you can apply document properties to the document templates.

You need to make sure that the *document units* have been set to meet the needs of your design. Unless you are absolutely positive that you are using a template with the proper units, you should make sure that these are set properly before modeling by doing the following:

1. Click the Options button in the menu bar.

2. In the previous chapters, you made some changes in the system options that affected the actual SolidWorks program. This time, select the Document Properties tab at the top of the System Options window.

3. The very first screen you will see after selecting the Document Properties tab will allow you to select the overall drafting standard that will be applied to the document. Depending on what part of the world you live in, different standards are used to control how dimensions are shown and applied. In the United States, we use the ANSI/ASME standard for the application of dimensions. Ensure that ANSI is selected in the Overall Drafting Standard field.

4. Next, select Units in the section on the left of the window.

5. Units are the unit of measurement used to create and measure parts, assemblies, and drawings. For this model, you need to ensure that IPS is the selected unit system.

 N O T E IPS stands for Inch, Pound, Second; these are standard units of measure used to describe length, weight, and time.

6. When modeling, it is often beneficial to view more digits to the right of the decimal point when placing linear dimensions. To do this, you need to adjust the decimal value in the Units section of the Document Properties tab. In the Length row, under the Decimals column, click the downward-pointing arrow.

7. Next, select the number of digits that follow the decimal point. Depending on your personal preferences or your company standards, the number of digits that must be shown in part models can vary. Many users prefer showing at least three digits to the right of the decimal. The more digits you show, the more precision you will have when adding dimensions. For this part, select the option that gives you three digits to the right of the decimal.

8. When finished adjusting the units, click OK to close the window.

Since you are making a modification to the standard settings for the ANSI drafting standard, a small balloon is displayed showing that the standard has been renamed to "ANSI-MODIFIED," as shown in Figure 3.1. The modified drawing standard can be renamed, saved, and used in other documents by multiple people. Since you don't need to be overly concerned with the drafting standards for this part, you can bypass this step for now.

Type	Unit	Decimals	Fractions	More
Basic Units				
Length	millimeters	.123		Overall drafting standard has been changed to "ANSI-MODIFIED"
Dual Dimension Length	inches	.123		
Angle	degrees	.12		

FIGURE 3.1 Notification of deviation from ANSI standard

This is a good time to explore the other document settings that are available. Throughout this book you will be making further adjustments to various other document settings in all three of the document types.

T I P If you are not sure what a particular option actually does, click the Help button at the bottom of the window. Depending on which screen you are in at the time of clicking Help, the help file will display useful information on what each option does.

Create a Base Extrusion

With the document settings adjusted to meet your needs, it is time to get down to some modeling. The first thing that you will be modeling is the base feature for the lamp base. As you may remember, the base feature of a part is the very first feature listed in the FeatureManager design tree. The base feature is usually created with a closed profile sketch that is then extruded or revolved.

Every user of SolidWorks has their own approach to base features, which usually depends on the part requirements. Some create a base feature that represents a raw stock of material such as a plate of steel or a rod of aluminum. The subsequent features then remove material to create the final part. This approach is often followed when creating parts that are meant to be machined, allowing the designer to ensure that the part is able to be manufactured.

Another approach is to create a sketch that captures as many of the features as possible prior to extruding or revolving. This approach minimizes the number of features in the FeatureManager design tree but may make each feature more complex. We are not fans of this approach since more complex sketches open you up to more potential errors that are harder to fix.

Still another approach is to make the base feature and each subsequent feature as simple as possible. This does create more features in the FeatureManager design tree, but with the FeatureManager design tree filter bar and folders, that is not really an issue. Besides, with simple features, it is easier to make adjustments as your design is finalized. As you can tell, this is the approach we tend to use more often, but each approach has its advantages, and you can use a number of modeling methods when working on different parts.

Not all base features are extruded or revolved. Base features can also be lofts, sweeps, boundaries, derived parts, or imported bodies.

Create a Sketch

Sketches are an important part of creating 3D models. A sketch is made of 2D entities such as lines, circles, and arcs that are then extruded, revolved, or lofted to create 3D features. Sketches must be created on one of the three standard planes, reference planes, or flat (planar) faces of 3D geometry.

For this exercise, you'll create the base feature of the lamp base by extruding a simple rectangle to a specified height. Since the sketch must be made on a plane, you will be using one of the standard planes that are already part of the model by default. To be honest, it doesn't really matter which plane you select to be used as the sketch, but we find, from experience, that it is easier to orient the part in 3D space as close to how it sits in the real world as possible. This helps in being able to visualize the design, and it makes the design intent of the part clear to other users who may need to revise your design at a later date. There is nothing more frustrating when working on other people's designs than needing to figure out how a part actually is intended to rest.

To start your sketch, do the following:

1. In the FeatureManager design tree, click the Top plane. The top plane in the graphics area will be highlighted.

2. After releasing the mouse button, a small context toolbar will be displayed with four commands: Sketch, Hide, Zoom To Selection, and Normal To. For now click the Sketch button to insert a new sketch on the selected plane.

 N O T E   **If you move the mouse pointer away from the context toolbar, it will disappear and will not reappear when you move the mouse pointer back. To show the toolbar again, you can select another plane and then reselect the top plane once again. You can also right-click the top plane and click the Sketch button in the context menu.**

In the FeatureManager design tree, a new sketch will be created and shown below the rollback bar. By default, the sketch will be named Sketch1, which means that this is the first sketch created in the model. Figure 3.2 shows the new sketch that was created in the FeatureManager design tree. Each time a new sketch is created, the number is incremented by one, and it will retain that designation even if previous sketches are deleted.

FIGURE 3.2 New sketch created in FeatureManager design tree

Sketch Prefixes

This is a good time to point out the prefix of the sketch shown in the FeatureManager design tree. Between the sketch icon and the sketch name, you will see a symbol enclosed by parentheses. This gives you a quick indication as to the status of the sketch. The following are the ways sketches can be prefixed in the FeatureManager design tree:

(-) This designates that the sketch shown in the FeatureManager design tree is *under-defined*. A sketch that is under-defined does not have the adequate number of dimensions or relations to prevent the sketch from being modified by dragging any of the *sketch entities*.

(+) This designates that the sketch shown in the FeatureManager design tree is *over-defined*. A sketch can be over-defined if it has more dimensions or relations than what is necessary to fully define the sketch. Usually removing a dimension or relation will fix the error.

(?) This designates that the sketch shown in the FeatureManager design tree cannot be solved for one reason or another. There are a number of reasons this may happen, and usually you can fix the sketch by removing sketch entities, relations, or dimensions.

No Prefix If there is no prefix shown before the sketch in the FeatureManager design tree, the sketch is fully defined with no errors. A *fully defined sketch*

means that all the sketch entities are located with either dimensions, relations, or both and cannot be moved in the sketch.

Draw a Rectangle

When the sketch was created in the FeatureManager design tree, the plane became active in the graphics area and changed its orientation to be normal to the screen. Normal to refers to a selected plane or face that faces the direction of the viewer. If you accidentally rotate the view, you can always make the sketch normal to the screen once again by clicking Normal To on the View Orientation flyout in the Heads-up View toolbar.

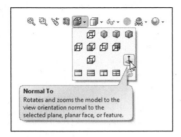

With the sketch active and plane facing toward you, it is now time to sketch the rectangle that makes up the base feature. As mentioned in earlier chapters, you can use menus, toolbars, or the CommandManager to create your sketch, but we are partial to the shortcut bar. To draw the rectangle, follow these steps:

1. With the mouse anywhere in the graphics area, press the S button on your keyboard to display the shortcut bar. It will be displayed next to the mouse pointer on your screen, as in Figure 3.3. You cannot move the shortcut bar by dragging it. If it is obstructing the view of something in the graphics area, move the mouse pointer to another spot in the graphics area and press S once again.

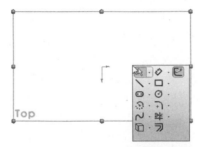

FIGURE 3.3 Sketch shortcut bar

2. Click the downward-pointing arrow next to the Corner Rectangle command to show the available rectangle types. Select Center Rectangle. This creates a rectangle from a center point in the sketch.

3. After selecting Center Rectangle in the shortcut bar, the mouse pointer will update to show the Sketch tool selected with a small icon next to a pencil, as in Figure 3.4. Select the sketch origin in the center of the screen by clicking and releasing the left mouse button with the tip of the pencil directly on top of the origin.

FIGURE 3.4 Creating a rectangle from a center point in the sketch

4. After releasing the mouse button when selecting the sketch origin, move the mouse pointer away from the origin. A rectangle will be shown but will not actually be created until clicking the mouse button again. Next to the mouse pointer, the X and Y coordinates of the mouse pointer will be displayed in relation to the rectangle origin instead of the sketch origin, as in Figure 3.5.

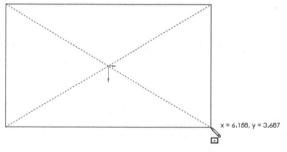

x = 6.158, y = 3.687

FIGURE 3.5 Coordinate display while sketching

5. To create the rectangle, after dragging to the shape of the rectangle, click the left mouse button once again. SolidWorks will apply the appropriate relations to the rectangle including making the edges horizontal and vertical and making the center point *coincident* to the sketch origin, as shown in Figure 3.6.

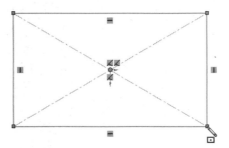

FIGURE 3.6 Undimensioned sketch with relations

More About Rectangles

You'll further define sketch relations throughout the book as the need arises.

When you were selecting Center Rectangle from the shortcut bar, you may have noticed that there are actually five different types of rectangles that can be used in sketches. Each of the five rectangles offers its own advantages, and you will be using each of them at least a few times during your time in SolidWorks. Here is a quick explanation of the five types of rectangles available in SolidWorks:

 Corner Rectangle   The *Corner Rectangle* option creates one of the most commonly used rectangles in SolidWorks. A corner rectangle is created by selecting two points that make up the opposite corners of the rectangle.

 Center Rectangle   The *Center Rectangle* option creates a rectangle by selecting the center point and then one of the corner locations. The opposite corners of the rectangle are connected with a hidden line, and a point is placed where the lines intersect.

 3 Point Corner Rectangle   The *3 Point Corner Rectangle* option creates a rectangle at an angle by selecting the location of three of the corners. The first point specifies the origin of one of the corners. The second point determines the angle of the rectangle in relation to the first point selected. The third point defines the width or height of the rectangle.

3 Point Center Rectangle   The *3 Point Center Rectangle* option is a combination of the Center Rectangle and 3 Point Corner Rectangle choices. It allows you to specify a center point of the rectangle; then the angle is defined with the second point and specifies the midpoint of one the sides. The third point defines the width of the rectangle.

Parallelogram　　The *Parallelogram* option is drawn much like a rectangle (which is a parallelogram as well). The parallelogram is defined with three points that coincide with three of the corners. The first point defines the origin of parallelogram, the second point defines the angle of the base of the parallelogram, and the third point defines the angle and length of the adjacent edge.

Define the Sketch

With the rectangle drawn, you could create the extrusion of the base feature and continue modeling, but it is considered very bad practice to not fully define your sketch. You will be tempted many times in the future to not fully define a sketch in order to save a little bit of time, but keep in mind that the extra couple of minutes you take to do something right the first time will save you even more time in the long run.

Not only will you avoid time-consuming errors by fully defining your sketch, but you will also be able to better capture your design intent. *Design intent* is how your part reacts as parameters are changed. For example, if you have a hole in a part that must always be .250≤ from an edge, you would dimension to the edge rather than to another point on the sketch. As the part size is updated, the hole will always be .250≤ from the edge.

> You can tell whether an active sketch is under-defined or fully defined by looking in the status bar, as described in Chapter 1.

Since this sketch only has a rectangle and no other sketch entities, the only design intent to capture is the overall size and orientation of the rectangle. When the rectangle was created, the orientation was defined with the center point becoming coincident to the sketch origin and the sides being made horizontal and vertical. That only leaves defining the size of the rectangle. This involves specifying the height and width of the rectangle by using *dimensions*. To specify the dimensions of your rectangle, do the following:

1. With the mouse pointer anywhere in the graphics area, press S on your keyboard to open the shortcut bar.

2. To view all the available dimension types in sketches, select the downward-pointing arrow next to the Smart Dimension icon.

3. Select the very first option, Smart Dimension. The mouse pointer will change to include an icon that represents the Smart Dimension tool.

4. There are a few ways to apply dimensions to sketch entities. One way is to *dimension to* points in the sketch to define their relationship to each other. Select the upper-left corner of the rectangle by clicking the corner. The corner will be highlighted with a small filled-in circle when the mouse pointer is in the correct position, as in Figure 3.7.

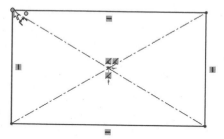

FIGURE 3.7 **Selecting a point in a sketch for a dimension**

5. Move the mouse pointer over to the upper-right corner of the rectangle, and click that point, as in Figure 3.8.

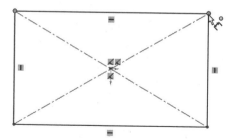

FIGURE 3.8 **Selecting second point for dimension on sketch**

6. A dimension will now be shown with the current width of the rectangle. Drag the dimension anywhere you want it to sit. We usually like to place it a short distance from the area being dimensioned since it makes it easier to determine which feature is being dimensioned in the sketch.

7. Click the left mouse button once again to place the dimension.

8. Once you place the dimension, the Modify window will pop up and allow you to specify the value of the dimension placed, as shown in Figure 3.9. You can choose to scroll the wheel that spans the entire

length of the number field, but this is extremely slow and inaccurate. Instead, using the keyboard, enter the width of the rectangle as **6**.

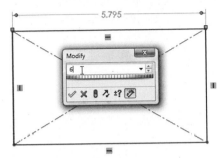

FIGURE 3.9 Defining the width of the rectangle

9. To accept the value entered and update the width of the rectangle, click the green check mark (or press the Enter key on the keyboard).

    The width of the rectangle will update, and the dimension will now show the new distance.

10. Now you need to specify the height of the rectangle. As mentioned earlier, there are a number of ways to place dimensions in a sketch. This time, instead of selecting the corners of the rectangle, select the line that makes up the left side of the rectangle, as shown in Figure 3.10.

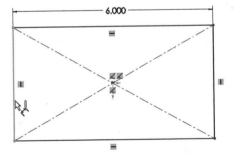

FIGURE 3.10 Applying dimension by selecting a sketch segment

11. The entire length of the line will automatically be dimensioned. Drag the dimension to the side of the rectangle, and place it by clicking the left mouse button once again.

12. Enter the new height of the rectangle to be 4, as shown in Figure 3.11. You do not need to specify a unit since you specified the units in the document settings.

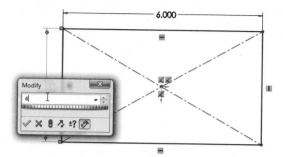

FIGURE 3.11 Defining the height of the rectangle

13. Click the green check mark to accept the new value and update the height of the rectangle.

14. To exit the sketch, click the Exit Sketch icon in the upper-right corner of the graphics area, as shown in Figure 3.12. This area of the graphics window is referred to as the *confirmation corner* and allows you to exit most editing modes while working in SolidWorks.

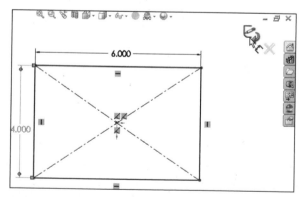

FIGURE 3.12 Confirmation corner of graphics area

Dimension Types in Sketches

When you selected the Smart Dimension tool in the shortcut bar while creating the sketch, you may have noticed that there were a few more dimension types available. The Smart Sketch dimension type will be the type you will use most of the time, but it still wouldn't hurt to become familiar with all the dimension types:

Smart Dimension   The *Smart Dimension* tool will be your most used tool when defining sketch elements. Smart Dimension automatically selects the dimension type that will be used based on the sketch entities that are selected. Not only does Smart Dimension determine the dimension type based on the type of entity selected, but it also can choose another dimension type, such as angles and point-to-point dimensions, based on where you place the dimensions.

Horizontal Dimension   The *Horizontal Dimension* tool creates a dimension where the dimension line is horizontal and the extension lines are vertical regardless of the entity selected in the sketch.

Vertical Dimension   The *Vertical Dimension* tool creates a dimension where the dimension line is vertical and the extension lines are horizontal regardless of the entity selected in the sketch.

Ordinate Dimension   In ASME Y14.5, *ordinate dimensions* are referred to as *rectangular coordinate dimensions without dimensions lines*—that's quite a mouthful. Luckily, in SolidWorks they are only referred to as *ordinate dimensions*, and you create them with the *Ordinate Dimension* tool. This type of dimension is shown with the dimension's value on the extension line without the addition of dimension lines or arrows. In a sketch, a zero dimension is specified, and then each subsequent dimension is shown with the value of the distance from the zero dimension. Like in smart dimensions, the Ordinate Dimension tool automatically determines the orientation of the dimension based on the entities selected.

Horizontal Ordinate Dimension   The *Horizontal Ordinate Dimension* tool creates a dimension with the value above the extension line without a dimension line or arrows. It will only place ordinate dimensions that are horizontally related to the selected dimension origin.

Vertical Ordinate Dimension   The *Vertical Ordinate Dimension* tool creates a dimension with the value next to the extension line without a dimension line or arrows. It will only place ordinate dimensions that are vertically related to the selected dimension origin.

Use Instant3D

With your first sketch created, you are now ready to create the base feature. As with most areas in SolidWorks, there is more than one way to create an extrusion. Most users will, for this feature, create an extrusion using the Extruded

Boss/Base command on the Features tab of the CommandManager. That is a perfectly fine approach to creating extrusions, but you'll learn how to quickly create extrusions by using Instant3D.

Instant3D was introduced to SolidWorks in the 2008 release; it allows you to create and modify features by using drag handles and on-screen rulers. Ultimately, this means fewer mouse clicks and less keyboard entry, which will make modeling and modifying parts and assemblies much quicker and easier. The Extruded Boss and Extruded Cuts options still serve an important role in SolidWorks, and you will definitely be spending some time on those commands later, but I wanted you to become familiar with using Instant3D since it is a method that is largely ignored by many users. Here's how to use it:

1. Using the middle mouse button to rotate the view, or by pressing Ctrl+7 on keyboard, rotate the sketch to an isometric view or somewhere close to isometric. Since using Instant3D requires dragging the sketch out to extrude, you need to have a good angle on the sketch in order to do this. It is not possible to drag a sketch that is normal to the viewing plane.

2. Before being able to use Instant3D, you need to ensure that the ability is enabled. Turn on Instant3D by clicking the Features tab in the CommandManager and clicking the Instant3D button, if disabled.

3. With Instant3D enabled, select any of the lines in the sketch. A green arrow, or *drag handle*, will be shown originating from the selected point on the sketch perpendicular to the sketch plane. If you do not see a drag handle when selecting the sketch line, ensure that you have exited the sketch and that Instant3D is enabled per the previous step.

4. Click and hold the left mouse button with the mouse pointer anywhere on the drag handle. You will know you are directly on the drag handle when its color changes from green to amber.

5. While still holding the left mouse button, drag the arrow away from the sketch. This will create the actual extrusion. Using the on-screen ruler, you can specify the extrusion height. With the mouse pointer directly on top of the on-screen ruler, specify the value of 1.5, and release the left mouse button, as shown in Figure 3.13.

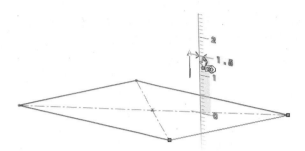

FIGURE 3.13 Creating an extrusion using Instant3D

Understanding the *on-screen ruler* is an important aspect of using Instant3D. The on-screen ruler allows you to precisely select the value of any operation that uses a drag handle to create or modify geometry. As you drag the drag handles, the ruler will appear on-screen running perpendicular to the feature being dragged. As you drag, the ruler will show the distance from the origin, and a green line and number with your current value in relation to the origin will be shown. Figure 3.14 shows the on-screen ruler as it appears while moving the mouse pointer.

Throughout this book you'll learn about tools such as Instant3D, FilletXpert, and others that reduce mouse clicks and save time.

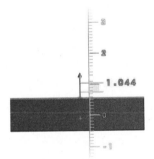

FIGURE 3.14 On-screen ruler in Instant3D

As you drag the location of your mouse pointer in relation to the on-screen ruler, you can snap the values to the ruler increments. If your mouse pointer is not directly over the ruler, the value does not snap, and you can change the value freely. This approach is not at all precise.

On the on-screen ruler, two levels of increments appear. The major increments are shown with longer ticks and a number value. The intermediate increments are shown with shorter lines and no numbers. The numbers and increments shown are based on your current view. As you zoom in closer, the increments become finer, giving you more accuracy, and as you zoom out, the increments are less accurate.

When dragging the drag handle, when the mouse pointer is over the outside of the ruler with the larger increments, the values will only snap to the number increment. At any point you can release the mouse button when your desired value is highlighted green. Figure 3.15 shows the mouse snapping to the larger increments of the on-screen ruler.

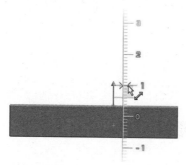

FIGURE 3.15 Snapping to major increments on the on-screen ruler

If the mouse pointer is over the inside of the ruler with the finer increments, you will be able to select a value that is a little more precise. The smaller hatch marks will be displayed with a value when the increment is active while dragging. Figure 3.16 shows how the mouse will snap to the smaller increments.

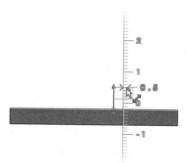

FIGURE 3.16 Snapping to minor increments on the on-screen ruler

 T I P   Even when Instant3D is not activated, the on-screen ruler can be used when using the Extruded Boss, Extruded Cut, Extruded Surface, Revolved Boss, Revolved Cut, Revolved Surface, and Base Flange commands.

Add an Extruded Cut

In the previous section, you created the base feature by drawing a sketch and then creating an extrusion with Instant3D. You can easily continue modeling the lamp base solely with this technique, but I want to make sure you are aware of the various ways to create a model. As you become familiar with the different approaches to modeling, you can use the technique that is best suited for the task at hand.

Create a Sketch on a Planar Face

For the next feature of the lamp base, you'll cut away an angled section of the base to create a more appealing look. Instead of creating the sketch first and then selecting the feature, you will need to select the feature first. This will eliminate a few mouse clicks, and when you are working, every mouse click saved saves you time. Here's how to do it:

1. With the lamp base in an isometric view, press S on your keyboard to display the shortcut bar. Select the downward-pointing arrow next to the Extruded Cut icon.

2. The menu will display the five cut features available in part modeling. For this particular feature, you will be creating just a simple linear cut, so select Extruded Cut from the top of the list.

3. After selecting Extruded Cut, the PropertyManager will inform you that must select a plane, planar face, or edge on which to create a sketch or select an existing sketch. Since you have not created a sketch yet, you will need to select a plane or face.

4. Select one of the side faces of the block, as shown in Figure 3.17. This is the face on which you will create the sketch for the cut.

5. As soon as the face of the block is selected, a new sketch will be created on the side. Although you could make the sketch from this viewing angle, it is often easier to change the view for the sketch plane to be normal to the viewing plane. To change the view to be normal to

the viewing plane, press Ctrl+8 on your keyboard, or select Normal To from the Heads-up View toolbar. You now have a canvas on which to create your next sketch.

FIGURE 3.17 Selecting a face on which to create a sketch

6. Press S on your keyboard to view the shortcut bar. Select the downward-pointing arrow next to the Line icon.

From the two commands shown in the flyout menu, click Line.

NOTE It is not necessary to view the menu flyout each time you want to select a command. For demonstration purposes, you will see all the available tools in each flyout. The last command selected in each flyout will become the icon in the shortcut bar. Selecting this button will initiate the command.

---

7. After clicking the Line command in this toolbar, the mouse pointer will change to a pencil with a blue line next to it to show that you can draw a line. Select the top-left corner of the face of the block by pressing and releasing the left mouse button. When the point can be selected, a small orange circle will be shown on the corner, as in Figure 3.18.

8. Move the mouse pointer horizontally along the top edge of the face a little more than half of the length of the edge. The edge of the part will be highlighted to show that the line being created is *collinear* with the edge. For this case, this is exactly what you want to achieve.

Click the left mouse button and release to draw the line, as shown in Figure 3.19.

FIGURE 3.18 Creating a sketch on a selected feature

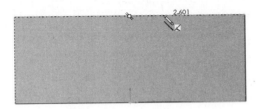

FIGURE 3.19 Drawing a line along an edge

9. Click and release the left mouse button while the mouse pointer has highlighted the left edge of the part, as in Figure 3.20.

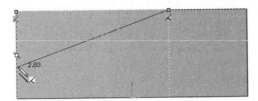

FIGURE 3.20 Drawing a line to create an angled cut

10. To complete the sketch, click and release the left mouse button with the mouse pointer directly over the original point at the upper-left corner of the part, as shown in Figure 3.21. Since the profile created is properly closed, moving the mouse will not create another line segment.

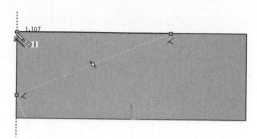

FIGURE 3.21 Closing the profile

Fully Define the Sketch

Two of the lines in the sketch are black to represent that these segment directions are fully defined. Although you did not specify any relations, SolidWorks assumed that the points you selected on the corner and the two edges are coincident. These automatically placed relations were enough to define these two segments, leaving only the hypotenuse (the angled segment) of the triangle drawn. You can tell that this segment is not fully defined since it is shown as a blue color. To fully define the sketch, you must follow these steps:

1. Press the S button on your keyboard, and select Smart Dimension in the shortcut bar.

2. The first step to fully define the sketch is to specify the length of one of the segments of the sketch. This is a perfect example of dimensioning a sketch for design intent. There are a number of ways to fully define the sketch, but you need to ensure that the top of the base always includes enough room for the shaft you will be modeling later. To do this, instead of dimensioning the length of the top segment, you will dimension the top-flat area of the lamp base. Click the top-right corner of the part and the corner of the sketch, as shown in Figure 3.22.

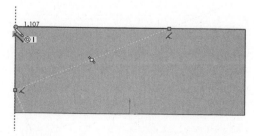

FIGURE 3.22 Dimensioning for design intent

3. Place the dimension, and update the dimension value to be **1.625**. This will ensure that no matter how the part dimensions are changed, the top of the part will always remain the same. The one end point of the hypotenuse is not defined, so it will change from blue to black.

4. You can tell by the blue line in the sketch that it is not fully defined yet. Once again, you can define the sketch any number of ways, but this time you'll specify the angle of the hypotenuse in relation to the top edge of the part. While still in Smart Dimension mode, select the hypotenuse of the triangle, as shown in Figure 3.23.

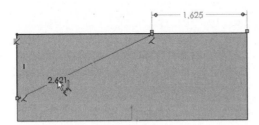

FIGURE 3.23 Applying dimension to the hypotenuse

5. Next select the top of the segment of the sketch, as in Figure 3.24. The dimension will change from a linear dimension to an angular dimension.

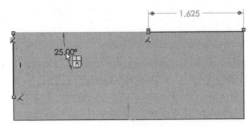

FIGURE 3.24 Specifying the angle of sketch segments

6. Just for demonstration purposes, without clicking the left mouse button, move the dimension around, and you will notice that the angular dimension changes based on the angle being defined. Place the dimension inside of the triangle, and click the left mouse button.

7. In the Modify window, enter the value **20**, and click the green check mark to accept the value. Figure 3.25 shows the resulting sketch.

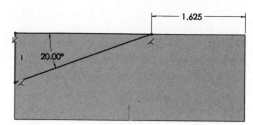

FIGURE 3.25 Sketch prepared to launch the Extruded Cut command

The sketch is now fully defined, as can be seen by all of the segment's black color. If you need to make sure, you can always glance at the status bar and see whether the status has changed to Fully Defined.

Explore Options for Creating an Extruded Cut

Now that the sketch is drawn, it will make sense why you started the process by initiating the Extruded Cut command instead of drawing a sketch separately and then doing an extruded cut. Once you exit the sketch, the *Extruded Cut* command will automatically launch, and the sketch that was drawn will be used for the cut. You can use a number of options to create an extruded cut, so here you'll take a couple of minutes to explore a few of them. Here is one option:

1. In the confirmation corner, click the Close Sketch icon (Figure 3.26).

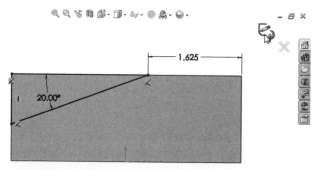

FIGURE 3.26 Closing the sketch in the confirmation corner

2. The Extruded Cut command will automatically start. The inside of the sketch profile will be highlighted to show that it will be used for the extrusion (see Figure 3.27), and the PropertyManager will show the parameters.

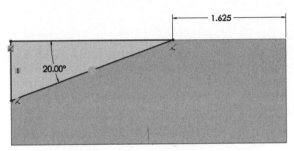

FIGURE 3.27 Highlighted portion of sketch profile to be used for extrusion

3. Switch to an isometric view in either the Heads-up View toolbar or by pressing Ctrl+7 on your keyboard.

4. Even though you are not creating the extruded cut using Instant3D, you can click and hold the left mouse button while the mouse pointer is over the drag arrow to drag out the extrusion.

While dragging, the on-screen ruler will be displayed, allowing you to select the depth of extrusion without entering a value, as in Figure 3.28. The depth of the extrusion will be updated in the Depth field of the PropertyManager.

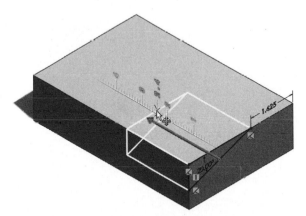

FIGURE 3.28 Specifying the depth of an extrusion using the on-screen ruler

5. Below the Depth field in the PropertyManager, there is a Flip Side To Cut check box, as shown in Figure 3.29. Select this box to cut everything on the model instead of the shape created with the profile of the sketch. Deselect Flip Side To Cut, and the extruded cut will be the profile of the sketch, as shown in Figure 3.30.

FIGURE 3.29 Flip Side To Cut option in the PropertyManager

FIGURE 3.30 Flip Side To Cut preview in the graphics area

6. At the top of the Direction 1 section of the PropertyManager, next to the End Condition field, click the Reverse Direction button, as shown in Figure 3.31. The preview of the cut will change directions. Using this option will allow you to specify the direction of the cut if the default direction of the extrusion was not what you actually intended to cut.

Since there is no model geometry in this direction, click the Reverse Direction button once again to return it to its previous direction.

FIGURE 3.31 Reverse direction of the extrusion in the PropertyManager

The last extrude parameter you'll see at this time is *End Condition*. The End Condition parameter specifies how the extrusion will be terminated on the model. For this particular model, there are a few different ways you can terminate the extrusion, and each will work, but there are a couple that are more fitting than others. Up to this point, you have been specifying the depth of the extrusion with a value whether it is entered in the PropertyManager or via the on-screen ruler. Specifying the depth of extrusion is required when the End Condition parameter is set to Blind. This is the default End Condition parameter of all extrusions, and it will probably be your most used, but you should look at a couple more examples.

To terminate the extrusion by changing the end condition, do the following:

1. Click the downward-pointing arrow next to the End Condition field. If you are not sure which one is the End Condition field, right now it should be set to Blind.

2. In the End Condition field, eight types of conditions are available, but not all of them will work for what you need to do with this condition. The first end condition that will work is Through All. Select Through All from the End Condition field.

In the graphics area, you will see the extrusion preview go through the entire part, as in Figure 3.32. This will work in this case, but it is not exactly the correct one. Through All should be reserved for when it is necessary to create an extrusion that goes through multiple features on a part.

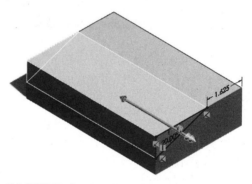

FIGURE 3.32 Using the Through All End condition for an extrusion

3. The next End Condition parameter that will work in this case is the Up To Surface condition. Select it from the End Condition field.

4. You will need to select a surface on which to terminate the extrusion. Select the back face of the model, and you will see the extrusion preview cut through the part, as in Figure 3.33.

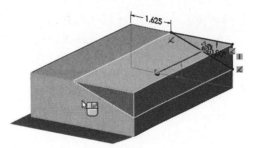

FIGURE 3.33 Using the Up To Surface end condition for an extrusion

The problem with selecting this condition is that if later during part revisions the face gets removed by a feature above this cut, this feature will fail and generate an error. For that reason alone, try to avoid this end condition unless it is absolutely necessary.

5. Lastly, the end condition that is perfect for the particular feature is Up To Next. Selecting this end condition terminates the current extrusion at the next face that is large enough to include the entire sketch profile. Select Up To Next, and you will see the extrusion preview go through the entire part, as shown in Figure 3.34.

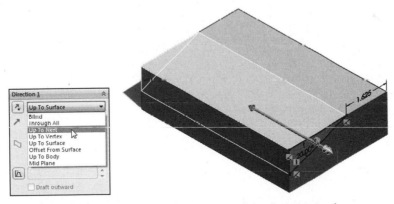

FIGURE 3.34 Using Up To Next end condition for an extrusion

6. At this point, you are finished with the extrusion, and there are no other parameters that need to be selected. Click the green check mark in the Extrude PropertyManager to create the cut.

7. It is now probably a good time to save your work so far just in case something happens. Click the Save button in the menu bar, or press Ctrl+S on your keyboard. You will notice that you were not prompted to enter a filename or location since you defined that information earlier.

Add Boss Extrusions

The next step in creating the lamp base is adding a boss on the part that will later be used to support the lamp shaft. In efforts to expose you to additional methods of modeling, you will create a sketch first and then initiate the command. You could easily create the boss using one of the two previously described methods, but it is a good idea to be familiar with as many techniques as possible.

To add a boss, do the following steps:

1. Select the top surface of the lamp base with the mouse pointer, and a context toolbar will be displayed providing you with the most commonly used tools available for the selected face. Click the Sketch Icon in the toolbar, as shown in Figure 3.35. A new sketch named Sketch3 will be created on the selected face and will show in the FeatureManager design tree.

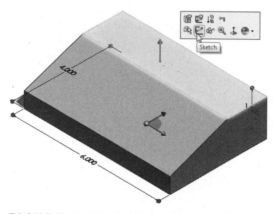

FIGURE 3.35 Creating a sketch for a boss

N O T E   As with the context toolbar when selecting items in the FeatureManager, the context toolbar in the graphics area will disappear if you move the mouse away. If the toolbar disappears, right-click the surface to click the Insert Sketch button.

2. Press Ctrl+8 on your keyboard or select Normal To from the Heads-Up View Toolbar toolbar to make the sketch plane parallel to the viewing plane.

3. Press S on your keyboard to display the shortcut bar, and click the downward-pointing arrow for the Circle button. You will see there are two available circle types for creating circles on a sketch. Select the Circle tool. The mouse pointer will change to include a pencil and a circle.

4. With the mouse pointer on the top surface of the lamp base, press and release the left mouse button to specify the center point of the circle, as shown in Figure 3.36. It does not matter where the circle is placed since you will be adding relations and dimensions to define its final location on the part in the next few steps.

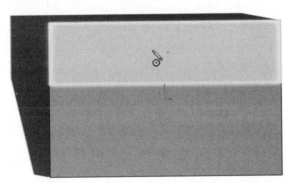

FIGURE 3.36 Selecting the center point of a circle

5. Drag the mouse pointer away from the center point specified in the previous step. As you move the mouse pointer, a circle will be shown as a preview, and the radius will dynamically update next to the mouse pointer. Since you will be specifying the actual diameter of the circle with a dimension, this value being shown is used as a reference only while creating the circle. Click and release the left mouse button once again to create the circle, as shown in Figure 3.37.

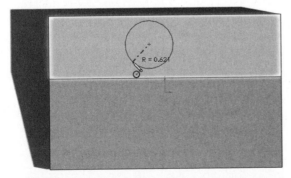

FIGURE 3.37 Drawing a circle for a boss extrusion

6. Now all that is left to do is specify the size and location of the circle to fully define the sketch prior to creating the boss extrusion. Press S on your keyboard to view the shortcut bar, and click Smart Dimension in the toolbar.

7. With the mouse pointer, select the circle circumference by clicking and releasing the left mouse button, as shown in Figure 3.38.

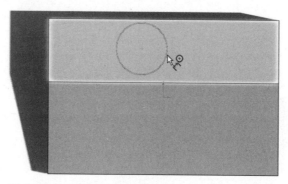

FIGURE 3.38 Selecting the circle to specify the diameter

8. A dimension for the diameter will be displayed by default since the circle is complete. If you were selecting an arc such as a fillet, the dimension will automatically display the radius value. Place the dimension anywhere in relation to the circle by pressing and releasing the left mouse button.

9. In the Modify window, enter the diameter value of **1.25**, and click the green check mark to accept this value, as shown in Figure 3.39.

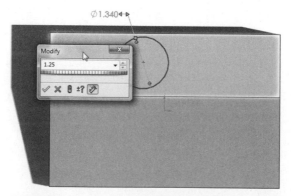

FIGURE 3.39 Using Smart Dimension to specify the diameter of a circle

10. Now you need to specify the location of the circle in relation to the rest of the part in order to define its design intent. Since this circle is going to be the boss that supports the lamp shaft, you want it to always be .900 inches from the back edge of the part. With the Smart Dimension tool still active, click the circumference of the circle again.

Once again, the Smart Dimension tool, based on your selection, attempts to predict your action by providing you with the diameter dimension. If this was the only selection made in the sketch, it would be the only option available, but you will need to define your selection even more to properly dimension the circle.

11. Move the mouse pointer directly above the back edge of the part. When the edge is highlighted, press and release the left mouse button, as shown in Figure 3.40. With this additional selection, the Smart Dimension tool now has enough information to determine that the feature requires a vertical dimension, and it is automatically updated.

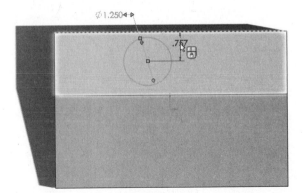

FIGURE 3.40 Defining a vertical location for a feature

12. Move the mouse pointer to the side of the circle, and press and release the left mouse button to place the dimension. In the Modify window, enter the value of .9 to make the center of the circle always be .900 inches from the back edge of the part no matter what dimensional changes that part may go through during a revision. Exit the Smart Dimension command by clicking the green check mark in the PropertyManager or by pressing Esc on your keyboard. The dimension will be shown as in Figure 3.41.

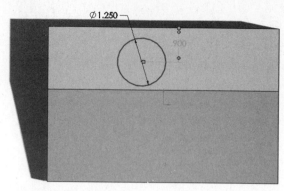

FIGURE 3.41 Defining a vertical location for a feature, step 2

13. All that is left to do is define the circle's horizontal position on the face of the part. You can do this with a dimension, but to better define its design intent, you will be using a *relation* to specify that the center of the circle will be in line with the center of the part. The first thing you need is to select the center of the circle. Move the mouse pointer to the center of the circle, and when the point is highlighted with a small orange circle, as in Figure 3.42, press and release the left mouse button.

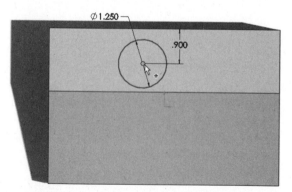

FIGURE 3.42 Specifying points of a sketch to apply relations

14. Press and hold the Ctrl button on your keyboard, and select the sketch origin.

T I P   Holding the Ctrl key allows you to select multiple entities in sketch, parts, assemblies, and drawings. To remove an item from the selection set, while still holding the Ctrl key, select the item once again.

15. As soon as you select both the points in the sketch while holding the Ctrl key, another context toolbar will be displayed next to the mouse pointer, providing you with the available tools for the selected items. For now select the Make Vertical tool, which is the button with a vertical line, as shown in Figure 3.43. This will make the center of the circle and the sketch origin always share the same line vertically.

 N O T E As with previous context toolbars, if you move the mouse away, the toolbar will disappear, but you can make it reappear by pressing Ctrl on your keyboard.

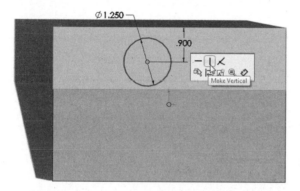

FIGURE 3.43 Selecting the Make Vertical tool in the context toolbar

In addition to selecting the relations using the context toolbar, you can also select relations in the PropertyManager.

16. With the sketch fully defined, switch to the isometric view, and click the Extruded Boss/Base button in the Features tab in the CommandManager.

17. In the Extrude PropertyManager, ensure that the end condition is set to Blind, and enter the extrusion height to be .375. Click the green check mark to accept the parameters, and the new boss will be created. Figure 3.44 shows the finished version.

Now is probably a good time to save the model. Although rare, crashes do happen, and it is a good habit to save your work as you go to prevent losing data when the unfortunate happens. I usually save my work every few minutes and definitely after completing a complex procedure.

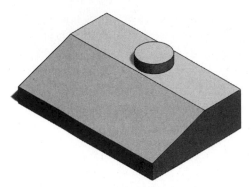

FIGURE 3.44 The part model with the extruded boss

Core Out the Part

Up to this point, you have been modeling a solid piece of metal with no cutouts or holes. As you can imagine, it would be extremely difficult to use a solid piece of metal for a lamp. You need to add a cavity on the bottom side for the wiring and model a hole for the power cord and for the lamp shaft.

Also, instead of switching through various modeling techniques, you are going to finish up this part with one technique that is well suited for this type of modeling. To create a core in the part, do the following:

1. Press Ctrl+6 on your keyboard, or select the bottom view from the Heads-up View toolbar.

2. Press S on the keyboard, and select Cut-Extrude from the shortcut bar.

3. To create a cutout, you need to create a sketch first. Since you already initiated the Cut-Extrude command, all you need to do is select a face on the part to create a sketch. Select the bottom plane of the part by pressing and releasing the left mouse button with the mouse pointer on the face, as in Figure 3.45.

4. The cutout you are creating will eventually house the wiring and any electronics needed for the lamp. The cavity must be located on the side of the part that the boss you created in the previous section is on. If you placed it on the incorrect side, the wires will not be able to be pass through the shaft to the bulb assembly. From the current view, it is impossible to tell on which side of the part the boss is located, so you need to make the part transparent enough to be able to see what

is only visible on the far side of the part. On the Heads-up View toolbar, click the downward-pointing arrow next to the Display Style button, and select Hidden Lines Visible.

FIGURE 3.45 Selecting the bottom face on which to create a sketch

5. With the hidden lines visible, you are able to see the geometry on the far side of the part shown as hidden lines (dashed). You can now create the sketch for what will become the cavity of the part. Press S on the keyboard, and click the downward-pointing arrow to show the rectangle tools.

6. The last time you created a rectangle, you used the Center Rectangle tool, but in this case you do not need to specify a center point of the rectangle. Instead, click Corner Rectangle.

7. To create the rectangle, move the mouse pointer to one of the corners of the part on the side that has the boss, as shown in Figure 3.46. Make sure that the mouse pointer is not directly over any edges or points and is still within the boundaries of the part, and click and release the left mouse button.

8. Drag the mouse pointer to the other side of the part creating a rectangle that runs the length of the part and is less than half the height of the part avoiding the horizontal hidden line, as shown in Figure 3.47, and press and release the left mouse button.

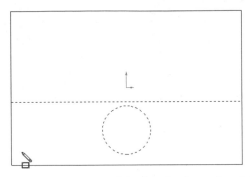

FIGURE 3.46 Selecting the first point of the rectangle

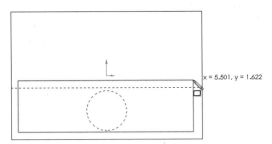

FIGURE 3.47 Selecting the second point of the rectangle

Define the Cutout Location

By the end of this book, you will probably be tired of hearing the phrase "design intent," but we cannot stress it enough. The cutout you are adding to the bottom of the part has some areas that must be considered when modeling to preserve its design intent. First, you need to ensure that the minimum wall thickness is maintained even if the size of the part is changed. Next, you need to make sure that the height of the cutout is maintained in order to make sure there is adequate room for the lamp electronics. You can control both of these areas with how the dimensions are placed in the sketch. Here is how to define the cutout location:

1. Press S on your keyboard, and select Smart Dimension from the shortcut bar.

2. Select the lower horizontal segment of the rectangle, and then select the corresponding part edge. Place the dimension, and make the value .20 in the Modify window, as shown in Figure 3.48.

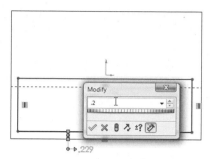

FIGURE 3.48 Defining the bottom wall thickness of the cutout

3. Do the same on the two vertical rectangle segments that are closest to the part edges.

4. Now all that is left is to define the height of the cutout. Select one of the two segments on the side of the rectangle, and place the dimension. Set the height of the rectangle to be 2 inches in the Modify window, as shown in Figure 3.49.

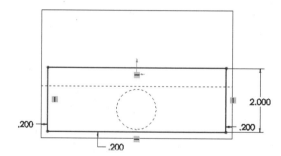

FIGURE 3.49 Fully defined sketch of the cutout

5. Exit the sketch by clicking the Exit Sketch button in the confirmation corner.

Cut Out the Cavity

Since you started the process by clicking the Cut-Extrude button prior to creating the sketch of the cutout, when the sketch was exited, the Extruded Cut command automatically initiated. This approach reduces the number of mouse clicks and in the long run will save you time while you are modeling, which is always a good thing.

1. Press Ctrl+7 on your keyboard, or select the isometric view in the Heads-up View toolbar.

2. In the Extrude PropertyManager, set the depth of the extrusion to be 1.00 inch deep, and click the green check mark to complete the action, as shown in Figure 3.50.

FIGURE 3.50 Setting the depth of extrusion in the Extrude PropertyManager

3. Press Ctrl+S on your keyboard or press the Save button on the menu bar to save the changes you have made to the model. Figure 3.51 shows an isometric view of the model so far.

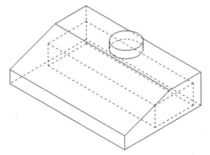

FIGURE 3.51 Part model showing a rectangular-shaped cavity cut out from the bottom

Add Cutout for Electronics Cover

When the lamp is manufactured and in use, the electronics and wiring will be housed in the cavity and cannot be allowed to just fall out. This could be a huge issue for the consumer, not to mention a hazard. This is why you need to add a cutout that a small plastic cover will sit in. The cutout has to be recessed since this is the side of the base that will ultimately be placed on a desktop, and if it is above the surface of the base, the base will tilt to one side and be very unstable. To add the cutout, do the following:

1. Press Ctrl+6 or select the bottom view in the Heads-up View toolbar.

2. Press S on the keyboard, and select Cut-Extrude in the shortcut bar.

3. Select the bottom face of the lamp base model to insert a blank sketch.

4. Since the cutout for the cover will follow the outline of the cavity cutout, you'll *offset* the edge rather than create a new rectangle. Press S on the keyboard, and select the Offset Entities button on the shortcut bar.

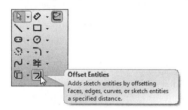

The *Offset Entities* command allows you to create sketch entities that are offset by a specified distance from existing sketch entities, model edges, or model faces. Using the Offset Entities tool, you'll offset the edges of the cavity you created earlier to ensure that the geometry for the cover cutout will be updated as dimensions are changed.

5. In the Offset Distance field in the PropertyManager, enter the value .1. This is the distance a line will be created from the edge of the cavity.

6. Ensure that the Add Dimensions option is selected in the PropertyManager. Without this option selected, the newly created sketch entities will not be defined. Also, make sure that the other selected options shown in the previous image are selected.

7. In the graphics area, select the bottom face of the cavity to offset the four edges by the specified dimension.

8. Click the green check mark to exit the command and create the offset, shown in Figure 3.52.

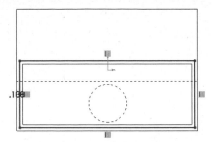

FIGURE 3.52 Creating an offset entity

The lines that are created by the Offset Entities command take on the Offset Entities relation, eliminating the need for additional relations such as Horizontal or Vertical since these relations should have been applied to the original edges. Also, by selecting the Add Dimensions option in the PropertyManager, you're able to create a fully defined sketch without the need to add more dimensions. With the sketch fully defined, all that is left to do is to create the extruded cut.

9. By clicking the Extruded Cut command prior to creating the sketch, you eliminated a couple of extra steps. Once the sketch is complete, click the Exit Sketch icon in the confirmation corner to initiate the Extruded Cut command.

10. In the Depth field in the PropertyManager, enter the value of .1, and make sure that the Blind end condition is selected. Since these are the only options you need for this feature, click the green check mark to make the cut. Figure 3.53 shows the part model with the offset entity.

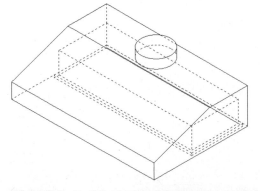

FIGURE 3.53 Part model showing extruded cut to use for cover cutout

Add Holes for Wiring

In the previous couple of sections, you created a cavity that will eventually be used to house the wiring and electronics for the lamp. But you may have noticed that there is nowhere for the wiring to go. Well, you do, in fact, need to remedy that, and you are going to do it by creating a hole in the boss from earlier in the chapter to pass the wires up to the bulb subassembly. You'll also create a hole in the back of the lamp base that will be used for the AC plug cord. First is the hole for running the wires up to the bulb assembly and the counterbore that will be necessary for the shaft nut.

Sketch a Circle with a Defined Diameter

Here are the steps for adding a hole for the counterbore:

1. If you changed the display style of the part back to Shaded With Edges, you will need to return to the Hidden Lines Visible view in order to create the next couple of features. In the Display Style pull-down on the Heads-up View toolbar, select the Hidden Lines Visible option.

2. Press S on your keyboard, and select Extruded Cut from the shortcut bar.

3. Rotate the part to show the bottom, and select the face on the bottom of the wiring cavity to insert a sketch for the extruded cut, as shown in Figure 3.54.

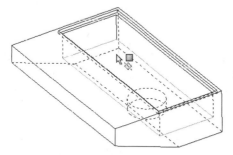

FIGURE 3.54 Selecting a face for an extruded cut sketch

The following step is another example of how design intent affects how a sketch is created. In the next step, you can easily decide to offset the edge of the round boss to specify the wall thickness, if that was indeed what your design intent required. Since the hole going through the boss and counterbore require that the shaft and shaft nut have enough room, you must instead specify the hole diameter.

The easiest way to do this is to create a circle and specify the circle diameter in the sketch.

4. Press S on your keyboard, and select the Circle button in the shortcut bar. Press Ctrl+8, or select Normal To in the Heads-up View toolbar.

5. To ensure that the circle drawing in the sketch is *concentric* with the boss, you will specify that the center of the circle shares the same center point of the boss. Without clicking the mouse button, hover over the edge of the boss with the mouse pointer until the four quadrants of the circle are shown with small yellow diamonds and the center is displayed with a small circle with a cross, as shown in Figure 3.55.

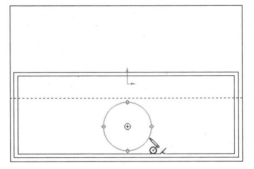

FIGURE 3.55 Drawing a circle concentric with the boss

6. Move the mouse pointer over the center mark for the boss, and press and release the left mouse button.

7. Drag the mouse slowly from the center point to create the circle. When the radius value displayed next to the mouse pointer shows the R value to be somewhere close to 0.500, click and release the left mouse button, as shown in Figure 3.56.

8. Press the S key, and click the Smart Dimension button in the shortcut bar.

9. Select the circumference of the circle with the mouse pointer, and click and release the left mouse button. Place the dimension on the outside of the circle, and enter 1 in the field of the Modify window. If you properly selected the center of the circle, the circle will be shown as black after applying the dimension, since the location and size of the circle will be fully defined, as shown in Figure 3.57.

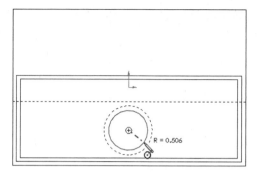

FIGURE 3.56 Drawing the circle, continued

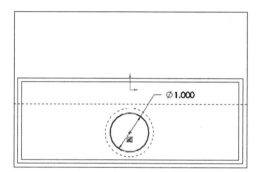

FIGURE 3.57 Fully defined concentric circle

The sketch with the 1.00≤ circle is what will become the counterbore that makes room for the shaft nut. When the lamp is assembled, the threaded end of the shaft will be held into place securely fastened to the lamp base with a nut.

Execute an Extruded Cut for the Counterbore

Now it is time to create the actual extruded cut feature that will become the counterbore. Here's how:

1. Click the Close Sketch icon in the confirmation corner in the upper-right corner of the graphics area. Once the sketch is exited, the Extruded Cut command will automatically be initiated. To make the next couple of steps easier, press Ctrl+7 on your keyboard to switch to an isometric view.

2. In yet another example of design intent dictating the modeling of features, instead of creating a blind extrusion, you will create the feature

to ensure that a specified wall thickness is met. To do this, you will need to select another end condition in the PropertyManager for the Extruded Cut command. Click the End Condition field to display the available ways to terminate the feature.

3. To ensure that the wall thickness is properly specified, select the Offset From Surface option in the End Condition field.

4. Although you should not have to select it, you should at least be aware that the Face/Plane field in the PropertyManager is highlighted and expecting the selection from the graphics area, as shown in Figure 3.58.

FIGURE 3.58 Face/Plane field in PropertyManager

The Face/Plane field, when using the Offset From Surface end condition, is the one that will be used to create the theoretically offset terminating plane for the feature created. Select the top face of the boss at the top of the lamp base, as in Figure 3.59.

5. The Offset Distance setting must now be specified in the PropertyManager. As with the Face/Plane field, you should not have to select the field in order to input the value since it should automatically gain focus after specifying the face of the boss. In the Offset Distance field, enter the value **.125** to represent the thickness of material that will be spared after creating the cut, as shown in Figure 3.60. After entering the value, click the green check mark to create the extruded cut.

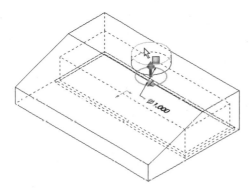

FIGURE 3.59 Specifying the face for the Extruded Cut offset

FIGURE 3.60 Offset Distance field in PropertyManager

The last feature was the counterbore that will be used for the shaft nut. Now you need to create the hole that allows the shaft to mount to the lamp base.

Create the Through Hole for the Lamp Shaft

This feature, like the counterbore, will be defined with another sketch of a circle with the diameter specified in order to ensure that the shaft will fit properly in place. At this point, you can also switch the view display back to Shaded With Edges since it will no longer be necessary to see the hidden lines of the model.

1. Once again, press S on your keyboard, and click the Extruded Cut command in the shortcut bar. This time, select the top face of the boss to insert a sketch for the extruded cut, as shown in Figure 3.61.

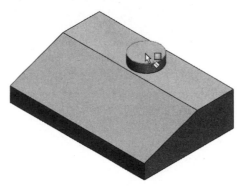

FIGURE 3.61 Selecting a face on which to draw the sketch

2. While in the sketch, open the shortcut bar, and click the Circle command.

3. Display the center mark for the edge of the boss by hovering over the edge with the mouse pointer. Specify that the center point of the circle will share the center point with the boss, as in Figure 3.62.

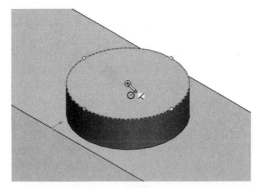

FIGURE 3.62 Creating the concentric circle for the thru hole

4. Create the circle, and specify the diameter to be .7, as in Figure 3.63. Exit the sketch to initiate the Extruded Cut command.

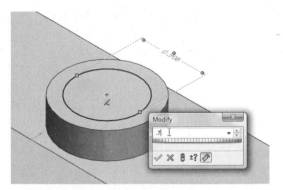

FIGURE 3.63 Setting the diameter of the circle

5. In the Extruded Cut PropertyManager, change the end condition of the feature to be Up To Next. This will terminate the hole on the next face it encounters, which in the case would be the terminating face of the counterbore.

6. Click the green check mark to create the hole. The boss with a hole for the lamp shaft is shown in Figure 3.64.

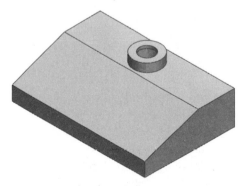

FIGURE 3.64 Boss with a hole big enough for a lamp shaft

Last but not least is the hole for the AC power cord in the back of the lamp base.

Create a Through Hole for the AC Power Cord

Even though you will not be going as far as creating the power cord or even the grommet that is snapped into the hole to protect the cord, you should still make sure that the features on this lamp base are as accurate as possible. At a later date when you become more comfortable with modeling parts in SolidWorks, it would be great practice to design these components to finish your assembly. Here's how to make that hole:

1. Click the Extruded Cut command in the shortcut bar, and select the back face of the lamp base to insert a sketch for the hole.

2. Press Ctrl+8 on your keyboard to change the view to be normal to the viewing plane.

3. With the sketch mode active, select the Circle tool in the shortcut bar.

4. Create a small circle in the lower-left area of the face, and apply a dimension to the circle by selecting the Smart Dimension tool in the shortcut bar, as shown in Figure 3.65. Make the Diameter of the circle .400 by entering the value in the Modify window.

FIGURE 3.65 Drawing a circle on the back face of the model

In the future revisions, it may be necessary to specify a new diameter for the hole created for the power cord. Since you want to ensure that the distance between the bottom edge of the part and the edge of the hole will always remain the same regardless of the hole diameter, you will specify the gap between the edges rather than to the center of the circle.

5. From the shortcut bar, select the Smart Dimension.

6. Instead of just selecting the circle to dimension to the center, press and hold the Shift button on the keyboard while selecting the bottom quadrant of the circle. This will specify that you are actually dimensioning the edge of the circle, as shown in Figure 3.66.

FIGURE 3.66 Selecting a circle while holding Shift to dimension to its tangent

7. While still holding the Shift key, select the bottom edge of the part, and place the dimension. Specify the distance to be .300 in the Modify window.

8. While the Smart Dimension tool is still active, select the circle once again, and select the sketch origin.

9. Place the dimension and specify that the center of the circle will be 2.00 inches from the sketch origin, as shown in Figure 3.67.

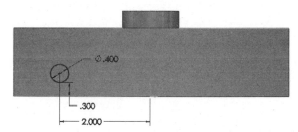

FIGURE 3.67 Circle with defined diameter, distance from sketch origin, and distance from bottom edge

10. Once the sketch is fully defined, click the Exit Sketch icon in the confirmation corner.

11. In the Extruded Cut PropertyManager, change the End Condition field to Up To Next, and click the green check mark. Figure 3.68 shows the lamp base with the newly created holes.

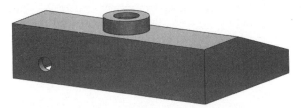

FIGURE 3.68 Solid part with holes added

Add Fillets and Chamfers

The main modeling of the lamp base is now complete, but the part is not yet ready to be manufactured. Even though the shape and size meet the requirements of the assembly, all the edges are considered sharp and not very appealing to the consumer. To finish the model, you need to add some chamfers and fillets to the many sharp edges to soften up the final look and in some cases make the part easier to manufacture.

In many designs, a *fillet* is used to add an overall softer appearance to a part, and it is rare that a part not utilize a fillet in one way or another. A fillet is often an edge of a part that is rounded to a specified radius. Depending on whether the fillet is on the outside or inside corner, the manufacturing process will differ, but the process in SolidWorks is the same. A *chamfer* is is used a lot less often in consumer products because it is not as "soft" as a fillet, but removing the edge is the same. A chamfer is used to break a sharp edge with an angled edge, often 45° at a specified distance.

In the lamp base, you will be using both fillets and chamfers, but how you choose which type to use will mostly depend on the function. For example, you can use fillets to soften the look of a part or make it easier to machine inside corners, but you can also use chamfers to create lead-in chamfers. Especially when it is necessary to insert a part into another part, lead-in chamfers make it easier for the person doing the assembly to quickly find the hole.

Add Fillets Using FilletXpert

You'll start by adding fillets to the four corner edges of the lamp base. Even though you can individually select each of the four edges separately, you will use the little used FilletXpert to help in edge selection to save time. To use FilletXpert, do the following:

1. Press S on the keyboard, and select the Fillet tool in the shortcut bar.

2. In the PropertyManager, instead of selecting each edge in the Items To Fillet section, click the FilletXpert button located near the top.

 N O T E The FilletXpert has a number of features that aid in the creation of fillets. The reason for using the FilletXpert in this case is to quickly create multiple fillets. This, in my opinion, is one of the best reasons for using the FilletXpert—it is an amazing time-saver, especially in larger parts.

3. With the Edges, Faces, Features, And Loops selection box in the PropertyManager selected, click one of the four outside edges of the lamp base in the graphics area.

4. After selecting the edge, a context toolbar will pop up next to the mouse pointer allowing you to specify which edge combination the fillets will be applied. Hovering the mouse pointer over each button on the toolbar will highlight the potentially selected edges on the part and will also display a tooltip explaining the selection set. For this particular fillet, the outside four edges need to be filleted. Click the Connected To End Loop button on the toolbar that shows these edges highlighted, as in Figure 3.69. The four selected edges will be displayed in the PropertyManager.

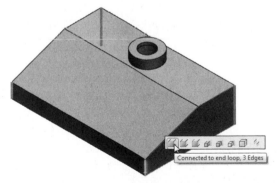

FIGURE 3.69 Selecting the edges to be filleted

5. In the Radius field in the Items To Fillet section of the PropertyManager, enter the value .250, and click Apply button.

With FilletXpert you can apply a fillet without exiting the command by clicking the Apply button instead of the green check mark.

6. While still in the FilletXpert, select the top edge of the base created by the angled cut you created earlier in the chapter. Since you are applying the fillet to only one edge, there is no need to select an option from the context toolbar.

7. In the PropertyManager, specify that the radius of the fillet is **1.00**, and click the Apply button to move onto the next fillet.

8. In the PropertyManager, change the radius value to **.500**, and select one of the top edges of the part. Since all the edges are connected with a curved edge, selecting one will select the top edge. This is called a *closed loop*, as shown in Figure 3.70.

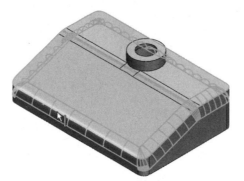

FIGURE 3.70 Applying a radius to a closed loop

9. Click the Apply button to continue.

10. Change the radius value to **.375**, and click the bottom edge of the boss on the top of the base, as shown in Figure 3.71.

11. Click Apply to create the fillet and move onto the next fillet.

12. Set the Radius value to **.125**, and select the top edge of the boss, as in Figure 3.72.

FIGURE 3.71 Adding a fillet to the bottom edge of the boss

FIGURE 3.72 Adding a fillet to the top edge of the boss

13. Since you are finished adding fillets for the time being, click the green check instead of the Apply button in the PropertyManager.

Reorder Features

If you rotate the part around to the backside by pressing and holding the scroll wheel while moving the mouse, you will notice that the last fillet you created is not continuous around the boss, as shown in Figure 3.73. The radius of the last fillet is slightly larger than the space between the boss and the edge of the part. There are two ways you could have avoided this issue; the first is using a smaller radius for the fillet. If the fillet was smaller, SolidWorks wouldn't have needed to change the geometry of the fillet to move around the boss. The second way you could have avoided this issue was to create the fillet before you added the boss.

FIGURE 3.73 Fillet affected by boss

For this part, you are not interested in changing the radius of the fillet, so that leaves creating the fillet before you created the boss. So, this is when you break out the time machine and go back a few minutes and add the radius. Of course, by time machine, we are referring to the FeatureManager design tree.

Here's how to use the FeatureManager design tree to change the order in which you added features to your part:

You can use the FeatureManager design tree to change the order in which features are applied to a part.

1. In the FeatureManager design tree, select the first fillet that was created, Fillet1, with mouse pointer and click and hold the left mouse button, as shown in Figure 3.74.

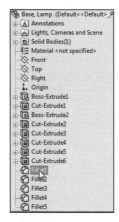

FIGURE 3.74 Selecting the fillet to be reordered in the FeatureManager

2. While still holding the left mouse button, drag the fillet feature up in the FeatureManager design tree, as shown in Figure 3.75. Since the boss was created as Boss-Extrude2, the fillet needs to be placed above this feature. When dragging a feature in the FeatureManager, the feature will be placed after a selected feature. Since the fillet feature needs to be placed above Boss-Extrude2, when Cut-Extrude1 is highlighted by the mouse pointer, release the left mouse button.

FIGURE 3.75 Moving fillet creation to precede another feature

---

 N O T E When reordering features in the FeatureManager, the mouse pointer provides you with a visual cue to show that the feature will be placed below the highlighted feature.

3. After moving Fillet1, do the same with the other two fillets, each following the previous. In the FeatureManager they must be listed in numerical order; otherwise, they will fail since they are each dependent on the previous.

Edit Fillet Feature

Despite how careful you may be when changing the order of features in the FeatureManager design tree, there will be times when reordering features will cause an error. As you might have noticed, reordering Fillet1, Fillet2, and Fillet3 caused Fillet4 to fail. Next to the Fillet4 feature in the FeatureManager, a red circle with an X is displayed. This is how SolidWorks displays that there is an error with the feature.

There are many reasons a feature might fail, and sometimes trying to figure out the error can be a little frustrating. SolidWorks does provide you with information about the error to aid you in debugging the issue. If you hover the mouse pointer over the error in the FeatureManager design tree, a brief explanation of the error will be display. Hovering over Fillet4 will display the error shown in Figure 3.76, and it explains that some filleted items are no longer in the model.

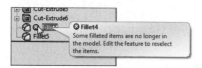

FIGURE 3.76 Error tooltip in FeatureManager

This was caused because Fillet4 could no longer find the original edge that was used to create the feature. Being able to fix errors in the FeatureManager design tree is an important skill when using SolidWorks, and this gives you a great opportunity to learn how easy it is to do.

Here's how to correct the error by moving the fillet features back in time:

1. In the FeatureManager design tree, select the Fillet4 feature by pressing and releasing the left mouse button.

2. In the context toolbar, select Edit Feature (Figure 3.77).

FIGURE 3.77 Editing a feature with errors

3. You will see in the PropertyManager that the fillet is missing an edge. At first glance, you may assume that all you need to do is select the edge once again, but that would be incorrect in this case. As you can see in Figure 3.78, reordering the feature caused the boss to no longer be able to make full contact with the part.

You can also select the Edit Feature command by right-clicking the feature if you moved the mouse away from the context toolbar.

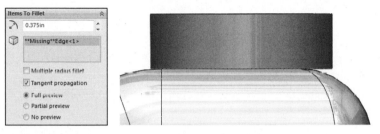

FIGURE 3.78 Boss no longer connected with the part

4. Instead of editing the fillet with the error, all you need to do is extend the bottom of the boss to make full contact with the part where the fillet resides. In the PropertyManager for Fillet4, click the red X to exit the command.

5. Select the feature for the boss, Boss-Extrude2, and select the Edit Feature button in the context toolbar, as in Figure 3.79.

FIGURE 3.79 Editing the boss created earlier

6. In the PropertyManager for Boss-Extrude2, select the Direction2 check box, as in Figure 3.80. This will create an additional extrusion in the opposite direction of the first extrusion.

FIGURE 3.80 Enabling Direction2 for the boss to reconnect to the part

7. In the end condition for Direction2 of the extrusion, select Up To Next to take the extrusion up to the next logical step. Click the green check mark to accept the changes.

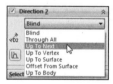

8. After making the change to the extrusion, the error will be resolved, and the fillet will be visible once again, as in Figure 3.81.

FIGURE 3.81 Solid part with correctly filleted edge

Select Edges Through Faces

The last couple of fillets that need to be added are the inside corners of the cavities on the bottom of the part. The following fillets will give you a chance to use a little-used process for selecting edges. These corner edges are under the part and currently out of sight. With the ability to select edges through faces that is available in the Fillet tool, you can create the fillets without changing the rotation of the view.

1. Press S on your keyboard, and select the Fillet tool in the shortcut bar.

2. In the Fillet PropertyManager, ensure that the Select Through Faces option is selected. If this option is not selected, the following steps will not be possible.

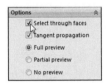

3. Change the Radius value to **.100**, and move the mouse pointer over the outside of the part to the approximate area where one of the inside edges of the cavity. If you are still viewing the part from the backside, you should be able to easily select the corner closest to the viewing plane, as in Figure 3.82. As the mouse moves over an edge, it will be highlighted orange. When one of the vertical edges is highlighted, press and release the left mouse button.

FIGURE 3.82 Selecting an edge that is not seen in the current view

4. Since you are using the FilletXpert to create your fillets, after selecting the vertical edge, the context toolbar will be displayed next to the

mouse pointer. Hover over the buttons in the toolbar until you find the button that highlights the other three edges of the cavity. This should be the button that displayed the tooltip "Connected to Start Loop," as shown in Figure 3.83. Select this button, and click Apply in the FilletXpert PropertyManager.

FIGURE 3.83 Selecting the vertical edges of the part's inner cavity

5. In the PropertyManager, change the Radius value to .200, and move the mouse pointer in the graphics area to right below that last edge you selected. This should be the edge of the cutout you created for the cover earlier.

6. Once the smaller vertical edge is highlighted in the graphics area, click the Connected To Start Loop button in the context toolbar, as shown in Figure 3.84.

FIGURE 3.84 Selecting the vertical edges of the cover cutout

7. Instead of clicking the Apply button in the PropertyManager, click the green check mark since this will be the last fillet that needs to be applied to the model.

8. Since you are more than likely new to applying fillets in this manner, it is not a bad idea to rotate the part to view the cavity. If you did it correctly, you should see the corners of the cavity with radii, as shown in Figure 3.85.

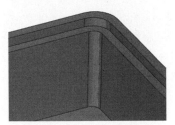

FIGURE 3.85 Inner cavity of a part with filleted edges

Add Chamfers

A chamfer is a beveled surface that connects to surfaces at an angle. The most common chamfers are usually applied at a 45° angle to the surfaces, and a height of the bevel is specified. Most often, chamfers are applied to parts to break the sharp edges, but they are sometimes used to act as a lead-in chamfer to allow for the easy assembly of parts. The chamfers that you will be applying to the lamp base are for the latter. The hole for the AC power cord and the shaft nut will both have generous chamfers to make it easier to assemble. The rest of the sharp corners will not be broken for this example, but typically you would break these edges to .005″ × 45° just to clean up the part.

To add chamfers, do the following:

1. Press and hold the scroll wheel to rotate the part to an angle that easily allows access to the top edge of the shaft nut counterbore, as shown in Figure 3.86. Once the appropriate view has been achieved, release the scroll wheel.

FIGURE 3.86 Rotated view to provide better access to the shaft nut counterbore

2. Press S on the keyboard to view the shortcut bar. Click the downward-pointing arrow next to the Fillet button to view the contents of the flyout.

3. In the menu, select Chamfer.

   Take a quick look at the Chamfer PropertyManager. One of the first things you may notice is that the PropertyManager is significantly different from that for fillets. First, there is no such thing as a "ChamferXpert," so there are no additional buttons at the top of the window to switch between the modes. Next you may notice a few more options are available for the Chamfer tool; throughout the book you will be taking a closer look at these. For now you will only be concentrating on the options that are required to create the chamfers for this part, since they are the most common options used for creating chamfers.

4. In the PropertyManager, ensure that the Angle Distance option is enabled, as in Figure 3.87. This will allow you to specify the angle of the beveled edge in relation to one of the adjacent faces and specify the distance of the chamfer.

FIGURE 3.87 Chamfer PropertyManager

5. In the Distance field, enter the value **.125**. This is the distance that the edge of the chamfer will be from the original edge.

6. As mentioned, the most common chamfer that is often applied to parts contains the angle of 45°. The reason for this is when you are creating a chamfer on two perpendicular faces, a 45° angle makes the chamfer equal distance from the original edges. The angle shown in the Angle field of the PropertyManager should already be set to 45°, but if it is another value, it should be changed at this point.

7. In the graphics area, select the top edge of the shaft nut counterbore. A preview of the chamfer will be shown as well as a tag displaying the values that were used to create the chamfer, as shown in Figure 3.88.

FIGURE 3.88 Creating a chamfer on the shaft nut counterbore

8. If the correct edge is selected, click the green check mark.

9. With the scroll wheel, rotate the part to show the AC cord hole that you created on the backside of the part.

10. Since the last command you used was the Chamfer tool, you do not need to select it again. Instead, the last command used can easily be opened without using the mouse. Press Enter on your keyboard, and the Chamfer command will once again be initiated.

11. In the Chamfer PropertyManager, change the distance value to **.025**, and select the edge of the hole on the back face of the part, as shown in Figure 3.89.

FIGURE 3.89 Adding a chamfer to the AC plug hole

12. Click the green check mark to create the chamfer.

Congratulations! You have just created your first 3D model in SolidWorks. If you haven't already done so already, save your model by clicking the Save button on the menu bar or by pressing Ctrl+S on your keyboard. This model that you have created will be used in the next couple of chapters and will also be used when you begin building the assembly.

Before moving on to the next chapter, you may want to try building the model again in order to become comfortable with all the tools and techniques that were discussed in this chapter. Many of the tools and techniques that were covered in this chapter are extremely common and can be used daily when you begin designing your own parts. It will be extremely helpful to be able to know how to quickly find and use the tools.

You can find a complete version of the exercise as `Base,Lamp.SLDPRT` on the companion website for this book:

`www.sybex.com/go/solidworks2010ner.com`

or on this website:

`www.swner.com`

Are You Experienced?

Now You Can...

- ☑ Create a new part model

- ☑ Start with a base extrusion

- ☑ Create simple sketches

- ☑ Fully define sketches

- ☑ Add and remove material using extrusions

- ☑ Reorder features in the FeatureManager design tree

- ☑ Add fillets and chamfers

CHAPTER 4

THE SKILLS FOR SUCCESS

SolidWorks

Creating Your First Drawing

▶ **Create a Drawing from a Part**

▶ **Add Views**

▶ **Annotate the Drawing**

▶ **Finalize the Drawing**

▶ **Share the Drawing**

P rior to the introduction of computers to the engineering world, drawings were painstakingly drawn by hand by drafters who were artists in their own right. Using straight edges, triangles, scales, and graphite pencils of varying hardness, drafters would create drawings that could be placed on the walls in any art museum. Not only were they created with a certain artistic flair, these hand-drawn drawings were precise instructions that gave the manufacturer all the information needed to accurately produce the product being depicted.

Gone is the era of hours, days, weeks, and even months of hand-cramping drawings. With today's 3D CAD applications such as SolidWorks, creating an accurate drawing is easier than ever. In SolidWorks, *models* are created to capture the design intent and to be 100 percent accurate. The models are then used to create the *drawings*. As the models are revised, the drawings will automatically update as well. This, of course, all depends on whether the correct procedures are followed.

Drawings that are incorrectly produced may still be dimensionally accurate, but revisions often take longer to document than the original drawing did. But by following the steps described in this chapter, you will be able to quickly create drawings that will be even easier to revise in the future. Some of the steps may seem like they create extra work, but we promise you that they will all be worth it in the future.

As you might have noticed so far in this book, many tasks in SolidWorks can be performed in different ways yet still have the same result. The steps described in this chapter are just one approach to creating drawings, but throughout the book we will be introducing you to alternative approaches as well.

Create a Drawing from a Part

In the previous chapter, you created a 3D model of the lamp base, and you will be using that model to create a drawing. There are more than a couple of ways to create drawings from models, but this chapter will concentrate on probably the quickest and easiest ways. This chapter will use a drawing template that has been created with predefined drawing views. Predefined drawing views are created in templates to automatically create orthographic drawing projections from a model. Without predefined drawing views, you would need to create the projections manually when creating a new drawing.

The most common way to make a drawing is to insert the part into a drawing and then create the necessary projections before applying dimensions. When compared to using a template that has predefined drawing views, this approach adds only a minute or two to the overall time it takes to create a drawing. But when you begin making many drawings for a large project, those couple of extra minutes per drawing can really add up. That is why we use a variety of drawing templates for each sheet size ranging from no predefined views up to all six views that would normally be used for an orthographic drawing.

Although this chapter concentrates on creating a drawing from a template with predefined drawing views, it is not the only, or even the best way, to create drawings. That is why we will show you how to use a variety of techniques to create drawing views throughout this book.

Download and Install the Drawing Template

Before going any further, you will need to download the drawing template named FDC Size B from the companion site. After downloading it, save the template to the Document Templates folder. If you don't place the template into the correct folder, it will not show up in the New SolidWorks Document window. Not only is the Document Templates folder used for drawing templates, but it is also used for part templates, assembly templates, and other templates. The folder can reside on your computer's hard drive, or it can reside on a network drive. In fact, many companies, to ensure that all drawing, parts, and assemblies are consistent, will store all of their templates in a public folder on the network that will be shared by all installations of SolidWorks.

If you do not know where your Document Templates folder is located, you can check where SolidWorks is looking for templates. You can find this information in the File Locations section of the System Properties window. The File Locations section not only specifies where document templates can be found but also where sheet formats, color swatches, the materials database, and other files are located. To look up the location of the Document Templates folder, do the following:

1. Enter the System Options window by clicking the Options button in the menu bar.

2. Click the File Locations link in the left pane of the System Options window.

3. In the File Locations section of the System Options window, click the Show Folders For field, and select Document Templates from the list if it is not already selected.

4. In the Folders field, you will see the full path of the Document Templates folder. Make note of the folder path shown in the field.

5. Using Windows Explorer, browse to the folder specified in the System Options window. Copy the template downloaded from the companion site, and close Windows Explorer.

In Chapter 15, you will learn how to create the template used in this chapter.

N O T E If you need to specify another folder for your document templates, click the Add button next to the Folders field, browse to the new location in the Browse For Folder window, and click OK.

Open the Drawing Template

Once you've downloaded the drawing template and copied it to the appropriate folder, the template will be available for use in the New SolidWorks Document window. Since you are using a drawing template that contains predefined drawing views, it's easier to create the drawing from the part model rather than inserting the model view into the drawing. To create a drawing from the part model, do the following:

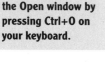

You can also access the Open window by pressing Ctrl+O on your keyboard.

1. Click Open on the menu bar, and browse to the folder that you saved the Base, Lamp model from Chapter 3.

2. Select the Base, Lamp model, and click Open.

3. Click the downward-pointing arrow next to the New button on the menu bar, and select Make Drawing From Part/Assembly.

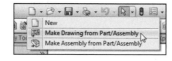

4. In the New SolidWorks Document window, click the Advanced button located in the lower-left corner of the window.

T I P You can always return to the simple interface for opening templates by clicking the Novice button in the lower-left corner of the New SolidWorks Document window.

5. In the Advanced view of the New SolidWorks Document window, select the FDC Size B drawing template, and click OK (see Figure 4.1). As soon as you click OK in the New SolidWorks Document window, the new drawing will be created with the predefined views displaying the projected views of the lamp base, as shown in Figure 4.2. This cuts out at least a couple of minutes that would otherwise be used to place the initial views and create the required projections.

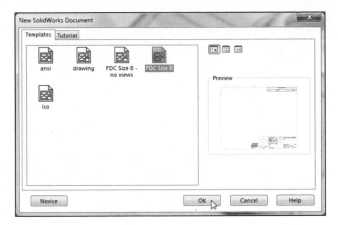

FIGURE 4.1 Advanced view of New SolidWorks Document window

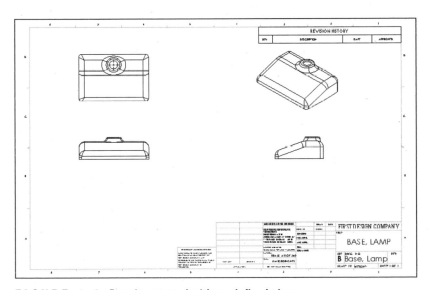

FIGURE 4.2 Drawing created with predefined views

6. Click the Save button on the menu bar, and ensure that you are in the current folder that the Base, Lamp model is saved. Enter **Base, Lamp** in the File Name field, and click Save.

Add Views

In the previous section, you saw firsthand the advantages of creating a drawing template with predefined views. Taking the extra couple of minutes of planning when creating the template will save time in the long run, especially when you consider how many drawings you may create in an average week. A couple of saved minutes per drawing adds up when you are responsible for making hundreds of drawings.

Even though you were able to eliminate the need to create all the views in the drawing by adding predefined views, it is impossible to add every view that is necessary to fully tell the story. So, in addition to the views that were created automatically, you will need to add a couple more views to the drawing. The drawing is going to require the addition of a section view, a projected view, a broken-out section, and a detail view, all of which are required to be able to fully describe what is going on with the part. Since this is a fairly simple part, you can get away with only a few views, but it is not unheard of to have some drawings with anywhere from one to hundreds of views just to describe one part.

Add Sectioned Views

Sectioned views are important in drawings to be able to show what is going on inside a part. Even though you could always show the part with hidden lines, this could be extremely confusing. Plus, if you have ever taken a drafting class, you may remember your instructor telling you that you cannot dimension to hidden lines. *Hidden lines* are meant just for reference and clarity and should not be used to actually manufacture the part.

So, what is a sectioned view? Imagine taking the finished part for the lamp base and cutting it in half with a band saw. The cross section allows you to see the shape and size of the inside geometry. That is what a sectioned view in a drawing allows you to do. It is a virtual cross section of the part and gives you access to the inside features of the part for dimensioning.

The section is necessary to be able to show the depth of the pocket and other information on the inside of the part that would normally be obscured. The following steps will walk you through the process of creating a cross section of the lamp base:

1. Click the Zoom To Area button in the Heads-up View toolbar, and drag a window around the Front view of the lamp base (see Figure 4.3).

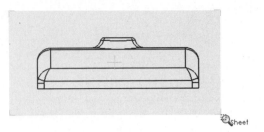

FIGURE 4.3 Zooming in on the Front view of the lamp base

2. Press S on your keyboard, and click the Drawings button on the shortcut bar. In the Drawings flyout, select the Section View flyout and then Section View, as shown in Figure 4.4. The mouse pointer will change to a pencil with a blue line under it to signify that a line must be drawn.

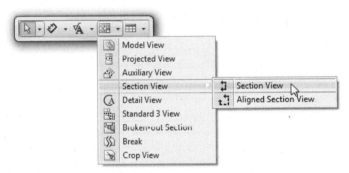

FIGURE 4.4 Selecting Section View in the shortcut bar

TIP Throughout this book, you'll use the shortcut bar almost exclusively. Instead of pressing S on your keyboard each time, you can assign the Shortcut Bar command to the mouse gesture guides. Select Tools ➢ Customize, and select the Mouse Gestures tab. Type **Shortcut** in the Search For field, and assign a direction to the command.

3. Move the mouse pointer to the midpoint of the top of the boss on the Front view, and slowly move it up once the pointer includes a small yellow icon representing the coincident relation, as shown in Figure 4.5.

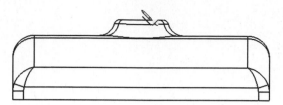

FIGURE 4.5 Icon next to pointer representing coincident relation

4. With the mouse pointer a small distance above the top of the boss, click the left mouse button and release to begin drawing a line.

5. Draw the line vertically down, bisecting the lamp base.

6. When the line extends slightly below the bottom of the lamp base, click and release the left mouse button to complete the line, as shown in Figure 4.6.

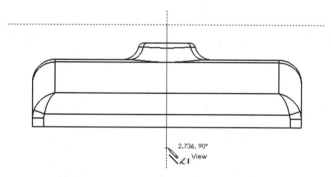

FIGURE 4.6 Drawing a line to bisect the part model

7. A section arrow will now be drawn where the line was created, and all that is left to do is place the section view. Press F on your keyboard or double-click the scroll wheel to fit the entire drawing on the screen.

8. Move the section view to the left of the Front view of the lamp base, and then click and release the left mouse button.

9. In the Section View PropertyManager, enable the Flip Direction option, as shown in Figure 4.7. Click the green check mark to accept the changes.

FIGURE 4.7 Section View PropertyManager

The part has now been sectioned, giving you access to the inner geometry for dimensioning. The new section view will automatically be labeled as Section A-A, as shown in Figure 4.8, and if you were to create a second sectioned view, it would be labeled as Section B-B.

 N O T E In later chapters, you will be exploring the section views in more detail, but in the meantime, we encourage you to explore the options available in the Section PropertyManager. Simply select the section view in the graphics area, and you will be able to make adjustments to the view in the PropertyManager.

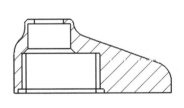

SECTION A-A

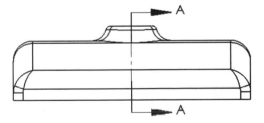

FIGURE 4.8 Newly created section labeled Section A-A

Add Projected Views

The drawing template downloaded from the companion site already has predefined views for the Front, Top, Right, and Isometric views. For many drawings, these views are more than sufficient to fully describe the part. For this particular part, you will need a couple of additional views in order to be able to show the features on the back and bottom of the part.

Using *projected views* allows you to add these views and take on the properties from the *parent view* such as Scale and Display Style. These new projected views will also be connected to the original views, which means that if one of the views is moved on the sheet, the dependant view will move along with it, ensuring that the integrity of the drawing layout is preserved.

The following steps describe the process for creating the two new views from the existing views instead of adding new views to the drawing:

1. Select the Right view by clicking and releasing the left mouse button with the pointer inside the bounding area of the view.

2. Press S on your keyboard, and click the Drawing Commands button. In the flyout, click the Projected View button.

3. Place the projected view of the back of the lamp base to the right of the view.

4. Select the Front view of the lamp base, and once again click the Projected View button in the shortcut bar.

5. Place the new projection below the Front view to create a view of the bottom of the lamp base, as shown in Figure 4.9.

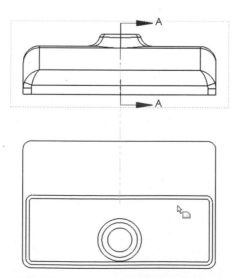

FIGURE 4.9 Projected view of bottom of lamp base

Once you place the projected views, you can move them around to clean up the arrangement of the views on your drawing. But, you will only be able to move the views in line with the projection unless you break the alignment of the view. Very rarely will you need to break the alignment, but when the time comes, it is a good skill to know. To be able to move a projected view elsewhere on the drawing, right-click the view, and select Break Alignment in the Alignment flyout of the menu.

Add a Broken-out Section

A *broken-out section* is similar to a section view in that it is used to show the internal geometry of a part, but instead of creating a new view that shows the section, the parent view shows a broken area. This is equivalent to getting a hammer and knocking off a chunk of the part to be able to see the inside. The rest of the view shows the outside geometry, but in the broken-out section, the inside geometry can be seen and dimensioned.

The advantage of using a broken-out section is that you will not need to create a new view, which is extremely important if space is a consideration. Plus, if you need to show only a small area of the part, it seems to be overkill to create a large section view. In the example drawing, instead of creating a new section view to be able to show the cross section of the AC cord hole, you'll use a broken-out section. Here's how to do it:

1. Zoom in closer to the Bottom view by using the Zoom To Area button in the Heads-up View toolbar or by using the scroll wheel on your mouse.

2. Select the Bottom view by clicking and releasing the left mouse button with the mouse pointer directly over the view.

3. In the Heads-up View toolbar, click the Display Style button, and click the Hidden Lines Visible button in the flyout.

4. Select the Sketch tab in the CommandManager, and click the Spline tool.

5. Create a *closed spline profile* that completely surrounds the hidden lines that represent the hole on the back of the base by clicking around the area as many times as required to create a spline that somewhat represents the one shown in Figure 4.10.

 N O T E *Splines* are 2D or 3D curves that are defined with multiple points. As points are selected, a continuous smooth line is created. Splines have many uses in SolidWorks, and you will be using them throughout your career as a SolidWorks designer. But in this section, you will be using the spline solely for creating the break-out section.

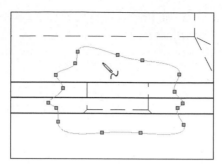

FIGURE 4.10 Creating a closed spline profile

6. After creating the closed spline profile, press S, and click the Drawings button on the shortcut bar.

7. Click Broken-Out Section in the flyout.

8. Pan to the Back view of the lamp base, and select the circumference of the hole, as shown in Figure 4.11. This will set the depth of the cutout to be exactly the center point of the hole.

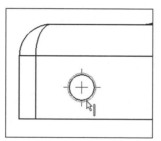

FIGURE 4.11 Defining the depth of a broken-out section

WARNING You can also define the depth of the broken-out section in the PropertyManager, but if you take that approach, the depth will not change as the surrounding geometry changes. This is why here you have selected the circle that makes up the hole in the back of the lamp base. If the location or size of the hole changes, the broken-out section will always be based on the center of the hole.

9. Click the Preview option in the Broken-Out Section PropertyManager to see what the broken-out section will look like when created (see

Figure 4.12). Make sure that the hole along with the lead-in chamfer can be seen clearly without hidden lines.

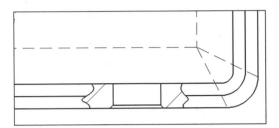

FIGURE 4.12 Previewing the broken-out section

10. Click the green check mark in the Broken-Out Section PropertyManager to complete the section.

11. Make sure the Bottom view is selected, and click the Hidden Lines Removed button in the Heads-up View toolbar.

The broken-out section is now ready to be dimensioned, but because of the size of the part, it may be a little difficult. So, in the next section, you will be creating a detailed view that will allow you to apply dimensions to a larger representation of the section.

Add a Detailed View

A *detailed view* is a partial view of a part that is most often at a larger scale than the original part, allowing for greater detail. Using detailed views allows you to dimension smaller features of a part without having to increase the overall scale of the drawing, which is another way to conserve valuable sheet real estate. The following steps will create a detail of the broken-out section created in the previous section:

1. Press S on your keyboard, and click the Drawing Commands button in the shortcut bar.

2. In the Drawing Commands flyout, click the Detail View button.

3. Click near the center of the cross section of the hole in the broken-out section you just created.

4. Drag the circle out from the center until the entire broken-out section falls completely inside. Click the left mouse button to create the circle, as shown in Figure 4.13.

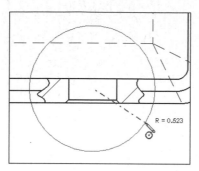

FIGURE 4.13 Selecting part of the model to view in detail

5. Move the mouse pointer (with the detail view attached) to an empty area of the drawing, and click the left mouse button to place the view (see Figure 4.14).

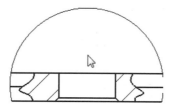

FIGURE 4.14 Placing a detail view in the drawing

Unlike projected views and sections, a detail view can be moved anywhere in the drawing sheet without limitations. In fact, if it is necessary, you can move the detail view to a completely different sheet in the drawing. This is hugely helpful if you are short on space in the drawing. Also, the scale of the detail view can be changed independently from the rest of the views in the drawing. If you think the current detail view is still too small at its current scale, select the view and adjust the scale in the PropertyManager.

Annotate the Drawing

With all the required views created on the drawing, it is time to start applying dimensions. Many users opt to add dimensions manually at this point, but that approach would cause you to miss out on one of the greatest advantages to creating drawings in SolidWorks—bidirectionality. When done correctly, not only are dimensions on the drawing updated when the part model is revised, but it can go the other way. If you make a change to a dimension in the drawing, the model will update at the same time.

Dimensions that are manually placed on the drawing are actually *reference dimensions*. Many users or organizations tend to change the system options of SolidWorks to display reference dimensions as regular dimensions. Although not technically correct, many users find that this approach to annotating a drawing is quicker and easier. Reference dimensions that are manually added to a drawing do not affect the part geometry but will update automatically as the part is updated. However, if the part was not created with fully defined sketches or the sketches were not defined with the design intent in mind, adding reference dimensions would be quicker and easier than making changes to the part model.

With the steps described in this section, you will learn how to use the preferred method of annotating a drawing, but we would like to stress that it is not the only accepted technique. Instead of adding dimensions to the drawing, you will be importing the dimensions that you used to fully define the lamp base model in both the sketches and features. This is one of the main reasons we're stressing the importance of design intent when defining sketches and features. If you did the model correctly, the *model dimensions* that are imported into the drawing would be those required to make the part per your design intent without the need for adding too many extra dimensions.

Of course, as we have mentioned a few times already, there is more than one way to do most things in SolidWorks. The steps described here are not the only way and may not be the preferred method to some users, but we find these are the easiest ways to annotate your drawing. In later chapters, you will be exploring more options for annotating drawings that will also meet the requirements.

UNDERSTANDING DIMENSIONS

Throughout this book, we will often mention the various elements of a dimension. It is important to understand what the different elements that make up a dimension are before continuing.

You can see a dimension, dimension line, and extension line here.

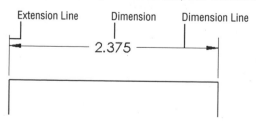

Dimension Lines

A *dimension line* is a straight or curved line with arrows used to specify the extents and the direction of the dimension being applied. The dimension line is often broken to include the dimension value, depending on the drafting standard used.

Extension Lines

Extension lines are lines drawn perpendicular to the dimension line and are used to connect the dimension line to the part surface or points. A small gap is made between the end of the extension lines and the area being dimensioned to prevent the extension line from obscuring the area. If space is a concern, the extension lines can be made oblique, or slanted, to the part.

Import Annotations

As long as the dimensions that you used to define the sketches in the part are marked for use in the drawing, you can import those dimensions directly into the drawing. Luckily, all the dimensions are automatically marked for drawing, but if that weren't the case, you could right-click dimensions and select Mark For Drawing from the menu.

The dimensions that will be inserted into the drawing are the ones used in the sketch and features to create the model. This is one of the reasons that when creating sketches, the sketch should be dimensioned to define the design intent. If you just arbitrarily placed dimensions in the sketches, the dimensions imported into your drawing would not make any sense, and you might be forced to manually dimension the drawing views.

Here are the steps to perform the import:

1. Press S to view the shortcut bar, and click the Annotations button to view the tools available in the flyout.

2. Select Model Items from near the top of the menu.

3. In the Source/Destination section of the Model Items PropertyManager, ensure that the source is set to Selected Feature. Also, make sure that the Import Items Into All Views option is enabled in the same section.

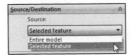

4. Depending on the feature being annotated, different types of dimensions may be necessary. In the Dimensions section, you can specify the type of dimensions that will be used for the selected feature. In the Dimensions section of the PropertyManager, select the buttons Marked For Drawing, Instance/Revolution Count, and Hole Callout.

5. In the Options section of the PropertyManager, select Include Items From Hidden Features and Use Dimension Placement In Sketch. This will make use of the layout that was used in the sketch of the part. This is another example of why the extra steps taken in the creation of the part can help with time management later in the process.

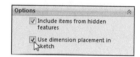

6. Rather than spending the time to fully dimension the drawing at this time, only a couple of features will be annotated to save time. You can always go back later to finish the rest of the features. For the time being, start by zooming in on the Section A-A view. While the Model Items PropertyManager is still active, click the inside face of the counterbore for the boss, as shown in Figure 4.15.

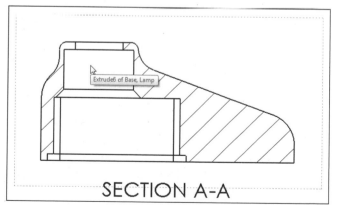

FIGURE 4.15 Selecting a feature to import annotations

7. After selecting the inside face of the counterbore, the dimensions used when creating the feature, including the chamfer, are imported into the drawing. If those were the only dimensions that were meant to be imported, you could click the green check mark in the PropertyManager to fully import the dimensions and exit the command. But since you need to select more features, you will keep the PropertyManager open so you can continue importing dimensions. However, you can take this opportunity to rearrange the dimensions before the view becomes too busy with the other features. Rearrange the dimensions by clicking and holding the left mouse button while dragging the dimensions into a better position.

8. As you arrange the dimensions already imported into the view, you may find it impossible to arrange the dimensions to avoid crossing over the view label, Section A-A. Rather than spend too much time with the dimensions, you can move the label a little lower in the view. Just like with dimensions, to arrange a label, click and hold the left mouse button while you drag the label to a better position. After you are done, the view should look something like what is shown in Figure 4.16.

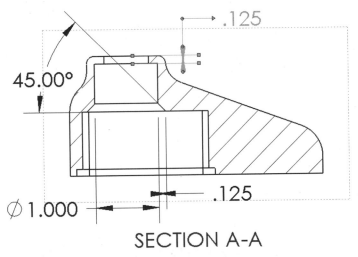

FIGURE 4.16 Arranging imported dimensions in the drawing view

9. Before exiting the Model Item PropertyManager, you need to import one more feature at this time. Click the bottom line of the section view to import the annotations for the width and the height of the base, as shown in Figure 4.17. Notice that not only are dimensions imported into the section view for the base, but there is also a dimension added to the top view. This is because the Import Items Into All Views option

was previously selected. The dimension added to the top view cannot be shown in the section view, so the most logical place for the dimension was automatically selected.

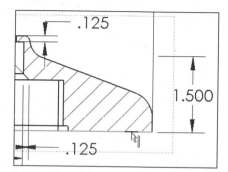

FIGURE 4.17 Importing dimensions for the base feature of the part

10. Click the green check mark in the Model Items PropertyManager to exit the command.

Move Dimensions Between Views

After importing the annotations from the part model into the drawing views, it is often necessary to clean up the dimensions. Since the annotations and dimensions that are inserted are based on the location in the sketches and features of the parts, they do not always translate well to the drawing space. Because of this, you will need to rearrange the dimensions and annotations on the drawing by distributing them throughout all the views and arranging them neatly. To demonstrate this, you will be moving one of the dimensions for the base of the part into another view that is a little more fitting.

Sometimes dimensions are imported into views that do not show the feature being defined by the dimension. As you look through the dimensions that were imported, you will see a dimension that is not attached to any feature. This dimension will need to be moved to the view that actually contains the feature. The following steps allow you to do this and still maintain the link to the part models:

1. Zoom and pan until you can see Section A-A and the Right view as clearly as possible by spinning the scroll wheel to zoom and pressing and holding the wheel while moving the mouse to pan.

2. Move the mouse pointer on top of the vertical 1.500 dimension in Section A-A. When the dimension turns orange, click and hold the left mouse button and hold down the Shift button on the keyboard.

3. While still holding the left mouse button and Shift on the keyboard, drag the 1.500 dimension to the Right view, as shown in Figure 4.18.

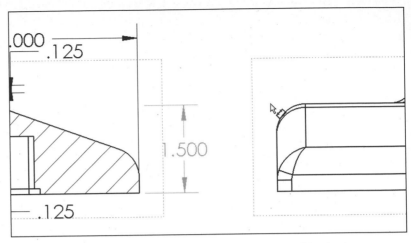

FIGURE 4.18 Moving an imported dimension to another view

 T I P **You can also copy dimensions to other drawing views by holding the Ctrl button on the keyboard while dragging instead of holding the Shift button.**

4. It is safe to release the left mouse button once the mouse pointer icon changes from a red circle with a line going through it to a blue dimension icon. Once you release the left mouse button, the dimension will be moved to the view.

Arrange Dimensions

After moving dimensions to their appropriate drawing views, you can arrange them in the views to eliminate dimensions that are crossing or are inside the visible lines of the part. Also, in the case of the 1.500 dimension that was moved from the section view into the Front view, sometimes the extension lines may be shown on the wrong side of the part and should be fixed. Not only is this for aesthetic purposes, but it also ensures that the reader of the print will be able to interpret the drawing correctly.

How dimensions are shown on a drawing can have a huge impact on how well it is interpreted. If dimensions are crossing over each other or lie within the part itself, the reader of the drawing can make potentially expensive mistakes. Sometimes dimensions having to be placed in less than desirable spots on the drawing are unavoidable, but they can often be resolved by adding extra views or just moving them to another view. To arrange dimensions, do the following:

1. Zoom in on the Top view of the lamp base with whatever method you have become most comfortable with so far.

2. Select the vertical 4.000 dimension by clicking and holding the left mouse button while the mouse pointer is directly over the dimension and it turns orange, as shown in Figure 4.19.

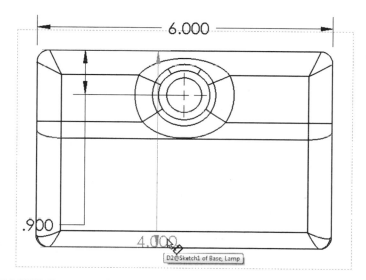

FIGURE 4.19 Select dimension to be moved to another drawing view

3. Drag the dimension while holding the left mouse button horizontally to the other side of the part away from the edge. As you move the dimension, it will snap to different distances from the model edge. The distance is used to ensure that all dimensions on the drawing have a uniform distance between the model edge and first dimension, as well as stacked dimensions. Move the dimension to the first snap point beyond the visible edge of the part, as shown in Figure 4.20. When

arranging the dimensions, try to avoid placing dimensions inside the visible outline of the part. If at all possible, make every attempt to arrange the dimensions in such a way that they do not cross over each other. Sometimes it may be easier to move the dimension to another view to eliminate the chance of dimensions crossing each other.

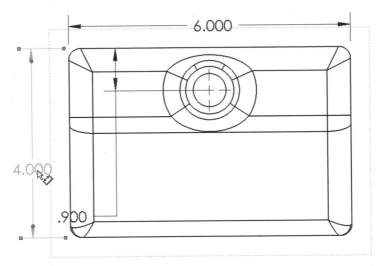

FIGURE 4.20 Moving a dimension to make the drawing more legible

Extend the Extension Lines

After moving the 1.500 dimension, you may have noticed that the extension line does not extend all the way to the part. To have a clean-looking drawing, you will need to extend the extension lines up to the features being defined. This is probably the only drawback to importing dimensions from the model and then distributing them to the various views. But luckily it is a simple task that can be taken care of quickly:

1. Zoom in closer to the Front view.

2. Click the vertical 1.500 dimension by clicking and release the left mouse button with the mouse pointer directly over the dimension.

3. Click and hold the blue handle point on the dangling extension line of the dimension, and drag it horizontally until the point on the model being dimensioned is highlighted with an orange dot. Release the left mouse button. After extending the line to the part, the dimension should appear as shown in Figure 4.21.

> You can adjust the offset distance of dimensions in the Document Properties tab of the Option window. In the Document Properties tab, select Dimensions in the left pane and then adjust the value in the Offset distances section.

You may be asking yourself why one would even care about the gap between the feature and extension line. It is considered good drafting practices, per ASME Y14.5, to ensure that there is a uniform gap between the outline of the part and the extension line. Sometimes this is not possible because of the feature being defined, but when you can control it, there should be a gap.

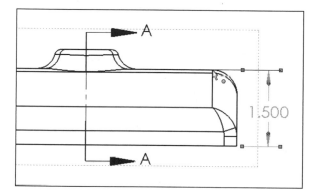

F I G U R E 4 . 2 1 Lengthening the extension line of a dimension

 N O T E You can adjust the default gap distance that is automatically inserted by SolidWorks in Document Properties. Select Dimensions in the left pane of the window and adjust the value in the Gap field in the Extension Line section.

Change Diameter Dimensions

You can specify a diameter dimension for a circle on a drawing in many ways. Although not very common, it is perfectly fine to keep the linear diameter dimensions that are currently being shown in the example drawing. But we prefer showing diameters of a circle with a *leader dimension*.

Instead of deleting the current diameter dimensions, you can just adjust the display to be shown with leaders instead of a linear dimension. Perform the following steps on all diameter dimensions that are currently shown with a linear dimension:

1. Select Model Items in the Annotations flyout of the shortcut bar.

2. Zoom into the Back view of the part, and select the inner circle of the AC cord hole to import the dimensions, as shown in Figure 4.22. The dimensions that locate the hole in the back of the lamp base will be shown. Since the option for importing items in all views is selected,

the dimension for the size of the hole will automatically be inserted into Detail B. Click the green check mark in the PropertyManager to exit the command since you will not need to import any other dimensions at this time.

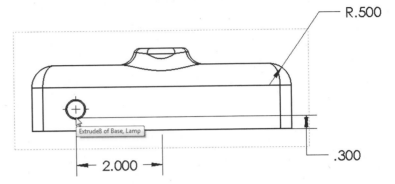

FIGURE 4.22 Importing the dimensions for AC cord hole

N O T E   If the Import Items Into All Views option was not selected, the diameter dimension would have been imported into the Back view. Normally, for this feature, this would have been the ideal situation, but for the sake of demonstration, we will allow the diameter dimension to be imported into the detail.

3. While holding the Shift key, move the .400 diameter dimension from Detail B to the Back view. After moving the dimension, do not close the Dimension PropertyManager for the selected dimension.

4. In the Dimension PropertyManager, select the Leaders tab.

5. In the Witness/Leader Display section, click the Diameter button.

6. Select and hold the diameter dimension, and arrange it in the view so it sits outside the part and does not cross over any other dimension in the view.

When you are finished arranging the dimensions, they should look something like the views shown in Figure 4.23.

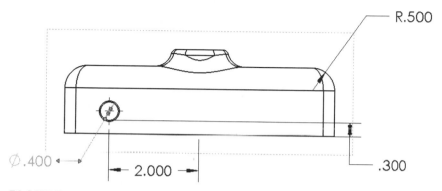

FIGURE 4.23 Dimensions in cleaned-up drawing views

Reverse Directions of Dimension Arrows

Sometimes, depending on the size of the feature begin dimensioned, the arrows will cross over each other, obscuring the area being defined. Since you can't enlarge the feature to make the arrows appear properly on the dimension, you can reverse the arrow direction. An example of this is the diameter dimension for the AC cord hole. Since the diameter is so small, the arrows are on the inside of the hole, so you need to reposition the arrows to be on the outside. To reverse the direction of the arrows, do the following:

1. Zoom in closer to the .400 diameter dimension. If it's not selected already, select the dimension by clicking and releasing the left mouse button. Not only will the dimension be highlighted, but the point where the dimension attaches to the hole edge and the endpoints of the arrows will be highlighted on the fattest end of the arrow, as shown in Figure 4.24.

2. To flip the arrowheads of the dimension, click one of the highlighted arrow endpoints. The arrowhead attached to the leader will flip sides to the outside of the circular edge, and the second arrow will disappear, as shown in Figure 4.25.

Not only can the arrowheads for diameter dimensions be reversed, but all dimensions, even on linear dimensions, can be reversed. As you scan the rest of the drawing, you may see a few dimensions that may need to be updated in this manner; if that is the case, this is the best time to update the dimensions.

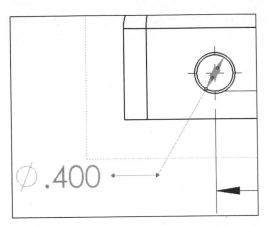

FIGURE 4.24 Highlighted points of the selected dimension

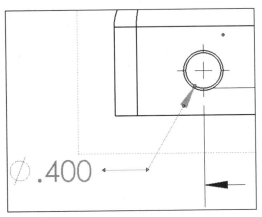

FIGURE 4.25 Arrowhead changed to the outside of the dimensioned hole

Hide/Show Annotations

Sometimes it may be necessary to remove a dimension that was imported into the drawing from the model. Although it would work to simply delete the dimension, we prefer to hide the dimension just in case it is needed for future use. For this drawing, you'll hide the dimensions that detail the chamfers on the part. There are two main reasons for hiding the chamfer dimensions. First, we wanted to show you how to apply a single chamfer dimension in the next section. Second, we needed an excuse to hide a dimension so you can be aware of the process. If, when you are creating drawings of your own, you decide to leave the chamfers dimensioned as they are imported, it is perfectly legit to do so.

Hide Dimensions

Hiding dimensions and annotations in drawing views allows you to show them at a later time if you find it necessary. If you need to edit the linked dimension that will update the part, you can show the hidden dimensions again. To hide a dimension on the sheet, do the following:

1. Zoom in closer to Section A-A, and move the mouse pointer on top of the 45.00° dimension for the internal chamfer, as shown in Figure 4.26.

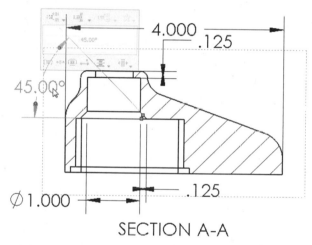

FIGURE 4.26 Selecting a dimension to hide

2. When the dimension turns orange, click and release the right mouse button to display the menu of options for the selected dimension.

3. In the menu, select Hide, and the dimension will be hidden from view (see Figure 4.27).

4. Using the same process, hide the horizontal .125 dimension for the chamfer and the vertical .125 dimension for the thickness at the top of the boss as well.

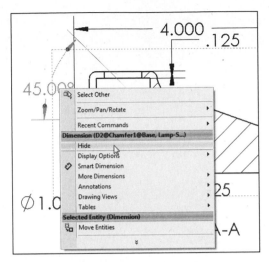

FIGURE 4.27 Hiding a dimension

Show Hidden Dimensions

Using the Hide/Show Annotations command allows you to select multiple dimensions to be hidden or shown again. Once the command is initiated, dimensions that are currently hidden will be shown in a light gray color. Selecting the light gray item will change its color to black and will make it visible once you exit the command. You can also select visible dimensions while in the Hide/Show Annotations mode that you want to be hidden once you exit the command. The following steps describe the process for showing one of the dimensions that was hidden in the previous section:

1. Hover over or click the SolidWorks logo in the menu bar, and select Hide/Show Annotations in the View menu.

2. Dimensions that have been hidden will be shown in light gray (see Figure 4.28). To show the hidden dimensions again, click the vertical .125 dimension with the left mouse button.

3. To exit the Hide/Show Annotations mode, press Esc on your keyboard.

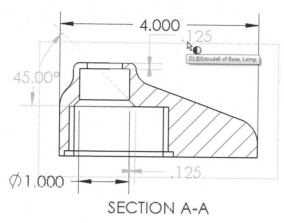

SECTION A-A

FIGURE 4.28 Hidden dimensions shown in gray

Dimension a Chamfer

In the previous section, we opted to have you hide the default dimensions that were imported from the part model for the chamfers. Not only did we do that to illustrate the process for hiding and showing dimensions, but we did that to apply a single chamfer dimension. If you are familiar with dimensioning per ASME Y14.5, then you should know that you can specify a 45° chamfer with a single note callout. You can use this approach only on chamfers that have a 45° angle since the linear dimension can apply to either direction. If you need to dimension a chamfer that has an angle other than 45°, you should use separate dimensions. To use a single note callout for dimensioning a 45° chamfer, do the following:

1. Zoom in closer to Section A-A, and press S to access the shortcut bar. Click the downward-pointing arrow next to the Smart Dimension button.

2. Click the Chamfer Dimension button.

3. First select the angled line that makes up the chamfer of the hole, as shown in Figure 4.29.

4. Then select one of the adjacent vertical or horizontal lines.

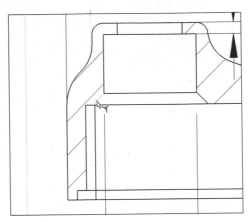

FIGURE 4.29 Selecting a chamfer to add a dimension

5. After selecting the second edge for the chamfer dimension, a circular symbol called the Rapid Dimension Manipulator will be shown next to the arrowhead, as shown in Figure 4.30. You use the Rapid Dimension Manipulator to quickly place a new dimension that is added to a drawing view. As you move the mouse pointer over one of the four quadrants of the circle, the leader of the dimension will rotate to the highlighted direction. Select one of the four sections to place the dimension.

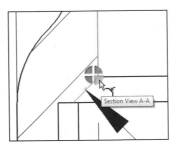

FIGURE 4.30 Rapid Dimension Manipulator for the chamfer dimension

 N O T E In addition to selecting one of the sections of the Rapid Dimension Manipulator, you can quickly switch between the available positions by pressing the Tab button on the keyboard. When the preferred location is selected, pressing the spacebar will place the dimension.

6. Using the same procedure, add a chamfer dimension to Detail B.

7. Once you've added the chamfer dimension, hit Esc on your keyboard to exit the command.

After placing the dimensions for the chamfers, you will notice the color difference. Since the chamfer dimensions were not imported from the model, they are considered reference dimensions and are not parametrically linked to the actual model. In fact, if you were to modify the actual dimension value in the drawing, the part model would not update with the change. Instead, the link to the part geometry will be broken, and even if the part model is updated separately, the dimension will still show the edited value. Even though the dimensions show as gray on the screen, they can be printed as black; we will be covering this later in this chapter.

N O T E It is generally considered poor practice to change the value of a reference dimension since the link to the part geometry will be broken. This will cause the dimension value to remain static regardless of how the part geometry changes in the course of normal revisions. If you can avoid it, do not edit reference dimensions in a drawing; instead, update the part model, and the change will be reflected in the drawing.

Use the Dimension Palette

So far, all the dimensions that were added to the drawing were shown with no tolerance other than the tolerance applied in the title block. It is rare that a part drawing doesn't have at least one dimension with a tolerance. This is especially true when the part is destined to be mated to other components. Only in a perfect world would every part of an assembly be manufactured exactly to the dimensions on a drawing. Variations in the manufacturing process will cause a dimension to drift from its nominal value. It is important to keep these variations in mind when dimensioning a part to ensure that the part conforms to its intended form, fit, and function.

Prior to SolidWorks 2010, the only way to add a tolerance to a dimension was by selecting the Tolerance Type and Unit Precision settings in the PropertyManager. Even though that approach was sufficient, SolidWorks introduced the Dimension Palette to make it even easier to add tolerances as well as to adjust the precision, style, text, and other formatting options for a dimension. The benefit to using the Dimension Palette is that it appears right next to dimension and gives a clearer picture of the modifications being made to a dimension.

In this section, you'll add some tolerances to a couple of the dimensions in the drawing by using both the PropertyManager and Dimension Palette. Either approach is acceptable, but we think after you have used the Dimension Palette that you won't go back to the PropertyManager. To add tolerances to dimensions by using both methods, do the following:

1. To add a symmetric tolerance to a dimension, zoom in to the Section A-A view, and select the .125 dimension for the wall thickness at the top of the boss.

2. In the Dimension PropertyManager, select the Tolerance Type field in the Tolerance/Precision section. After selecting the field, a drop-down list will display the available tolerance types. In the tolerance type field, select the Symmetric tolerance, as shown in Figure 4.31.

FIGURE 4.31 Selecting the Symmetric tolerance type in PropertyManager

3. Below the tolerance type field, set the Maximum Variance option to be .003, as shown in Figure 4.32. In the graphics area, the dimension will be updated to include a +/-.003 tolerance.

FIGURE 4.32 Setting the Maximum Variance value of the symmetric tolerance

4. The counterbore in the same view also requires a tolerance, but instead of using the PropertyManager, you will be using the Dimension Palette. The Dimension Palette will always appear next to a selected dimension but not always in the same position. The location of the window next to the dimension will vary depending on the location of the dimension in relation to other dimensions, but most of the time it will be either directly above or on either side of the dimension. Select the 1.100

diameter dimension, and move the mouse pointer to the side and top of the dimension until the palette is displayed, as shown in Figure 4.33.

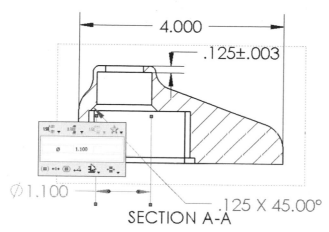

FIGURE 4.33 Displaying the Dimension Palette

 N O T E If you move the mouse pointer away from the Dimension Palette and it disappears, you can make it reappear by pressing Ctrl on your keyboard.

5. Many of the same controls that exist in the PropertyManager are also available in the Dimension Palette, including the tolerance type control. The button in the upper-left corner of the palette, after being clicked, will display the same list of tolerance types that you saw in the PropertyManager. In the list select the Bilateral tolerance type, as shown in Figure 4.34. In addition to updating the tolerance in the graphics area, the dimension displayed in the palette will update as well.

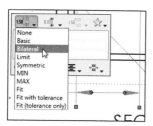

FIGURE 4.34 Selecting the tolerance type in the Dimension Palette

6. In the middle of the Dimension Palette, the dimension along with the tolerance is displayed. Instead of specifying the variance in the PropertyManager, you can specify the values in this area of the palette. Select the top-upper limit of the tolerance, and type in .003, as shown in Figure 4.35. Leave the lower limit as .000. After you update the values, just move the mouse pointer away from the palette, and it will dissolve from view automatically.

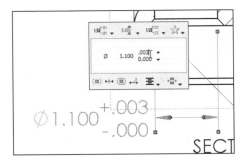

FIGURE 4.35 Setting the tolerance value in the Dimension Palette

7. Press and hold the mouse wheel, and pan over to the Back view of the base plate.

8. Select the .400 diameter dimension, and move the mouse pointer to the Dimension Palette.

9. On this dimension, the tolerance will be another symmetric tolerance with the variance of .003. Luckily, since you have already applied this tolerance recently, you can just apply the same tolerance you added before in the Style area of the palette. In the upper-right corner of the palette, click the button that has a big yellow star. This button will display the most recent tolerance styles as well as any saved styles.

10. In the Style window, select the tolerance that shows the variance of +/-.003, as shown in Figure 4.36. The tolerance will be instantly updated.

11. If you moved the mouse pointer away from the Dimension Palette, press Ctrl on your keyboard to display it once again. Below the dimension display in the palette, click the Inspection Dimension button, as shown in Figure 4.37.

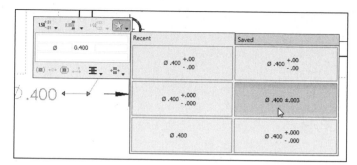

FIGURE 4.36 Applying a previous tolerance style to a dimension

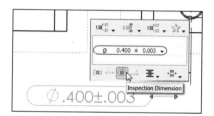

FIGURE 4.37 Specifying an Inspection dimension in the Dimension Palette

At this point, you do not need to make any additional changes to any more dimensions. This section was meant to be just a quick introduction to the Dimension Palette. A few options are still available in the palette that you did not get a chance to explore. We strongly recommend you play around with a couple of the editing options available in the palette by adding text to a dimension, changing the justification of the dimension text, adjusting the unit precision, and more.

Add Reference Dimensions

Despite the dimensions and annotations being imported from the model that were used to define the part, some vital dimensions may not be shown. This happens when the location of some parts were defined with relations instead of dimensions. When you created the lamp base model, you created some of the features in relation to reference geometry. When you created some of the features, they were made in relation to the sketch origin instead of adding a dimension to specify the location.

Earlier in the chapter, you added a chamfer dimension that did not exist in the model. By adding the dimension, you created a reference dimension. In fact, any dimension that is added to a drawing manually is a reference dimension since it is not vital to the definition of part geometry in the model itself. Reference dimensions do not affect the 3D model you created, but they do serve a purpose in that they convey the part information to the print reader.

In the model, the boss location was defined by making the center vertical to the sketch origin. As you can imagine, this is not good enough information to a manufacturer. So, in addition to the dimensions that were imported from the model, you will be adding a dimension to specify the location. The following steps will add a dimension to the part to define the horizontal location of the boss:

1. Zoom in on the Top view in the graphics area, open the shortcut bar, and click the Smart Dimension button.

2. Move the mouse pointer to the left edge of the part until the line is highlighted orange, as in Figure 4.38.

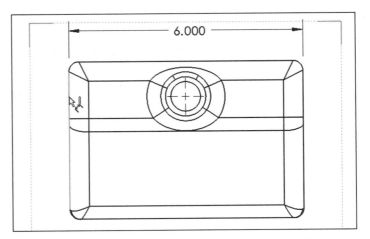

FIGURE 4.38 Selecting first edge for a linear dimension

3. Click and release the left mouse button to select the edge as the first point for the dimension.

4. Move the mouse pointer over the top line of the center mark for the boss. When the center mark is highlighted in orange, click and release the left mouse button (see Figure 4.39).

5. After selecting the center mark, select the top half of the Rapid Dimension Manipulator, as shown in Figure 4.40. The 6.000 dimension will automatically move up, and the new dimension will be placed between the part and the 6.000 dimension.

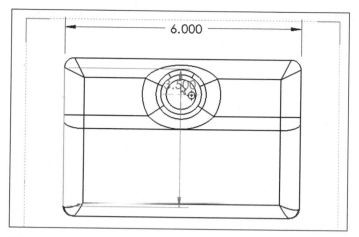

FIGURE 4.39 Dimensioning to a center mark

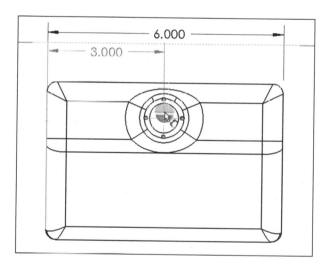

FIGURE 4.40 Placing the new dimension using the Rapid Dimension Manipulator

As with the chamfer dimension you added earlier, the newly added dimension will show as gray on the drawing. This is to signify that the dimension is a reference dimension and is being driven by the part geometry. When the part model is revised, the dimension will be updated as long as the original geometry exists in the model. However, there may still be issues when using reference dimensions. For example, if any of the features of the model used for the dimension are removed or replaced, the dimension will no longer be attached properly and will be considered dangling. That is one of the major downfalls to using reference dimensions, especially if you use many reference dimensions to dimension a part that goes through a major revision.

Add Centerlines and Center Marks

Centerlines and *center marks* are a very important but often overlooked aspect of a properly created drawing. The addition or omission of a centerline or center mark can drastically affect how a print is interpreted. For example, without a centerline, a cylinder looks like a rectangle in a 2D drawing, but with a centerline, it becomes a rod. We have seen designers receiving prototypes from a machinist that looked nothing like the model because of an omitted centerline.

Centerlines and center marks serve two purposes in a drawing. First, they represent the center point or axis of a circular or cylindrical feature. Second, they give a theoretical point to a dimension in the drawing. Another common use for a centerline is to represent symmetry of a noncylindrical part, but we try to avoid that approach.

Depending on your system settings for SolidWorks, center marks are often automatically inserted with the drawing views. Centerlines are not automatically inserted in drawings, so you will need to add them manually. The following steps will describe the simplest and quickest way to add centerlines to drawing views. And just for good measure, we will describe the process for adding center marks. Some organizations do not automatically have center marks inserted into drawing views, so it would be up to you to add them.

Add Centerlines

To add a centerline, do the following:

1. Press F on the keyboard or double-click the scroll wheel on your mouse to fit the entire drawing in the graphics area. Then zoom into the Back view of the lamp base.

2. Press S and click the Annotations button in the shortcut bar to view the commands available on the flyout.

3. In the Annotations flyout on the shortcut bar, select the Centerline tool.

4. Move the mouse pointer until it is inside the dashed lined box that makes up the Back view boundary. Once the box becomes orange, click and release the left mouse button. Centerlines will automatically be added to any areas of the view that require a centerline. Since

the only feature that requires a centerline is the boss, only one centerline was added, as shown in Figure 4.41.

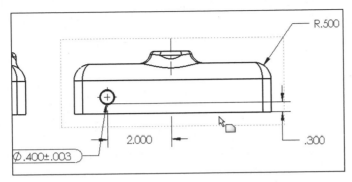

FIGURE 4.41 Adding a centerline to the part boss

5. When you are finished placing the centerline on the drawing view, press Esc on your keyboard to exit the command.

6. The dimension at the bottom of the view, the 2.000 dimension, really should be connected to the centerline since the dimension is based on the center of the boss. Select the dimension, and drag the endpoint of the extension line to the centerline with a short gap between the two.

Add Center Marks

Since center marks were automatically inserted when the drawing views were created, you really do not need to add any to the example drawing. But before moving on, we want to make sure you at least understand the process behind adding center marks. To do this, you will need to remove one of the center marks and add a new one. We know this is kind of repetitive, but it is such an important aspect of drawing creation that we're willing to take a couple of seconds here to show you this procedure.

1. Zoom in closer to the Bottom view of the lamp base.

2. Move the mouse pointer directly on top of the center mark for the boss. Once the mouse pointer is directly on top of it, it will be highlighted orange, and the mouse pointer will change to include a center mark symbol below the arrow, as shown in Figure 4.42. Click and release the left mouse button to select the center mark, and press Delete on the keyboard.

> You can also add centerlines individually to features by selecting the two visible edges of the cylinder.

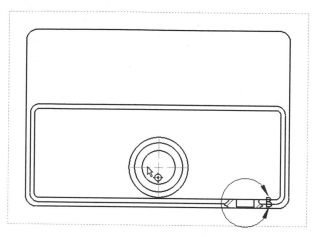

FIGURE 4.42 Selecting a center mark in a drawing view

3. Before adding another center mark to the view, you'll add a dimension to the view to illustrate another enhancement in SolidWorks 2010. If you are familiar with drafting standards, you may know that a short gap should be made between an extension line of a dimension and a line of a centerline or center mark. Prior to SolidWorks 2010, adding a center mark to a dimension circle or arc would result in a single solid line because the center mark would lie directly on top of the extension line. In SolidWorks 2010, when a center mark is added to a dimensioned arc or circle, the extension line is automatically shortened to create that gap. To illustrate this, first select the Smart Dimension tool and then select the bottom edge of the part.

4. Next select one of the concentric circles that represents the bottom of the boss. Using the Rapid Dimension Manipulator, place the dimension to the left of the part, as shown in Figure 4.43.

5. Once the dimension is added to the view, you can add another center mark. Press S on the keyboard, and click the Annotations button in the shortcut bar.

6. In the Annotations flyout, select the Center Mark button.

7. In the Center Mark PropertyManager, ensure that the Single Center Mark option is selected.

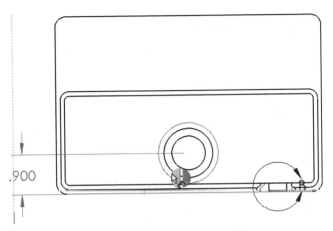

FIGURE 4.43 Dimensioning to a circle without a center mark

8. Make sure that the Use Document Defaults option is set in the Display Attributes section. This option allows you to adjust how the center mark is displayed, whether it is displayed without extension lines, how large the mark is displayed, and whether the center mark lines use the centerline font. You can also set these options in the system properties, but at this time you have no need to overwrite these settings.

9. Since there are no other settings you will be changing at this time, select the largest circle on the Bottom view that makes up the lamp base boss. The new center mark will be inserted, and you will notice in Figure 4.44 that a gap was automatically created between the extension line of the dimension and the center mark.

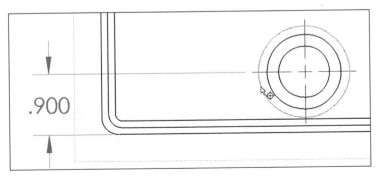

FIGURE 4.44 Adding a center mark

10. Since at this time you are finished adding center marks, click the green check mark in the PropertyManager.

Finalize the Drawing

At this point, you are finished updating the drawing views of the lamp base, but you are still not finished with your drawing. Although the drawing views are important in telling the story, they do not tell the whole story. The often underappreciated areas of the drawing are the title block, the general notes, and the revision table. Without this vital information, it would be impossible to properly control a design and ensure that the design intent is fully documented.

The information that is presented in the title block, the general notes, and the revision table are just as critical as the part dimensions. Without title blocks, tracking the many parts that your organization makes cannot be done without names and control numbers. Accountability is not possible if you don't know who created the drawing, revised the drawing, or even approved the changes. Without the title block or general notes, material specifications cannot be specified. All the steps required for manufacturing cannot be delineated for the print reader. And if there is no revision table on the drawing, changes to the part or drawing cannot be readily available to the print reader.

In the next few sections, you will be finishing the drawing by adding all the pertinent information that is required to manufacture and control the drawing.

Fill in the Title Block

The steps you took while creating the drawing template will make the task of filling out the title block extremely easy. Prior to SolidWorks 2009, the title block would be filled out by editing the properties that were linked to the title block text items or by directly editing the text in the Sheet Format setting. Although editing the linked properties was the correct manner of filling out the title block, many users also thought it to be the quickest and easiest approach. But with the Title Block Manager, filling in the title block is even easier, and it updates the properties that are linked. So, there is no reason not to use this approach, and the next couple of steps will demonstrate how easy it really is to do:

1. Zoom in on the title block area of the drawing until the text is readable. Depending on your monitor size and screen resolution, you may need to do the following steps in sections in order to allow you to have the text being entered as readable on the screen.

2. Move the mouse pointer to the title block within the boundaries of the title block hotspot you defined in the drawing template.

3. Activate the Title Block Manager by double-clicking the left mouse button with the mouse pointer within the hotspot.

4. Select the field in the Title section of the title block by moving the mouse pointer directly onto the blue field, and click the left mouse button (see Figure 4.45).

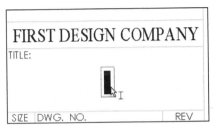

FIGURE 4.45 Updating the drawing description using the Title Block Manager

5. Type in the title of the drawing in all uppercase: **BASE, LAMP.**

6. Click the Name field to update the DrawnBy custom property with your name, and then change the date to the date you created the drawing, as shown in Figure 4.46.

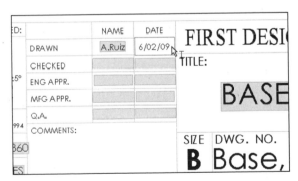

FIGURE 4.46 Adding the name and date to the drawing

7. Click the block in the Material section, and type **BRASS, ALLOY 360.**

8. Click the block in the Finish section, and type 8 **MICROINCHES.**

9. Once you've correctly filled out the title block, accept the changes by clicking the green check mark in the Title Block Data PropertyManager.

Add Notes to the Drawing

Notes on a drawing are just as important as the drawing views themselves, since the notes describe additional manufacturing and quality instructions that cannot be described in the views. Notes that are added to a drawing are normally considered to apply to the drawing as a whole; however, with the use of flagnotes notes, they can also apply to specific areas of a drawing.

For this drawing, you will have a small set of notes that apply to the entire drawing and will be numbered in sequential order. The following steps will demonstrate the process for adding notes to the drawing:

Flagnotes consist of a symbol such as a triangle, square, or diamond pointing to a specific area on the drawing.

1. Press F on the keyboard or double-click the scroll wheel to fit the entire drawing into the graphics area.

2. Press S on the keyboard, and click the Annotations button in the shortcut bar.

3. Select Notes from the Annotations flyout.

4. A number of settings for notes are available in the Notes PropertyManager, but you need to be concerned with only a couple at this time. In the Text Format section of the PropertyManager, ensure that the Left Align button is selected. This will left justify all the text of the note.

5. Also in the Text Format section, ensure that the Use Document Font option is enabled.

N O T E   With the Use Document Font option enabled in the Text Format section, the format of the font will be controlled with the Document Properties dialog box of the active drawing. This saves time when company standards or sheet sizes are revised, allowing the user to update one format parameter and have it be propagated throughout the drawing. If notes and dimensions are created without this option enabled, any changes to the font parameters will have to be made manually and to each item individually.

6. Once you've set the options in the PropertyManager, you can create the drawing notes. Attached to the mouse pointer is a small box that represents the text box that will be placed. Move the mouse pointer to the approximate area of the upper-left corner of the drawing sheet. Don't worry too much about its position at this time since you will be able to fine-tune its position after the note is created. When the mouse pointer is in the upper-left corner of the drawing sheet, click and release the left mouse button to place the note box, as shown in Figure 4.47.

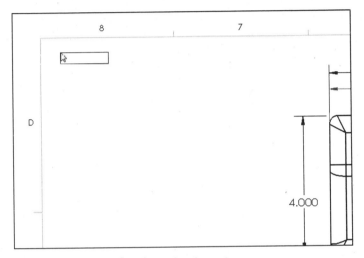

FIGURE 4.47 Creating a drawing note

 WARNING When placing notes into a drawing, ensure that the note is not placed within the highlighted boundary of a drawing view; otherwise, the note will become part of the view.

7. After placing the text block, press the Caps Lock button on the keyboard since text on drawings are generally shown in uppercase, and type the words **GENERAL NOTES** followed by a colon. This will be the title for the notes. Don't worry about the formatting at this point; you will go back and adjust the formatting in a few minutes.

8. Hit Enter to start a new line, and click the Number button on the Formatting toolbar. Enter the notes shown here. Pressing Enter at the end of each line will add a new number.

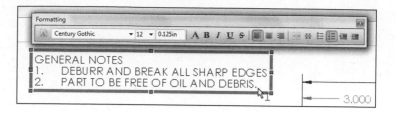

9. After filling in the notes, highlight the note title, and select Bold in the formatting toolbar.

10. Once finished with the notes, click anywhere outside the note.

11. Depending on where you placed the note, it may be necessary to adjust its position on the drawing to prevent it from running into the drawing views. It may also be necessary to move a drawing view to make more room for the notes.

12. Select the notes again, and in the PropertyManager, click Lock/Unlock Note in the Text Format section. The notes can still be edited, but the positions will not change until the Lock/Unlock Note option is deselected.

Update the Revision Table

It is a good idea to lock notes into position to prevent accidentally moving them when selecting other drawing objects.

The revision table is used to track the changes made to the drawing to meet the needs of document control. When the drawing template was created, you added the revision table, which eliminates the need for inserting it at this time. All that you need to do is add a revision to the drawing stating that the drawing is ready for manufacturing. To add revisions to the revision table, do the following:

1. Zoom in closer onto the revision table in the upper-right corner of the drawing sheet.

2. Select anywhere inside the revision table by clicking and releasing the right mouse button.

3. In the menu, select Revisions and then Add Revision, as shown in Figure 4.48. A new row will be added to the revision table with the revision and current date already added.

4. Select the cell in the Description column in the newly created row.

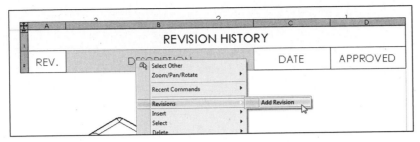

FIGURE 4.48 Adding a revision to the revision table

5. Enter **INTIAL RELEASE** for the description. Click anywhere outside the revision table to accept the changes.

	3	2	1	
REVISION HISTORY				
REV.	DESCRIPTION		DATE	APPROVED
A	INITIAL RELEASE		6/2/2009	

If you look at the revision field in the title block, you will notice that it now displays *A* as the revision. In the future as revisions are added to the revision, the latest revision will automatically be displayed in the title block. That is one of the main advantages to linking properties; it removes a lot of the guesswork and ensures that you won't forget important information.

Share the Drawing

Congratulations! You have now officially created your first SolidWorks drawing. Of course, even the best drawing is not very helpful if no one can see it, and there a few different ways to share your drawings with others in your organization. The following sections will describe the most commonly used process for sharing drawings. The steps shown are by no means all the methods you may encounter in your career as a SolidWorks designer.

Print Your Drawing

The most common way to share drawings within an organization is to create a hard copy. This often involves using a large-format printer to create a full-scale drawing on the specified sheet size. The following steps will vary slightly for each person, depending on the printer that is installed onto your system. Keep that in mind that when doing the following steps; it is impossible to give details depending on your specific print drivers. To keeps things simple, we will go over the most basic settings, and you should look into the particular requirements for your printer.

1. Click the Print button in the menu bar or press Ctrl+P on your keyboard to initiate the Print command.

2. In the Document Printer section of the Print window, select the printer you want to use for your drawing.

3. Clicking the Properties button next to the Name field will allow you to specify the settings that are specific to the selected printer. This is often the area where you can select the resolution, image quality, printer tray, and other settings your printer may allow.

4. Click the Page Setup button in the same section.

5. The Page Setup window is where you can specify the sheet size, orientation, scale, and other specifications for your drawing. First, in the Resolution And Scale section, click the option Scale, and make sure the value is set to 100%.

6. In the Drawing Color section, you should be presented with three choices: Automatic, Color/Gray Scale, and Black And White. In most cases, any of these options will suffice, but in this case you want to select Black And White. Since your drawing contains reference dimensions that are displayed in gray, specifying this option will print the gray dimensions as black. The reader of the print does not need to see that the dimensions you added are not linked to the part features.

7. In the Paper section, select the box next to the Size label. This field allows you to specify the sheet of paper that will be printed. Depending on your printer options, you may need to select either Size B or 11″ x 17″.

8. In the Orientation section, select Landscape. This option specifies that the drawing will be printed horizontally, matching the drawing you created. If this option is not selected, the drawing will be cut off.

9. Once you've set the required options, click the OK button to return to the Print dialog box.

10. The Print Range setting of the Print dialog box allows you to specify exactly what you want to print. For this drawing, you can select

the Current Sheet option or All Sheets, since this drawing has only one sheet.

11. With all the options set, click the Print button, and you will be rewarded with a fresh new drawing to route for approvals.

As we mentioned, this is just a basic example of printing your drawing. We suggest experimenting with the additional options available for your drawing.

Create a PDF of Your Drawing

In recent years the popularity of PDF files has grown to the point where some organizations have abandoned hard-copy prints completely. PDF stands for Portable Document Format, and it was created by Adobe Systems in 1993. The advantage of PDF is that it is a fairly lightweight file format that completely captures the appearance of 2D documents. The use of PDF files for drawings also allows for the viewing of drawings without SolidWorks. SolidWorks has the capability to save drawings as PDFs without the need of any additional software. The options are limited, and if you require more options for PDF creation, you will need to purchase Adobe software for printing to PDF.

PDF files also allow you to send the drawing via email to vendors, suppliers, and manufacturers without the need to send the model data that would be required when sending a SolidWorks drawing. The following steps will allow you to create a PDF of your drawing:

1. On the menu bar, select the downward-pointing arrow next to the Save icon, and select Save As from the flyout.

2. Click the File Type field, and select Adobe Portable Document Format (*.PDF) from the menu.

3. Near the bottom of the Save As window, click the Options button.

4. Select the High Quality option to make sure that the drawing will have the property quality needed to be able to view the drawing clearly. Click OK to accept the changes.

5. In the Save As dialog box, click Save to create the PDF.

6. To view the PDF file created, you must have a reader for PDF files installed on your system. Navigate to the folder where the file was created in Windows Explorer, and double-click the file to view the document.

▶

Sharing PDFs of drawings saves on transmission time and also helps prevent the release of proprietary model data.

One drawback to using a PDF is that the dimensions that were created as reference dimensions will still be displayed as gray. When the PDF file is printed, the option to print as black and white can be set in the Print Options. Refer to the help file for the PDF reader for information on how to set the option.

Make a Detached Drawing

The last option for sharing your drawing that we will cover in this chapter is creating a detached drawing. A detached drawing allows you to share the actual SolidWorks drawing with other SolidWorks users without the need for the model data. The advantage to using a detached drawing over a print of PDF is that the user can measure, add reference dimensions, and even edit notes on the drawing as needed. It is a great way to send information to vendors and manufacturers. In some cases, the end user can decide to save the drawing as another file format, such as a DWG, DXF, AI, or other 2D file format for other CAD packages.

1. On the menu bar, click the downward-pointing arrow next to the Save button, and select Save As from the menu.

2. In the Save As dialog box, select the File Type field, and select Detached Drawing from the menu.

3. Navigate to the folder that will be used to save the drawing, and edit the filename if necessary.

4. Click Save to create the detached drawing.

If you open the detached drawing in SolidWorks, you will notice that all the drawing views shown in the PropertyManager are still shown but now include an icon representing that the view link is broken. Depending on the size of your drawing, you may also notice that the load time for the drawing was greatly reduced since the model data was not loaded into memory.

Are You Experienced?

Now You Can...

- ☑ **Create a drawing from a SolidWorks model**

- ☑ **Add projections, sections, and details to drawings**

- ☑ **Import model data into a drawing**

- ☑ **Move and arrange dimensions in drawing views**

- ☑ **Add reference dimensions**

- ☑ **Add centerlines and center marks**

- ☑ **Fill in the title block using the Title Block Manager**

- ☑ **Add revisions to the revision table**

- ☑ **Add notes to a drawing**

- ☑ **Print a drawing**

- ☑ **Create a PDF of a drawing**

- ☑ **Create a detached drawing**

CHAPTER 5

Creating a Revolved Part

▶ Create a Sketch for a Revolved Part

▶ Draw Arcs

▶ Dimension Sketches with Centerlines

▶ Mirror a Sketch

▶ Trim Sketch Entities

▶ Revolve the Sketch

▶ Add a Threaded Boss

▶ Add a Revolved Cut

▶ Finish the Shaft

I n Chapter 3, "Creating Your First Part," your first model for the desktop lamp was the base. The part you modeled would be machined most likely using a milling machine. In a milling machine, a piece of metal or other hard material is held down on a plate that moves in linear directions along the x- and y-axes. A spindle holds various cutting tools that spin at a high rate, cutting into the material to create the features specified in the model or print.

In this chapter, you will be creating the shaft of the lamp that attaches to the base and holds the shade assembly. Unlike the lamp base, the shaft of the lamp will be created using a lathe. Parts that are machined using a lathe are spun at a high rate, while cutting tools are used to cut features into the material based on the solid model or a print. SolidWorks parts that are designed to be turned on a lathe have features that share the same centerline on a revolved part. Most features on a revolved part will be revolved 360° around a centerline that corresponds to the axis of revolution in the lathe.

Create a Sketch for a Revolved Part

Creating a sketch for a revolved part is the same as another sketch except for one key aspect. A sketch that is meant to be revolved must have a centerline that will act as the axis of revolution. The sketch for a revolved part is a closed profile that can be created with normal sketch entities such as lines, arcs, circles, and polygons. The lamp shaft, although a fairly simple part, has a great modern look to it and is actually fun to model. So, let's get started on the part by first creating a new part file. Here's how:

1. Click New in the menu bar.

2. Select Part in the New SolidWorks Document window, and click OK.

3. Just like you did in earlier chapters, you need to make sure the document settings that pertain to the units are set if not already done so in the part template. Click the Options button in the menu bar, and select the Document Properties tab. On the right side of the window, select Units.

4. In the Units section of the Document Properties tab, select the IPS option to set the unit system of the part to use Inches. Then set the number of places to the right of the decimal point to three places. Click OK to accept the changes to the document properties.

5. Click Save in the menu bar, and browse to the location where you are saving the models for the lamp project. Name the part **Shaft, Lamp,** and click Save.

6. Select Front Plane in the FeatureManager, and select Sketch from the context menu.

7. Select Centerline in the shortcut bar in the Line flyout.

8. Move the mouse pointer directly above the sketch origin until the point is highlighted orange. Click and hold the left mouse button to begin drawing the centerline.

9. Drag the line up while still holding the left mouse button down until the length is approximately 8.000 inches long, as displayed below the mouse pointer (see Figure 5.1). When the desired length is achieved, release the left mouse button.

FIGURE 5.1 Drawing a centerline

10. Press S on the keyboard, and click the Smart Dimension button in the shortcut bar.

11. Select the centerline, and place the dimension to the side of the line. In the Modify window, make the dimension 8.000, as shown in Figure 5.2.

FIGURE 5.2 Modifying the dimension of a centerline

12. Select the Centerline tool again in the shortcut bar, and slowly move the mouse pointer along the line until the midpoint is highlighted (see Figure 5.3).

FIGURE 5.3 Finding the midpoint of a centerline

13. Press and hold the left mouse button, and drag a new line to the right perpendicularly to the centerline until the length is approximately .500″ long. Release the left mouse button when the desired length is achieved (see Figure 5.4). The reason for the line will make sense in later steps.

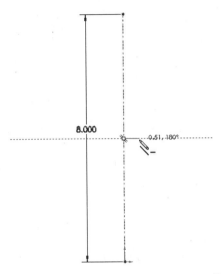

FIGURE 5.4 Drawing a line perpendicular to the centerline

14. Select the Line command in the shortcut bar.

15. Press and release the left mouse button with the mouse pointer directly over the sketch origin, and drag the line horizontally to the right until the length is once again about .500″ long. Click and release the left mouse button to complete the line. Notice how the Line command is still active.

 N O T E Holding or not holding the left mouse button while drawing a line makes a difference. Holding down the left mouse button while drawing the line will create only one segment. Clicking and releasing the mouse button while specifying the endpoints of the line will create a continuous line with multiple segments.

16. Move the mouse pointer vertically, and click and release the left mouse button when the length of the next segment is approximately .250″ long. To end the Line command, double-click your left mouse button or press Esc on your keyboard.

Draw Arcs

An arc is a continuous section of a circle. In SolidWorks there are three different ways to create arcs, each of which can be seen in the Arc flyout on the shortcut bar. Figure 5.5 shows the available Arc tools. Each arc tool serves its own purpose in sketches. The first arc tool, Centerpoint Arc, allows you to specify the center of the arc just as you would a circle. The next point specifies the radius of the arc and the starting point of the arc. The last point specifies the length of the arc. The Tangent Arc tool creates an arc that is automatically tangent to the connecting sketch segment. The position of the second point of the arc specifies the radius and endpoint of the arc. The last arc tool, 3 Point Arc, specifies three points on the arc. The first and second points specify the start and end of the arc. The third point specifies the radius.

FIGURE 5.5 Arc tools in the shortcut bar

As you become more familiar with SolidWorks and sketches, you will be able to determine the appropriate situation for using each arc type. For instance, in the following sketch, you will be using only two of the arc types to create the profile of the shaft:

1. Press S on the keyboard to show the shortcut bar, select the downward-pointing arrow next to the Arc tool, and click the Tangent Arc button. Select the endpoint of the last line you created in the earlier exercise.

2. Move the pointer until the arc has an approximate angle of 60° and a radius of .200″, as displayed next to the mouse pointer in Figure 5.6. Once again, don't get too hung up with how accurate the arc is at this point since you will be fully defining the sketch in later steps.

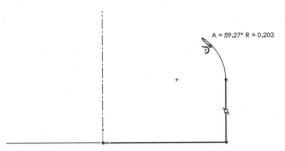

A = 59.27° R = 0.203

FIGURE 5.6 Drawing a tangent arc

3. In the Arc PropertyManager, click the 3 Point Arc button, and select the endpoint of the last arc segment drawn.

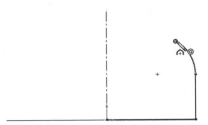

4. Select the endpoint of the horizontal centerline that was created from the midpoint of the vertical centerline, as in Figure 5.7.

5. Depending on what direction you move the mouse pointer, the arc will be convex or concave in relation to the centerline of the sketch. Move the mouse pointer away from the centerline until the arc is convex, as in Figure 5.8. Click and release the left mouse button to draw the arc.

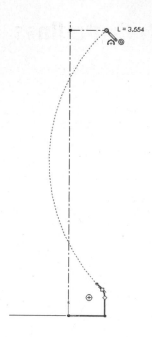

FIGURE 5.7   Drawing a 3 point arc

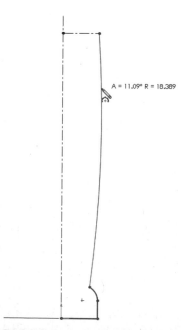

FIGURE 5.8   Making an arc convex

Dimension Sketches with Centerlines

By now you have surely become comfortable with adding dimensions to fully define sketches. Now it is time to introduce another cool dimensioning trick with sketches. As you know, clicking two points or sketch segments will define the distance between the two entities. But since your sketch has a centerline that represents the axis of revolution for the part, you can use that centerline to define the diameter of the part even though only half is shown in the sketch. This is a great way to control the design intent of the part since you are probably more apt to require the diameter controlled rather than the radius. Specifying the diameter of a sketch feature is extremely easy if you already know how to add a dimension, as you will see in the following steps:

1. Select Smart Dimension in the shortcut bar.

2. Select the vertical centerline, and then select the short vertical segment at the bottom of the sketch.

3. The dimension placement is important for how you want to define the sketch. On one side of the centerline, the dimension will be the distance from the centerline to the sketch segment or the radius of the shaft (see Figure 5.9).

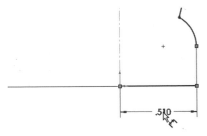

FIGURE 5.9 Defining the radius of a part

4. Move the mouse pointer to the other side of the centerline, and the dimension changes to show the diameter of the shaft. With the

dimension showing the diameter, click and release the left mouse button to place the dimension (see Figure 5.10).

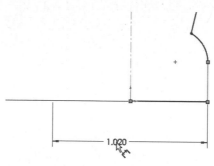

FIGURE 5.10 Defining the diameter of a part

5. In the Modify window, make the diameter **1.000**, and click the green check mark.

6. Making a dimension a diameter also works with points on the sketch. With the Dimension tool still active, select the centerline again, and select the undefined endpoint of the small arc, as shown in Figure 5.11.

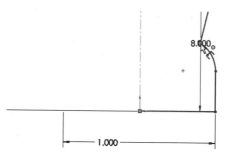

FIGURE 5.11 Defining the diameter from a point on the sketch

7. Move the mouse pointer to the opposite side of the centerline again to make the dimension a diameter dimension, and accept its location.

8. In the Modify window, add the value .900 for the diameter of the shaft at the end of the arc.

9. In addition to lines and points, you can also specify the diameter for an arc at the tangency. Select the centerline again, but this time press and hold the Shift button on your keyboard while selecting the large arc (see Figure 5.12).

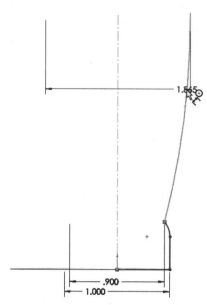

FIGURE 5.12 Defining the diameter for an arc at the tangent point

10. Move the mouse pointer to the other side of the centerline, and accept the dimension once it changes to a diameter dimension. In the Modify window, specify the value **1.100**, and click the green check mark.

Rather than specifying the radius of the arc, this approach specifies the diameter of the shaft at the largest part of the arc, allowing the radius and length of the arc to float depending on the other dimensions in the sketch.

Mirror a Sketch

Mirroring a sketch or part of a sketch is a great time-saver when areas of the sketch are symmetric. Using a centerline as the mirror point, items that you select can be mirrored so they take on the relations and dimensions specified in the original section. If you haven't used another CAD package that has a mirror function, the length of the mirror line does not matter; instead, the actual angle used is important. This should become clear as you use the Mirror tool in the next few steps.

1. Before mirroring the sketch, you need to finish dimensioning some items. Select the small vertical segment that makes up the 1.00 diameter, and place the dimension to the side. In the Modify window, add the value .250.

> ◀
>
> A centerline representing the axis of revolution for a part can be used to define the diameter of the part.

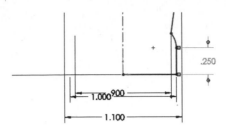

2. Next, select the horizontal line at the bottom of the sketch. Then select the under-defined point at the end of the short arc, and place the dimension so that it is shown as a vertical dimension. In the Modify window, make the value .350.

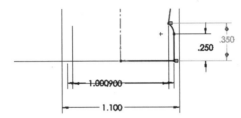

3. Press Esc on the keyboard to exit the dimension mode.

4. Double-click the scroll wheel or press F on your keyboard to fit the entire sketch into the graphics area.

5. Select the Sketch tab on the CommandManager, and click the Mirror Entities button.

6. Select all the sketch entities that are not centerlines. The easiest way to do this is to window over the sketch selecting all the items. Then while holding the Ctrl key on the keyboard, deselect the centerlines.

7. Ensure that Copy is selected in the Mirror PropertyManager.

8. Next click the Mirror About field in the Mirror PropertyManager.

9. In the graphics area, select the horizontal centerline. A yellow preview will show what the mirrored entities will look like in the graphics area (see Figure 5.13).

10. Click the green check mark in the PropertyManager to accept the mirror sketch entities. The sketch now contains the mirror image of the lower half of the shaft above the mirror line with the same size and relations defined in the original section (see Figure 5.14).

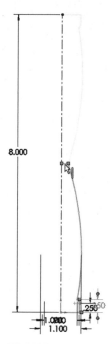

FIGURE 5.13 Preview of mirrored entities

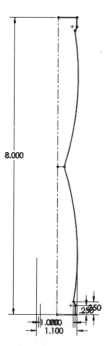

FIGURE 5.14 Part of a sketch created through mirroring

Trim Sketch Entities

Even the most perfectly planned sketch will require segments to be trimmed. As you build your sketch by adding sketch entities, you will often be required to trim a segment using an existing sketch entity as the trimming plane. Even the smallest line that is not properly terminated will cause issues when you attempt to create a feature. In your sketch, you will be adding one last sketch entity that will be used to complete the profile, and you will need to trim all the segments to create one continuous profile. But first you need to add the last entity. Here's how:

1. Select the Circle command in the shortcut bar.

2. Move the mouse pointer to the middle of the sketch, onto the point where the two large arcs merge, and click the left mouse button.

3. Move the mouse pointer away from the point selected until the radius of the circle is about .150, as shown next to the mouse pointer in Figure 5.15. Click and release the left mouse button to create the circle.

FIGURE 5.15 Using the Circle command

4. Open the shortcut bar, and select Trim Entities.

In the Trim PropertyManager, you will notice there are five different ways to use the Trim tool. Each has its strengths and weaknesses, and rather than show you how to use each of them at this point, we'll just briefly touch on each of them.

Power Trim   The *Power Trim* option allows you to trim multiple sketch entities by dragging the mouse pointer across the segments to be trimmed. This is extremely helpful when you have many items that would be too tedious to individually select.

Corner Trim   The *Corner Trim* tool trims or extends line segments to create a corner. If a selected segment is too short to meet where the obvious corner should be created, the segment will extend.

Trim Away Inside   The *Trim Away Inside* tool allows you to select two sketch entities and then trim away nonclosed sketch entities that intersect with both of the selected entities or none of them. An example of a closed sketch entity would be a circle. That means even if a circle crosses both of the selected items, it could not be trimmed with the Trim Away Inside option.

Trim Away Outside   The *Trim Away Outside* tool acts the same as the Trim Away Inside option except sketch entities that fall outside the two entities selected can be trimmed.

Trim To Closest   The *Trim To Closest* option is my most frequently used trimming option. We find that this option is the most useful since it trims anything to the nearest sketch entity without the need to preselect a trimming entity. In fact, in this particular sketch, it will be the option that will be used to clean up the profile.

To perform the trim, do the following:

1. Select Trim To Closest in the Trim PropertyManager.

2. Select the two arc segments that fall inside the circle to trim off the segment.

3. Then, select the two segments of the circle that fall inside the sketch profile to remove them, making one continuous profile.

4. Click the green check mark in the PropertyManager to exit Trim.

5. Since the ends of the large arcs were trimmed back, the relationship to the original endpoint was lost. You need to ensure that the arcs are still connected to the endpoint of the horizontal centerline to maintain the integrity of the sketch. While holding the Ctrl key on your keyboard, select one of the large arcs and the endpoint of the horizontal centerline.

6. Release the Ctrl key, and select the coincident relation in the context toolbar.

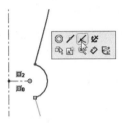

7. Add the coincident relation to the second large arc as well.

8. Select Smart Dimension in the shortcut bar, and click the remaining section of the circle at the middle of the sketch.

9. Place the radius dimension, and enter the radius value of **.100** in the Modify window.

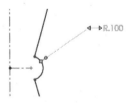

10. Now, select the vertical centerline of the sketch, and hold the Shift button on the keyboard while selecting the middle arc segment.

11. Place the dimension, and set the value to **1.250** in the Modify window, as in Figure 5.16.

12. The sketch should be fully defined, as you will be able to tell by all the sketch segments shown in black and the words Fully Defined in the status bar. If the sketch is not fully defined, recheck your sketch for all relationship and dimensions.

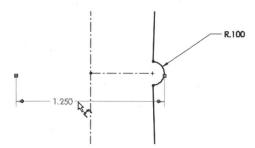

FIGURE 5.16 A trimmed sketch segment

Revolve the Sketch

Now that you have fully defined the sketch that makes up the profile for the lamp shaft, you can create the revolved part. All that is required in the sketch is that a centerline be present to use as an axis of revolution and that all the sketch entities be on one side of the centerline only. The profile that will be used must also be a closed profile, but since you created the sketch with an obvious dividing line, SolidWorks will be able to place a line along the centerline to close the sketch. To revolve the part, do the following:

1. Select the Features tab on the CommandManager, and click the Revolved Boss/Base button.

2. A SolidWorks message box will prompt you stating that the sketch needs to be closed and asking whether you would like to automatically close the sketch. Since you do need it to be closed, click Yes.

 N O T E Depending on how the sketch was created, SolidWorks will not always be able to properly determine how to close the sketch. This sketch is fairly simple, and it will have no problem, but if there is any doubt, it would not be a bad idea to close the sketch manually with a line connected to the two open ends of the sketch.

3. Since there is more than one centerline in the sketch, the Revolve tool doesn't know which one will be used to revolve the sketch. This can be seen by the lack of a selected axis of revolution in the Revolve PropertyManager. This means that you must select the vertical centerline that makes up the axis of the sketch manually (see Figure 5.17).

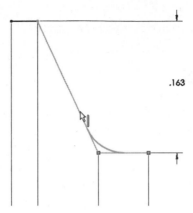

.163

FIGURE 5.17 Selecting a centerline around which to rotate the sketch

The preview in the graphics area will show what the revolved part will look like when created.

4. In the Revolve PropertyManager, the only options that you need to be concerned with are *Revolve Type* and *Angle Of The Revolution*. The Revolve Type setting should already be set to One-Direction, and the angle should be set to 360°. If that is the case, click the green check mark to create the revolved part. The base feature for the lamp shaft has been created! See Figure 5.18.

FIGURE 5.18 Preview of a revolved part

Now you need to add a few more features to complete the model.

Add a Threaded Boss

In lieu of adding separate fasteners to assemblies, it is often advantageous to build the fastening feature directly into the part. In this instance, a threaded boss is needed to attach the lamp shaft to the lamp base that would be held in place with a nut. Some designers enjoy modeling threads on a part because they want to show how the threads actually look on the part. Although this approach is very pleasing to look it, it is often still a waste of system resources, not to mention time in modeling the threads. Instead of taking the time to model threads onto a part, we always encourage designers to use the Cosmetic Thread option.

Using the Cosmetic Thread option in SolidWorks, a simple representation of the thread is shown in the part and assembly. The information also transfers well onto the drawing, giving the reader a representation of the thread that adheres to common drawing standards and that also displays the pertinent thread information for the manufacturer.

 N O T E Although it is not the case for this project, there will be times when modeling a true thread is required. In those times, the advantages of the actual thread geometry far outweigh the disadvantages. For example, if your part model is to be used for injection-molded parts, using a cosmetic thread may not work with your process, and you would be forced to actually make the thread.

Before you can add the threads to the lamp shaft, you first need to add a boss to the bottom of the shaft. This is the portion of the shaft that goes into the hole in the top boss of the lamp base. The next few steps should be pretty straightforward to you at this point since we have covered this process before.

1. Rotate the part around to give you access to the bottom view of the part.

2. Select Extruded Boss/Base in the shortcut bar.

3. Select the bottom face of the revolved part to insert a sketch for the threaded boss.

4. Select the Circle tool in the shortcut bar, and select the origin of the sketch that corresponds to the center point of the circular face.

5. Create a circle and add a diameter dimension of .750 using the Smart Dimension tool selected in the shortcut bar (see Figure 5.19).

6. Click the Exit Sketch button in the confirmation corner to initiate the Extrude command.

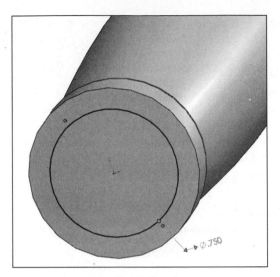

FIGURE 5.19 Sketching a boss

7. In the Depth field in the Extrude PropertyManager, set the depth of extrusion to .375, and click the green check mark.

8. Click or hover over the SolidWorks logo on the menu bar. Select Insert ➤ Annotations ➤ Cosmetic Thread.

9. Select the top circular edge of the boss (see Figure 5.20).

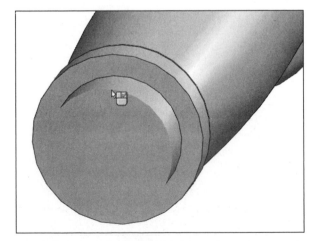

FIGURE 5.20 Specifying an edge for a cosmetic thread

10. In the Cosmetic Thread PropertyManager, select the Standard field to display a list of available thread standards. From the list, select Ansi Inch. After you specify the standard, two additional fields that pertain to the Ansi Inch thread standard will appear below the field. In the first of the two new fields, the Type field, ensure that the Machine Threads option is specified.

11. Below the Type field, the second new field is used to specify the thread. In previous versions of SolidWorks, you were required to manually enter the thread size. Unless you already knew the size of the thread you were going to specify, you would need to look up the thread that worked with the diameter of the boss selected. In SolidWorks 2010, based on the diameter of the selected edge, the Size field should already be set to the most thread callout. Many times the coarse thread is considered the most common, but for this design, you require a fine thread since the length of the boss is only .375". To select the fine thread, click the Size field, and select the 3/4-10 thread size, as shown in Figure 5.21.

FIGURE 5.21 Specifying the thread size in the Cosmetic Thread PropertyManager

12. Make sure that the End Condition setting, near the bottom of the Thread Settings section, is set to Up To Next. This will make the

cosmetic thread end at the next feature, which is where the boss ends on the shaft.

THREAD SIZE

The callout that you used here is a standard thread callout that can be interpreted by most manufacturers in the United States. Each part of the callout gives the machinist the information necessary to create the thread.

▶ The first part, ¾, refers to the actual nominal size of the thread displayed in fractions.

▶ Next, the -10 tells the machinist that the thread will have 10 threads per inch.

13. Click the green check mark to create the thread on the boss. A circle shown in a dash line will be added to the part to represent the minor diameter of the thread, and the shaded thread will be shown on the cylindrical face of the boss, as in Figure 5.22.

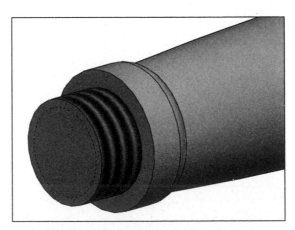

FIGURE 5.22 Minor diameter of a thread

 N O T E   If you do not see a shaded thread as shown in Figure 5.22, you'll need to update your document properties. In the Document Properties tab of the Options window, click Detailing in the left pane, and then select the Shaded Cosmetic Thread option in the Display Filter section.

Add a Revolve Cut

The next feature you need to add to the lamp shaft is a revolved cut that will be used to create a thread relief at the base of the threaded boss. A thread relief is often preferred by machinists since it makes it easier for them when they cut the threads to remove the material that comes off the cutting tool. A thread relief can be done a few different ways, but we like to make the smallest diameter of the relief slightly smaller than the minor diameter of the thread. The relief does not need to be very large, just large enough to allow the machinist to remove the material.

To create the thread relief, you need to create a profile of the cutout that will be revolved around the axis. The profile is different from the one that you used for the shaft itself since the profile is not connected to the axis. That and being a cut are the only two things that are different about this revolve feature for this part. But first, you need to add a couple of features to the boss to complete it prior to creating the revolve cut; follow these steps:

1. Select the Chamfer tool in the shortcut bar.

2. Select the bottommost circular edge of the boss.

3. In the Chamfer PropertyManager, set the Distance value to .025, as shown in Figure 5.23.

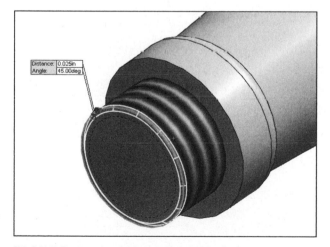

FIGURE 5.23 Adding a chamfer to the boss

4. Accept all the other defaults and select the green check mark to create the chamfer on the threaded boss.

5. Open the shortcut bar, select the downward-pointing arrow next to the Extruded Cut tool, and select Revolved Cut.

6. In the upper-left corner of the graphics area, the flyout FeatureManager can be accessed by clicking the plus (+) next to the model name.

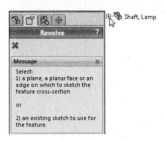

After expanding the FeatureManager, select Front Plane to insert a sketch for the revolved cut.

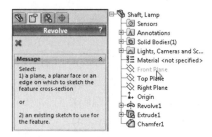

7. Press Ctrl+8 on the keyboard to change the view to normal to the Front Plane.

8. Zoom in closer to the threaded boss since you will be creating a sketch in that area.

9. Select the Centerline tool in the shortcut bar. Draw a centerline from the origin of the part down, creating a vertical centerline through the threaded boss, as shown in Figure 5.24.

10. Open the shortcut bar, select the downward-pointing arrow next to the Convert Entities button, and click the Intersection Curve button.

The *Intersection Curve tool* is one of the most used tools in our arsenal. The tool creates a sketch segment where the sketch plane and a select face intersect. It is extremely handy, such as in this case, when you require a point or line to reference in your sketch that is based on the surrounding geometry. Even though the tool will result in a single straight line in this instance, you can also use the tool can to create a complex line, such as a spline, that traces the contours of a complex face.

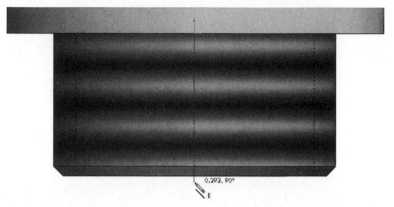

FIGURE 5.24 Adding a centerline for thread relief

11. Select the cylindrical face of the boss (Figure 5.25), and then click the green check mark in the Intersection Curves PropertyManager.

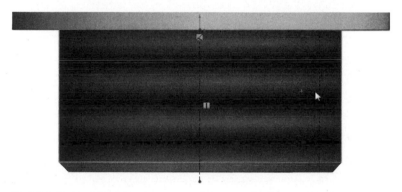

FIGURE 5.25 Selecting a curved face on which to use the Intersection Curve tool

You can use the Intersection Curve tool to create a line or spline that traces the contours of a face.

12. Click the red X in the PropertyManager to exit the Intersection Curve command.

13. Since you need only one of the lines drawn, select the other line and press Delete on your keyboard to remove the line from the sketch (see Figure 5.26).

Two separate lines were created when you selected the cylindrical face of the threaded boss since the face is one continuous face that intersects the sketch plane in two places. If you had instead chosen a face that intersects the sketch plane only once, then only one line would be created.

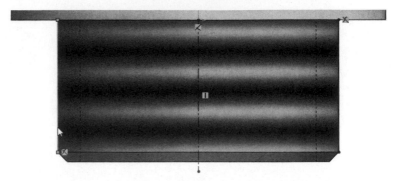

FIGURE 5.26 Deleting a line where the cylindrical face intersects the sketch plane

14. Select the Line tool in the shortcut bar, and begin the line at the upper endpoint of the line created in the previous step. Click and release the left mouse button to begin drawing the line (see Figure 5.27).

FIGURE 5.27 Drawing a line to define the trim

15. Draw the line horizontally toward the center of the shaft until the line extends beyond the vertical dashed line that represents the minor diameter of the thread. Click and release the left mouse button to draw the line.

16. While the Line tool is still active, draw a short vertical line downward to a length of approximately .050 inches.

17. Next, draw another segment that is approximately 135° from the last segment with the endpoint of the line coincident with the line that was created with the Intersection Curve tool (see Figure 5.28).

18. Press Esc or click the green check mark in the PropertyManager to exit the Line command.

19. Select the Trim tool in the shortcut bar, and ensure that the Trim To Closest option is selected in the Trim PropertyManager.

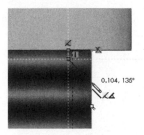

FIGURE 5.28 Drawing another line to define the trim

20. Trim the excess length of the line that was created using the Intersection Curve command, as in Figure 5.29. Then click the green check mark in the PropertyManager to exit the command.

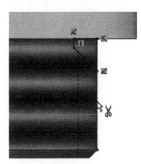

FIGURE 5.29 Executing the Trim command

21. Select the Smart Dimension tool in the shortcut bar, and add a diameter dimension using the centerline and the short vertical line. Make the diameter .625.

22. Select the leftmost vertical line to add a vertical dimension of .050.

23. Select the leftmost vertical line and the angle line to make the angle between the two 135° (see Figure 5.30).

24. With the sketch fully defined, click the Exit Sketch button in the confirmation corner to initiate the Revolved Cut command.

25. Since there is only one centerline in the sketch, it is automatically selected in the Cut-Revolve PropertyManager. Accept the defaults by clicking the green check mark. The thread relief is now created by cutting away the material from the threaded boss (see Figure 5.31).

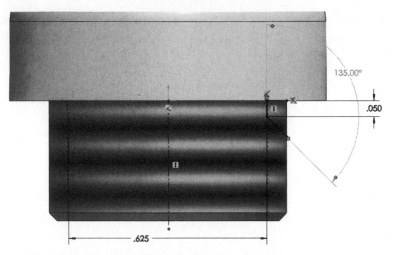

FIGURE 5.30 Defining the angle for the revolved cut

FIGURE 5.31 Thread relief

Finish the Shaft

Now that you're familiar with many of the tools you have been using, the steps will be less detailed.

You are just a few steps away from finalizing the lamp shaft. First you need to create a hole that extends through the length of the part that will allow the wiring to pass from the lamp base up to the shade assembly. In addition to the through hole, you also need to add a threaded hole at the other end of the shaft that will be used to mount the lamp shade assembly. This will help you reinforce the knowledge you have by allowing you to review the steps that you take. If at any point in the next few steps you forget how to do any of the task, we recommend returning to where the function is described in this or earlier chapters.

1. Select the Extruded Cut tool in the shortcut bar, and select the bottom of the shaft on the face of the threaded boss to add a sketch.

2. When the sketch is inserted, select the Circle tool in the shortcut bar, and place the center of the circle on the sketch origin.

3. Move the mouse pointer away from the center point, and click the left mouse button to create the circle.

4. Select the Smart Dimension tool in the shortcut bar, and select the circle. Specify the diameter of the circle to be .550 (see Figure 5.32).

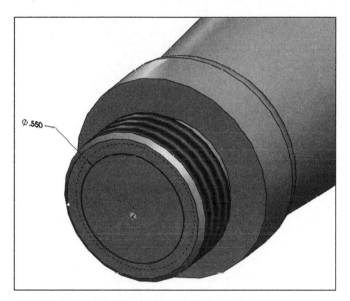

FIGURE 5.32 Preparing to do an extruded cut

5. Click the Exit Sketch button in the confirmation corner to open the Cut Extrude PropertyManager.

6. In the Direction1 section of the Extrude PropertyManager, change the End Condition option to Through All, as in Figure 5.33.

FIGURE 5.33 Extrude PropertyManager

We tend to not use the Through All End Condition very often since it can be confusing when the dimension is inserted into the drawing. In most cases, a *blind hole* and the Up To Next End Condition fit most needs, but this is one of the times when Through All is the best option — there are a few different features on the part, and the part is pretty long, Through All is the best, and in the drawing the hole callout will also include the note "Thru All."

7. Click the green check mark.

8. Hit Enter to recall the Cut Extrude command.

9. Rotate the part around, and select the top circular face of the shaft.

10. Sketch another circle with the center coincident to the sketch origin. Make the diameter of the circle .6417. Since you set the number of digits to the right of the decimal point to be three places, the value in the dimension will be rounded up, as shown in Figure 5.34, but the true value will be as entered.

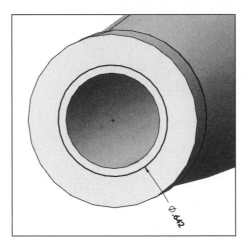

FIGURE 5.34 Circle with center coincident to the sketch origin

11. Click Exit Sketch in the confirmation corner.

12. Ensure that the End Condition option is set to Blind, and set the depth of the cut to .500. You don't need to set any other options at this time. Click the green check mark to create the cut.

13. Select Insert ➢ Annotations ➢ Cosmetic Thread in the menu.

14. Select the outer edge of the cut you just created, as shown in Figure 5.35, and select Ansi Inch in the Standard field.

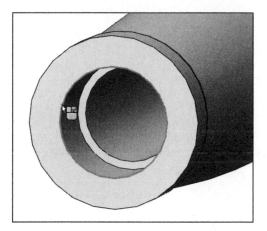

FIGURE 5.35 Setting the diameter of a thread

15. Change the Type setting to Machine Threads, and select 3/4-10 in the Size field. Click the green check mark to create the cosmetic thread.

16. Add a .050-wide chamfer to the inner edge of the threaded hole (see Figure 5.36).

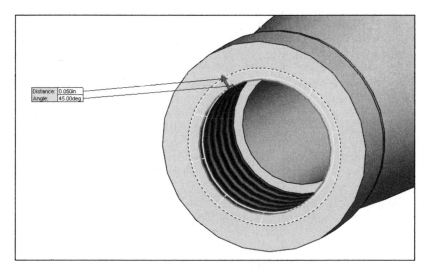

FIGURE 5.36 Adding a chamfer to a threaded hole

That concludes the modeling of your first revolved part.

If You Would Like More Practice...

As you can see, making a revolved part is pretty simple once you get the process of creating sketches down. For that reason, rather than spending too much time creating revolved parts, practice your drawing skills. Since you will not be creating any more part drawings in this book, we suggest trying to create a part drawing of the lamp shaft with some of the techniques described in the previous chapter. If you want to check your work, you can find a copy of the drawing for the lamp shaft on the companion website at `www.swner.com` and also at `www.wiley.com/go/solidworks2010ner`.

Are You Experienced?

Now You Can...

- ☑ **Create a sketch for a revolved part**

- ☑ **Create arcs in sketches**

- ☑ **Use the centerline in a sketch to specify the diameter of a part**

- ☑ **Use the mirror to mirror sketch entities**

- ☑ **Understand the trim tool options**

- ☑ **Create a revolved boss and revolved cut**

- ☑ **Insert cosmetic threads into your part**

CHAPTER 6

THE SKILLS FOR SUCCESS

SolidWorks

Creating a Subassembly

- ▶ Model a Washer
- ▶ Model a Washer Cover
- ▶ Create a Subassembly
- ▶ Use Mates
- ▶ Change the Appearance of Parts in an Assembly

Up to this point, you have been creating individual part models, but many of the design projects you will more than likely work on in SolidWorks will not consist of only one part. Assemblies and subassemblies are an important part of most designs, and in this chapter we will show you how to build a simple subassembly that will be used multiple times in your design. An *assembly*, in regards to SolidWorks, is a document that consists of parts, features, and other assemblies that are assembled using mates. Most of the time, the parts and subassemblies that make up the assembly are files that are referenced only by the assembly.

In this chapter, you will be modeling two components: a washer and a brass cover for the washer. You'll then assemble the two parts together and define the relationship with mates. *Mates* are geometric relationships between parts that often replicate real-world conditions such as when components are concentric, parallel, coincident, and perpendicular. Without the addition of mates, the location of parts would be under-defined, and they would just float in space with no relationship to bind the parts together.

Before creating the subassembly, you first need to model the parts. The next couple of sections will introduce you to a couple of new ways to create revolved parts that we hope you will find extremely helpful. Instead of describing every step as we did in previous chapters, we're concentrating on the new commands and concepts. If at any point you are not exactly sure how to do any of the actions described, feel free to jump back to previous chapters as a reminder.

Model a Washer

The first component that you will be modeling is the washer. You'll create it using the Revolve command, but unlike the shaft from the previous chapter, you'll model the washer with a hole in the part by specifying it in the sketch instead of a separate feature. This limits the number of features in the FeatureManager, which has a few advantages, including making it easier to edit the part in the future.

Before you can begin modeling the washer, you need to create a new part file and set the units as you did in previous chapters. Name the new part Washer, and save it with the other parts you have created so far. In the new SolidWorks part, follow these steps to create the washer:

1. In the shortcut bar, select the downward-pointing arrow next to the Extruded Boss/Base tool, and select Revolved Boss/Base from the flyout.

2. Select the front plane in the graphics area to insert a new sketch.

3. Select the Centerline tool in the shortcut bar, and select the sketch origin to create the centerline while holding the left mouse button.

4. Draw a vertical centerline to an approximate length of .250.

5. Select the Line tool in the shortcut bar.

6. Move the mouse pointer to the right of the sketch origin. A blue dashed line will be displayed showing the mouse pointer is horizontally aligned to the origin (see Figure 6.1).

FIGURE 6.1 Beginnings of a sketch with centerline

INFERENCING LINES IN SKETCHES

In step 6 of modeling the washer, you saw that as you moved the mouse pointer in line with the sketch origin, a blue dashed line appeared. This line is referred to as an *inferencing line*, and it is used to display the possible relation between a point in the sketch and the mouse pointer. Instead of adding a relation, such as a coincident and midpoint, to a sketch entity, SolidWorks attempts to anticipate what relation is needed. In addition to the inferencing line, the pointer shows the relation that will be added, and sometimes highlighted cues such as endpoint and midpoints are displayed. Throughout this book you will be using *inferencing* to save time during sketch creation. In this sketch, inferencing is used to add a horizontal relation to a line that will also be coincident with the sketch origin, saving you the time of adding the relation manually.

7. Using the Line tool, sketch the profile shown in Figure 6.2. Using inferencing, SolidWorks will automatically add a horizontal and coincident reference between the sketch origin and the bottom line of the sketch as long as the first sketch segment is the horizontal line.

8. Select Smart Dimension in the shortcut bar, and apply the dimensions shown in Figure 6.3.

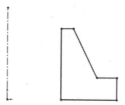

FIGURE 6.2 Undefined sketch of the washer

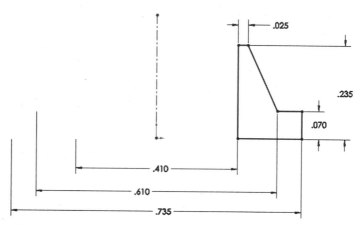

FIGURE 6.3 Dimensions applied to washer sketch

9. Click Exit Sketch in the confirmation corner to exit the sketch and show the Revolve PropertyManager.

10. In the Revolve PropertyManager, since there is only one centerline in the sketch, there is no need to select it; the centerline will already be selected and displayed in the Axis Of Revolution field. Also, although it should already be selected, ensure that the Revolve Type option is set to One Direction and the Angle setting shows 360°. Click the green check mark to create the washer.

11. Press Ctrl+S or click Save in the menu bar to save the part file.

Add Draft to a Part

When manufactured, the washer will most likely be injection molded. *Injection molding* is the process in which a liquid plastic material is forced into a mold cavity. When the material cools, it takes on the shape of the cavity producing the desired part. To make it easier for the injection-molded part to be extracted from the mold, draft angles are added to surfaces that are perpendicular to the parting line. The *parting line* of a part is where the two halves of the mold meet.

To facilitate the manufacturing of the washer, you will need to add a *draft angle* to any surface that may make it difficult to remove the part from the mold. Since this is a fairly basic part, you will only need to add draft to a couple of surfaces. The Draft tool is available in the set of tools used for creating molded parts. Although you can access the required tools in the menu, we prefer enabling the tab in the CommandManager for the Mold tools. Here's how to add the draft angles:

1. Right-click one of the tabs in the CommandManager, and select Mold Tools to enable the Mold Tools tab, as shown in Figure 6.4.

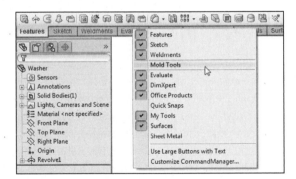

FIGURE 6.4 Enabling the Mold Tools tab in CommandManager

2. Click Draft on the Mold Tools tab in the CommandManager.

3. Ensure that the Manual button is selected at the top of the Draft PropertyManager.

4. In the Type Of Draft section, ensure that the Neutral Plane option is selected.

5. Set the Draft Angle setting to 1°. This is the angle that will be applied to the selected surfaces. 1° may not seem like a lot — in fact, it is not even noticeable — but it will make a huge difference when trying to eject the part from the mold, and the manufacturer will thank you.

6. With the Neutral Plane field active in the PropertyManager, select the top face of the lip of the washer, as shown in Figure 6.5.

FIGURE 6.5 Selecting the neutral plane

SPECIFYING THE NEUTRAL PLANE

When applying draft to faces, you must specify the *neutral plane*. The neutral plane is where the cross section of the drafted face will maintain the true size. For example, in the washer model, the outer diameter before the draft is .735″. After the draft is applied, the diameter of the outer diameter will remain .735″, and the rest of the face will be drafted. The neutral plane does not need to intersect the surfaces selected for the draft. In fact, if you were to pick another surface, such as the top surface of the washer, the diameter of the face would still be .735 at the neutral plane. This would cause the drafted face to become even smaller.

7. Click the Reverse Direction button next to the Neutral Plane field. After clicking the Reverse Direction button in the PropertyManager, the arrow in the graphics area will flip and will be pointing down to represent the direction of pull when the part is molded.

8. With the Faces To Draft field active, select the two vertical faces of the washer. These two faces, as shown in Figure 6.6, are the only faces that are perpendicular to the neutral plane, and without an added draft, they will cause issues for the molding process.

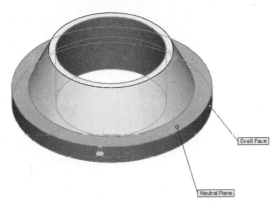

FIGURE 6.6 Selecting which surfaces to draft

9. Click the green check mark to create the drafted surfaces.

Check the Draft of a Part

Now that you have added draft to the washer, you need to ensure that it is indeed drafted properly to meet the manufacturing requirements. You can check the draft and how it is applied to your part by using the Draft Analysis tool. This tool not only verifies the draft but can show the angle changes on a face as well as determine the optimal areas for the parting lines, injection, and ejection surfaces in parts.

The Draft Analysis tool uses colors to show whether faces on the part have a positive draft, have a negative draft, or have the needed draft based on the draft angle specified and the neutral plane selected. Faces that have a *positive draft* meet the minimum angle required for the mold to be pulled in the direction specified; these faces are shown green by default. Faces shown in red are designated as having *negative draft* and are faces that cannot be extracted with the mold being pulled in the designated direction. Often, the faces shown as having negative draft are ones that will sit on the other half of the mold, unless the surface or features is an undercut. Flipping the direction of pull will often swap the colors. Faces that are shown in yellow require more draft applied to them, or the draft angle in the Draft Analysis PropertyManager needs to be decreased.

The great thing about the Draft Analysis tool is that it allows you to continue making modifications to your part while the tool is active. This gives you real-time feedback while you modify the model. The colors designating positive, negative, and needed draft will remain on the part until the tool is deselected. The following steps will set your requirements for the draft of the washer, and you will leave the analysis running while you finish your part to ensure that changes you make do not affect the overall moldability.

1. Select the Mold Tools tab in the CommandManager, and click the Draft Analysis button.

2. With the Direction Of Pull field active in the Draft Analysis PropertyManager, select the face of the washer that was used as the neutral plane. Then click the Reverse Direction button to match the direction you specified when creating the draft.

> You can also enable the Draft Analysis tool in the menu by selecting View ➢ Display ➢ Draft Analysis.

3. Set the Draft Angle option in the Analysis Parameters section to 1°. This will represent the minimum draft that is required by the manufacturer. Then click the green check mark to finish selecting options.

Positive draft
Requires draft
Negative draft

Add Multiple Fillets Using FilletXpert

With the Draft Analysis tool running, you are now going to add some radii to the edges of the washer. Running the Draft Analysis tool while you finish your model will allow you to see whether the drafted faces need to be tweaked as the fillets are added. As in an earlier chapter, you'll use the FilletXpert to add the radii to the washer because it allows you to add the fillets without needing to select the tool after each fillet. After adding the necessary fillets, you will also be adding a chamfer to one of the edges. Unfortunately, the Chamfer tool does not have an Xpert option like the Fillet tool does, but that won't slow you down this time since you only need to add one chamfer. To add radii to the washer, do the following:

1. Select Fillet in the shortcut bar.

2. Click the FilletXpert button at the top of the Fillet PropertyManager.

3. In the Radius Value field, enter the value **.010**, and select the top-outside edge of the washer, as in Figure 6.7. Click Apply in the FilletXpert PropertyManager.

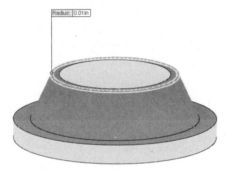

FIGURE 6.7 Adding a fillet to the washer model

4. Change Radius value to **.025**, and select the outer and inner edges of the lip of the washer, as in Figure 6.8. Click the green check mark to create the second set of fillets, and close the Fillet PropertyManager.

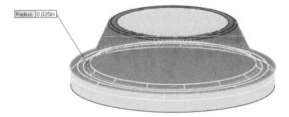

FIGURE 6.8 Adding another fillet to the washer model

5. Select Chamfer in the shortcut bar, and change the value of the chamfer distance to **.010**. There is no need to specify the angle since the default is already set to 45°. Then select the upper-inner edge on the inner diameter of the washer, as in Figure 6.9. Click the green check mark to exit the Chamfer PropertyManager.

6. Once you have confirmed that the additional fillet and chamfer features did not affect the draft requirements of the part, deselect the Draft Analysis button on the Mold Tools tab by clicking it once again.

FIGURE 6.9 Adding a chamfer to the washer model

Configure a Part

Configurations in parts are extremely helpful when you want to create different versions of a part. Instead of creating multiple parts that are only variations of the original, you can include those variations in the parent part. Take the washer, for instance. You may have different sizes of the washer that are used in your company, but instead of having multiple models, you can include the dimensional variations within configurations of the original washer.

You can use a *part configuration* for more than just dimensional variations with a part. You can use configurations to specify different materials, custom properties, suppressed or resolved features, or even appearances. This can be extremely helpful when you have whole families of parts, and it is also a great time-saver since you will not need to create multiple models. You can use configurations in a variety of ways, and there are even a few different ways to create them. We will not be able to get to each version here, but we can at least get you started exploring configurations.

In the following steps, you'll create a second configuration to the washer that will contain a larger diameter version. You will be using the Modify Configurations window in SolidWorks to create the configuration and also modify the dimensions in each version. Although there are a couple of ways to create configurations, we find this method the quickest and easiest way since it allows you to create configurations on the fly and it gives you a tabular view of the dimensions being modified.

1. Click the plus (+) next to the Revolve1 feature in the FeatureManager to show the child sketch.

2. Select the sketch, and click the Edit Sketch button in the context menu.

3. While holding the Ctrl key, select the three diameter dimensions and the overall height in the sketch, as shown in Figure 6.10.

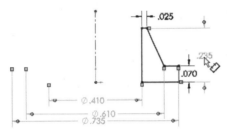

FIGURE 6.10 Selecting the dimensions to configure in the sketch

T I P If only one dimension needs to be configured, you can skip the step of opening the sketch. Selecting the sketch in the FeatureManager will display the dimensions used in the sketch without opening it. You can then right-click one of the dimensions to configure it.

4. Right-click, and select Configure Dimension in the menu.

5. In the Modify Configurations window, select the field labeled <Creates A New Configuration>, and type **Config2** (see Figure 6.11).

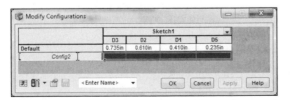

FIGURE 6.11 Modify Configurations window

6. Since the new Configuration is named Config2, you might as well change the name of the original configuration that is currently named Default to Config1. Right-click the field labeled Default, and select Rename Configuration in the menu.

7. In the Rename Configuration window, type **Config1**, and click OK.

T I P Renaming the configurations makes it easier to determine which configuration is being referenced in drawings and assemblies. In many organizations, the configuration names match the part number for the configuration of the part.

8. Change the values for the dimensions in the Modify Configurations window by selecting each cell and typing in the new value. Change the values to those shown in Figure 6.12.

	Sketch1			
	D1	D2	D3	D6
Config1	0.410in	0.610in	0.735in	0.235in
Config2	0.510in	0.710in	0.835in	0.335in
< Creates a new configuration. >				

FIGURE 6.12 New values for washer configurations

9. Click OK to accept the changes. You may be prompted to rebuild the document; click Rebuild in the window to continue.

The Modify Configurations window is not exclusive to configuring dimensions. You can configure features of a part and parts in an assembly using the same process. When you right-click a feature in a part and select Configure Feature, you can specify whether the specified feature is suppressed or resolved in a part. In assemblies, you can use the Modify Configurations window to specify the part configuration used in the assembly as well as specify that the part is suppressed or resolved in each assembly configuration.

Switch Between Configurations

When a part contains configurations, the graphics area will update depending on the active configuration. As you switch between configurations in the part, the model will change to include the variations specified, whether they are dimensional variations or just a simple appearance change to the part. The FeatureManager will also display the active configuration being shown in the graphics area. Figure 6.13 shows how the name of the active configuration appears next to the part name at the very top of the tree.

FIGURE 6.13 Name of active configuration in FeatureManager

The configurations in a part can be viewed, modified, and activated in the ConfigurationManager. In Figure 6.14, you will see a tab that is available above the FeatureManager design tree to give you access to the ConfigurationManager. Clicking the tab will hide the FeatureManager design tree and show the ConfigurationManager.

FIGURE 6.14 ConfigurationManager tab in FeatureManager

View the FeatureManager Design Tree and ConfigurationManager at the Same Time

Sometimes it is helpful to be able to view the FeatureManager design tree and the ConfigurationManager at the same time. Instead of switching back and forth between the two tabs, it is possible to show both of the panes at the same time. This allows you to continue to make modifications to your features and then switch between configurations quickly. To show them both at once, do the following:

1. Move the mouse pointer to the double line directly above the FeatureManager until the mouse pointer changes to include double lines. The double line bar is referred to as the *horizontal split bar* and is used to split the left pane into two windows.

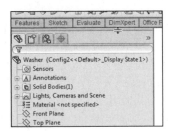

2. While holding the left mouse button, drag the split bar down below the rollback bar, and release the mouse button. The FeatureManager is now shown in both sections of the pane (Figure 6.15).

FIGURE 6.15 FeatureManager split into two panes

3. Click the ConfigurationManager tab in the lower pane of the FeatureManager to view the available configurations.

T I P Double-clicking the horizontal split bar will return it to its last position. If the FeatureManager is split, it will return to the top of the FeatureManager. If the FeatureManager is not split, double-clicking it will place the split bar at its last position.

4. In the ConfigurationManager, the available configurations will be displayed. The active configuration will be shown in black, and the rest of the configurations will be shown in gray. To activate a configuration, double-click the configuration name, and the part will be updated in the graphics area.

Something to keep in mind when switching between configurations is that changes made to the model can impact other configurations. Depending on the option selected in the Modify Dimension window, changes to dimensions can apply to the active configuration only, to all configurations, or even to selected configurations. The same holds true to applying appearances, suppressing and resolving features, and adding new features.

Model a Washer Cover

The washer from the previous section will more than likely be made of a black rubber-like material that does not really add to the appearance of the overall desk lamp. The washer cover model you are about to create has no other purpose other than covering the washer to provide a clean look to the overall product. The cover will be made of the same brass material that will be used on the other metallic parts on the lamp.

The washer cover also gives you an opportunity to explore another way to create a revolved part. Up to this point, you have been creating revolved parts with closed profile sketches to create a solid cross section. Most of the revolved features you will need to create will indeed require a closed profile, but there are times when you can create what is referred to as a *thin feature*. A thin feature is when a feature, such as a revolve, is created from an open profile, and the thickness is added at the feature level. Using a thin feature is equivalent to offsetting the sketch to the required thickness and closing the ends to create a closed profile. But instead, the sketch can be left open, and the thickness is specified in the PropertyManager, saving you the time it would take to close the sketch.

The following steps should make it easier to understand the concept of using thin features as you create the model for the washer cover:

1. Open a new part template, and save the file as Washer Cover.

2. Set the number of decimal places used in length to three places in the document properties.

3. Select Revolved Boss/Base feature, and create a sketch on the front plane.

4. Create a vertical centerline originating from the sketch origin that is approximately .300 long.

5. Using the dimensions shown in Figure 6.16, create the sketch of the washer cover.

> It's a good idea to switch between configurations occasionally to see whether you have inadvertently made changes to other configurations.

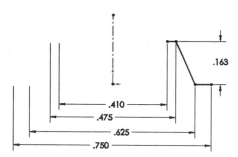

FIGURE 6.16 Sketch of washer cover

Add Sketch Fillets

Up to this point, you have been adding fillets using the fillet tool on the model. This is usually the preferred method since too many fillets added at the sketch level will affect the overall speed performance of parts and assemblies. However, sometimes it is more beneficial to add fillets at the sketch level, especially for models such as the washer cover. Since the feature that will be used to create the model is a thin feature, it is better to add the fillet in the sketch to keep from having to create multiple fillets on both sides of the part. By adding the fillet in the sketch, when the thickness is added to the feature, the outside fillet on the model will change in radius depending on the thickness specified.

In this sketch, you require two different radii to be specified for the fillets. But instead of using the same method for both, we want to illustrate a couple of different ways of adding the radii. The first method requires selecting two adjacent sketch entities. After specifying the radius and selecting both entities, the sharp corner will be replaced with a radius. The second method only requires specifying the radius and then selecting the point where the two adjacent sketch entities meet. Both methods are accepted practices, but we find the second method a lot quicker and easier, and we are sure you will see why.

1. Select the Sketch Fillet tool in the shortcut bar.

2. In the Sketch Fillet PropertyManager, set the Radius value to .050.

3. Select the bottom line of the sketch and the angled line that is connected to it, as in Figure 6.17.

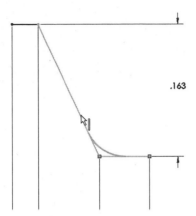

FIGURE 6.17 Adding a sketch fillet

4. If the preview of the fillet, shown in yellow, meets your expectations, click the green check mark in the PropertyManager to create the fillet.

This method is probably the most widely used approach to adding fillets in sketches, but in our opinion it is not always the best way. The next method is often quicker and provides the same result, and we always prefer the faster method as long as the integrity of the part is not sacrificed.

5. Change the Radius value in the Sketch Fillet PropertyManager to .020, and select the point that makes the top corner of the sketch, as shown in Figure 6.18. Click the green check mark to add the sketch fillet.

FIGURE 6.18 Adding sketch fillet by selecting point

6. When you are finished adding the fillets, click the green check mark once again to exit the command.

Create a Revolved Thin Feature

The sketch is now complete and ready to be revolved to make the cover. You probably have a nagging feeling that the sketch is incomplete, but we assure you that as long as the sketch is fully defined, it is more than sufficient to create the necessary model. To create a thin feature, you don't need to select any special tool. You will be able to use the same Revolve Boss/Base tool that you have already used in previous chapters. The only difference is that you will specify the thickness of the revolve in the PropertyManager.

1. Click the Exit Sketch button in the conformation corner to begin the Revolve command.

2. When prompted to automatically close the sketch, click No.

 W A R N I N G   It is important that you do not select to automatically close the sketch when prompted. If you select Yes, SolidWorks will attempt to create a closed profile resulting in a model that does not meet the design intent of the part.

---

3. In the Revolve PropertyManager, the check box in the header of the Thin Feature section should be selected. If it is not already expanded, click the chevron in the header to view the Thin Feature options (Figure 6.19).

FIGURE 6.19 Revolve PropertyManager

---

4. In the Direction1 Thickness field, enter the material thickness of the washer cover as .025, and click the green check mark to create the part.

5. Look at the preview in the graphics area (Figure 6.20). The sketch you drew is supposed to represent the inner surface of the part. If the preview does not show the sketch being the inner surface, click the Reverse Direction button in the PropertyManager.

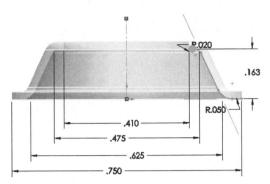

FIGURE 6.20 Preview of revolved thin feature

6. Click the green check mark to create the revolved part.

7. Save your changes by pressing Ctrl+S or by clicking the Save button on the menu bar.

The model for the washer cover is now complete. Since you included the fillets in the sketch, you don't need to add any fillet features. To see the advantage of adding the fillet at the sketch level, take a look at the inside and outside faces of the part. The same fillet now has different radii depending on the direction of the offset.

Create a Subassembly

With the parts you created in the previous sections, you can now begin to build your first assembly. As far as assemblies go, this one will be one of the easiest ones you can possibly make, so it is good one to use to introduce the process. In the assembly, you'll mate the washer and washer cover together to allow you to quickly insert them into the top-level assembly later. You could actually individually insert the components into the top-level assembly, but that approach is not considered good practice for a couple of reasons. First, the more components that are individually inserted into the top-level assembly, the more it can affect the overall system performance. Next, in our opinion, the more parts that you have showing in the FeatureManager, the more overwhelming it can be, especially on very large assemblies. Also, think about how many extra times you need to apply mates to all the instances of the part in a large assembly.

So, to build the assembly, follow these steps:

1. If you did not close the washer from the earlier section, press Ctrl+Tab on the keyboard to switch between the open documents. If you closed the washer, open it at this time.

T I P   Pressing R on your keyboard will display a thumbnail for the most recent documents opened in SolidWorks. Selecting one of the thumbnails will open that document in the graphics area.

2. Click the downward-pointing arrow next to the New button on the menu bar, and select Make Assembly From Part/Assembly.

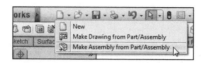

3. In the New SolidWorks Document window, select the assembly template, and click OK.

4. In the Begin Assembly PropertyManager, select the file named Washer in the Part/Assembly To Insert section, and click the green check mark. The part will automatically be inserted at the origin in the new assembly file.

5. Save the assembly as Washer Sub-Assembly, Desk Lamp.

In the FeatureManager, instead of listing features for the part, the parts that make up the assembly are shown. Since you have only one part added to the assembly so far, there is only one listed. On the same line that shows the name of the part that exists in the assembly is a wealth of information. First, in front of the name of the part is the symbol showing the document type of the model. Since the washer is a part document, the symbol for a part is shown. If you inserted another assembly, the icon would show the symbol for an assembly. After the icon, in parentheses, is the letter *f*. This shows that the part is fixed in place and cannot be moved. At least one part in an assembly should be fixed, and the other components are then mated to the base part — otherwise, the whole assembly will be able to move, and that is not a good thing. Because you created the assembly from a part, the part is automatically fixed. If you were to create a blank assembly and insert the part manually, it would not necessarily be fixed.

After the name of the component shown in the FeatureManager, inside the brackets, is the number of instances of the component. If you were to insert more washers into this assembly, this number would increment up with each subsequent part. This number cannot be changed and will not be reused in the assembly for the part named even after a component is deleted from the assembly.

Last, inside the parentheses following the instance count, the active configuration and display state names appear. In later chapters, we will be covering display states, so for the time being you can concern yourself only with the configuration that is displayed. When you created the model for the washer, you made it with two configurations. This is the time that you need to specify which configuration the current assembly will be utilizing. The next section describes the process for selecting the configuration of a part in an assembly.

Select a Part Configuration

As we mentioned in the previous section, since you created the washer with two configurations, you need to specify which one will be used in the assembly. Depending on the active configuration when the part was saved, the correct configuration may very well be displayed in the FeatureManager at this point, but just in case, follow these steps for specifying the configuration in the Component Properties window:

1. Select the washer in the FeatureManager, and select Component Properties in the context toolbar.

2. In the Reference Configuration section of the Custom Properties window, ensure that Config1 is selected.

3. Click OK to accept the selected configuration, and close the window.

After clicking OK in the Custom Properties window, the name of the configuration in the FeatureManager should now show Config1. Once the washer is set to the appropriate configuration, move to the next section to learn how to insert the washer cover into the assembly.

Insert Components into Assembly

Now it is time to insert the washer cover into the assembly. There are a couple of quick and easy ways to insert components into an assembly, and we will be addressing a few of them in later chapters, but for now you will be using the Insert Components tool. When you initiate the command, the PropertyManager might seem familiar to you, and in fact it should. The Insert Component PropertyManager is the same as the Begin Assembly PropertyManager. The only difference is the name.

1. Press S on the keyboard, and select Insert Components in the short-cut bar.

2. In the Part/Assembly To Insert section of the Insert Component PropertyManager, select the washer cover .
   The washer cover will be present only in the Open Documents field if the model is currently opened in SolidWorks. If you closed the model for the washer cover after creating it, you will need to select the Browse button in the Part/Assembly To Insert section and select the model in the Open window.

3. In the graphics area, place the washer cover by clicking and releasing the left mouse button (see Figure 6.21). Once the washer cover is placed, there is no need to exit any command.

FIGURE 6.21 Inserting washer cover into assembly

There may be times in the future while you are using SolidWorks that you will need to insert multiple components into your assembly. Instead of selecting the Insert Components tool each time you need to add a model, you can keep the PropertyManager open. Selecting the pushpin icon next to the red X at the top of the PropertyManager will keep the pane open as long as you need it. Once you are finished inserting all your components, clicking the red X will close the pane.

Move Floating Components in an Assembly

Until the position of a component in the assembly is fully defined, you can freely move the part around the graphics area. To determine whether the component's position is fully defined, just look at the component in the FeatureManager. If there is a minus (-) shown between the component icon and the component name, the position is not fully defined.

Moving components in an assembly is really simple. In fact, you don't even need to use any commands other than the buttons of your mouse. Using the left and right mouse buttons, you can rotate and move a floating component in your assembly. For example, to move the washer cover, select the washer cover with the mouse pointer while clicking and holding the left mouse button. Move the mouse around, and the part moves in the X and Y directions in relation to the viewing plane. Release the left mouse button to place the part. To rotate the washer cover, select the washer cover with the mouse pointer while clicking and holding the right mouse button. Move the mouse around, and the part will rotate in the direction the mouse moves.

Add Mates in Assemblies

Parts as they are entered into an assembly have six degrees of freedom. Degrees of freedom refer to the directions a part can freely move in 3D space. In 3D environments, there are three basic directions; X, Y, and Z. For a graphical representation of these directions, one does not have to look further than the reference triad in the lower-left corner of the graphics area. The red arrow shows the X direction, which is horizontal. The Y direction, shown in green, is the vertical direction. The Z direction, shown in green, is the direction moving either toward or away from you. The other three degrees of freedom are how a part rotates around the x-, y-, and z-axes.

To fully define a part in an assembly, you must restrict all six degrees of freedom. This is done by using mates, which are the geometric relationships added to a part in relation to other parts or planes. For example, in the Washer Sub-Assembly part, the washer cover needs to be mated to the washer. The way we like to describe mates to new users is that mates can be used to replicate the way that the parts would interact with each other in real life. In real life, the washer and the washer cover would have a threaded post inserted through their inner diameters. This would make the washer and washer cover concentric, and there is a mate for that. Next, when the washer and washer cover are installed, the inside-top face of the washer cover will be touching the top face of the washer. In SolidWorks, this can be done with a coincident mate. The next few steps will show you how to apply these mates to the washer cover to complete the subassembly.

1. Press S on the keyboard, and select Mate in the shortcut bar.

2. Select the conical faces on both the washer and the washer cover. The two components will become concentric based on the selected faces (see Figure 6.22).

FIGURE 6.22 Concentric components

You can use the concentric mate with any circular edge or cylindrical or conical face. There are many edges and faces in the two components that could have been used to make the two components concentric. The only reasons we chose these two faces is because they had the largest surface area and they were easier to select, but feel free to select other faces to see how they work for the mate.

3. Click the green check mark in the PropertyManager or the context menu to accept the mate.

4. Click the top face of the washer. Then select the top-inside face of the washer cover to make the two surfaces coincident. Accept the mate by clicking the green check mark, and click the green check mark once again to exit the Mate command.

5. You can confirm how the two parts mate together by creating a cross section. Select the Section View button in the Heads-up View toolbar.

6. In the Section View PropertyManager, click the Front Plane button, and click the green check mark (see Figure 6.23).

7. On the reference triad in the lower-left corner of the graphics area, click the z-axis to change the orientation of the view to be able to see the cross section of the assembly.

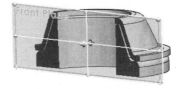

FIGURE 6.23 Section View PropertyManager

8. Instead of zooming in on the part, press G on the keyboard to display the magnifying glass. The magnifying glass allows you to zoom in to areas of the model without needing to change the overall scale of the graphics area (see Figure 6.24).

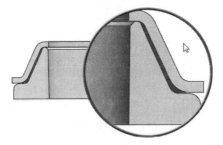

FIGURE 6.24 Viewing cross section with magnifying glass

9. The mouse pointer will be able to move freely inside the magnifying glass, but when the mouse reaches the outside of the circle, it will push the view around the graphics area.

10. Spinning the scroll wheel on your mouse will cause the view in the magnifying glass to zoom in and out depending on the direction you spin the wheel.

 TIP Pressing and holding the Alt key while spinning the scroll wheel on your mouse will create a section view within the magnifying glass normal to the viewing angle.

11. To exit the magnifying glass, click and release the left mouse button.

12. To exit the section view, deselect the Section View button on the Heads-up View toolbar by clicking the button once again.

As you work in SolidWorks, you may discover that the two most common mates you will apply to assemblies are the concentric and coincident mates. That is because these two mates match the most common ways parts are put together in real life. However, as you may have noticed, there are many more mates to choose from in the Mates PropertyManager. In later chapters, you will be taking a look at a few of the other available mates as well as alternate methods to apply the most commonly used mates.

Change the Appearance of Parts in an Assembly

In the previous section, when you sectioned the part to see how the mate was applied, you might have thought that is was difficult to tell the difference between the two components. This is actually a very common issue when you have multiple components that all have the same color or appearance. Luckily, there are a couple really easy ways to change how a part looks in your assembly.

Some may think that changing the color of components in assemblies, or even adding material appearances, is a waste of time, but we do not agree. The ability to quickly determine where one component ends and the other begins can sometimes be difficult, especially in very large assemblies. You may not have problems telling components apart, but remember that there may be other users or even vendors who will be studying your assemblies and they won't know the components as intimately as you will. Anything that can make things easier for all parties involved, we are always a fan of doing.

Change Colors Using Appearances

The most common way to change the appearance of your components in an assembly is to simply change the color. In our opinion, there is no drawback to applying colors to components in an assembly. It's quick and easy, makes it easier for users, and has absolutely no effect on the system performance. The following steps will show you the easiest way to apply a color to a component:

1. Select the washer in the graphics area by clicking and releasing the left mouse button.

2. In the context menu, click the downward-pointing arrow next to the Appearances button.

3. In the Appearances flyout, select the first item in the list that shows the assembly icon next to it. This will apply the appearance only at the subassembly level and will not affect the part itself.

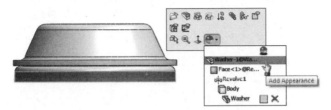

4. In the Color section of the PropertyManager, select the desired color in the swatch, as in Figure 6.25. The washer in real life is completely black, but we often find that selecting a pure black color makes it difficult to distinguish the features of the part. Because of this, select the dark gray color box directly above the pure black.

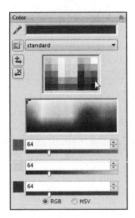

FIGURE 6.25 Applying a color to a part

5. At this time, no other options are needed for the color of the washer, so click the green check mark to close the PropertyManager and apply the color.

Add Realistic Material Appearances to Models

Sometimes you have the time to add a little more style to your models. Using appearances and RealView, your models can look like the material they are made of. It is a little like rendering the model, but unlike rendering, you can still continue to work on the part, and the material look will update with the geometry.

In the previous section, you made the washer color black, or dark gray, to mimic the final color of the injection-molded part. So, that leaves the washer cover, which still has that dull gray color applied to it. When the part is produced, it will be made from a shiny brass material. You could just change the color of the washer cover to yellow and be done with it, but what is fun about that? Luckily, with appearances, you can actually make the part look like the brass material it will be made out of:

1. Click the Appearances/Scenes tab on the task pane.

2. Click the plus (+) next to Appearances to view the available material types.

3. Expand the Metal folder, and select the folder named Brass. In the lower section of the Appearances tab, all of the available Brass materials will be listed, as in Figure 6.26.

4. Select the thumbnail for Polished Brass by pressing and holding the left mouse button. Drag the thumbnail directly on top of the washer cover in the graphics area, as in Figure 6.27.

5. Release the left mouse button, and a small toolbar will appear to allow you to choose the level at which the material will be applied. Select the icon for an assembly to apply the material to the washer cover only at the assembly level, as in Figure 6.28. The washer cover model will not be updated with the material appearance except at the assembly level.

Turn on RealView

Unless you already have RealView enabled, the washer cover now has a dull dark yellow color to it. Not really as exciting as you probably expected, but that is because the SolidWorks environment does not show the full material appearance by default. To be able to view your parts in RealView, you must have one of the many supported video cards. You can check to see whether your video card supports RealView graphics on the SolidWorks website:

www.solidworks.com/sw/videocardtesting.html

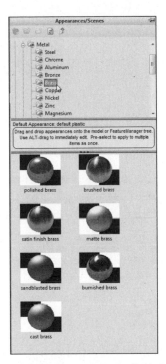

FIGURE 6.26 Available brass material appearances

FIGURE 6.27 Applying a material to a model

FIGURE 6.28 Applying a brass material to model at the assembly level

If you have a supported card, you can update the view by selecting RealView Graphics in the View Settings flyout on the Heads-up View toolbar, as shown in Figure 6.29.

FIGURE 6.29 Enabling RealView

If You Would Like More Practice...

You might have noticed that when you made the additional configuration for the washer, you did not do the same for the washer cover. For the subassembly you will be using in the desk lamp, the larger size is not needed, but this gives you a great opportunity to get some practice creating configurations. Using the Configure Dimensions command, create a new configuration in the washer cover, and increase the diameters by the same amount as what was added to the washer. Configurations are a very powerful tool in SolidWorks, and it would be beneficial to gain more experience creating them.

In later chapters, you will be learning how to create configurations in assemblies. You can always go back to the Washer Sub-Assembly part to create an additional configuration with what you learned.

Are You Experienced?

Now You Can...

- ☑ **Add fillets to a sketch**

- ☑ **Add drafted surfaces to a simple molding part**

- ☑ **Create a revolved part with a thin feature**

- ☑ **Create an assembly**

- ☑ **Use the concentric and coincident mates**

- ☑ **Change the appearance of models**

CHAPTER 7

Creating a Simple Assembly Drawing

▶ Create the Drawing Views

▶ Add a Bill of Materials

▶ Add Balloons to the Drawing

▶ Finish the Bill of Materials

I n previous chapters, you created parts, a simple part drawing, and an assembly. In this chapter, you'll make a simple assembly drawing for the assembly that you created in Chapter 6, "Creating an Assembly." Unlike the drawing you created in Chapter 4, "Creating Your First Drawing," an assembly drawing does not contain dimensions in most cases. Instead, an *assembly drawing* is used to show which parts are used to build an assembly or subassembly and how they are put together.

Before you can begin creating your assembly drawing, you need to download the drawing template from the companion site that you will be using throughout this chapter. The drawing template is the same template you used in Chapter 4, but it does not contain any predefined views since you will be adding the necessary views manually. After downloading the template, save the file in the same folder with the rest of the drawing templates, as described in Chapter 5, "Creating a Revolved Part."

If you have not completed Chapter 6, you can download the parts and assembly from the companion site as well. Save the parts and assembly in your working folder.

Create the Drawing Views

In Chapter 4, when you created your first drawing, you opened the part first and created the drawing from the part using predefined views. In this chapter, you will be creating the views manually by inserting the appropriate views. This is probably the most common way users choose to create drawing views, because unless you create many templates with different predefined views, you will not be able to anticipate which views you will need to use. To create the assembly drawing with the needed views, do the following:

1. Select New in the menu bar.

2. In the New SolidWorks Documents window, select the template named FDC Size B – No Views, and click OK to create a new drawing.

    In the graphics area, the new drawing will be displayed, and the Model View PropertyManager will appear. The Model View PropertyManager, shown in Figure 7.1, is used to select the model that will be used to create the views on the drawing. The Model View PropertyManager will automatically be displayed when a new drawing is created, but you can choose to disable it. Just for demonstration purposes, disable the option to start the Model View command when creating a new drawing, and then we will show you how to initiate the command manually.

FIGURE 7.1 The Model View PropertyManager

3. In the Model View PropertyManager, deselect the option to automatically start the Model View command when creating a new drawing. Then click the red X to exit the Model View PropertyManager.

The next time you create a new drawing, the Model View command will not automatically launch. This is merely a personal preference, and if you prefer to have the command launch automatically, you can always reselect the option in the Model View PropertyManager. However, if you decide to leave the option turned off, it is quite easy to launch the Model View command manually.

4. With your mouse pointer in the graphics area, press S on your keyboard, and click the Drawings button to view the items in the flyout.

5. Select Model View in the Drawing flyout to initiate the command. You will notice that the PropertyManager that opens is the same PropertyManager you disabled previously.

N O T E The Model View tools are also available in the View Layout tab of the CommandManager and in the Insert ➢ Drawing View menu.

Explore the Model View PropertyManager

Now that you know how to access the Model View command, whether or not it is launched automatically when creating a new drawing, it is time to specify what model will be used to create the drawing. The next steps will require that you have the parts and assembly that were created in the previous chapter. If you do not have these files on your system, you can always download them from the companion site. Once the files are located on your system, you can create the drawing views by doing the following:

1. Click the Browse button in the Part/Assembly To Insert section of the Model View PropertyManager.

2. Browse to the location where the parts and assembly from the previous chapter are located on your computer, select the washer subassembly, and click Open.

The Model View PropertyManager will now be updated with the options necessary to properly select your drawing view requirements. Before moving on, let's take a couple of minutes to quickly look at a few sections in the PropertyManager.

Reference Configuration Section

This section is pretty straightforward; if you have multiple configurations in the part or assembly you selected, you can specify which configuration will be shown in the created drawing view. Since this assembly does not have any configurations, the configuration named Default is the only option available in the section.

Orientation Section

The Orientation section of the Model View PropertyManager allows you to specify which view of the model will be shown in the drawing when created. At the top of the section is an option called Create Multiple Views, which allows you to create multiple views, such as Top, Front, and Right, with one operation. This is extremely helpful when you create part drawings that require multiple projections of the part to fully document the part.

Below the Create Multiple Views option are a set of buttons that allow you to specify the standard views of the part. If the Create Multiple Views option is selected, you can select more than one view of the part with these buttons; otherwise, only one view can be selected at a time. These buttons correspond with the standard views that are available in the part model. This means that the Top view in the part model will also be the Top view in the drawing. If you are sure which button corresponds to which view, you can hover your mouse pointer over the button, and a tooltip will provide you with the view name.

The More Views box allows you to select any named views that were created in the part. If none were created, the only views that will be shown are the Dimetric and Trimetric views. The Isometric view is not shown in the box since it is already available as a button in the Standard Views section. Also, if you currently have the part file open in the background, you can select Current View in this box.

Last, at the bottom of the Orientation section is the option named Preview. This option is available as long as the Create Multiple Views option is not selected. We normally like to select the Preview option when creating drawing views since it gives a preview of the drawing view instead of just a blank box.

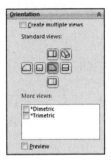

Import Options Section

The Import Options section is used to import the annotations and dimensions that were used to define the sketches and features of the part model into the drawing. You can then arrange and move the annotations between the various views to create a fully dimensioned drawing. Since in most cases assembly drawings do not contain any dimensions other than those required to assemble the parts, you will not need to import anything in your drawing.

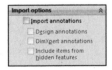

Display State Section

If the selected model uses display states, you can specify which display state will be used when creating the drawing views. Since your assembly does not have any display states other than the default one, the only display state shown in the section is Display State-1.

Options Section

In later chapters, we will be discussing display states in more detail.

In the Options section of the Model View PropertyManager, you can set the Projected View command to automatically start after adding the drawing view. This section is available only when the Create Multiple Views option in the Orientation section is not selected. We prefer to keep the Auto-Start Projected View option selected most of the time since more often than not you will need to create additional projected views after inserting the model view. If after inserting the drawing view you do not need to create an additional projected view, you can always press Esc on the keyboard. However, sometimes it is beneficial to turn the option off when you know for sure that you will not be making any projected views, such as in the example in this chapter.

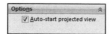

Display Style Section

The Display Style section allows you to specify which style will be applied to the drawing views you create. In our opinion, you should keep the Hidden Lines Removed button selected since most of the drawing views you will create will be displayed this way. You can always specify the display style for selected drawing views in the Heads-Up View toolbar. But if you know ahead of time that the views need to be shown as shaded or with hidden lines, you can specify this during the view creation in this section.

Scale Section

The Scale section is used to specify the scale that the newly created drawing view will be set as. Selecting the Use Sheet Scale option is the best option in most cases since the scale of the drawing will match that of the sheet itself and will match the value displayed in the title block if it is set to reflect the value. Selecting a custom scale will cause the view to no longer match the sheet scale, and because the value is changed in the sheet, the drawing view will not be updated. If after you create the drawing view you decide that the scale needs to be updated, you can change it in the Drawing View PropertyManager.

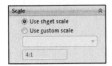

Dimension Type Section

The Dimension Type section is an often-overlooked section but can cause major issues with your drawing if the wrong option is selected. Basically, the two options determine how the value of the dimension is derived from the drawing view. In all orthogonal views, such as Top, Right, and Front, the Projected option must be selected since it specifies the dimension as it is projected onto the 2D drawing plane. The True option is used when trying to apply dimensions to nonorthogonal views such as Isometric, Dimetric, and Trimetric views. The True option is used in these views since a projected dimension will often be larger or smaller than the actual dimension for the selected features. You should never need to change these options since SolidWorks will automatically set the appropriate dimension type when the drawing view is created, but if you think the dimensions shown in the drawing do not match the value that should be displayed, make sure the appropriate option is selected.

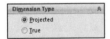

Cosmetic Thread Display Section

The Cosmetic Thread Display section controls how the threads will be displayed in the drawing. Rarely do we change this option since this option is also controlled in the Detailing section of the Document Properties dialog box. But if you need to change the display option for cosmetic threads, you should know that the High Quality option can have an effect on your overall system performance depending on the threads that are being displayed.

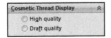

Now that you have seen the various options available in the Model View PropertyManager, it is time to create the drawing view by doing the following:

1. In the Orientation section, select the button for the Front view, and select the Preview option, as shown in Figure 7.2.

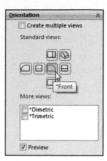

FIGURE 7.2 Specifying the Front view for the new drawing view

2. Ensure that the Auto-Start Projected View option is selected in the Options section.

3. In the Display Style section, ensure that the Hidden Lines Removed button is selected.

4. In the Scale section, ensure that the Use Sheet Scale option is not selected.

5. Move the mouse pointer into the graphics area, and the preview of the drawing view will move with the pointer. When the drawing view is approximately in the middle-left side of the drawing sheet, as shown in Figure 7.3, click and release the left mouse button.

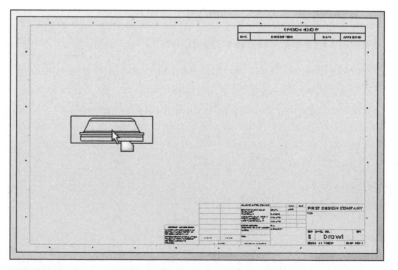

FIGURE 7.3 Placement of the washer subassembly drawing view

Now is a good time to save the drawing. If you look at the menu bar at the top of the SolidWorks interface, you will see that the drawing has taken on the same name of the part/assembly when the drawing view was created. Since there is no need to change the name, you will keep the same name in the Save As window, but you will still need to specify the folder location of the file before saving.

Section the Washer Subassembly

In the previous section, you added the Front view of the washer subassembly, and you can just leave the drawing with the one view and finish the rest of the drawing. But, as you can see from Figure 7.4, it may not be clear to the reader of the drawing where one part ends and the other begins. That is why, in drawings such as this one, we like to add a section view to clear up any confusion there may be as to how the parts are put together.

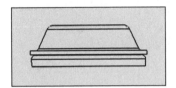

FIGURE 7.4 Front view of the washer subassembly

It can help to add a section view to eliminate confusion about how parts are put together in an assembly.

In Chapter 4, we already went through the process of creating a section view, so the following steps should be a quick review of the process:

1. Select Section View in the shortcut bar or on the View Layout tab in the CommandManager.

2. Move the mouse pointer to the middle of the top line of the washer subassembly until the midpoint is highlighted and the mouse pointer changes to include the midpoint relation, as shown in Figure 7.5.

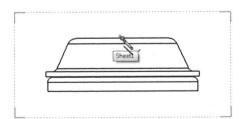

FIGURE 7.5 Highlighting the midpoint of a segment in drawing view

3. Slowly move the mouse pointer vertically, ensuring that the coincident relation appears next to the mouse pointer while moving. When the mouse pointer is a short distance from the top of the washer subassembly, as shown in Figure 7.6, click and release the left mouse button to specify the first end of the section line.

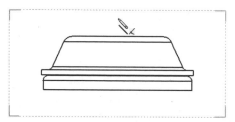

FIGURE 7.6 Using the midpoint of a drawing view for section

4. Move the pointer to just below the bottom line of the washer subassembly at approximately the same distance in the previous step, as shown in Figure 7.7. Click and release the left mouse button to create the section line.

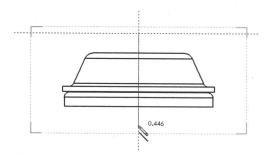

0.446

FIGURE 7.7 Drawing a section line

The Section View window, as shown in Figure 7.8, is something you did not encounter when you sectioned the lamp base in Chapter 5 since you sectioned only one part. Now that you are applying a section to more than one component, you are presented with a couple more options.

The first thing that you may notice in the Section View window is the large blue box on the left side of the window. This window lists any parts that you do not want to be sectioned. Since you actually want to section both parts in the drawing view, you will not be adding anything. However, if you were to decide to exclude a component from the section, you would just select the component in either the graphics area or the FeatureManager design tree.

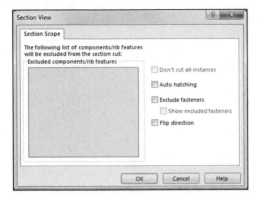

FIGURE 7.8 The Section View window

The Section View window appears when you apply a section to more than one component.

To the right of the Excluded Components/Rib Features box are additional options that you can apply to the section. The first option, Don't Cut All Instances, doesn't become active until components are specified first. If a component is shown in the excluded component list and the Don't Cut All Instances option is deselected, all the copies of the same component will be sectioned with the line created. If the option is selected, only the instances of the same component that are in the excluded list will be sectioned.

The next option in the list, Auto Hatching, is used to specify how SolidWorks will apply section lines to components that are made of the same material and are next to each other in the section view. As you may know, each material type has a different hatch pattern to help identify the material. But since many users do not specify materials for their parts in SolidWorks, all the parts in the section will have the same hatch pattern. Selecting the Auto Hatching option will automatically adjust the hatch pattern by changing the angle and/or scale of the pattern to allow the reader to easily identify the components in the assembly.

The Exclude Fasteners option, when enabled, will prevent standard components that were added to the assembly via the Toolbox from being sectioned. If the Exclude Fasteners option is selected, the Show Excluded Fasteners option will be available and will provide a preview of the fasteners that will not be sectioned.

The last option, Flip Direction, will toggle the direction of the cutting plane when the section is made. This option is also available in the Section PropertyManager.

To complete the section, do the following:

1. Select the Auto Hatching option, and click OK to close the Section View window.

2. Move the section to the right of the Front view, and click and release the left mouse button to place the view. The New section will be

labeled Section A-A, and the section line on the Front view will be drawn as well.

3. Since there are no other options that you need to worry about at this point, close the Section PropertyManager by clicking the green check mark. Figure 7.9 shows what the drawing views should look like.

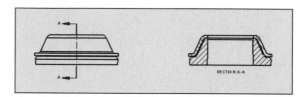

FIGURE 7.9 Drawing views created in assembly drawing

4. Before moving on to the next section, notice that the section view that was created does not have a centerline going through the center of the parts. This is a minor thing, but it always good practice to add centerlines to revolved parts in a drawing. Select Centerline in the Annotations flyout on the shortcut bar.

5. Select one of the lines that makes up the inner diameter of the washer, as shown in Figure 7.10.

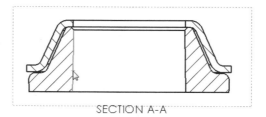

SECTION A-A

FIGURE 7.10 Selecting the first edge for adding centerline to drawing view

6. Select the second line of the inner diameter of the washer. The centerline will now be added to the view. Hit Esc or click the green check mark in the Section PropertyManager to exit the command.

After the centerline was added to the view, you may notice that the centerline is a little shorter at the top of the section view, and it crosses over the section label at the bottom of the view. It is always good to take care of some simple housecleaning as the need arises rather than waiting until the end. So, at this time, you will need to extend the centerline a little more beyond the top of the view and also move the section label down until the centerline is no longer running into it.

7. Zoom in close to the section view by spinning the scroll wheel down with the mouse pointer over the approximate center of the section view. Or if you prefer, you can click the Zoom To Area button in the Heads-up View toolbar and drag a window around the section view.

8. Move the mouse pointer directly on top of the section label, and click and hold the left mouse button.

9. While still holding the left mouse button, move the label to just below where the centerline ends, giving a short gap between the label and the centerline.

10. Move the mouse pointer to the centerline itself, and select it by clicking and releasing the left mouse button. The centerline will be highlighted, and drag handles will appear at both ends of the line.

11. Move the mouse pointer to the top drag handle, and click and hold the left mouse button.

12. Drag the end of the centerline until it extends approximately the same distance from the top of the section as from the bottom. Once the desired length is achieved, you can click anywhere on the drawing or hit Esc to deselect the centerline, after which the section view should look something like the one shown in Figure 7.11.

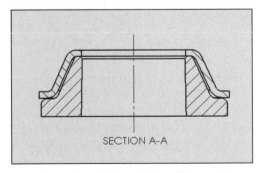

SECTION A-A

FIGURE 7.11 Section view after cleanup

 N O T E Don't forget to save your work often to prevent any loss of data in the off chance that SolidWorks experiences a crash.

Add a Bill of Materials

A bill of materials (BOM) is a list of components that tells the print reader what components are used in the assembly shown in the drawing. Although every company has their own standards in what information in the BOM is displayed, they all have the same minimum information such as the item number, part number, description, and quantity of each component in the assembly. Additional entries such as Vendor Name, Material Type, Next Assemblies, and Used On can also be found on some BOMs.

SolidWorks comes preinstalled with a set of BOM tables that will fill the needs of many organizations, but often it is necessary to update the templates to meet special needs. At this point, we will not be covering the process of how to create your own BOM template. This will be covered in detail later in the book, so for now you can download the BOM template that will be used in this chapter from the companion site. After downloading the BOM, save it in the same folder that you have been saving the rest of the templates to make it easier to find when the time comes.

With the BOM template downloaded and added to the folder that contains the rest of your templates, it is time to add it to the assembly drawing you have been working on. To add a BOM to the assembly drawing, do the following:

You can find the requirements for BOMs or part lists in ASME Y14.34-1996.

1. Select the Tables flyout on the shortcut bar.

2. In the Tables flyout, click the Bill Of Materials button.

3. Before you can insert the BOM into the drawing, a message in the Bill Of Materials PropertyManager tells you that you must first select a view in the drawing that will be used to populate the list. You would at this point select any view that displays the components that you want to be shown in the table. Since you only have two views in this drawing, you can select either one of them.

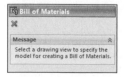

Explore the Bill of Materials PropertyManager

After selecting the view that will be used to populate the BOM, you will be presented with many options for creating the BOM in the PropertyManager. It may seem like a lot of information to take in, but if you break it down into sections, it is easier to understand. Some of the sections shown in the PropertyManager at this time are available only when inserting a BOM, and the others will remain available when the BOM is already inserted.

Table Template Section

The Table Template section is available only when inserting a BOM. This section allows you to specify a standard or custom BOM table that will be inserted in the drawing. Since this section is available only when inserting a BOM, once you insert a BOM, you must delete it to change the template being used. Next to the name of the template selected for insertion is a button named Open Table Template For Bill Of Materials, which will launch the browse window to locate the desired template.

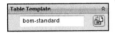

Table Position Section

The Table Position section contains the option to attach the inserted BOM to an anchor point on the drawing sheet. Each table type in SolidWorks, including the BOM, has its own anchor point in the drawing sheet that is used to attach the table to prevent it from being moved. The major advantage to using an anchor point for tables is that the position of the tables will be consistent in all drawings.

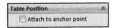

BOM Type Section

The options in the BOM Type section are used to determine which components will be shown in the BOM that is created. The first option, Top-level Only, is probably the most common. This option shows only the top-level parts and sub-assemblies of the current assembly. If the assembly being depicted in the drawing has subassemblies, then only the subassembly will be shown and not the components that make up the subassembly. If the Parts Only option is selected, all of the parts, including those in the subassemblies, will be shown, but the subassemblies themselves will not be listed in the BOM. Lastly, the Indented option allows you to show an indented parts list that shows the top-level parts and subassemblies. Then the parts that make up the subassemblies will be shown in an indented manner on the BOM.

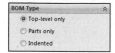

Configurations Section

Sometimes configurations are used in assemblies to create different versions of assemblies that contain different components and quantities to eliminate the need for multiple drawings. The Configurations section allows you to select the configurations that will be used to populate the BOM. The next section will then be used to specify how the different configurations are displayed in the BOM.

Part Configuration Grouping Section

If more than one configuration is selected in the Configurations section, the Part Configuration Grouping section is used to determine how the parts are grouped in the BOM. Each configuration will have its own QTY column in the BOM with the name of the configuration included. Since you will not be using this option in this book, we will not be spending any more time covering this option, but you may need to read up on these options in the SolidWorks help file if your organization plans to incorporate this approach to assembly drawings.

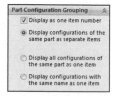

Item Numbers Section

In the Item Numbers section, you can specify how the numbering of the items in the BOM is handled. In most cases, you will not need to change these settings. The first option allows you to specify where the numbering starts, and in almost all cases that we have encountered, this should remain as 1. The second option allows you to specify how the numbers will increment from the starting number. Leaving the option as 1 will number the items sequentially as 1, 2, 3, 4, and so on. If you enter another number in this section, the item numbers will increment by that value. The last option is used to prevent the item numbers in the BOM from being changed if the item's numbers are updated elsewhere.

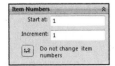

Border Section

If your organization requires that the outside border of the BOM be thicker than the inside lines or if you want to adjust the thickness of all the lines to make them easier to read on the print, then changing the values in this section will do the job. Of course, you can always select the Use Document Settings option to let the value that is specified in the document properties control the display of the lines in the BOM.

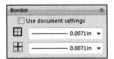

Layer Section

The Layer section is used to specify which layer the BOM will be created on in the drawing. This is an option that is rarely used. The use of layers has gone out of practice since the advent of laser printers and since selecting different pins for the various line types is no longer necessary. We will not be using layers in any of the areas of this book, but if your company uses layers, this is where you can select the layer that will be used.

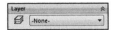

Now it is time to select and insert the desired BOM into the assembly drawing. Do the following to insert the BOM:

1. Click the Open Table Template For Bill Of Materials button in the Table Template section. In the Open window, browse to the folder that contains the BOM template you downloaded from the companion website. Select the BOM, and click Open.

2. In the BOM Type section, select Top-Level Only.

3. Since there are no other selections to be made at this point, click the green check mark to insert the BOM into the drawing.

4. The BOM will now be attached to the mouse pointer, waiting for you to specify where it needs to reside in the drawing. Since you have not defined an anchor point so far, just place the BOM anywhere in the drawing for the time being, as shown in Figure 7.12.

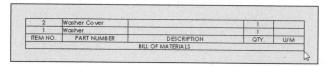

2	Washer Cover		1	
1	Washer		1	
ITEM NO.	PART NUMBER	DESCRIPTION	QTY.	U/M
		BILL OF MATERIALS		

FIGURE 7.12 BOM ready to be placed in the drawing

Specify the Anchor Point for the Bill of Materials

 TIP Anchoring the BOM and other tables in drawings creates a consistent position for all the tables throughout all your drawings.

Before you can attach the BOM to an anchor, you need to specify the anchor point on the drawing itself. This would normally be done once when creating the drawing template, but this is a good time to cover the procedure. To adjust the anchor point and attach the BOM to the anchor, do the following:

1. In the FeatureManager, click the plus (+) next to the Sheet1 item to display its contents.

2. Then click the plus (+) next to the Sheet Format1 item to display the items that are attributed to the sheet format that can be modified.

3. Right-click the item labeled Bill Of Material Anchor1 below Sheet Format1, and select Set Anchor from the menu, as shown in Figure 7.13.
    The drawing contents will disappear in the graphics area, and the sheet format will become active. As you move the mouse pointer in the graphics area, you will notice that it snaps to wherever there is an endpoint and the endpoint is highlighted with an orange dot. This point is the proposed anchor point based on where you currently have the mouse pointer.

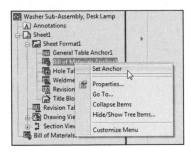

FIGURE 7.13 Setting the BOM anchor from the FeatureManager

4. Move the mouse pointer to the top-right corner of the title block, as shown in Figure 7.14, and click and release the left mouse button when the point is highlighted.

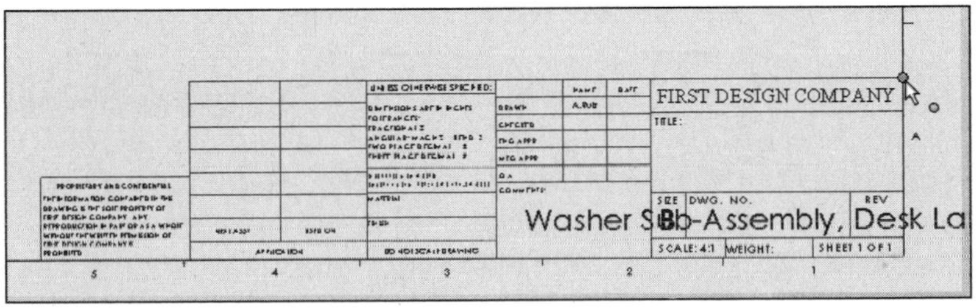

FIGURE 7.14 The anchor point highlighted on the drawing title block

Once the point is specified, the drawing will return, and it is time to specify that the BOM is now to be anchored to the point.

5. Move the mouse pointer over the BOM that you inserted earlier. Select any cell of the table to display additional items on the table including a cross in the upper-left corner of the table. Select this cross, as shown in Figure 7.15, to display the Bill Of Materials PropertyManager.

	A	B	C	D	E
	2	Washer Cover		1	
	1	Washer		1	
	ITEM NO.	PART NUMBER	DESCRIPTION	QTY.	U/M
			BILL OF MATERIALS		

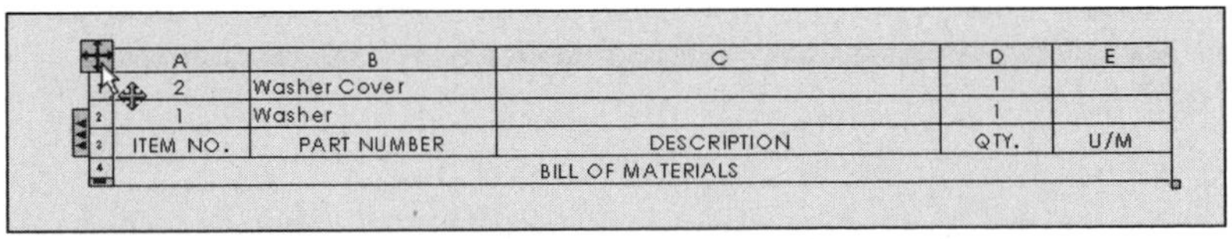

FIGURE 7.15 Displaying the Bill Of Materials PropertyManager

6. In the Bill Of Materials PropertyManager, select the Attach To Anchor Point option in the Table Position section, and click the green check mark. The table will now be moved to just above the title block based on the position you defined in the previous steps, as shown in Figure 7.16.

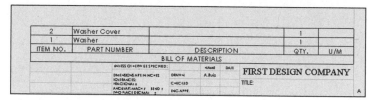

FIGURE 7.16 BOM attached to its anchor point

Add Balloons to the Drawing

Now that you have added the BOM to the drawing, you need to add balloons to identify each part. The numbers in the balloons will correspond to the items listed in the BOM. As items in the BOM are reordered, the numbers in the balloons will be updated as well as long as the balloons are created correctly. You can add balloons to the drawing in a couple of ways, but we'll cover what we think is the easiest way. To add the balloons, do the following:

1. Select the section view by moving the mouse pointer inside the boundary area of the view, and click and release the left mouse button.

2. Press S on the keyboard, and select the Annotations flyout to view the commands that are available, as shown in Figure 7.17.

3. Click the AutoBalloon button.

Explore the AutoBalloon PropertyManager

Before you actually add the balloons to the drawing, we'll take a couple of minutes to examine the options available in the AutoBalloon PropertyManager. Each section contains options that are used to control how the balloon looks and acts. Some of the sections are common, so you'll see them in various PropertyManagers for other commands.

FIGURE 7.17 Available commands in the Annotations flyout

Style Section

The Style section is a common section that can be found in annotations and dimensions throughout SolidWorks. The Style section allows you to save and recall customized styles.

Balloon Layout Section

The Balloon Layout section allows you to specify how the balloons will automatically be arranged when adding them to your drawing. The six buttons shown will get you started in arranging the balloons, and you can go back afterward to rearrange individual balloons to better suit your needs. The Ignore Multiple Instances option will eliminate duplicate balloons when there is more than one copy of the same component in an assembly. The last two options, Balloon Faces and Balloon Edges, define where the leader will terminate. With the Balloon Faces option, the leader will terminate on the face of the component, and the Balloon Edges option will terminate the leader on the edge of the components. All the options in this section reflect the personal preference of the drawing creator and should be adjusted to provide the best information to the reader of the print.

Balloon Settings Section

Depending on your company standards, the balloon styles on the drawing can take many different shapes including circles, squares, triangles, diamonds, and more. The most common balloon is probably the circle. The second option determines what the size of the balloons will be based on and the number of characters that will be shown in the balloon. The diameter of the balloons can also be defined using the user-defined option and specifying the diameter in the field. The last option, Balloon Text, specifies what text will be displayed in the balloon. For our purposes, the item number will be specified throughout the book since you need to ensure that the number displayed matches the item numbers in the BOM. Selecting any other option will mean that they do not match.

Leader Style Section

The Leader Style section adjusts how the leader's line style and weight will be displayed. Selecting the Use Document Display option means the style will be controlled by the document properties and ensures consistency throughout your drawing.

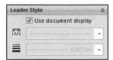

Frame Style Section

The Frame Style section acts the same as the Leader Style section, but it adjusts the line style and weight of the balloons.

Layer Style

The last section in the AutoBalloon PropertyManager is the Layer section. This section is common among different PropertyManagers, and it specifies which layer will be used when creating the balloons.

Now that you have an idea of the basic options available in the AutoBalloon PropertyManager, you need to make sure that the settings are specified before you add the balloons. Perform the following tasks to create the balloons in the drawing:

1. In the Balloon Layout section, click through the six and see how the balloons in the drawing are affected. For this drawing, the Left option is probably the best one, but feel free to select whatever one you like.

2. In the Balloon Settings section, make sure that the style is set to Circular and the balloon text is set to Item Number.

3. At this point, there is no need to adjust any other settings, so click the green check mark to create the balloons. The section view with the balloons should look like the example in Figure 7.18.

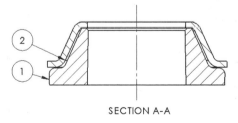

SECTION A-A

FIGURE 7.18 Balloons in section view

Look closely at the section view and how the balloons are shown; you might need to adjust where the leader terminates or how long the leader is on the screen. You can do this quickly and easily without needing to initiate any commands.

4. To adjust where a leader terminates on the part, select the balloon by clicking and releasing the left mouse button with the pointer directly

on the balloon or leader. The balloon and leader will be highlighted, and the endpoint of the leader will have a drag handle.

5. Move the mouse pointer to the drag handle at the end of the leader, and click and hold the left mouse button.

6. Move the endpoint to another segment of the section view. The lines of the view will be highlighted as you move the mouse over them. Once the appropriate edge is selected, release the left mouse pointer.

7. To lengthen the leader of the balloon, select the balloon by clicking and holding the left mouse button.

8. While still holding the left mouse button, drag the balloon to increase or decrease the length of the leader.

Once you have completed adjusting the balloons in the view, it should look something like the view shown in Figure 7.19.

 T I P The exact appearance of the balloons doesn't matter as long as it is readily apparent to the reader of the drawing which component in the section view is being specified. Make sure the leaders do not cross each other.

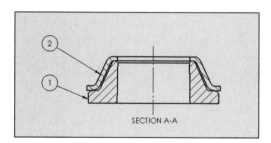

SECTION A-A

FIGURE 7.19 Balloons and leaders adjusted in the section view

Finish the Bill of Materials

Now that you have the BOM inserted into your assembly drawing and it is anchored in its correct position, it is time to fill in the missing values. In later chapters, when we discuss the process of how to create the BOM template you are currently using, we will cover in greater detail the intricacies of the BOM. Until then, you just want to make sure that the BOM is filled completely all while updating the custom properties of the components.

The values displayed in the BOM are taken from the custom properties of the part models. As you make a change to the custom properties of the components, the fields are updated automatically. In the past, you were not able to update the BOM without breaking the link to the part model, but in SolidWorks 2008 the BOM became bidirectional. This means that as long as the link is maintained, the properties of the components will be updated when the cells of the BOM are updated. Since you did not define the values of the properties of the components prior to making the assembly, you can easily update them now by following these steps:

As you change the components' custom properties, the BOM fields are updated automatically.

1. Select the cell for the Part Number column for the first row, which should be the washer.

2. In this cell, you will assign a part number for the washer. Just for demonstration purposes, you will assign the number 901236 to the washer. As you begin to type the number, you will be prompted with the window shown in Figure 7.20.

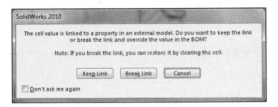

FIGURE 7.20 Prompt to keep link between BOM and part file

3. Click Keep Link to allow the part model custom properties to be updated with the new value. Continue typing in the number in the field.

4. Repeat steps 1–3 for the Part Number cell for Item 2, except this time make the number 902458.

5. Now select the description cell for the first row, and make the description **WASHER, WASHER SUB-ASSEMBLY**. Make sure that you keep the link.

6. Make the description for item 2 **WASHER COVER, WASHER SUB-ASSEMLY**.

7. In the U/M column, make the unit of measure for both components EA, which stands for Each. After the values have all been updated, the BOM should look like Figure 7.21.

2	902458	WASHER COVER, WASHER SUB-ASSEMBLY	1	EA
1	901236	WASHER, WASHER SUB-ASSEMBLY	1	EA
ITEM NO.	PART NUMBER	DESCRIPTION	QTY.	U/M
		BILL OF MATERIALS		

| UNLESS OTHERWISE SPECIFIED: | | NAME | DATE | FIRST DESIGN COMPANY |
| DIMENSIONS ARE IN INCHES TOLERANCES: | DRAWN | A.RUIZ | | |

FIGURE 7.21 Completed BOM

If You Would Like More Practice...

Although we are finished with the points that are going to be covered in this chapter, the drawing is still not complete. The title block is still empty and should be filled out completely as well. Using what you learned in previous chapters, complete the drawing by using the Title Block Manager and the custom properties for the drawing.

Are You Experienced?

Now You Can...

- ☑ **Create views in a drawing using model view**

- ☑ **Understand the Model View PropertyManager**

- ☑ **Exclude components in a section view**

- ☑ **Insert a BOM into an assembly drawing**

- ☑ **Specify the anchor point for tables in a drawing**

- ☑ **Add balloons to an assembly drawing**

- ☑ **Understand the AutoBalloon PropertyManager**

- ☑ **Update the custom properties of components using the BOM**

Creating a More Complex Part Model

So far in this book you have created a couple of simple parts and subassemblies. Now things start to get a little more interesting, because you will create a part model that will introduce you to some new commands and also give you more practice in creating sketches. The part you will be making in this chapter is the shade mount that is screwed into the top of the shaft you modeled in Chapter 6, "Creating a Subassembly." The shade mount will then be used to hold the lamp shade and the bulb receptacle.

If this part were to be manufactured for real, it would more than likely be made in separate parts and then welded together. The welds would then be cleaned up and hidden with the plating process. Lucky for you, you are not actually going to build this lamp, so you can get away with a little artistic license. You'll instead model the whole part as one.

Create the Base Feature of the Shade Mount

The first feature you'll create in the model is the part of the mount that will be screwed into the lamp shaft and also support the arms of the mount. This feature will be a simple, fully revolved feature, but don't think it is going to be a breeze. The feature itself might be a simple revolve, but the magic is all in the sketch. Unlike some of the sketches you have created so far in this book, this sketch will be comprised of mostly arcs to give the feature a nice spherical look.

Before you can begin, you need to create a new part and set up your environment. By now you should be comfortable with specifying your document settings, so we won't be going into detail about the process here. Instead, you will jump right into modeling the base feature for the model.

1. Click the New button in the menu bar, and select the part template. Click OK to create the new part.

2. Click Options in the menu bar, and select the Document Properties tab. On the Document Properties tab, set the Overall Drafting Standard option to ANSI.

3. In the Units section of the Document Properties tab, set the Unit System option to IPS, and specify that length dimensions display values with three decimal places. Click OK to apply the new settings and close the window.

 TIP   You can always create a part template to save the time of updating the document properties each time you create a new part.

4. Select Revolved Boss/Base in the shortcut bar, and select the front plane to create the sketch.

5. Select the Line tool in the shortcut bar. Select the sketch origin as the first point of the line by clicking and releasing the left mouse button.

6. Move the mouse pointer vertically, making the line approximately 1.25 inches long. Click and release the left mouse button to create the first line.

Transition Between Lines and Arcs in Sketches

When most SolidWorks users need to create arcs in sketches, the Arc tools are often their first thought. But as with many things in SolidWorks, there is more than one way to create an arc in a sketch. While still in the Line tool when sketching, you can quickly and easily switch to an arc without even selecting another tool. By using your mouse, you can switch to the Arc command to draw an arc and return to drawing lines. Switching between lines and arcs in a sketch is referred to as autotransitioning, and it is a great time-saver. Using autotransitioning, you can finish the sketch by doing the following:

1. If you move the mouse pointer, you can create another line segment, but this time you'll do something different. Move the pointer back to the endpoint of the line and move it away again, and the line will change to an arc, as shown in Figure 8.1.

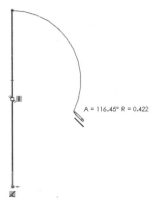

A = 116.45° R = 0.422

FIGURE 8.1 Autotransitioning between the line and arc

You can also transition between a line and arc by pressing A on your keyboard while in the Line command.

2. Using the values displayed next to the mouse pointer, draw an arc that has an approximate radius of 0.425 and angle of 115°. It will be near impossible to draw the arc to the target radius and angle, but that will not be an issue since you will be further defining the arc with the addition of relations and dimensions. Click and release the left mouse button to draw the arc.

3. After drawing the arc, the next segment will automatically transition back to a line. Move the mouse pointer back to the endpoint of the last arc to transition back to an arc segment.

4. Once again, using the values displayed next to the mouse pointer, create an arc that has an approximate radius of .075; this time the angle does not matter as long as the endpoint of the new arc is horizontal to the center of the arc, as shown with the inference line between the center and endpoint. Figure 8.2 shows the new arc with the inference lines. Click and release the left mouse button to create the arc.

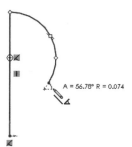

FIGURE 8.2 New arc segment showing inference lines

5. Using the same technique, create another arc that has an approximate radius of .125 and once again has the endpoint horizontal to the center of the arc. Click and release the left mouse button to create the arc.

6. Move the mouse pointer vertically down from the endpoint of the last arc. Notice that next to the mouse pointer a symbol for tangency is displayed. This will automatically make the line segment tangent to the last arc created. When the pointer displays an approximate value of .100 and an angle of 90°, click and release the left mouse pointer, as shown in Figure 8.3.

7. Now move the mouse pointer horizontally toward the first line you sketched. Once the value shows that the line is approximately .150 long and has an angle of 90°, click and release the left mouse button.

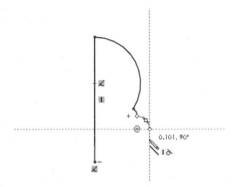

FIGURE 8.3 Adding a line tangent to the last arc

8. Move the mouse pointer down vertically until an inference line is shown between the first endpoint of the sketch and the endpoint of the new sketch segment, as shown in Figure 8.4. Click and release the left mouse button to create the new line.

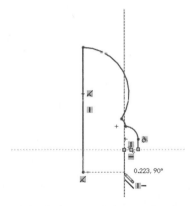

FIGURE 8.4 Inference line between the origin of the sketch and the endpoint of line

9. For the final sketch segment, move the mouse pointer back to the sketch origin (where the sketch began), and click and release the left mouse button when the pointer displays the concentric icon. The profile should look like Figure 8.5. If all went well, the line segment that you just drew will automatically have a tangent relation added between the arc and the line. If for some reason the tangency is not automatically added, select both segments while holding the Ctrl key, and then select Tangent in the PropertyManager.

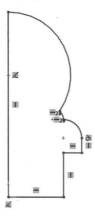

FIGURE 8.5 Under-defined profile created

Change a Line to a Construction Line

Sometimes as you are sketching in SolidWorks, you want to change a solid line into a construction line that could be used as an axis of revolution, for diametrical dimensioning, or just as a reference for other sketch segments. In the shortcut bar, under the Line flyout, you can access the Centerline tool, but sometimes you may want to convert a line after it has been created. Luckily, there are a couple of quick and easy ways to convert solid lines into construction lines or change construction lines to solid lines. In your sketch, you will need to convert the line that will be used as the axis of revolution when the part is revolved to a construction line. A solid line can be used as an axis of revolution, but you need to be able to add dimensions that specify the diameter of the feature. The following steps will show you how to change the line to a construction line and fully define the sketch.

1. Press Esc on the keyboard to exit the Line command, and then select the vertical line that is coincident with the sketch origin.

2. On the context toolbar, click the Construction Geometry button or the For Construction option in the Line PropertyManager.

3. Using the Smart Dimension tool, apply the dimensions shown in Figure 8.6. It may be necessary to apply any relations that were not added automatically; for example, the R.075 arc may need the centerpoint made horizontal to the endpoint of the adjacent arc.

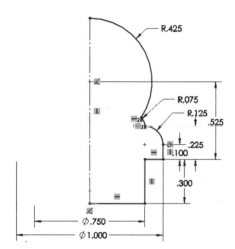

FIGURE 8.6 Fully defined sketch profile

You can also change the selected line to a construction line by selecting the For Construction option in the Line PropertyManager.

Create a Revolved Feature for the Shade Mount

Now that you've created and fully defined the sketch, you are able to create the revolved feature that will be the base feature for the shade mount. Since you initiated the Revolved Boss/Base tool prior to creating the sketch, the moment you exit the sketch, the command will begin. Do the following to create the feature:

1. Click the Exit Sketch icon in the confirmation corner to initiate the Revolved Boss/Base command. When asked to automatically close the sketch, click Yes.

 N O T E Even though the sketch appears to be closed, SolidWorks does not take the construction line into consideration when checking to see whether the sketch is closed. After clicking Yes, a solid line will be added to the sketch exactly where the original solid line existed.

2. Since you specified a centerline in the sketch, there is no need to select an axis of revolution in the Revolve PropertyManager. The Revolve

PropertyManager will automatically specify that the revolution will be in one direction and will have an angle of 360°. Since this meets the requirements for the feature, click the green check mark to create the revolved feature. The feature created should look like Figure 8.7.

FIGURE 8.7 Revolved feature created

 N O T E   If no construction line or centerline exists in a sketch that is meant to be revolved, a solid line would have to be specified to act as the axis of revolution.

3. Now is also a good time to save the part. When saving the part, give it the name **Shade Mount, Desk Lamp.**

Create a Swept Feature

Although extruded and revolved features are common in SolidWorks parts, they are not the only types of features you will need to be familiar with when modeling. Another common feature type that you will encounter the need for at times is a swept feature. A swept feature is comprised of a profile that is extruded along a path. The profile must be a 2D sketch that is made up of a closed profile, and the path is another sketch that can be a single line, arc, spline, or combination thereof.

You'll create a couple of swept features to create one of the arms of the shade mount. The arms of the shade mount are not only used to support the shade but are also used as conduits to pass the wire through from the base to the bulb receptacle.

Add a Reference Plane

Before you can create the swept features that will be used to create the arm, you need to add a reference plane to the part. Up to this point you have only made use of the default planes in parts to create sketches that cannot be added to faces of the parts. Since there are no faces that can be used to create the sketch you require for the path of the swept feature, you will need to add a plane that is offset from existing geometry in the part. You can then use this plane as many times as necessary to create new sketches or even for other features in the model. Perform the following steps to add a new reference plane to the model:

1. Rotate the part to allow access to the bottom surfaces.

2. In the shortcut bar, select the Reference Geometry flyout to view the available tools.

3. In the flyout, select the Plane tool.

4. Select the bottom face of the part ledge as the first reference of the plane, as shown in Figure 8.8.

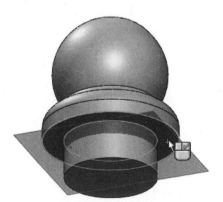

FIGURE 8.8 Selecting first references for the new plane

5. In the First Reference section of the Plane PropertyManager, enter the distance of the plane offset from the selected face to be .525, as shown in Figure 8.9.

6. Below the input field for the offset distance in the Plane PropertyManager, select the Flip option. By default, a plane is offset in the direction that the selected face is pointing. For the example's purposes, you need the plane to be created on the other side of the face. Click the green check mark to create the new plane. Figure 8.10 shows what the new plane should look like.

FIGURE 8.9 Specifying the offset distance for the new plane in PropertyManager

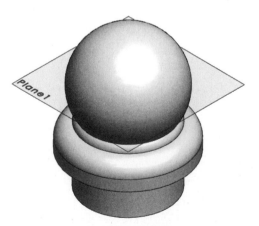

FIGURE 8.10 New reference plane created

Create a Path for Swept Feature

Sometimes it does not matter which comes first, the path or the profile, when creating the sketches for a swept feature, but we often find it is easier to create the path first. The path for a swept feature can be a single sketch consisting of a set of curves, a single curve, or even a set of model edges. The path for a swept pattern must not intersect itself, and it can be made up of continuous segments only. The path must also intersect the plane of the profile. By creating the path first, you can ensure that the profile plane is normal to the end of the path, and it also gives you a good point to work from in your profile sketch, as you will see.

The path for the arm of the shade mount is a simple path that will consist of two lines that are connected with a tangent arc or fillet. To create the path on the sketch plane that was added in the previous section, do the following:

 WARNING   Be careful when sketching the path to ensure that the resulting solid is not self-intersecting. This can often be caused by an angle in the path that is too acute or a radius that is too small.

1. Select the new plane, Plane1, and click the Sketch button on the context toolbar.

2. Select Normal To in the Heads-Up View toolbar.

3. Create a line that originates at the sketch origin, and draw it horizontally to the right about 5 inches long as displayed next to the mouse pointer. Click and release the left mouse button.

4. Drag the mouse pointer up vertically to create another sketch segment that is approximately 3.500″ long. Click and release the left mouse button to draw the line. Press Esc on your keyboard, or double-click the left mouse button to exit the Line command.

5. Using the Smart Dimension tool, apply the dimensions shown in Figure 8.11.

6. Select the Sketch Fillet command, and specify the radius in the Sketch Fillet PropertyManager to be 1.25.

7. Select the corner where the two sketch lines meet to create the R1.25 fillet. Click the green check mark to create the fillet, and then click it again to exit the command.

8. Click the Exit Sketch button on the confirmation corner.

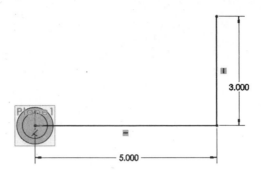

FIGURE 8.11 Dimensioning the line segments of the sketch

Create a Profile Sketch for Swept Feature

A profile for a swept feature can range from the simplest sketch to the most complex sketch. The sketch for a profile must be closed, meaning that there are no gaps in the profile or segments that do not terminate elsewhere on the profile. The only exception to this rule is if you are creating a surface swept feature, but we will not be covering surfacing in this book.

The profile that you need for the arm will consist of just a circle to represent the outer face of the tube. In most cases, you can create the profile to contain both the outer and inner diameters of the tube by sketching two concentric circles. However, because of the way the arm intersects other features in this model, you cannot add the inner diameter at this time. You will be able see why later in this chapter. For now, let's just go ahead and create the profile with a single circle. To create the profile sketch that will be used for the swept feature, do the following:

1. In the FeatureManager design tree, select the right plane, and select the Sketch button in the context menu.

2. Select Normal To in the Heads-Up View toolbar.

3. Select the Circle tool, and select the point from the last sketch at the center of the ball. The point should be highlighted with an orange dot, and the mouse pointer will include a coincident relation icon, as shown in Figure 8.12.

4. Draw the circle and specify the diameter using a smart dimension to be .375.

5. Click the Exit Sketch icon in the confirmation corner.

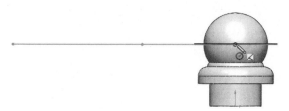

FIGURE 8.12 Center of circle to share point with previous sketch

Create a Swept Feature from Sketches

With the sketches for both the profile and path complete, you can now create the swept feature. There are a couple of ways to create the swept feature from the sketches you created. You can preselect the sketches, and the Sweep tool will automatically differentiate between the profile and the path. You can also initiate the Sweep tool and then select the path and profile sketches. Either way will work, and you will be doing both in this chapter just to see how they both work equally as well. To create the swept boss, perform the following steps:

1. Press S on your keyboard, and select the downward-pointing arrow next to the Extruded Boss/Base button to view the items listed.

2. In the flyout, click the Swept Boss/Base button.

3. In the Sweep PropertyManager, there is a section named Profile And Path. In this section, the profile and the path that it will follow are specified. Each one is color-coded, with blue representing the profile and pink representing the path. These colors correspond to how the sketch segments will be highlighted in the graphics area. The first field is automatically highlighted, meaning that it is expecting the profile to be selected. Select the circle that you created in the second sketch.

4. After selecting the profile for the swept feature, the Path field will automatically be highlighted and be expecting the next selection. In the graphics area, select the path sketch.

5. The view in the graphics area will update with a preview of what the swept feature will look like when created, as shown in Figure 8.13. Since you do not need to make any more selections in the PropertyManager, click the green check mark to create the swept feature.

FIGURE 8.13 Preview of swept feature in the graphics area

Add a Swept Cut Feature

Now that you have created the first arm for the shade mount, you need to make it hollow in order to allow the passage of the wiring. You could have added a concentric circle in the sketch for the swept boss/base to create the inner diameter of the tubing, but it would have not obtained the result wanted here. If you were to include the inner diameter in the first sketch, it would not have succeeded in creating a hole in the base feature of the shade mount, and you would have been required to add another feature to create the cutout. So, it would have not been much of a time-saver anyway.

The requirements for creating a *swept cut feature* are the same as with a swept boss/base. Just like with a swept boss/base feature, you require a path sketch and a profile sketch. Just to mix things up and explore different techniques, you'll go with a slightly different approach to this feature. First, instead of re-creating the path sketch, you'll use the same sketch that was used to create the boss. The advantage to this approach is that when one feature path is updated, the second will automatically reflect this change. Second, rather than selecting the sketches after initiating the swept cut command, you will preselect the sketches so you can see how the PropertyManager will automatically differentiate between the two sketches. To create a swept cut feature, do the following:

1. Select Right Plane once again in the FeatureManager, and select Sketch in the context toolbar.

2. Make the sketch plane normal to the viewing plane, and select the Circle tool.

3. Move the mouse pointer to the center of the spherical body until the circle used to create the swept feature and its center point is highlighted, as shown in Figure 8.14. Click and release the left mouse button to specify the centerpoint for the circle.

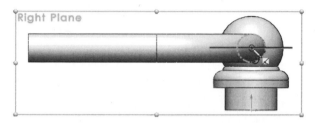

FIGURE 8.14 Specifying the centerpoint of a circle with hidden sketches

4. Draw the circle, and specify its diameter to be .300 using a smart dimension. Click the Exit Sketch button in the confirmation corner.

Share Sketches Among Multiple Features

Sharing sketches whenever possible has a couple of advantages that cannot be overlooked. First, it saves time re-creating a sketch multiple times. When you share a sketch, the original sketch is used and is not a copy, so there cannot be any modifications to either sketch without affecting all the dependent features. There is an advantage to this as well: changing only one sketch to affect multiple features can be a huge time-saver, especially if major changes need to be made to the sketch. To share a sketch, do the following:

1. In the FeatureManager, expand the Sweep1 feature created earlier to view its sketches. Select Sketch2, which is the path used to create the swept boss, and press and hold the Ctrl key while selecting Sketch4, which you just created (see Figure 8.15).

2. With the sketch preselected, select the downward-pointing arrow next to the Extruded Cut button in the shortcut bar to view the available tools.

FIGURE 8.15 Preselecting sketches for the swept cut feature

3. In the flyout, select the Swept Cut tool. Since the sketches were preselected, there will be no need to specify the profile and path in the Cut-
Sweep PropertyManager. The preview of the swept cut will be displayed
in the graphics area. You may need to rotate the view to get a better
look at the preview, as shown in Figure 8.16. If you are happy with the
result, click the green check mark to create the swept cut feature.

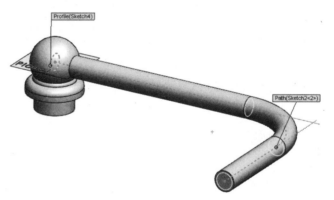

FIGURE 8.16 Swept cut feature preview in the graphics area

Notice in the FeatureManager how the sketch that was used as the path
in the swept boss/base and the swept cut, Sketch2, has been updated to
include a hand below the sketch icon. This represents that the sketch is
shared among multiple features (see Figure 8.17).

FIGURE 8.17 Shared sketches in the FeatureManager

Model the Shade Retainer

The shade retainer is the part of the arm that will be used to hold the shade in place. It consists of a threaded shaft that passes through a hole in the shade. The shade is held in place with the washer subassembly on one side and a nut. One of the shade mounts will also be used to hold the bulb receptacle. Perform the following steps to create one of the two shade retainers:

1. Select the face of the end of the tube you created, and select Sketch in the context toolbar.

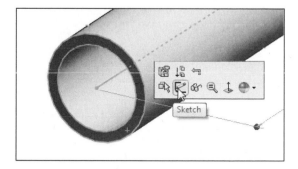

2. Make the sketch normal to the viewing plane, and select the Line tool.

3. Move the mouse pointer over the right quadrant of the outer diameter of the tube until the point is highlighted with a diamond. Slowly move the mouse pointer to the right of the circle while dragging the inference line along with the pointer, as shown in Figure 8.18. When

the pointer is a short distance from the tube, click and release the left mouse button to begin drawing the line.

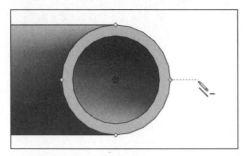

FIGURE 8.18 Specifying the first point of the sketch to be horizontal to a quadrant of a circular edge

---

4. Draw the line horizontally across the face of the tube until it extends a short distance beyond the other edge of the circular face. Click and release the left mouse button to draw the line.

5. Draw a vertical line that is about .225″ long. Click and release the left mouse button.

6. Move the mouse pointer back to the endpoint of the last sketch segment to transition to an arc.

7. Create an arc to the right that has an approximate radius of .075 and an angle close to 135°, as shown in Figure 8.19. Click and release the left mouse button.

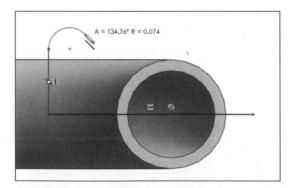

FIGURE 8.19 Autotransitioning to an arc in sketch

---

8. Transition to another arc, making sure that it is not an arc that is tangent to the previous arc. You may find it necessary to go back and forth between the endpoint and the arc until you are able to achieve the arc required. At this point, it is going to be difficult to get the radius that you need. Just make a radius that is slightly smaller than the last arc, and make sure that no inference lines are being shown.

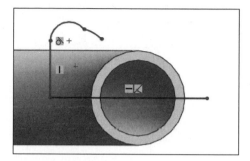

9. For the last sketch segment, transition to another arc, and terminate the arc on the endpoint of the first line that was created.

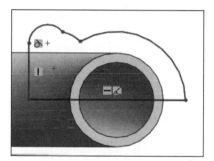

10. Exit the Line command, select the horizontal line of the sketch, and change it into a construction line that will be used for creating diameter dimensions. After completed, the under-defined sketch should look like the one shown in Figure 8.20.

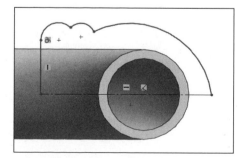

F I G U R E 8 . 2 0 Under-defined sketch of the shade retainer

Fully Define the Sketch of Shade Retainer

Before you can create the revolved feature for the shade retainer, the sketch needs to be fully defined. By now you have become very comfortable with adding dimensions and relations to a sketch to fully define it. Before you can begin adding dimensions to the sketch, you need to add a relation to the sketch.

1. You need to add one relation to the sketch that was not added automatically. Select the centerpoint of the last arc you created, and while holding the Ctrl key on the keyboard, select the outer diameter of the tube. In the context toolbar or the PropertyManager, select the concentric relation to ensure that spherical diameter will remain concentric with the end of the tube.

 T I P   Make sure that you select the outer edge of the tube; otherwise, you will have issues in later steps.

---

2. Using smart dimensions, fully define the profile using the dimensions shown in Figure 8.21.

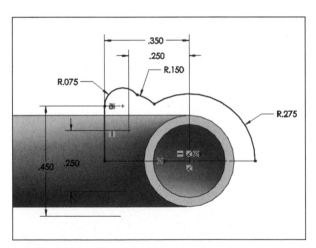

FIGURE 8.21 Fully defining the shade retainer profile

---

3. Exit the sketch, and create a revolved boss using the centerline as the axis of revolution. When prompted, allow SolidWorks to automatically close the profile. Once created, the revolved feature should look like Figure 8.22.

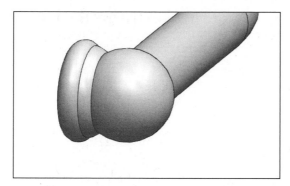

FIGURE 8.22 Revolved feature for the shade retainer

Complete the Shade Retainer Feature

The revolved feature created in the previous section is not the only part that makes up the shade retainer. To be functional, you still need to add a threaded boss onto the revolved feature that will be used to hold the washer subassembly, the shade, and the nut that will hold everything in place. Then you need to reorder the feature that makes up the inner diameter of the tube in order to add a cutout to the retainer in order to let the wiring get to the bulb receptacle. Perform the following steps to complete the shade retainer feature:

1. Select the Extruded Boss/Base tool, and select the flat face of the last feature created to create a sketch.

2. Create a circle that is concentric to the edge of the face, and make the diameter .4361.

3. Exit the sketch, and in the Extrude PropertyManager make the depth of extrusion .800.

4. Change the orientation of the part to show the top, and change the Display State option to show the hidden lines.

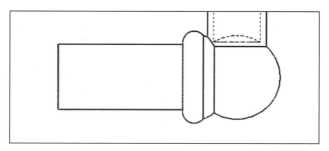

5. In the FeatureManager, select the feature for the Revolve2 feature, the one for the revolved part of the shade retainer, and move it up in the tree directly on top of the Sweep1 feature. This will make the revolve feature happen before the sweep cut feature that was used to create the inner diameter of the tube.

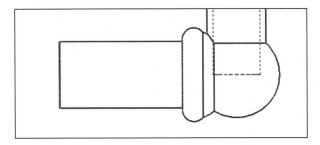

Introduce the Hole Wizard

The Hole Wizard is an extremely helpful tool that allows you to add a tapped or drilled hole to a part or assembly that meets the requirements of various standards. The Hole Wizard has a couple of advantages over creating a regular extruded cut or revolved cut. Most notably is the ability to select a standard hole or tap size per standards such as ANSI Inch, ANSI Metric, ISO, DIN, JIS, and others. Selecting a hole per a standard saves you the time that would otherwise be used to research the dimensions and create the sketch.

The Hole Wizard PropertyManager consists of two tabs, Type and Position. The Type tab is used to specify the hole type, size, depth, and other options. The Position tab is then used to specify the location of the hole or holes in the model after being specified in the PropertyManager.

Specify Types of Holes

The Type tab of the PropertyManager is broken down into the following sections:

Favorite The Favorite section of the Hole Specification PropertyManager allows you to manage a list of hole specifications.

Hole Type   The Hole Type section of the Hole Specification PropertyManager is used to specify the type of hole that will be created. The top of the section contains six buttons: Counterbore, Countersink, Hole, Straight Tap, Tapered Tap, and Legacy Hole. The Legacy Hole option is used for holes created in versions of SolidWorks prior to SolidWorks 2000.

Below the hole type buttons is the Standard field, which allows you to select which standard will be used to determine the size and dimensions of the holes. As we have discussed in previous chapters, you can apply many different standards in designs for different regions of the world. In the United States, the two most commonly used standards for holes are ANSI Inch and ANSI Metric.

The options in the Type field vary depending on the hole type selected. For instance, if you decide to make a tapped hole, you will have the options of Bottoming Tapped Hole, Straight Pipe Tapped Hole, and Tapped Hole. But if you select a countersunk hole, you will have the options of Flat Head Screw With A 100° head, Flat Head Screw With A 82° head, Oval Head, and Socket Countersunk Head Cap Screw.

Hole Specifications   The Hole Specification section is where you will specify the actual size of the hole to be created based on the hardware. The options available change depending on the hole type selected in the previous section. The sizes and fits (if available) are based on the standard and hole type selected.

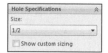

End Condition   Just like with a regular extruded cut, you can specify how the hole created will terminate. When working with a counterbored, countersunk, or regular hole, the end condition will apply just to the depth of the hole and does not include the drill tip, which is usually left unspecified in drawings. When creating a straight tap or tapered tap, two end conditions are available.

With the Hole Wizard, you know the selected hole size will match the requirements of the hardware (screws, bolts, and so on).

The first end condition is used to specify the depth of the drilled hole, and the second end condition is for the thread.

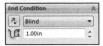

Options   The Options section provides you with a different set of options such as Near Side Countersinks, Clearances, and Thread Options. Each hole type has its own set of options available.

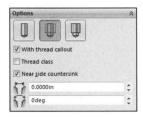

Specify Positions of Holes

After setting the options for the hole or holes that need to be created, you click the Positions tab. There are no options on the Positions tab. The only task that can be completed when the tab is activated is the placement of the hole or holes in the model. When adding holes to a flat surface in the model, click the left mouse button when the hole preview displayed next to the mouse pointer meets your approximate location on the model. A sketch point will be added to a sketch that is created on the selected face. Each point will then be used by the Hole Wizard to create the hole designated in the Type tab.

In previous versions of SolidWorks, you would have to select the face of the model for the hole prior to initiating the Hole Wizard common. If the face was not preselected, the Hole Wizard would create the hole by using a 3D sketch. In this situation, it would not make a difference as to whether the hole was created with a 2D or 3D sketch. However, if you needed to add dimensions to define the location of the hole, a 3D sketch would make it a little more difficult because of the way the dimensions would be projected. A 2D sketch would cause the dimensions to all be on the same plane of the sketch, but a 3D sketch would make things difficult when trying to dimension to other points in the model that do not reside on the same sketch plane. In SolidWorks 2010, regardless of whether you preselect a 2D face prior to initiating the Hole Wizard command, the default sketch type is a 2D sketch. If you do require a 3D sketch, when you click the Positions tab, you can choose to create a 3D sketch by clicking the 3D Sketch button in the PropertyManager.

Unless you place the point on another point in the model, there will be no relations or dimensions to specify the location of the hole or holes. You can go back at a later time and edit the sketch to add relations or dimensions. You can also add the desired dimensions or relations while still in the Hole Wizard. Pressing Esc once will exit the placement mode of the Hole Wizard but will not escape the command itself. After adding the location definition, you can return to the Type tab or finish the command by clicking the green check mark.

Add a Hole to the Shade Retainer

Using the Hole Wizard, you will now add a drilled hole to the shaft of the shade retainer to allow the wiring to reach the bulb receptacle. One benefit of using the Hole Wizard is the ability to choose a standard drill size instead of specifying an arbitrary diameter for a hole. This may seem like a minor thing, but ask any machinist, and you'll learn that specifying a nonstandard diameter for a hole can create extra work. For years, one of us kept a chart of standard drill sizes near our workstation to ensure that we always select a standard drill size, but with the Hole Wizard we rarely need to even look at the chart.

In the previous section, you took a brief look at the Hole Wizard PropertyManager, and now you are going to put it to use. Perform the following steps to add a hole to the shade mount:

1. Rotate the part to allow you to see the face of the extruded boss that will become the threaded shaft of the shade retainer. Select Hole Wizard on the Features tab of the CommandManager.

2. In the Hole Type section of the Hole Specification PropertyManager, click the Hole button, as shown in Figure 8.23. This will be used to add just a simple hole with no threads or countersinks. Ensure that the Standard is set to Ansi Inch and that Type is also set to All Drill Sizes.

FIGURE 8.23 Specifying the hole type

3. In the Size field in the Hole Specifications section of the PropertyManager, select the size $5/16$ for the hole that will be created, as shown in Figure 8.24.

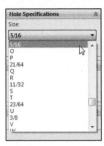

FIGURE 8.24 Specifying the drill size to be used

4. In the End Condition section, set End Condition to Blind, and specify the depth of the hole to be **1.250in**, as shown in Figure 8.25.

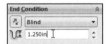

FIGURE 8.25 Specifying the depth of the drilled hole

5. At the top of the PropertyManager, select the Position tab.

6. Select the face of the extruded boss. A point will be created on the face that will be used to mark the location of the drilled hole. Since only one hole is needed at this time, hit Esc on your keyboard to exit the Sketch Point command. You can then add the required relations or dimensions to define the location of the hole.

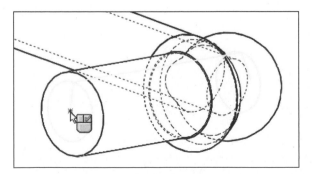

7. Select the point shown on the face of the boss, and while holding the Ctrl key, select the circular edge of the shaft. In the context toolbar, select the concentric relation. Click the green check mark to create the hole and exit the Hole Wizard.

 N O T E   **You can also define the location of the hole when not in the Hole Wizard command by editing the sketch and adding the necessary relations.**

Add Cosmetic Threads

We already covered adding cosmetic threads to parts in previous chapters, so we will not be spending too much time on them here. You need to add the thread to the shaft of the shade mount feature that will be used by both the bulb receptacle and the shade retaining nut. Using the following steps, add the cosmetic thread to the part:

1. In the menu bar, select Insert ➤ Annotations ➤ Cosmetic Thread.

2. With the Circular Edges field in the Cosmetic Thread PropertyManager active, select the outer edge of the shaft, as shown in Figure 8.26.

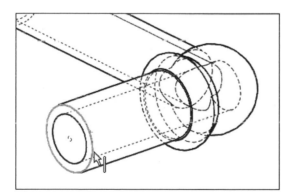

FIGURE 8.26 Selecting circular edge for cosmetic thread

3. In the PropertyManager, select Ansi Inch as the Standard setting, and select Machine Threads as the Type setting. Based on the diameter of the edge selected, SolidWorks will attempt to automatically specify the thread that is appropriate. In this case, it should automatically select 7/16-14. Set the End Condition option to Up To Next, and then click the green check mark to create the thread.

Mirror Features

You may have noticed that up to this point we have been concentrating only on one half of the overall model. You can repeat the steps described in previous sections to create the second arm of the shade mount, which it would be great practice, but it would not exactly be the best use of time. Luckily, there is an extremely handy tool in SolidWorks that allows you to mirror features in a model.

You can use the *Mirror tool* to create a copy of a feature, features, or bodies. The selected features are mirrored about a planar face or plane and maintain a link to the original features. As the original features are updated, the mirrored features will update to reflect the changes. Using the Mirror feature is a great time-saver, and with practice you will be able to determine the best situation for using it.

In your current model, by using the Mirror tool to create the second arm, not only do you eliminate a few steps, but you also ensure that any adjustments made to one of the arms will be directly reflected in the second arm. If you were to model the features in the second arm manually, you only open yourself up to the chance of having the geometry of the two arms not match up. To mirror the features of the arm to the other side of the model, do the following:

1. Press F on your keyboard or double-click the scroll wheel on your mouse to fit the entire model in the graphics area.

2. In the FeatureManager, select the right plane.

3. On the Features tab of the CommandManager, select Mirror.

4. Since Mirror Plane/Face was selected prior to starting the Mirror command, the Features To Mirror field will be active. Instead of selecting the features in the graphics area, click the plus (+) next to the model name in the top-left corner of the graphics area (Figure 8.27). This will display the Flyout FeatureManager to allow you to select the features while still in the Mirror PropertyManager.

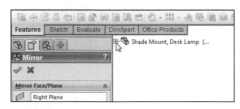

FIGURE 8.27 Expanding the Flyout FeatureManager

5. In the Flyout FeatureManager, select the last five features in the tree that make up the arm of the shade mount. As you select the features in the tree, they will be added to the Features To Mirror field, as shown in Figure 8.28.

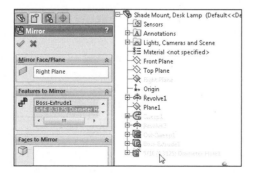

FIGURE 8.28 Features added to Mirror PropertyManager by selecting in Flyout FeatureManager

6. Since there are no other options that you need to specify, click the green check mark, and the selected features will be mirrored to the other side of the model with the right plane as the center. The model with the mirrored features should look like Figure 8.29.

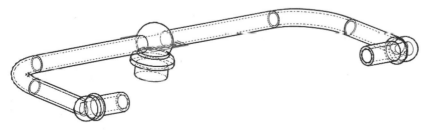

FIGURE 8.29 Arm features mirrored in model

Finish the Model

Your model is now almost complete. All that is left to do is add one last hole to the center feature for the part and add the thread that will be used to mate to the shaft. First you will begin by adding another hole that will be used to pass the wiring through the center feature and into the arms that will eventually terminate at the bulb receptacle. Do the following to add the hole:

1. Rotate the part to provide access to the bottom of the center feature of the model. Select the bottom face, and select the Hole Wizard.

2. In the Hole Specification PropertyManager, specify the hole type as Hole and the Standard setting as Ansi Inch.

3. Set the size of the hole to be ½, enter **1.000in** for the depth, and click the Positions tab.

4. Press Esc on the keyboard since you do not need to add any more holes than what is already shown.

5. Specify the point to be concentric with the circular edge of the face. Click the green check mark to create the hole, as shown in Figure 8.30.

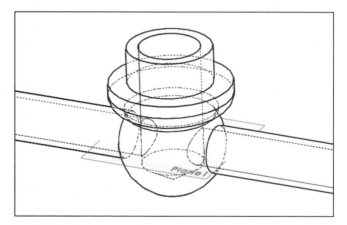

FIGURE 8.30 Center mounting hole added to part

6. Since you no longer need to use the plane you added earlier, you can hide it from view. This will make the overall look of the model cleaner. To hide the plane, select Plane1 in the graphics area, and select Hide in the context toolbar. The plane can be shown again by selecting the plane in the FeatureManager and clicking Show in the context toolbar.

 WARNING   If you begin adding a large number of planes to a part, it will sometimes become very difficult to see what is going on in the model.

7. Since you are no longer concerned with the inside geometry of the part, you can change the view back to the shaded view. Change the display mode in the Heads-Up View toolbar to Shaded With Edges, and save the model.

Model a Threaded Feature

So far, you may have noticed that you have been using the Cosmetic Thread tool exclusively for adding threads. There are a couple of really good reasons for this. The main reason, in our opinion, is that cosmetic threads have little to no impact on the overall system performance.

Some users prefer to actually model the threads onto parts by creating a helical path and creating a swept cut to create the threads. This approach has the advantage of representing how the part will actually look with the thread, but it comes at a price. One or two threaded features in a part or assembly probably won't make a huge difference, but when the number of threaded features add up, your PC can slow considerably, which can be extremely frustrating. And in most machined parts, there is no real advantage to creating the thread manually since the machinist will most often go by the thread callout on the drawing and not look at the actual geometry in the model.

That is not to say that there are not cases where modeling a thread is important. Although we often find it is unnecessary to model threads in a machined part such as the one you are making in this chapter, many times we have found that it is necessary when modeling parts that are destined to be injection molded. This is because the threaded features are sometimes machined into the mold cavities.

We don't want to send you out in the world without at least having a basic idea of how to create a threaded feature. In the next couple of steps, just for demonstration purposes, you will be creating a helical path and cutting the thread into the center feature of your part. The thread you will be adding will be a ¾-16 UNF thread, and unfortunately you need to be able to determine all the values for the thread without the help of SolidWorks. The values that you will be using in this section are derived from the 27th edition of the *Machinery's Handbook*.

1. Rotate the model to give you better access to the bottom boss for the center feature.

2. Select the bottom face of the feature, as shown in Figure 8.31, and click Sketch in the context toolbar.

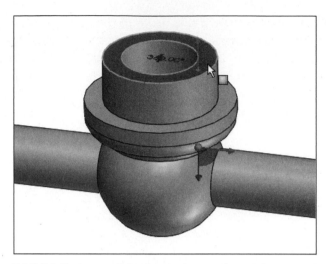

FIGURE 8.31   Selecting the bottom face of the center feature

3. Press S on the keyboard, and select Convert Entities in the shortcut bar. Since you selected the face of the feature, Convert Entities will "trace" the outside edge of the face, creating a parametric sketch that will automatically update if you change the geometry for the feature at a later time.

4. Click the green check mark to close the Convert Entities PropertyManager.

5. In the menu bar, select Insert ➢ Curve ➢ Helix/Spiral.

Use the Helix/Spiral PropertyManager

The key part of creating a threaded feature is creating the helical path of the thread. Before you can create a helix, or spiral, you must have a sketch of a circle that will act as the diameter of the helix when creating a curve with a constant pitch. After selecting the Helix/Spiral tool, you will see a preview of the helix in the graphics area, and you will be able to make adjustments in the PropertyManager. The following are the parts of the Helix/Spiral PropertyManager:

Defined By   The first section in the Helix/Spiral PropertyManager is the Defined By section. In this section, you have four choices to define the helix that will be created: Pitch And Revolution, Height And Revolution, Height And Pitch, and Spiral. You will make your selection based on the information that you have for your helical requirements. This is what the terms mean:

Pitch   *Pitch* refers to the number of threads per inch. For example, since the thread you will be creating has 16 threads per inch, as defined by the -16 in the thread callout, you can determine the pitch by dividing an inch by the number of threads. If you are still not sure what the pitch is, imagine cutting a screw lengthwise to view the cross section of the threads. If you were to measure the distance between the peaks of two adjacent threads, this would be the pitch.

Height   The height of the helix is the physical height of the helix, or the thread length. The height can be specified in lieu of the pitch or the revolutions but not both.

Revolution   Revolution is the actually number of revolutions that the helix will make. This can be used to replace the actual height of the helix if it is more important to maintain a certain number of threads.

Spiral   A *spiral* differs from a *helix* in that it is flat, unlike a helix, which actually has some height to it.

Parameters   Depending on what you selected in the Defined By section, the options available in the Parameters section will be different. The following is a list and brief explanation of each parameter that is available:

Constant Pitch   Selecting the Constant Pitch setting means that the entire helix will be made up of one value. This is the most common type used, in our experience.

Variable Pitch   Sometimes you need to specify different pitches at different points in the helix. This is normally not done when modeling threads, but it is very common when designing springs since some springs will have the coils closer together at the ends than in the middle.

Region Parameters   The *region parameters* are used when creating a helix with a variable curve. When the Variable Pitch option is selected, a small table is shown in the PropertyManager, which allows you to specify the revolutions, heights, diameters, and pitch for each variable pitch section of the helix.

Reverse Direction   This option toggles the direction of the helix from the sketch created.

Start Angle   Sometimes it may be necessary to specify the starting point of the helix based on the angle of the point in relation to the center of the circle.

Clockwise and Counterclockwise   These options differ from the Reverse Direction option. The Reverse Direction option just affects the direction that the helix points, whereas the Clockwise and Counterclockwise options affect the directions of the turns.

Taper Helix   The last section in the Helix/Spiral PropertyManager is the Taper Helix section. This section is used to create a helix that shrinks or grows in diameter over the length of the curve based on a specified angle. To use this section, the check box next to the Taper Helix section title must be selected.

Create a Helical Path

Now it is time to create the helical path that will be used to cut the threads into the center feature. That last step you did was to create a sketch that will act as the major diameter of the thread itself. Do the following to complete the helix:

1. In the Defined By section, select Height And Pitch. The Parameters section will be updated with the required options.

2. Ensure that the Constant Pitch option is selected at the top of the Parameters section.

3. Specify the height of the helix to be .295, which is the height of the shaft that the thread will be cut into.

4. In the Pitch field, set the pitch to be .0625, which is the result of dividing 1 by 16.

T I P   Instead of doing the math ahead of time, you can type $^1/_{16}$ in the field. This will tell the field that the value is 1 divided by 16. The calculated value of.0625 will then be shown in the field.

5. If the helical path shown in the graphics area is floating in space and is not directly on the cylindrical face of the shaft, then the direction of the helix needs to be updated. Click the Reverse Direction option.

6. No other values need to be specified for this particular thread. Click the green check mark to create the helix and to exit the PropertyManager. Figure 8.32 shows what the helix should look like.

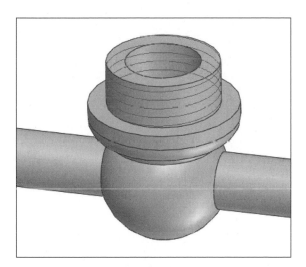

FIGURE 8.32 Helical path created

Add Sketch of Thread

To create a thread, you need to add a sketch for the cutting tool that will follow the helical path. The key to creating a sketch that is meant to be swept along the path is that the sketch must be created perpendicular to the end of the helical path. If you specified the Start Angle setting of the path to be either 0°, 90°, 270°, or 360°, you can create the sketch on one of the predefined sketch planes. Sometimes that is not possible or viable, and you will need to create a new sketch plane that will be perpendicular to the path. The following steps will add a new plane and create a sketch for the thread:

1. Select the helix created in the previous section, then select the Reference Geometry button in either the shortcut bar or the Features tab in the CommandManager, and finally select Plane, as shown in Figure 8.33.

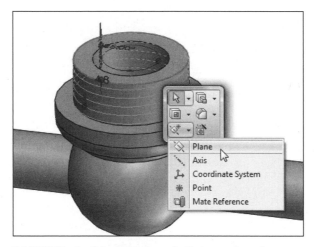

FIGURE 8.33 Selecting a helix to create a plane

2. The plane preview should now be shown in the graphics area at the end of the helix closest to the point selected. In the Plane PropertyManager, the Perpendicular option should be preselected. Select the Set Origin On Curve option to allow the endpoint of the helix to act as the sketch origin, as shown in Figure 8.34.

3. For the second reference, select the endpoint of the helix closest to the bottom face of the extrusion. Click the green check mark to create the plane.

4. Select the newly created plane, and click Sketch in the context toolbar.

5. Select Normal To in the Heads-up View toolbar, or press Ctrl+8 on your keyboard.

6. Starting from the sketch origin, sketch a triangle, as shown in Figure 8.35.

FIGURE 8.34 Creating a plane perpendicular to the helix

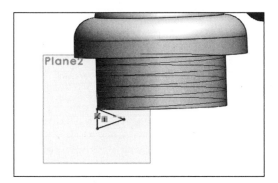

FIGURE 8.35 Under-defined sketch for thread

7. Sketch a construction line that originates at the apex of the triangle and terminates at the midpoint of the triangle base, as shown in Figure 8.36. After sketching the construction line, set the relation of the line to Horizontal.

8. Using the dimensions shown in Figure 8.37, fully define the sketch. Feel free to add extra detail to the sketch such as fillets and chamfers, but be aware that any additional sketch entities will increase the regeneration time for the completed model. Since this thread will be used for reference only, you do not need to add any other sketch features.

9. Click the Exit Sketch button in the confirmation corner.

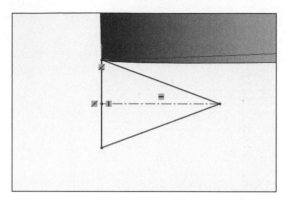

FIGURE 8.36 Construction line added to thread sketch

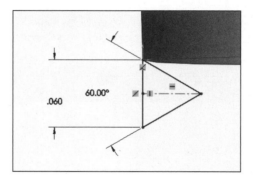

FIGURE 8.37 Fully defined thread sketch

Cut the Threads

With the helical path and the cutting tool sketch created, all that is left to do is create the swept cut feature. Do the following to create the thread and finish the model:

1. Select the helical path, and while holding the Ctrl key, select the sketch created in the previous section.

2. Select Swept Cut in the shortcut bar or the Features tab in the CommandManager.

3. The preview shown in the graphics area should look like Figure 8.38. There are no other options that need to be adjusted for this particular swept feature. Click the green check mark to create the thread.

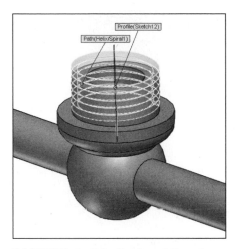

FIGURE 8.38 Preview of thread

4. Hide the plane that was used to create the thread sketch. The newly created thread should look like Figure 8.39.

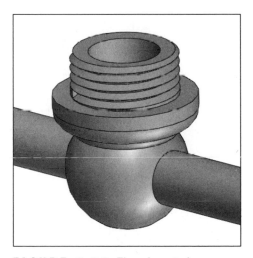

FIGURE 8.39 Thread created

Understand that you are merely adding the thread for demonstration purposes. Before anybody points out that the thread is not exactly machineable, we would agree. If this were a real model that was destined for manufacturing, we would have asked you to add a thread relief at the base of the shaft to make it easier for the threading process. We would also have you add a few strategically placed chamfers.

With that said, the model is now complete. Congratulations! You are now ready to move onto the next chapter where you will be using this part and a couple parts created previously to build the shade assembly.

Are You Experienced?

Now You Can...

☑ **Automatically transition between lines and arcs**

☑ **Add a reference plane**

☑ **Create swept base/boss and swept cut features**

☑ **Use the Hole Wizard to create a variety of hole types**

☑ **Mirror features in a model**

☑ **Create a helical path and model threads**

CHAPTER 9

Modeling Parts Within an Assembly

▶ Create the Shade Subassembly

▶ Create an In-Context Model

▶ Finish the Shade Model

▶ Finish the Shade Subassembly

▶ Add Configurations to an Assembly

Sometimes when creating parts for an assembly, it is difficult to anticipate changes that will be made to the various components and how they will affect other components in the assembly. So far, you have created all the components for the desk lamp separately, and then you built subassemblies from them. This is often referred to as *bottom-up design*. One drawback to this approach is that as a component in the desk lamp is updated, it may be necessary to manually make the changes to other components.

In this chapter, you will be using a different approach when you create the model for the shade. Instead of making the shade as a separate model and inserting it into the subassembly, you will be creating the model from within a subassembly. By modeling the shade from within an assembly, as any components in the assembly are updated, any required changes will automatically be applied to the shade.

Create the Shade Subassembly

Before you can create the shade, you need to begin building the shade subassembly. The base part of the assembly will be the shade mount model you created in the previous chapter. The washer subassembly that you created in Chapter 7 will also be used in this assembly. If you have not completed the models in the previous chapters, you can always download them from the companion site. In addition to the parts and subassemblies from the previous chapters, you also need to download a couple of models in order to complete the shade subassembly.

Once you have downloaded all the necessary models for this chapter, you can begin building a new assembly using the following steps:

1. Click New in the menu bar, and select Assembly in the New SolidWorks Document window. Click OK to create a new assembly model.

2. Click Browse in the Begin Assembly PropertyManager.

3. Browse to the folder that contains the shade mount, which is the Desk Lamp.sldprt file created in Chapter 8, and select the model. Click the Open button.

4. Instead of placing the part and using mates to fix its location in the 3D environment, you'll accept its default location. Since this is the first component being inserted into the assembly, SolidWorks can automatically specify the location of the part. Clicking the green check mark in the PropertyManager will specify that the part orientation will match the assembly environment.

N O T E When building assemblies, at least one component should be fixed in place; otherwise, the entire assembly will be under-defined and will be able to move freely in all six degrees of freedom. This will cause issues with higher-level assemblies and drawings.

5. Update the units in the document properties to display the length dimensions using three decimal places.

6. Save the assembly as Shade Sub-Assy, Desk Lamp.sldasm.

Insert the Washer Subassembly

Now it is time to add the washer subassembly you created in Chapter 7, "Creating a Simple Assembly Drawing." By now you have probably become comfortable with the process for inserting components, so we will not need to spend too much time detailing the process. However, you will need two instances of the washer subassembly, which will give you the opportunity to explore some more options. Start by inserting the first instance, as described here:

1. In the shortcut bar or the Assembly tab of the CommandManager, select Insert Components.

2. In the Part/Assembly To Insert section of the Insert Component PropertyManager, click the Browse button.

3. Navigate to the folder containing the washer subassembly. If the assembly files are not visible, you may need to specify that the file extension be shown. In the flyout next to the File Name field, select Assembly (*.asm,*.sldasm), as shown in Figure 9.1.

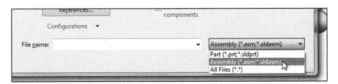

FIGURE 9.1 Specifying the file type in the Open window

4. Select the washer subassembly, and click Open.

5. The washer subassembly will be shown next to the mouse pointer. Moving the mouse pointer around, you will notice that the washer moves as well. Until you specify an insertion point, the subassembly is technically not part of the assembly. Click anywhere in the graphics area to insert the subassembly.

Mate the Washer Subassembly

Before inserting the next instance of the washer subassembly, you should mate the first instance. Using the concentric and coincident mates, you will be able to almost fully define the position of the washer subassembly. The only degree of freedom that will not be restricted is the rotation around the shaft of the shade mount. This means that the washer subassembly will be free to spin around the shaft, which for this design intent is acceptable. Apply the required mates as described in the following steps:

1. Select the Mate tool in the shortcut bar or the Assembly tab of the CommandManager.

2. Select the inner diameter of the washer assembly, as in Figure 9.2.

FIGURE 9.2 Selecting the inner diameter of the washer for mating

3. Select the cylindrical face of the shade retainer shaft, as shown in Figure 9.3. Click the green check mark in the Mate PropertyManager to apply the concentric mate.

4. Select the top face of the washer subassembly, as shown in Figure 9.4.

5. Select the face of the shade retainer, as shown in Figure 9.5. The position of washer subassembly will be updated, as shown in Figure 9.6. If the washer subassembly is not aligned in the manner shown in Figure 9.6, click the Anti-Align button in the Mate PropertyManager. Click the green check mark in the PropertyManager to apply the mate.

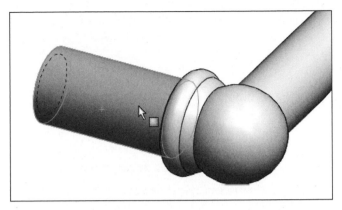

FIGURE 9.3 Selecting the cylindrical face of shaft for mating

FIGURE 9.4 Top face of washer cover selected for mating

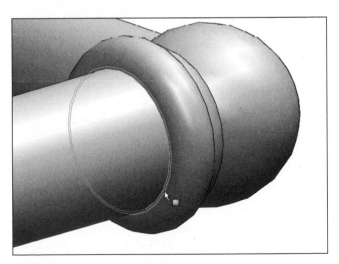

FIGURE 9.5 Face of shade mount selected for mating

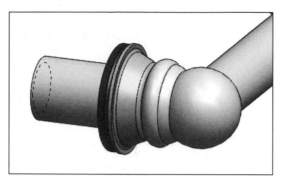

FIGURE 9.6 Washer subassembly mated to shade mount

Insert the Second Instance of the Washer Subassembly

Now it is time to add the second instance of the washer subassembly. Luckily, since the subassembly was inserted once, you can eliminate the step of using the Insert Components command. Instead, you will be making a copy of the subassembly without the use of any command. There are a couple of ways to create copies of parts and subassemblies in an assembly, but this time you will use our most-used procedure. Doing the following will create a copy that you can then mate:

1. Select the washer subassembly in the FeatureManager design tree by pressing and holding the left mouse button. While still holding the left mouse button, press the Ctrl key on your keyboard, and move the mouse pointer into the graphics area. A new instance of the washer subassembly will be inserted into the assembly. To insert the new instance into the assembly, release the left mouse button before releasing the Ctrl key; otherwise, the new instance will not be created.

 T I P You can use the Ctrl key to create copies of parts in the graphics area by clicking and dragging a part in the graphics area while holding down the key on your keyboard.

2. Mate the second instance of the washer subassembly just as you did with the first instance. When mated properly, the two washer subassemblies should appear as shown in Figure 9.7. Click the green check mark to exit the Mate PropertyManager.

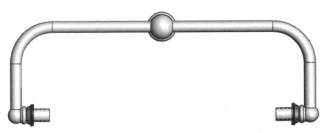

FIGURE 9.7 Both washer subassemblies mated in place

Create an In-Context Model

In-context models are models that are created in reference to existing geometry in an assembly. Oftentimes, some dimensions of the part relate to other parts in the assembly, and as the referenced geometry is changed, the in-context model will update automatically. As you can imagine, this could be a huge advantage because it eliminates the need to manually update all the parts in an assembly as the design is refined.

This is exactly how the shade model will be modeled. The steps described here will enable the overall length of the shade model to automatically update if you decide to change the distance between the arms of the shade mount. If, however, the length of the shade is manually edited in the model itself, the link to the assembly will be broken. To create an in-context model, do the following:

In-context models eliminate the need to manually update all the parts in an assembly as the design is refined.

1. Select the downward-pointing arrow next to the Insert Components button on the shortcut bar, and select New Part from the flyout.

2. Select the face of the washer, as shown in Figure 9.8, to create a new sketch on the face of the washer. After selecting the face, the rest of the components in the assembly will become transparent.

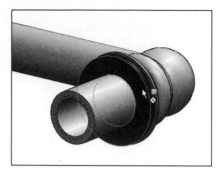

FIGURE 9.8 Selecting the face to insert a sketch for the shade model

The new part shown in the FeatureManager will look different from what you have seen up to this point, as shown in Figure 9.9. We will cover the reason for this later in this chapter.

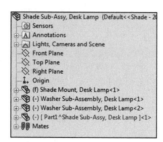

FIGURE 9.9 New part displayed in the FeatureManager design tree

3. Select Normal To in the Heads-Up View toolbar, or press Ctrl+8 on the keyboard.

4. Using the Line command and making use of autotransitioning to an arc, duplicate the sketch shown in Figure 9.10. It is important to note the tangencies between the three arcs.

N O T E Regardless of the orientation of the shade mount, the sketch of the shade must be drawn in the orientation shown.

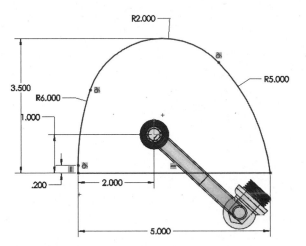

FIGURE 9.10 Fully defined sketch of the shade component

Extrude up to Existing Geometry

With the sketch for the shade created and fully defined, it is time to create the base extrusion. You will be using the Extruded Boss/Base command, which has probably become very familiar at this point, but instead of specifying a depth of extrusion, you will reference a face in the assembly to extrude up to. To use the command in this manner, do the following:

1. Select the Isometric view in the Heads-up View toolbar, or press Ctrl+7 on your keyboard.

2. Select Extruded Boss/Base on the Features tab in the CommandManager.

3. In the Direction1 section of the Boss-Extrude PropertyManager, select Up To Surface in the End Condition field.

4. Select the face of the washer on the other side of the shade mount, as shown in Figure 9.11.

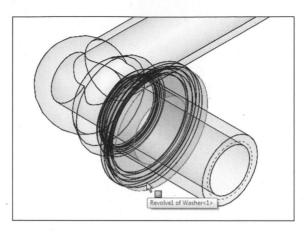

FIGURE 9.11 Terminating the face of the shade model

 N O T E   Terminating the extrusion of the shade on the face of the opposing washer subassembly will allow the extrusion to adjust to any changes in the distance between the two sets of washers.

5. The preview in the graphics area, as shown in Figure 9.12, will show the shade extending from the sketch and terminating on the other washer. If the distance between the two is updated in the shade mount model, the length of the shade will automatically be updated. Click the green check mark to create the shade.

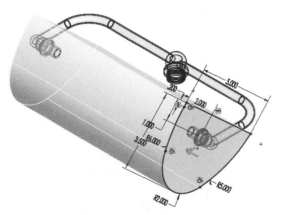

FIGURE 9.12 Preview of shade base extrusion

6. Click the Exit Model icon in the confirmation corner.

7. The new part will be shown in the FeatureManager, as shown in Figure 9.13, as a virtual component. You can also see in the figure, following the instance count, an arrow made up by a hyphen and a bracket (->). This arrow indicates that the model contains an external reference. The shade references the assembly and the location of the washers to specify the length of the extrusion.

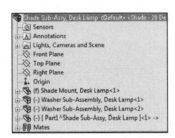

FIGURE 9.13 Virtual component in the FeatureManager design tree

ABOUT VIRTUAL COMPONENTS

Virtual components are a fairly recent addition to SolidWorks. They allow you to save a component inside the assembly itself without externalizing the component. This makes the model exist only in the assembly and not as a part that can be opened separately without first opening the assembly.

There are a couple of ways to use virtual components. When designing a new component in an assembly, it gives you the opportunity to see how the part fits in your scheme without making the commitment of an external part. Another common practice is to use virtual components for bulk items (glue, grease, solder, and so on) that do not normally require an actual model but should still be displayed in the bill of materials.

Existing components that are external to an assembly can also be changed to virtual components. Some users will find it easier to make all components in an assembly virtual before sending an assembly to other users via email. This approach creates a single assembly file without references to external components. We will be addressing this approach in Chapter 14, "Sharing Your Documents with Others."

Save Virtual Components Externally

Parts that are created inside an assembly are automatically created as virtual components.

This time when you save the assembly, you will have the opportunity to specify whether the shade model is meant to be an external file or should remain a virtual component. Since the shade is a stand-alone component, it would probably be a good thing to save it as an external file. This would give you the ability to send the model to a vendor or to create a drawing. Perform the following steps to save the models as an external file:

1. Click Save in the menu bar, or press Ctrl+S to save the work so far. When prompted to save modified documents, as shown in Figure 9.14, click Save All.

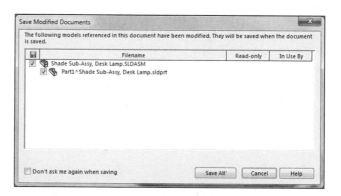

FIGURE 9.14 Save Modified Documents window

N O T E The Save Modified Documents window is often seen when saving an assembly that contains referenced components that also need to be saved.

2. After clicking Save All, you will be prompted to save the shade part internally or externally. Select the Save Externally (Specify Paths) option.

3. The Save As window will expand to include a field displaying the part to be saved externally. Select the part shown in the field, and click the Specify Path button, as shown in Figure 9.15.

FIGURE 9.15 Saving the virtual component externally

4. In the Browse For Folder window, specify the folder in which to save the shade model. Click OK to accept the selected folder.

5. With Part1 still selected, select the part again to allow you to edit the filename. Change the name of the part to **Shade, Desk Lamp**, and click OK to save the file (see Figure 9.16).

FIGURE 9.16 Changing the name of the virtual component to be saved externally

 N O T E Virtual components saved in an assembly can also be externalized by right-clicking the part in the FeatureManager and selecting Save Part (In External File) in the menu.

Finish the Shade Model

With the part saved externally, you can now open the model to continue to model the shade. The shade is a pretty simple part, and you can finish the model while in the assembly, but we often find it can be a bit distracting. Just to make things easier, you will open the model and add the last couple of features before finishing the rest of the shade subassembly.

Open the Part from Within an Assembly

Instead of opening the part with the Open tool on the menu bar, you can select the shade in the graphics area and make it the active document. After opening the shade, you will finalize the external geometry by adding fillets. To open the shade and add the fillets, do the following:

1. In the graphics area, select the shade, and click the Open Part button in the context toolbar.

2. In the shade model, select the Fillet command.

3. In the Items To Fillet section, set the radius of the fillet to **1.000**.

4. Select the two top edges of the shade, as shown in Figure 9.17. Click the green check mark to create the fillets.

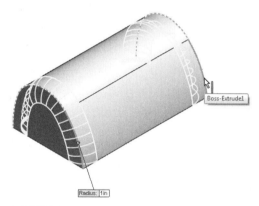

FIGURE 9.17 Adding fillets to the outside of the shade

Create a Shelled Feature

So far, you have only gone as far as modeling the outside of the shade. If you have ever seen a banker's desk lamp, you will notice one major problem with the shade that you have created so far. To complete the rest of the shade subassembly, you need to remove the material on the inside of the shade model.

You could always add an extruded cut to the model to remove the material on the inside of the shade, but the fillets make it near impossible to achieve the look that you want here. Another option is to move the rollback bar above the fillet feature and then do the cut extrude. The problem with this option is that you would need to add a fillet feature on the inside corners of the shade. It could work, but if you need to modify the radius of the fillets, you would need to remember to edit the second fillet feature.

Although an extruded cut could work, it would introduce too many variables and could cause trouble if and when the model needed to be modified. To make things a whole heck of a lot easier, you will instead be using a *Shell* feature to finish the model. The Shell feature allows you to specify a constant wall thickness on the model with just one feature. It also allows you to specify where the open face of the shade will be. The Shell command is a simple tool that will save you a lot of time. To shell out the shade model, follow these steps:

1. In the Features tab in the CommandManager, select the Shell command.

2. In the Parameters section of the Shell PropertyManager, there is a field labeled D1. This field is used to specify the thickness of the material after the model is shelled. Set the thickness to be .085.

3. Below the D1 field in the Parameters section, the Faces To Remove field will be highlighted. Select the bottom face of the shade to remove the face when the part is shelled, as shown in Figure 9.18. Click the green check mark to shell the part.

FIGURE 9.18 Selecting the face of the shade to be removed

Add Holes to the Shade for Mounting

The shade should be looking pretty good by now, but you still need one more thing before it can be used in the model. You need to add a couple of holes to the shade that will be used to allow the shade mount shafts to interface with the shade. Without these holes, there is no way to hold the shade in place.

1. Select the outside face, and select Sketch in the context toolbar, as shown in Figure 9.19.

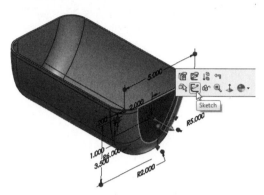

FIGURE 9.19 Selecting the outside face of the shade for mounting holes

2. Select Normal To in the Heads-up View toolbar, or press Ctrl+8 on your keyboard.

3. With the center coincident with the sketch origin, draw a circle with the diameter .500″.

4. Select Extruded Cut on the Features tab in the CommandManager.

5. Set the end condition of the extruded cut to be Through All, and click the green check mark.

 N O T E   Using the Though All end condition of the mounting holes ensures that no matter what changes are made to the width of the shade, the mounting holes will always go through both sides of the shade.

Add Appearances to the Shade Model

All the necessary features have been added to the model, so at this point you could just save the changes and return to the assembly. As far as fit and function are concerned, the part is now complete, but you would be missing out on a great opportunity to add a little flair to the part. If you look on the cover of this book, you will see that the shade is made of a semitransparent green glass or plastic to allow for some of the light to be seen through the shade. The following steps will describe the process for adding the approximate appearance to the part:

1. Select the Appearances/Scenes tab in the task pane.

2. In the top pane in the Appearances/Scenes pane, browse to Appearances ➤ Plastic ➤ Satin Finish, as shown in Figure 9.20.

FIGURE 9.20 Satin finish plastic material selected in the Appearances tab

3. Find the appearance named Green Satin Finish Plastic in the lower pane, as shown in Figure 9.21. Select the appearance by pressing and holding the left mouse button.

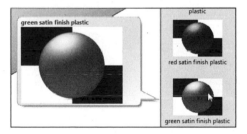

FIGURE 9.21 Green satin finish plastic selected

4. Drag the material into the graphics area directly over the shade model, as shown in Figure 9.22. Release the left mouse button to apply the material.

FIGURE 9.22   Applying the material appearance to the shade

5. As soon as you release the mouse button, a small toolbar will be displayed next to the mouse pointer to specify how the appearance is applied. Click the Part button on the toolbar, as shown in Figure 9.23.

FIGURE 9.23   Specifying that the appearance applies to the entire shade part

 N O T E   Adding an appearance to a part is not the same as specifying a material and will not affect calculations or be reflected in the document properties.

Edit an Appearance for a Part

Despite having many materials and appearances to choose from, sometimes the choices available on the Appearances tab will not meet your exact needs. Rather than settling on an appearance that doesn't quite cut it, you can edit the look of the appearance to come closer to the look you are trying to achieve. With some basic controls, you can tweak any appearance to get the material to the point where you like it. Don't go thinking that editing an appearance is hard and should be left only to the experts. That couldn't be further from the truth. In fact, editing appearances is extremely easy and more than a little bit fun.

You won't be making many modifications this time around. The only thing that you need to make the appearance work for you is to make it slightly transparent. There is more that can be done with appearances than what we discuss in this chapter. We strongly encourage you to continue to explore appearances and play with the various options. Don't worry about hurting anything; if you mess up, you can always cancel without saving the changes to the appearance. To edit the appearance to add a slight transparency, perform the following steps:

1. Select the shade model in the graphics area, and click the downward-pointing arrow next to the Appearances button. In the flyout, select the box next to the line showing the part icon and name of the current part to edit the appearance applied to the entire part, as shown in Figure 9.24.

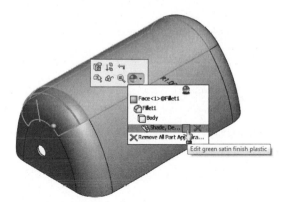

FIGURE 9.24 Selecting the appearance added to a part for editing

2. In the Optical Properties section of the PropertyManager, specify the transparency to be 0.10. Click the green check mark to apply to change to the appearance.

3. Save and exit the part to return to the shade subassembly. If prompted to rebuild the assembly file, click Yes.

Finish the Shade Subassembly

Once you exit the shade part model, the changes that were made to the model will automatically be made to the model in the assembly. Now it is time to finish the rest of the assembly. First you will need to add some mates to the shade to limit its movement in the assembly. You will do this with the addition of some configurations that will be used for different positions of the shade. After adding the mates and configurations, you will then add the rest of the components for the assembly.

Define the Position of the Shade in the Assembly

By creating the shade as an in-context model, it already has some in-place mates that will not be modified. As it is currently defined, the shade can only rotate around the axis of the shaft on the shade mount. You will find in the first step in this section that the shade can rotate, which does not meet the requirements of the assembly. When the desk lamp is built, the end user would be able to adjust the position of the shade by loosening the nuts and rotating the shade. You will simulate this by adding some positions in the assembly that can then be referenced in drawings and higher-level assemblies.

First you will define the base position of the shade. This is when the shade is pointing down toward the base of the lamp. Later you'll be adding positions at 10° intervals. To add the first mate, do the following:

1. Select and hold the left mouse button with the mouse pointer directly over the shade. While still holding the left mouse button, move the mouse around, and the shade will rotate around the shade retainer.

2. Select the Mate command in the shortcut bar.

3. Select the flat face near the bottom back of the shade, as shown in Figure 9.25.

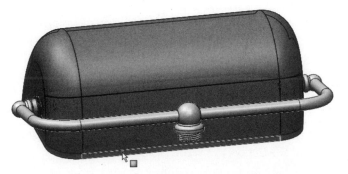

FIGURE 9.25 Selecting the face of shade for mating

4. Select the plus (+) next to the model name in the upper-left corner of the graphics area to display the Flyout FeatureManager. In the FeatureManager, select Front Plane, as shown in Figure 9.26.

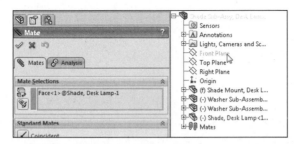

FIGURE 9.26 Selecting Front Plane in the Flyout FeatureManager

5. Select the Parallel mate in the Standard Mates section. The orientation of the shade will be displayed in the graphics area, as shown in Figure 9.27. Click the green check mark to apply the mate. Click the green check mark again to exit the Mate PropertyManager.

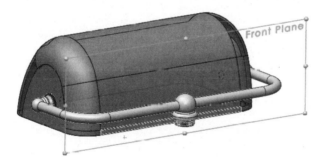

FIGURE 9.27 Position of shade fully defined

Add Washers for the Shade Inside

Before adding the bulb subassembly and locking nut to the assembly, you need to add two more washer subassemblies. No new tricks here — you will be using the same process as you did earlier to add two new instances from the FeatureManager:

1. Select the washer subassemblies in the FeatureManager, and click and hold the Ctrl key.

2. Drag another two instances of the washer subassembly into the graphics area. Mate the washer subassemblies as before to the inside of the shade, as shown in Figure 9.28.

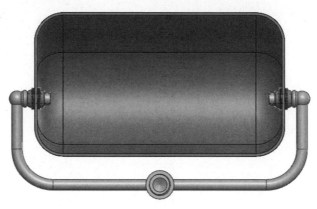

FIGURE 9.28 Washer subassemblies mated to the inside of the shade

Add the Shade Nut

To save some time, instead of modeling the shade nut and the bulb subassembly, make sure you download the models from the companion website. The first component that you will be adding is the shade nut. The shade nut screws onto the threaded post of the shade mount and holds the shade in place.

1. Select the downward-pointing arrow next to the Insert Components button on the shortcut bar. In the flyout, click the Insert Components button.

2. Click the Browse button in the Part/Assembly To Insert section of the Insert Component PropertyManager.

3. Browse to the folder that contains the models downloaded from the companion site. Select the part named Shade Nut, Desk Lamp. Click the Open button.

4. The shade nut will be shown in a preview mode next to the mouse pointer in the graphics area. Click and release the place the nut in the assembly.

5. Enter the Mate command once again, and select the shaft of the shade mount on the left side of the assembly, as shown in Figure 9.29, and the inner diameter face of the nut.

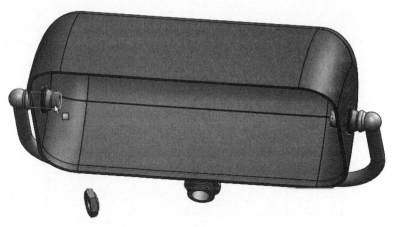

FIGURE 9.29 Selecting the shaft to mate locking nut

6. Next make the bottom face of the nut coincident with the top face of the washer. When mated, the nut should look like the one shown in Figure 9.30. Click the green check mark to exit the Mate command.

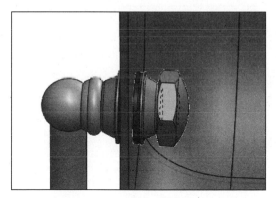

FIGURE 9.30 Locking nut mated in place

Insert a Subassembly into an Assembly

Adding subassemblies to an assembly is the same as adding a single part. When a subassembly is inserted, it acts just as a component would act. A subassembly, when inserted into an assembly, will act as a single rigid component, regardless of how many components the subassembly contains. You can change the subassembly to a flexible subassembly, which will allow the subassembly to move within the constraints that the mates allow.

N O T E Subassemblies in an assembly are designated either as rigid or flexible. A *rigid subassembly* acts as a single component, and a *flexible subassembly* can move as it was designed to do in the assembly.

The following steps will insert the bulb subassembly and define its location with some mates that you have probably become very comfortable with.

1. Select Insert Components in the shortcut bar, and select the Browse button in the Insert Components PropertyManager.

2. At the bottom of the Open window, change the file type field from Part (*.prt, *.sldprt) to Assembly (*.asm, *.sldasm). Select the bulb subassembly, and click the Open button to insert the assembly.

3. Click and release the left mouse button to place the bulb subassembly into the active assembly.

4. Enter the Mate mode, and select the inner diameter face of the nut on the end of the bulb subassembly.

5. Select the cylindrical face of the shade mount shaft on the right side of the model.

6. Make the bottom face of the bulb receptacle nut coincident with the top face of the washer.

7. Select the plus (+) next to the assembly name in the upper-left corner of the graphics area. In the FeatureManager, select the plus next to the bulb subassembly, as shown in Figure 9.31.

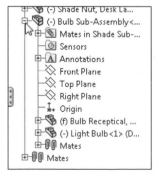

F I G U R E   9 . 3 1 Expanding the bulb subassembly in the Flyout FeatureManager

8. Select the Front Plane item that is listed as a child of the bulb subassembly.

9. Select the Front Plane item that is a child of the shade subassembly in the FeatureManager.

10. You may receive an error message saying that the default mate would over-define the assembly. When selecting two planes, SolidWorks assumes that you are attempting to add a coincident mate but in this case that particular mate is impossible with the current set of mates that have been applied to the bulb receptacle (Figure 9.32).

FIGURE 9.32 Default mate over-defining assembly

To remove the error, you need to select the appropriate mate to apply to the selected planes. In the Standard Mates section of the PropertyManager, select the *Parallel mate*, and click the green check mark. Click the green check mark to exit the Mate mode.

When selecting two planes, SolidWorks assumes that you are attempting to add a coincident mate.

Add Configurations to an Assembly

The shade is meant to be adjustable to achieve a variety of angles. The previous mate you added will allow only for the shade to point directly down toward the base. Rather than updating this one mate every time you need to rotate the shade, you will add some configurations for different shade positions. In previous chapters, we discussed using configurations to apply a different set of dimensions to a part to create different sizes, add features, or remove existing features. In assemblies, the most common use of configurations is to add and remove components, show movement, change the appearances, or as in this case add, remove, or modify mates.

In the next few steps, you will add a couple of configurations that will be used to show some basic positions of the shade.

1. Click the ConfigurationManager tab at the top of the FeatureManager design tree, as shown in Figure 9.33.

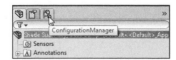

FIGURE 9.33 Selecting the ConfigurationManager tab

2. Right-click while the mouse pointer is inside the ConfigurationManager but not directly on top of any item listed. Select Add Configuration in the menu.

3. In the Configuration Name field in the Configuration Properties section of the Add Configuration PropertyManager, type **Shade - 10 Degrees**. If you were creating a configuration of the assembly that would require a different set of components, the configuration name could be used in the bill of materials. But since the changes that are applied in this configuration do not actually affect the parts list, you will not need to make any indication of this in the Configuration PropertyManager. The configuration name can instead be used to identify the active configuration of the assembly in the FeatureManager design tree.

 N O T E   When naming a configuration, it is important to know that the name cannot include either a forward slash (/) or an at sign (@). If you include any of these characters in the name, you will be prompted with an error message stating that the name is invalid.

4. Click the green check mark to create the configuration. The configuration description, based on the configuration name, will be available for use in the FeatureManager or in the ConfigurationManager.

5. Instead of clicking the FeatureManager design tree tab, double-click the split bar directly above the ConfigurationManager, as shown in Figure 9.34. The pane will be split into two equal panels. The top panel contains the FeatureManager, and the lower panel contains the ConfigurationManager. We often use this approach when working with parts or assemblies with configurations since there is still easy access to both the FeatureManager and ConfigurationManager.

FIGURE 9.34 The FeatureManager split bar

 N O T E   After creating the new configuration, it will become the active configuration, allowing any changes made to the assembly to be applied to the current configuration.

6. In the FeatureManager, the very last line is labeled as Mates. This is where all the mates that have been applied to the assembly so far are stored. Click the plus next to the label, as shown in Figure 9.35, to view the mates.

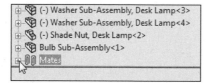

FIGURE 9.35 Expanding the Mates folder in the FeatureManager

Suppress a Mate

If you attempted to add a mate to the shade that will change the angle to 10°, it would over-define the assembly. The reason for this is that the Parallel mate you added fully defined the position of the shade, and SolidWorks would not be able to determine how the additional mate should be applied. Before you can add a mate to adjust the angle, you need to suppress the Parallel mate.

Suppressing a feature, or in this case a mate, does not remove the feature; instead, it only disables it in the active configuration. The previous configuration will still have the Parallel mate active. To suppress a mate, do the following in the FeatureManager:

1. Locate and select the Parallel mate in the Mates folder in the FeatureManager that was added in the previous section. Because it was the first Parallel Mate that was applied, it will be the first in the list. If you are not sure where the mates listed in the Mates folder are applied in the assembly, hover over the mate, and the entities used for the mate will be highlighted in the graphics area. Select the Parallel mate, and click the Suppress button on the context toolbar, as shown in Figure 9.36. When suppressed, the mate will be shown in the folder with gray text, and the shade can once again be rotated freely.

FIGURE 9.36 Suppressing the mate

N O T E   To unsuppress a suppressed mate, select the mate again, and click the Unsuppress button in the context toolbar.

Add an Angle Mate

Now that the position of the shade is once again under-defined and can be rotated freely, you can add the mate that will specify the angle of the shade. The Angle mate is used to specify the angle between faces, axes, lines, cones, and planes in an assembly. When the Angle mate is applied to an assembly, you can either specify the numerical value of the angle or use the angle that exists between the two selected entities.

In this instance, you will be specifying that the angle between the back face of the shade and the front plane of the assembly will be 10° in the current configuration. The following steps will show which entities need to be selected and how to apply the mate. Earlier in this chapter when you added the Parallel mate, you initiated the Mate tool prior to selecting the entities. To show you another approach, you will be selecting the entities prior to initiating the Mate tool.

1. In the FeatureManager, select Front Plane for the top-level assembly. While pressing and holding the Ctrl key, select the back face of the shade, as shown in Figure 9.37.

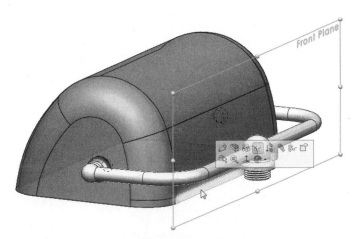

F I G U R E   9 . 3 7   Selecting entities for the Angle mate

2. Select the Mate tool in either the shortcut bar or the CommandManager.

3. In the context toolbar or the Mate PropertyManager, select the Angle mate. You may find it necessary to select the Anti-Aligned button in the FeatureManager to have the shade shown in the correct orientation.

4. In the field next to the Angle button in the Mate PropertyManager, specify the angle 10°. Instead of clicking the green check mark, hit Enter on your keyboard to see how the mate is applied in the graphics area.

5. After specifying the angle and hitting Enter, you will see that the shade opening moves 10° closer to the shaft. In this instance, that is not the direction that you require the shade to point. At first, you may be tempted to select the *Aligned* or *Anti-Aligned button* in the PropertyManager. If you were to actually do this, you would see that the shade rotates 180°, making the opening of the shade point up. This is not the effect you are hoping to achieve. Instead of selecting the Aligned or Anti-Aligned button, select the *Flip Dimension* option directly above the Angle field. If configured properly, the shade should be in the position shown in the side view in Figure 9.38. Click the green check mark to apply the mate and once again exit the Mate PropertyManager.

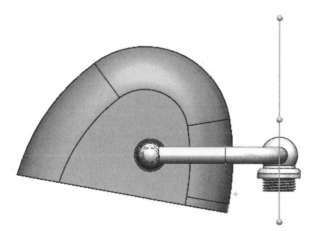

FIGURE 9.38 Shade shown at 10° angle

6. If you haven't saved your work so far, now would be a good time to do so. Click the Save button in the menu bar, or press Ctrl+S on your keyboard.

Add a Configuration to Modify the Mate

The last configuration you will add will be one to show the shade at an angle of 20°. Unlike the most recent configuration you added, you will not need to suppress any mates. Instead, you will be modifying the angle value of the existing mate to be 20° in the new configuration.

To start, you need to ensure that the configuration that contains the Angle mate is the active configuration. When creating new configurations, the active parameters are copied into the new configuration. If the default configuration is the active configuration, you will need to suppress the Parallel mate and unsuppress the Angle mate. To save the extra steps, it is always a good idea to create a new configuration from one that contains close to as many parameters that are needed. After that, all that you need to do is update the angle value. To do this, use the following steps:

1. In the Configurations section of the ConfigurationManager, select Add Configuration in the right-click menu.

2. Name the new configuration **Shade - 20 Degrees**, and enter the same in the Description field. Click the green check mark to create the configuration.

3. With the new configuration active, once again enter the Mates folder in the FeatureManager design tree.

4. Instead of creating a new mate for the angle, you will be changing the angle of the existing mate in the current configuration. Locate and select the Angle mate created in the previous section. The dimension that specifies the angle will be visible in the graphics area in blue.

5. In the graphics area, right-click the dimension, and select Configure Dimension in the menu, as shown in Figure 9.39.

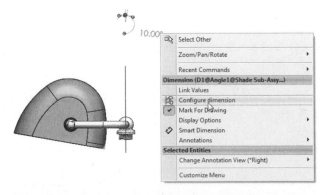

FIGURE 9.39 Configuring the dimension for the Angle mate

6. Select the cell that corresponds with the Shade – 20 Degrees configuration in the Modify Configurations window. Change the value from
10° to 20°, as shown in Figure 9.40. Click OK to accept the change.

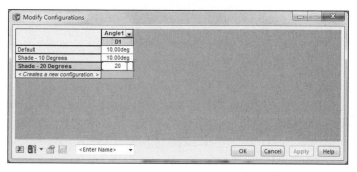

FIGURE 9.40 Updating the value of the Angle mate in the Modify
Configurations window

Switch Between Configurations

Switching between the available configurations allows you to see the differences
between them. In this assembly, switching between the three configurations will
give the illusion that the shade is moving between the three predefined locations.
Switching between configurations will also allow you to make additional modifications to the assembly. When you added the Angle mate to the second and third
configurations, it also added the same mate to the Default configuration. As we
mentioned earlier, this will cause a conflict and over-define the assembly. You
can now switch back to the Default configuration to address the error.

You can activate a configuration in a couple of ways. One way is to right-
click the desired configuration and select Show Configuration in the menu
(Figure 9.41).

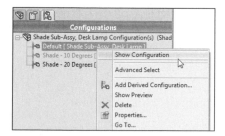

FIGURE 9.41 Selecting Show Configuration in the right-click menu

The second, and in our opinion the easier, way to activate a configuration is to simply double-click the configuration in the ConfigurationManager. Using this technique, you will address the error created by adding the Angle mate.

1. Activate the Default configuration in the FeatureManager.

2. After activating the Default configuration, you will see that the FeatureManager design tree lights up like a Christmas tree with red and amber colors. That is because there is an error somewhere in the assembly. Oftentimes you will not know what the error actually is until you do a little detective work. The first place you should look is in the status bar below the graphics area. There you will see a message giving a hint as to what the issue is in the assembly, as shown in Figure 9.42. Click the error shown in the status bar.

FIGURE 9.42 Over-defined message in status bar

3. Clicking the error message in the status bar will display a window showing the mates that are causing the assembly to be over-defined, as shown in Figure 9.43. Since you already know that this configuration should not have the Angle mate active, you can select the mate to suppress it in the window. Select the mate, and click the Suppress button in the context bar.

FIGURE 9.43 View Mate Errors window

4. After suppressing the offending mate, the View Mate Errors window will become empty, and the colored error messages in the FeatureManager will disappear as well. Click the red X in the upper-right corner of the View Mate Errors window to close it.

After fixing the error, you will be able to switch between all the assembly configurations to see how the shade moves between its three predefined locations. Save the assembly, and you are ready to move to the next chapter.

Are You Experienced?

Now You Can...

- ☑ **Create in-context models**

- ☑ **Use the Shell tool**

- ☑ **Save virtual components externally**

- ☑ **Modify appearances**

- ☑ **Add and show multiple configurations in an assembly**

- ☑ **Suppress and edit mates in configurations**

CHAPTER 10

Making Modifications

▶ Update Components in Isolation

▶ Update the Drawing Document

▶ Update Components Within Assemblies

▶ Replace Components in Assemblies

Changes to the model are to be expected. They are unavoidable and part of the design process. Before they are even prototyped, most parts and entire assemblies will often get redesigned and altered for many different reasons, such as to fit within size or weight restrictions, to reduce cost of manufacturing, to compensate for substitutions made because of lack of availability or excessive cost of materials, or even to comply with laws and regulations of the particular region where the product will be manufactured, used, or disposed of. However, this doesn't mean you'll have to remodel the whole thing from scratch over and over again to incorporate these alterations; rather, you can make small modifications, also called *revisions*, to the original models.

So far, you've learned how to use different features available in SolidWorks to create the parts for your model, and you've joined them together in assemblies and subassemblies. You've also learned how to generate a drawing from a part.

In this chapter, you will now learn how to make modifications to your model and how to update those changes into your assembly and drawing documents. We will demonstrate how to make changes to sketches and features inside a part, how to make modifications to parts within an assembly, how to update the revision table in your drawing to document the changes made to the model, and how to replace components in an assembly.

Update Components in Isolation

Continuing with the traditional bottom-up design approach that you've used so far, you will now make changes to a part in isolation. For this purpose, you'll open and edit the part individually, in its own window. Changes made to the part will later propagate to other documents. This method is usually preferred when editing off-the-shelf parts and other standard components.

The most basic and also the most common modifications that will usually need to be made to a model are changes to dimensions in sketches and features.

Changes to dimensions can be made the "old-fashioned" way, by editing sketches and features separately as needed, or in a much faster and easier way, as long as Instant3D is enabled.

In Chapter 3, "Creating Your First Part," you used Instant3D to create an extruded boss in your part simply by selecting and dragging a sketch. Here we'll demonstrate how, when Instant3D is enabled, you can resize features by editing sketch dimensions directly in the graphics area, without even having to go into Edit Sketch mode. This method is simple and can save you a few extra steps in the editing process, thus allowing you to make better use of your time.

N O T E   Remember, Instant3D is enabled by default, but it can be toggled on and off by clicking Instant3D on the Features tab. Parts and assemblies support Instant3D. Inside an assembly, you can use Instant3D to edit components within the assembly, edit assembly-level sketches and features, and modify mate dimensions. You will learn how to edit a component within an assembly later in this chapter.

Change Dimensions in Sketches with Instant3D

We will first demonstrate the way to make changes to sketch dimensions while Instant3D is enabled. For this purpose, you'll change the dimensions of one of the extrude features in the Base, Lamp part from Chapter 3.

1. Open the Base, Lamp model you created in Chapter 3.

2. Select Extrude6 in the FeatureManager. Notice that all dimensions associated with this feature will immediately show up in the graphics area.

3. In the graphics area, select the dimension for the diameter of 1.000 by clicking and releasing the left mouse button once.

4. After selecting the dimension, a small field will appear next to the dimension with the current value. In the field, change the value from 1.00 to **1.100**, as shown in Figure 10.1. To apply the updated value, hit Enter on your keyboard, or click anywhere outside the field.

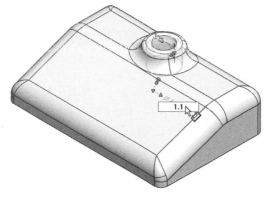

FIGURE 10.1 Applying the updated dimension value

Change Dimensions in Sketches Without Instant3D

As we mentioned, it was only recently that Instant3D technology was introduced in SolidWorks. Some users still prefer to disable this option and make modifications to features and sketches the way it was done in the past, before Instant3D was available. We will now demonstrate how it's done by changing another dimension of the same Base, Lamp model with Instant3D disabled. As you will see, this method requires a few extra steps and takes just a little longer than the previous one, but it's always a good idea to learn different ways to do the same in SolidWorks. There's no particular "right" way to do things, although some methods could save you some time and effort.

1. On the Features tab of the CommandManager, deselect the Instant3D button to disable it (see Figure 10.2).

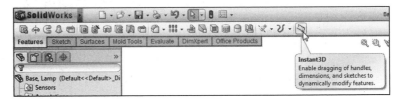

FIGURE 10.2 Disabling Instant3D

2. Select the Extrude7 feature in the FeatureManager, and notice that the dimensions of the sketch are no longer displayed in the graphics area.

3. Click the plus (+) next to the Extrude7 feature to display the child sketch.

4. Select the child sketch, Sketch7, and click the Edit Sketch button on the context toolbar (see Figure 10.3). Clicking this button will take you to Edit Sketch mode, or you can also double-click the sketch name in the FeatureManager design tree.

FIGURE 10.3 Edit Sketch button on context toolbar

5. Double-click the .700 diameter dimension in the graphics area to edit the dimension.

6. In the small Modify window that is displayed next to the mouse pointer, change the value to .755, as in Figure 10.4. Click the green check mark or hit the Enter key on the keyboard to accept the change.

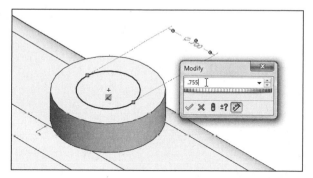

FIGURE 10.4 Modifying the dimension of the diameter

7. Click the Exit Sketch button in the confirmation corner to accept the change made to the sketch and to update the part geometry.

8. For future operations, click the Instant3D button on the Features tab once again to enable it.

9. Save the changes to the model, and click the X in the upper-right corner of the graphics to exit the file.

Prevent Loss of Data

At this point it is wise to observe that any changes made to the model will become permanent only once the document has been saved. If you fail to save and exit the document, all changes will be lost. It's good practice to save your work often during the session to prevent loss of data in the unfortunate event of a computer crash or power outage.

Save Notification

If you are likely to become so engrossed in your work that you forget to save often, you can choose to have SolidWorks remind you to do it every certain amount of time that you specify in advance. If the active document hasn't been saved within that interval, a transparent message will show up in the lower-right corner of the graphics area as an unsaved document notification, reminding you that you haven't saved your document yet. Click the appropriate command in the message to save the document.

Follow these steps in order to enable this option:

1. Select Tools ➢ Options.

2. Select Backup/Recover on the System Options tab.

3. Under Save Notification, select the option to show a reminder.

4. Type in the proper field the number of minutes for the time interval between reminders.

5. Click OK to accept changes.

Document Recovery

You can also have SolidWorks automatically save information about your active document every certain amount of time that you specify in advance. This option is known as Auto-Recovery, and its purpose is not to back up your active file but to save information of your model that you can retrieve in the event of an abnormal termination.

Auto-Recover won't save the information on top of your original file; it actually creates new files for the active document every time it saves changes. These files are always closed and deleted as soon as the original file is saved. If your computer crashes and you had this option enabled, the next time you start SolidWorks, the recovered files will appear on the task pane. You can choose to save any of these recovered files on top of your original file if it happens to include recent changes you made to the model and that are not present in the original file.

Follow these steps in order to enable this option:

1. Select Tools ➢ Options.

2. Select Backup/Recovery on the System Options tab.

3. Under Auto-Recover, select Save Auto-Recover Info.

4. Type the number of minutes for the time interval between saves.

5. Either accept the default folder or browse to a different location of your choice where these temporary recovery files will be stored.

6. Click OK to accept the changes.

Update the Drawing Document

Once you save your Base, Lamp model, all modifications you've made to the part will propagate to all other documents associated with it, such as assemblies and drawings. This is because parts, assemblies, and drawings are all linked documents in SolidWorks.

In Chapter 4, "Creating Your First Drawing," you created a drawing document from your Base, Lamp part. You will now see that the changes you've just made to the part document have been also included in the drawing document, and the modified dimensions will automatically update themselves the next time the drawing document is loaded.

This certainly saves a lot of time and trouble, but you still need to document the changes you've made to the drawing for future reference. You'll do this by updating the revision table and adding revision symbols to those entities and dimensions that have been altered.

Update the Revision Table

Unlike the rest of the drawing, the revision table doesn't automatically populate itself with fresh information every time a change in the model occurs. You need to update the revision table yourself in order to document all alterations made as they occur. It's important to remember to do it as soon as changes in the model take place.

The process is very simple and was already briefly introduced in Chapter 4. The following steps will show you how to update the revision table to account for the modifications made to the part and, therefore, to the drawing:

1. Open the drawing that was created in Chapter 4 named Base, Lamp. The changes that were made to the part model will automatically be updated in the drawing when it loads.

2. Zoom into the revision table in the upper-right corner of the drawing.

3. Right-click anywhere inside the table, and select Revisions ➢ Add Revision from the menu. Add Revision will add a new row to the table with the date of the revision and a letter assigned to it (see Figure 10.5).

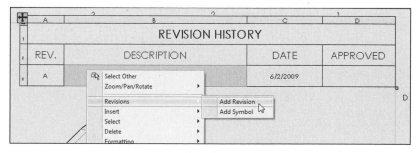

FIGURE 10.5 Adding a new revision to the table

Place Revision Symbols

Depending on your organization's standard operating procedures, you may be required to place *revision symbols* in your drawings. If that is not the case, you can skip the step of adding revision symbols by clicking Esc on your keyboard, but for the purpose of demonstration, you will be adding the symbols to this drawing. Here's how:

1. In the graphics area, a circle will be displayed with the current revision letter inside. Place the symbol next to the dimensions that were modified previously in the model by clicking and releasing the left mouse button, as shown in Figure 10.6. You can add the symbol to the drawing as many times as needed before clicking Esc.

    Notice also that if you ever need to add a symbol for an existing revision, even if it's not the latest one, simply right-click with your mouse on the row that corresponds to the revision in the table, and select Revisions ➢ Add Symbol; then follow the same procedure described earlier to place the symbol in the drawing.

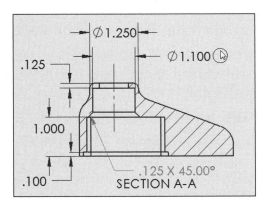

FIGURE 10.6 Adding revision symbols to the drawing

 N O T E **You can find more information regarding revision symbols in ASME Y14.35M-1997.**

2. In some organizations, the use of circular symbols may already be associated with other tasks. You can make changes to the appearances of selected symbols in the Revision Symbol PropertyManager. In the Border section of the PropertyManager, select the top field that currently displays Circular. In the flyout you can select an alternate symbol for the revision.

N O T E Change the revision symbol only if your organization requires a different symbol. The ASME standards allow for the omission of the revision symbol if the circular symbol conflicts with other symbols in the drawing since the revision description in the revision table will suffice.

3. Once you have placed the symbols next to the two dimensions that were updated, you can exit the Revision Symbol command by pressing Esc on your keyboard or clicking the green check mark in the PropertyManager.

4. Once the symbols have been added to the drawing area, the table should then be updated as well. Zoom in once again to the revision table in the upper-right corner of the drawing.

5. In the Description column, select the cell that corresponds to revision B in the table by clicking it once. Prior to SolidWorks 2010, you were required to double-click a cell to edit its value. Now all that you need to do after selecting the cell is begin typing the description of change. In the cell, provide enough information to the print reader to be able to determine the changes made to the part, as shown in Figure 10.7.

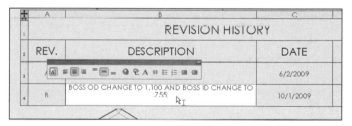

FIGURE 10.7 Entering changes in the revision table

6. To accept the changes made to the revision table, click anywhere outside the table.

7. Save the changes made to the drawing, and exit the document by clicking the X in the upper-right corner of the graphics area.

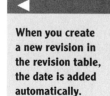

When you create a new revision in the revision table, the date is added automatically.

The next step will be to modify a component that is part of an assembly but without opening the component in a separate window. Don't worry! It's not really difficult to do. In fact, once you get the hang of it, you'll agree that it can actually be a very convenient approach.

Update Components Within Assemblies

So far, all the modifications or revisions that you've made to your model have been taken care of using the approach known as bottom-up design, which was previously described in Chapter 2, "Learning the Basics." As we mentioned, using this approach, you can create and modify a part in its own window, where only that part is visible and only the geometry inside that part can be used as reference. This way, changes made to that part will not propagate to other components in the assembly.

Use In-Context Editing

As we also mentioned in Chapter 2, SolidWorks allows the user not only to create new parts in the context of an assembly but also to edit parts within the assembly, regardless of how they were created, either independently or while working in the assembly. This approach is known as top-down design, or in-context editing.

The biggest advantages of editing the part using the top-down approach are being able to see the part in its correct location in the assembly while making modifications to it and that geometry from other components in the assembly will become available to you to copy, dimension to, or use as reference geometry for new or existing features in your part.

Adjust Transparency During In-Context Editing

By default, when editing a part in-context, the component that is being edited will appear opaque, while all other components in the assembly that are not being edited are made transparent in order to improve visibility. Even though the components have been made transparent, their geometry is still available and can be easily selected from the graphics area.

It is possible to adjust the default display settings that will be used for the components that are not being edited during in-context editing. The following steps will guide you in the process:

1. Click the Options button in the Standard toolbar, or select Tools ➤ Options.

2. On the Systems Options tab, select Display/Selection.

3. Under Assembly Transparency For In-Context Editing, you will be able to choose from three different options:

   Opaque Assembly   This option will make all components not being edited appear opaque.

Maintain Assembly Transparency   This option will allow all components not being edited to retain any individual transparency settings they may already have.

Force Assembly Transparency   This is the option selected by default. When using this option, all components not being edited will use the same transparency level that you set here.

Force Assembly Transparency is the best option for you at this moment.

4. Move the slider on the right side to the desired level of transparency. A level of 0 percent transparency will make the components opaque, and a level of 100 percent transparency will make them completely transparent. Click OK to accept the changes.

Create External References

If, while editing a component in the context of the assembly, you use a second component's geometry to dimension to or as reference geometry in the definition of a feature, an external reference to that second component's geometry will be created. It is actually during in-context editing that most of the external references are created.

The creation of this external reference means that one or more features in the document you just edited are now dependent on another document for their solution. An example of this would be using a face in a component different from the one you're editing as an end condition for an extruded boss feature. Your extruded boss would then become an in-context feature with an external reference to the face of the other component.

Any changes made to the referenced component will propagate to the one that is referencing its geometry, as long as the update path is available. Since the update path is contained in the assembly where the reference was created, this simply means that you'll need to open the assembly in order for updates made to the referenced component to propagate to the referencing one.

In the FeatureManager design tree, a suffix will be added to all items that have an external reference. This suffix indicates not only that an external reference exists in that component but also the status of this external reference. Each suffix is explained here:

▶ The suffix -> indicates that the external reference is up-to-date and a solution has been found for the in-context features in the referencing document.

▶ The suffix ->? indicates that the external reference is out-of-context and no solution has been found yet for the in-context features in the referencing document. You need to open the assembly that contains the update path.

▶ The suffix ->* indicates that the external reference is locked, the existing in-context features will no longer update, and you can't add any more external references to this component. Locked references can always be unlocked.

▶ The suffix ->x indicates that the external reference is broken, the existing in-context features will no longer update, and the external references can never be restored. You can, however, add new references to the component. External references can be broken intentionally or as result of improper file management.

N O T E   You also have the option not to create external references while in-context editing. You can still make use of the geometry of other components, but no external references will be created. To specify that no external references are created, click the No External References button on the Assembly tab, or select Tools ➢ Options and select External References on the System Options tab, and then select Do Not Create References External To The Model. You can select or deselect this option as needed to create external references for some components but not for others.

The modifications we'll make to your components in this chapter, however, consist only of changes to dimensions. No reference to geometry from other components in the assembly will be needed. The result will be similar to updating the part in isolation using the bottom-up approach, meaning that no changes will be propagated to any other components in the assembly and no references to outside geometry will be created. Technically, this is not considered top-down modeling, but it's still a very convenient way to do updates to a component.

Detect Interference Between Components

Before you can proceed with any changes, you need to find out what components should be updated and how. You can use interference detection to help you with this task.

It often happens that after updates are made to the individual parts that form an assembly, some of the components overlap or interfere with each other. In a small assembly, it may be easy to spot those interferences right away just by looking at it, but as assemblies grow larger and more complex, it also becomes more and more difficult to identify these areas of overlap between components.

By using interference detection, not only can you find the interferences between components, but you can also display the true volume of the interference, distinguish between a coincidence and a true overlap between components, change the display settings to make the interference easier to visualize, ignore certain kinds of interferences such as press fits and threaded fasteners, and treat a subassembly as a single component in order to ignore all interferences inside the subassembly and concentrate only on those between the subassembly and the rest of the components in the top-level assembly.

You can find the Interference Detection tool on the Evaluate tab in the CommandManager or listed in the Tools menu.

The following steps will demonstrate how to use interference detection to locate interferences between the components in the shade subassembly.

1. Open the shade subassembly you created in the previous chapter.

2. Click the Evaluate tab in the CommandManager, and select the Interference Detection button, as shown in Figure 10.8. You can also access Interference Detection in the Tools menu in the Standard toolbar.

FIGURE 10.8 Interference Detection button

3. Look at the Selected Components section of the Interference Detection PropertyManager, and notice that the shade subassembly is already selected by default. This works for the purpose of this demonstration because you are interested in finding all existing interferences in the assembly, but keep in mind that you could always clear this selection and select only a handful of components instead. Click the Calculate button.

4. The Results section of the Interference Detection PropertyManager will display a list containing all the areas of the assembly that were detected to contain interference. As you select an item listed in the window, the area will be highlighted in the graphics area. Select the first entry listed and the area where the washer cover and the mounting shaft overlap will be highlighted. For more clarity, you can see exactly which components are involved in the interference by clicking the plus (+) next to it (see Figure 10.9). It is obvious that the inner

diameter of the washer cover will have to be increased to eliminate the interference. At this point, you will only be making a mental note that the ID must be adjusted.

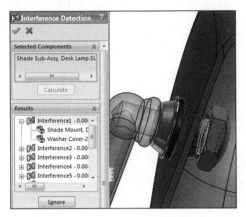

FIGURE 10.9 Interference between components

5. Moving on in the list, you will notice that the ID of the washer must also be updated. This makes sense because the washer and washer cover both have the same inner diameter.

For the moment, you will disregard these two interferences and continue in the list until you reach the interference shown between the bulb subassembly and the mounting shaft. This is not a true interference since the tool does not take into account that the interference is actually the threads interacting.

Instead of having these instances pop up again, you can choose to ignore the interference. Below the results window, click the Ignore button. The interference will be removed from the results and the next item in the list will be highlighted.

Continue to ignore any interference shown that is the result of threads. In other words, ignore two interferences between the shade mount and the bulb subassembly (Figure 10.10), one interference between the light bulb and the bulb receptacle (Figure 10.11), and one interference between the shade mount and the shade nut (Figure 10.12). That will leave you only with the interferences that were caused by the undersized washer and washer cover.

Click the green check mark to exit the PropertyManager.

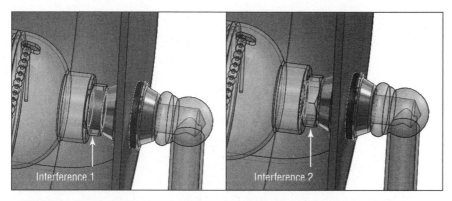

FIGURE 10.10 Two interferences between shade mount and bulb receptacle

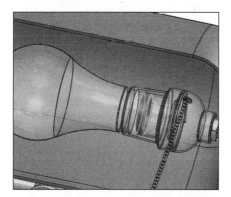

FIGURE 10.11 Interference between shade mount and shade nut

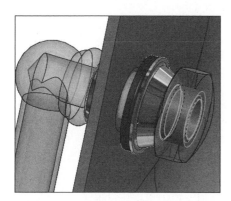

FIGURE 10.12 Interference between light bulb and receptacle

Now that the problem areas have been located, you can make the necessary modifications to the dimensions in the features of the washer and washer cover. For convenience and for illustration purposes, you'll do the editing of these two parts in the context of the assembly.

Make Modifications to the Washer Cover

Instead of opening the washer and washer cover separately in order to make the changes to the ID, you can make the changes while still in the assembly. Here's how:

1. In the FeatureManager, click the plus (+) next to the washer subassembly to view its components.

2. Click the plus (+) next to the washer cover in the FeatureManager to view its features.

3. Select the Revolve-Thin1 feature, and click the Edit Sketch button on the context toolbar (see Figure 10.13). Revolve-Thin1 has only one internal sketch; that's why you can access the Edit Sketch button by clicking the feature instead of the sketch.

FIGURE 10.13 Entering Edit Sketch mode from the context toolbar

4. Press Ctrl+8 or click the Normal To button in the Heads-up View toolbar, and zoom in closer to provide a better view of the sketch.

5. Select the .410 dimension in the graphics area.

6. You can also update the value of the dimension in the PropertyManager. In the Primary Value section, change the value to .450 (see Figure 10.14).

FIGURE 10.14 Updating the dimension

The Primary Value section also provides information on the name of the dimension and the sketch to which it belongs.

7. Using the same process, change the .475 dimension to .485. Click the green check mark to accept the changes.

8. Click the Exit Sketch button in the confirmation corner to accept the changes.

9. In the CommandManager, deselect the Edit Component button to toggle back to the main assembly (see Figure 10.15). You can also exit Edit Component mode by clicking the icon in the upper-right corner of the graphics area where the sketch confirmation corner usually resides. Notice that regardless of which tab is active in the CommandManager, the buttons for editing the components remain available. Once you go back to Assembly mode, the document will update to include the changes made to the part.

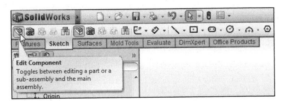

FIGURE 10.15 Deselecting the Edit Component button

Make Modifications to the Washer

To make things easier to view when editing the washer, you will isolate the part. This gives you the advantage of being able to edit the part without other assembly geometry obscuring the dimensions as they did when you edited the washer cover. This approach also allows you to remain in the assembly, so it is the best of both worlds.

When using the *Isolate command*, all other components except the one being edited are set to be transparent, wireframe, or hidden, allowing the user to concentrate only on the selected component. The display setting by default is hidden, but you can always change it to any of the other two directly from the Isolate pop-up toolbar.

The following steps will guide you in the process of isolating the washer and editing its dimensions in the context of the assembly:

1. Select the washer in the graphics area, and right-click. In the menu, select Isolate (see Figure 10.16). Remember, you can also select Washer in the FeatureManager design tree.

FIGURE 10.16 Isolating the component

2. All the other components in the assembly are hidden from the view, and you can now edit the diameter of the washer. Select the washer in the graphics area, and click the Edit Sketch button in the context toolbar, as shown in Figure 10.17.

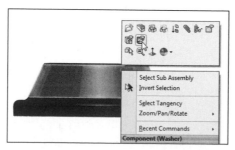

FIGURE 10.17 Entering Edit Sketch mode in the context toolbar

Isolate improves visibility, but you have no access to the geometry of other components in the assembly.

3. Double-click the .410 dimension to display the modify window. Change the value of the inner diameter to .450.

4. Click the Exit Sketch button in the confirmation corner, and click the Edit Component button in the confirmation corner to toggle back to the main assembly.

5. Clicking the Exit Isolate button in the floating toolbar will unhide the rest of the components in the assembly.

Check for Remaining Interferences

Now that you've successfully updated the dimensions of those two parts, you'll check for any remaining interferences in the assembly that you may have overlooked and may still need to be taken care of.

1. Click the Interference Detection button on the Evaluate tab of the CommandManager again.

2. Click Calculate to check the assembly again for any interference that was missed. The Results section should return a list of four items that you did not address yet. These four areas are the interference between the washer and the washer cover. This interference is by design since the washer is made of a rubber material that is meant to be slightly compressed by the cover to ensure a tight fit. Click the Ignore button four times until the list shows No Interferences, as shown in Figure 10.18. Note that the list also tells you that eight interferences have been purposely ignored. Click the green check mark to exit the PropertyManager.

FIGURE 10.18 No interferences remaining

You are now able to find and eliminate interferences between components in an assembly by making necessary updates to features and dimensions. In addition, you are able to do all the editing while in the context of the assembly.

Next, you'll go one step ahead and learn about how to replace components in the assembly. Does it sound complicated to you? Don't worry — the following example is very simple, and it's designed to help you learn the basic procedure. Are you ready? Keep reading!

Replace Components in Assemblies

All throughout the design process, you can expect that your assembly and most of its components will have to go through several revisions. So far, you've learned how to update components already inside the assembly, but what if what you really need is to completely replace a component with a different one?

You can find an example of this practice in a multiuser environment, where several users are working on individual parts and subassemblies that join together in a much larger model. To avoid confusion, it is considered safer and more efficient to update the assembly this way, by replacing components with their most recently revised versions and documenting all changes.

It is also possible that you're making substantial modifications to your design and have decided to replace a part for a subassembly, or vice versa. This is common practice when designing plastic products. Often, several parts in the assembly that were glued or fastened together will get redesigned and combined into one larger part that will perform in the same way and will replace them in the assembly. This is done to reduce the cost of manufacturing by having to design only one mold as opposed to several. It can also be done to reduce the need for post-manufacturing processes, reducing the cost even more. In such cases, the subassembly containing all the original parts will be replaced with the new part in the assembly document.

If you have multiple instances of one component in the assembly, you can replace all instances at the same time or choose to replace only one or a few of them.

The following steps will guide you through the process of replacing the shade nut component with a revised version of the same part that was previously downloaded from the companion website:

1. Select the shade nut in the graphics area by clicking and releasing the right mouse button.

2. Click the chevron at the bottom of the menu, shown in Figure 10.19, to display the hidden menu items. You could arrive to this same menu by clicking the shade nut with your right mouse button in the FeatureManager design tree.

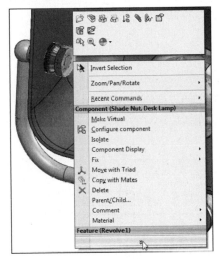

FIGURE 10.19 Displaying hidden menu items

3. Select Replace Components in the menu, as in Figure 10.20. Notice that you need to preselect a component in the assembly for this option to become available.

FIGURE 10.20 Replacing the component in the assembly

4. The Selection section of the Replace PropertyManager contains two windows. The first window, Replace These Component(s), displays the selected item that will be replaced. The second window, With This One, is currently empty because no other documents are open, but it will eventually display the new component. Click the Browse button to search for the new document (see Figure 10.21).

FIGURE 10.21 Selections for replacing components

5. In the open window, browse to the folder that contains the new shade nut model that was downloaded from the companion site, Shade Nut .375, Desk Lamp.sldprt. Select the part, and click Open at the bottom of the window.

 N O T E In this case, you have only one instance of this component in the assembly. If you had several instances, you could replace them all at once with the same new component by selecting only one instance and selecting All Instances. You could also replace only a few of them by selecting the instances you want to replace and leaving the option All Instances deselected.

6. Under Options, select Reattach Mates. When this option is selected, the software will try to reattach existing mates to the replacement component. Also, when selecting this option, the Mated Entities PropertyManager appears.

7. Click the green check mark in the PropertyManager to accept the selection of the new component.

8. Because you selected the option Reattach Mates, the Mated Entities PropertyManager will now be displayed to show any mate errors that

were caused by the new part, as shown in Figure 10.22. Since the new part is based on the old one, the mates used previously will continue to work.

Green check marks will show up next to the names of the two mated entities in the component, indicating that everything is fine with them. If you click any of these two mate entities, they will be highlighted in the graphics area. Click the green check mark to accept the mates and to finish replacing the nut.

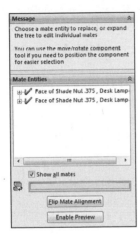

FIGURE 10.22 No errors appear in the Mated Entities PropertyManager.

9. Save the changes, and close the assembly.

Just so you know, in step 8, if any mate errors had indeed been caused by the replacement component, they would've shown as missing entities in the Mated Entities PropertyManager. Instead of green check marks, red question marks would appear next to each of the two missing entities. If you clicked any of the two missing entities on that list, a window would appear to show a picture of the original component with the missing entity highlighted. In addition, the Missing Entities pop-up toolbar would appear to allow you to select and delete any conflicting mates or flip mate alignments.

Congratulations! You have successfully replaced a component inside the subassembly by its most recent revised version. In the following chapters, you will use this subassembly and other components to put together the top-level assembly of the desk lamp.

If You Would Like More Practice...

You are finished making changes to the components in the assembly. However, you can still practice what you learned in this chapter. Try selecting other components in the assembly, and click the Edit Component button to enter Edit Component mode and examine their sketches and dimensions, the same way you did with the washer cover. Do not make any changes to the dimensions in the sketches. The idea is for you to feel comfortable getting in and out of Edit Component mode, not to modify the models any further. If you do make any changes by accident, make sure you don't save them.

You can also practice isolating other components in the assembly by following the same procedure you used to isolate the washer. If you want, change the display settings in the Isolate pop-up toolbar to make the components that are not being edited wireframe or transparent, and see whether you like those settings or whether you prefer the components to be hidden.

Are You Experienced?

Now You Can...

☑ **Change dimensions in sketches with Instant3D enabled**

☑ **Change dimensions in sketches with Instant3D disabled**

☑ **Save changes to your model and protect yourself from data loss**

☑ **Update the revision table**

☑ **Find interference between components in an assembly**

☑ **Modify a part within an assembly**

☑ **Replace components in an assembly**

CHAPTER 11

Putting It All Together: Part 1

▶ Create the Top-Level Assembly

▶ Use the Design Library

▶ Use the Width Mate

▶ Use SmartMates to Mate Components

▶ Finish the Appearance of the Assembly

n previous chapters of this book, you learned how to create and modify parts and how to join them together in subassemblies. Little by little you've been building all the different components that you'll need for your desk lamp. Now that you have everything you need, you're finally ready to put it all together and build the *top-level assembly*. For this purpose, you will use some of the tools and concepts already introduced in previous chapters, as well as a few new techniques and tricks that we will explain along the way.

Create the Top-Level Assembly

Open a new document for your top-level assembly, and save it as **Desk Lamp.sldasm**. These steps will guide you through the process:

1. Click New in the menu bar.

2. In the New SolidWorks Documents window, select the Assembly template, and click OK.

3. If the Begin Assembly PropertyManager does not open when opening a new SolidWorks assembly, click Insert Components in the shortcut bar.

4. In the Begin Assembly or Insert Components PropertyManager, click the Browse button in the Part/Assembly To Insert section.

5. Locate the Base, Lamp model updated in Chapter 10, "Making Modifications." In the Open window, select the part file, and click Open. The file will be displayed in the window of the Part/Assembly To Insert section. If you can't see it, make sure you have Graphics Preview selected under Options.

6. Instead of specifying the location of the lamp base in the assembly, you are going to allow SolidWorks to place the part in the same position it was created in. Clicking the green check mark in the PropertyManager without placing the base in the assembly will accept its default positions, and the origins of the part and assembly will be made coincident. After clicking the green check mark, the part will snap into its location, and the PropertyManager will close.

7. Save the assembly as **Desk Lamp.sldasm**.

T I P Remember, you can also create a new assembly document from an active part document by selecting File ➢ Make Assembly From Part or by clicking the downward-pointing arrow next to the New button on the menu bar and selecting Make Part From Assembly. The process of inserting the part into the assembly is the same as described earlier, except the part will already be displayed in the window of the Part/Assembly To Insert section.

Fully Define the Mates for the Shaft

Now that you've created an assembly document and successfully inserted your first part, you'll continue adding components to it. You could add all the components and define their locations later, but I find that this approach can be confusing especially for newer users. To avoid any confusion, you will mate each component as it is added to the assembly. To add and mate components, do the following:

1. Once again, select the Insert Components command in the shortcut bar.

2. Click the Browse button in the Insert Components PropertyManager and locate the Shaft, Lamp part created in Chapter 5. Click Open to add the part to the PropertyManager.

3. The shaft will be displayed in the graphics area of the assembly, but it is still not technically part of the assembly until it is placed. You will notice that as you move the mouse within the graphics area, the shaft will follow the pointer. Currently, SolidWorks is expecting a point in the graphics area to be selected to place the component. To place the shaft, click and release the left mouse button. Don't worry about its position since you will be using mates to define its location in the assembly.

4. Select the Mate command in the shortcut bar.

5. On the lamp base, select the inside cylindrical face of the hole for the shaft. Then select the cylindrical face of the threaded portion of the shaft, as shown in Figure 11.1. After selecting both faces, the Concentric mate will be selected by default in the Mate PropertyManager.

◄

Remember, you can access the shortcut bar by pressing S on your keyboard.

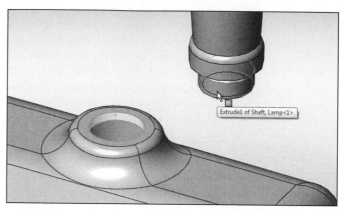

FIGURE 11.1 Selecting two cylindrical faces for mating

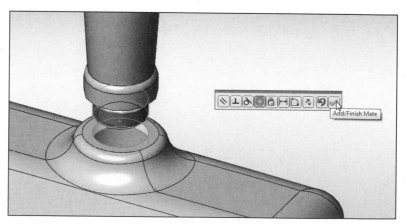

FIGURE 11.2 Aligning the shaft and mounting hole

Selecting two cylindrical faces or circular edges as entities for mating will always prompt the use of the Concentric mate.

6. At the same time, the shaft's location will update to show it in line with the mounting hole in the lamp base. To accept the Concentric mate, click the green check mark in the floating Mate toolbar, as shown in Figure 11.2.

The alignment is correct in this case, but if the shaft appears upside down, you can fix it by flipping the mate alignment in the Mate PropertyManager.

7. Next select the top face of the mounting boss, as shown in Figure 11.3, and the face of the shaft directly above the threaded boss. Click the green check mark to accept the Coincident mate.

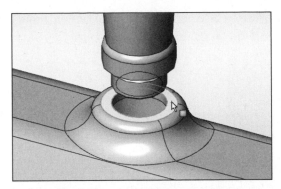

FIGURE 11.3 Selecting two planar faces for mating

At this point, the shaft's location is still considered under-defined, as you can see in the status bar. This is because even though the shaft cannot move from its location in the lamp base, it can still rotate freely.

Many times, you would not need to restrict a shaft's rotation in a hole because it would not have an effect on the assembly's design intent. An example of this would be a screw; many times it would not have an effect on how the screw functions, so it is often not necessary to restrict the rotation. However, since the lamp shaft supports another subassembly, it would have an adverse effect on the assembly if it was allowed to rotate freely.

> **Selecting two planar faces as mating entities will always prompt the use of the Coincident mate.**

Mate the Shaft with the Assembly

To prevent any issues, you will mate the front plane of the shaft with the front plane of the assembly. First you need to see the planes in order to mate to them. Here's how:

1. Click the plus (+) next to the assembly icon in the upper-left corner of the graphics area. This will open a flyout FeatureManager design tree.

2. Click the plus (+) next to the shaft in the flyout FeatureManager design tree to view the features, including the planes, as shown in Figure 11.4.

3. Select the front plane of the shaft, and then select the front plane of the assembly, as shown in Figure 11.5.

    As soon as you select both planes, SolidWorks tries to anticipate your selection and defaults to the Coincident mate. After selecting the two planes, SolidWorks will display an error message stating the selected mate would over-define the assembly, as you can see in Figure 11.6. This is because the two planes cannot be coincident, and if they were forced to be coincident, the Concentric mate you applied previously would no longer be able to be applied.

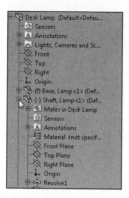

FIGURE 11.4 List of features in the lamp shaft

FIGURE 11.5 Selecting the front planes of the shaft and assembly

4. To fix the error and fully define the mates of the shaft, change the mate type from Coincident to Parallel. After selecting the Parallel mate in the PropertyManager or floating toolbar, click the green check mark once to apply the mate. Click the green check mark once again to exit the PropertyManager.

 N O T E   The *Parallel mate* places the selected entities so that they remain a constant distance apart from each other. You can add a Parallel mate between two planar faces, two planes, the two axes of a pair of cylinders, a planar face and a line, two lines, or a plane and a line.

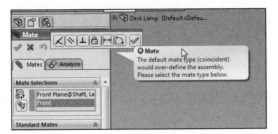

FIGURE 11.6 Selecting the proper mate type

Use the Design Library

Let's pause for a moment and talk about two very useful tools available in SolidWorks: the Design Library and the Toolbox. Since they are both accessible through the Design Library tab in the task pane, you may be tempted to think that they are both the same, but there are some substantial differences between them, which we will discuss next.

3D CONTENT CENTRAL AND SOLIDWORKS CONTENT

You will probably notice another two items also accessible through the Design Library tab in the task pane: the 3D Content Central and SolidWorks Content. The *3D Content Central* is a website where you can search and download for free from thousands of 3D models that have been previously uploaded by component suppliers and individual users. *SolidWorks Content* refers to additional content for blocks, Routing, CircuitWorks, and weldments that you can download for free and use with the Design Library. Both 3D Content Central and SolidWorks Content require an Internet connection.

Difference Between the Design Library and the Toolbox

SolidWorks Toolbox is an add-in that requires SolidWorks Professional or Premium. Toolbox gives you access to thousands of prebuilt standard hardware parts such as bolts and screws, gears, nuts, o-rings, bearings, pins, cams, and even structural shapes. SolidWorks Toolbox, however, doesn't actually store all those files but rather creates them on the fly from information supplied by the user, taking full advantage of configurations. The Toolbox library contains only a collection of master parts, plus a database and configuration information. Every time you use a part from the Toolbox, it either updates the master part according to the configuration information you supply or creates a new part file. This is very clever if you think about it! Instead of wasting space storing hundreds of kinds and sizes of screws, for instance, you can simply configure and create the one you really need.

SolidWorks Toolbox supports international standards, such as ANSI, AS, BSI, CISC, DIN, GB, ISO, IS, JIS, and KS. You can also customize the Toolbox to include your company's standard or only those that you use more frequently.

There are a few things to keep in mind about some of the components created by the Toolbox, however. In the first place, fasteners are merely a representation; they don't include accurate thread detail. The same goes for Toolbox gears, which are not true involute gears, but mere representations of a gear, and should not be used for machining purposes or included in a Finite Element Analysis study if you need accurate information about stress concentrations in these components.

SolidWorks Design Library, on the other hand, is used as a central location to access and store reusable elements such as features, parts, sketches, commonly used annotations, sheet metal forming tools, and even assemblies. It will not, however, recognize elements that are not reusable, such as text files, non-SolidWorks documents, or SolidWorks drawings. Even though some items have already been included for you in the Design Library, its purpose is really to become a collection of your own reusable items, meaning that you can add new content to it at any time. On the lower pane, you will find previews of all the available content. You can organize your content in folders and also drag items from one folder to another. Later, whenever the need arises, you can simply drag copies of these elements from the Design Library into the graphics area to use them in your active document.

Given that SolidWorks Toolbox is an add-in and it's likely that many readers of this book will not have it included in their license of SolidWorks, we won't deal with the particulars of installing it or configuring Toolbox parts and will focus instead on showing how to use the Design Library to your advantage.

When you open the Design Library tab, you will see four different icons that appear at the top. These are four different tools that will help you manage the Design Library contents. From left to right they are as follows:

 Add To Library File   Click this icon to add new content to the library. The content can be a part, an assembly, a feature, an annotation, and so on.

 Add File Location   Click this icon to add an existing folder to the library by browsing to its location on disk.

Create New Folder   Click this icon to create a new folder on disk and in the Design Library.

Refresh   Click this icon to refresh the view of the Design Library tab.

Add Components to the Design Library

Now that you understand what the Design Library is and what it's used for, your next step will be learning how to add items to it. You can do this easily through the Add To Library PropertyManager, which displays whenever you click the Add To Library button on the top of the task pane. From this PropertyManager, you can choose the items you want to add and assign a location for them among the different folders in the Design Library, a name, and a short description (also known as tooltip).

The Add To Library PropertyManager will also display whenever you attempt to drag an item (such as an assembly, a part, a feature, an annotation, or a sketch) from the FeatureManager design tree or even from the graphics area and drop it into the lower pane of the Design Library.

 N O T E It is also possible to add items to the Design Library simply by dragging them from Windows Explorer into the lower pane. In this case, however, the Add To Library PropertyManager will not display, and the item will be assigned the document's name. You can always rename the item later or move it to a different folder.

Parts and assemblies added to the Design Library will be, of course, saved with their regular extensions. To add a part or assembly to the Design Library, you need to select it from the FeatureManager design tree and either click the Add To Library button or drag it into the lower pane of the Design Library.

When copying features into the Design Library, they will be saved as library feature parts with the special extension .sldlfp. To copy a feature into the Design Library, you can select it from the FeatureManager design tree and either click the Add To Library button or drag it into the lower pane of the Design Library. In a part document, you can also select it and drag it directly from the graphics area into the lower pane of the Design Library.

To copy annotations or blocks into the Design Library, you can press Shift and then select and drag them from the graphics area into the lower panel of the Design Library. Blocks will be saved with the special extension .sldblk. Notes and symbols will be saved with their corresponding style extension: .sldnotestl for notes, .sldgtolstl for geometric tolerance symbols, .sldsfstl for surface finish symbols, and .sldweldstl for weld symbols.

N O T E   Creating and using library feature parts can become a very complicated task that involves more than simply dragging items into the lower pane of the Design Library. This is clearly beyond the scope of this book. We won't be dealing with annotations or blocks either. You are always encouraged to search for more information once you've mastered the basics covered in this book.

Even though you could simply insert the part custom bearing nut into the desk lamp assembly in the same way you have done for all other components in the past, for demonstration purposes you will first add the part to the Design Library and then use it as you would any other Design Library content.

The following steps will guide you through the process of adding a part to the Design Library:

1. Open the custom bearing nut model that was downloaded from the companion website.

2. Select the Design Library tab in the task pane, as shown in Figure 11.7.

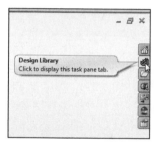

FIGURE 11.7   Design Library tab in task pane

3. Click the plus (+) next to the folders in the Design Library pane, and locate the folder Hardware in the Parts folder, as shown in Figure 11.8. Currently you should find a couple of hardware models that can be used within an assembly. Unfortunately, the component you need for the desk lamp does not exist in the Design Library. You will need to add the component to the Design Library before you can add it to your assembly.

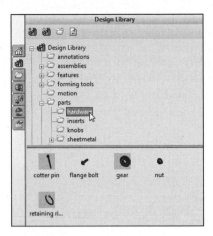

FIGURE 11.8 Hardware components available in Design Library

4. Click the Add To Library button above the folder view of the Design Library to open the Add To Library PropertyManager.

5. In the Add To Library PropertyManager, you need to specify which component will be added to the library first. Select the model in the graphics area, and the Items To Add field will update to include the custom bearing nut to the selection set, as you can see in Figure 11.9.

   The name of the component as it will be displayed in the Design Library is shown in the File Name field in the Save To section of the PropertyManager. You can change the name if you need to better describe the part, but for this component the description shown will suffice.

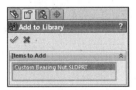

FIGURE 11.9 Items To Add field in the Add To Library PropertyManager

6. Ensure that the Hardware folder is specified in the Design Library Folder field, as shown in Figure 11.10. If the folder displayed is not correct, select the Hardware folder in the field.

FIGURE 11.10 Saving items in the Design Library

7. In the Options section, make sure that the correct file type is shown and add a word or phrase that will be shown as a tooltip when the mouse pointer is allowed to hover over the component icon, as shown in Figure 11.11.

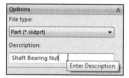

FIGURE 11.11 Entering a description that will become a tooltip

8. With the options set in the Add To Library PropertyManager, click the green check mark to add the component to the Design Library. The bearing nut will now be listed along with the other components in the Design Library, as shown in Figure 11.12.

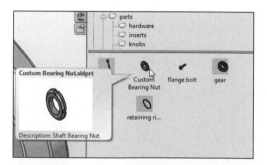

FIGURE 11.12 Preview image of the new item in the Design Library

9. Exit the Custom Bearing Nut model by clicking the X in the upper-right corner of the graphics area.

T I P If you ever need to remove an item from the Design Library, simply right-click it and select Delete. The item will no longer be included in the library, but the original document won't be deleted.

You have successfully added a part to the Design Library. The next step will be learning how to add the components you already have in the library to other documents in SolidWorks.

Add Components from the Design Library into an Assembly

You can easily add a part or subassembly from the Design Library into an assembly by selecting the component from the library and then dragging and dropping it into the graphics area. The following steps will guide you through the whole process as you add the custom bearing nut from the Design Library into the desk lamp assembly.

1. If you closed the desk lamp assembly previously, open it once again.

2. In the desk lamp assembly, click the Design Library tab in the task pane. Locate the Hardware folder that you placed the bearing nut into during the previous section.

3. Select the nut in the lower pane of the Design Library tab by clicking and holding the left mouse button. Drag the nut into the graphics area while still holding the left mouse button. Once inside the graphics area, release the left mouse button, and the component will be added to the assembly.

4. Once the nut is added to the assembly, you can exit the command by clicking Esc on your keyboard or by clicking the X in the PropertyManager. In this case, you need only one instance of this component. If more instances were required, you could add them all at once by clicking the graphics area with the left mouse button as many times as needed before exiting the command.

N O T E The part you just added to the assembly had no configurations. If configurations had been available for that part, you would've been prompted to choose the right one from a list as soon as you dropped the part into the graphics area.

5. Rotate the assembly to give you better access to the bottom of the lamp base.

6. Click S on the keyboard, and select the Mate tool in the shortcut bar.

7. Select the cylindrical face of the threaded shaft and the inner face of the nut, as shown in Figure 11.13. Click the green check mark to accept the Concentric mate.

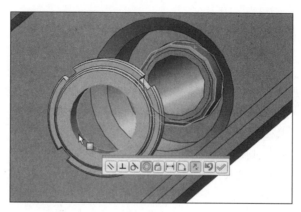

FIGURE 11.13 Selecting two cylindrical faces for mating

8. Next, select the face at the bottom of the cutout in the lamp base, and then select the bottom face of the nut, as shown in Figure 11.14.

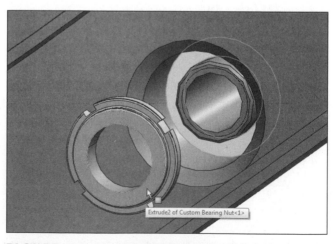

FIGURE 11.14 Selecting the two planar faces for mating

9. After selecting both faces, it might be necessary to click the Anti-Aligned button in the PropertyManager, as you can see in Figure 11.15. Clicking the Anti-Aligned button will ensure that the two selected faces face each other. You will probably notice that a pop-up window will show up at this point to let you know that the alignment of the Concentric mate was reversed to prevent mate errors. This is OK.

FIGURE 11.15 Using the Anti-Aligned button

10. Since this is one of the instances where the rotation of the component will not affect the design intent, you can choose not to add other mates to the nut. Instead, click the green check mark to accept the mates added and to close the PropertyManager.

 N O T E If you modify a component that was added from the Design Library, the component will be modified in the Design Library as well.

Congratulations! You have learned how to add content from the Design Library into another SolidWorks document. You will now continue adding components to your desk lamp assembly, and you'll also learn some more about mates along the way. You sure don't want to miss this, so keep on reading!

Use the Width Mate

In this section, you'll learn about a special kind of mate known as Width mate, which, for some strange reason, is often ignored even by the most experienced of SolidWorks users, despite that it's extremely practical and powerful.

You can use the *Width mate* to quickly and efficiently center a part inside a hole or cutout, a channel, or a slot in another component, while leaving a clearance between them. You can accomplish all this in just one step, with only one mate and without having to create any extra reference geometry. The component that needs to be centered is called a *tab* in the Mate PropertyManager.

Most commonly, both the tab and the hole, channel, or slot will have parallel planar faces, and the tab will be centered right in between those planar faces, but that's not always the case. The Width mate can also center a cylindrical face or axis between two parallel planar faces, and a tab with nonparallel planar faces, such as a wedge, can be centered in between another couple of nonparallel planar faces.

Once you add a Width mate, the components will align in such a way that the tab will remain centered between the faces of the hole, channel, or slot. The tab will not be allowed to translate or rotate from side to side, but it will still be able to move in and out of the hole, channel, or slot by translating along its center plane. It will also be able to rotate around an axis normal to that same center plane.

You can find the Width mate under Advanced Mates in the Mate PropertyManager. But don't let the *advanced* part scare you, because it's really easy to use. First, open the Mate PropertyManager, and click the Advanced Mates section. In the Width Selections field, select the planar faces of the hole, channel, or slot you want to center the tab in, and then select a couple of planar faces or a cylindrical face or axis in the Tab Selections field for the tab. The following steps will guide you through the whole process, and it will become clearer for you:

1. Press S on your keyboard, and click the Insert Components button on the shortcut bar.

2. Click Browse in the Insert Component PropertyManager, and locate the electrical cover model that you downloaded from the companion site. Click Open to show the component in the graphics area.

3. Click and release the left mouse button to insert the electrical cover into the assembly.

4. Click the Mates tool in the shortcut bar.

5. Select the bottom face of the electrical cover and the recessed face of the electrical cutout, as shown in Figure 11.16. After selecting the two faces, the Coincident mate is automatically selected. Depending on how the components were first placed in the assembly and whether you have previously moved or rotated anything, you may or may not need to use the Anti-Aligned button in the PropertyManager. If you aren't sure, check Figure 11.18 to verify that you achieved the proper alignment between the two components. If the alignment isn't right, click the Anti-Aligned button to flip the electrical cover to its correct position. Click the green check mark to accept the mate.

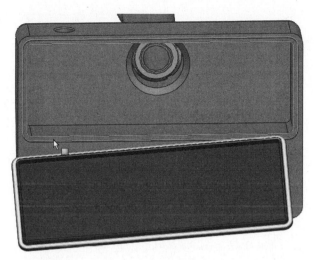

FIGURE 11.16 Selecting the two faces for mating

6. In the Mates PropertyManager, select the Advanced Mates section header to expand the list of available mates. Click the Width mate in the Advanced Mates section, as shown in Figure 11.17.

FIGURE 11.17 Width mate in the Advanced Mates section

7. After selecting the Width mate, the Mate Selections field will update to show two selection sets. The top field, Width Selections, will be the first highlighted field. Select the two opposing faces of the lamp base cutout.

8. After selecting the two faces that represent the Width selections, select the Tab Selections field in the PropertyManager. Next, select the two outside faces of the electrical cover, as shown in Figure 11.18. Click the green check mark once to apply the Width mate to the components.

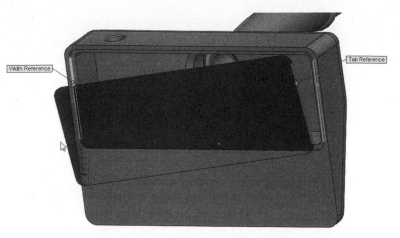

FIGURE 11.18 Width and Tab selections for mating

9. Select the Width mate a second time in the Advanced Mates section.

10. For the Width selections, select the two opposing adjacent faces in the cutout.

11. Click the Tab Selections field, and select the other two opposing faces on the electrical cover. You may need to move the face to the side of the lamp base in order to have access to both of the faces on the cover.

12. Click the green check mark in the PropertyManager twice—the first time to accept the new Width mate selections and the second time to close the PropertyManager. If you selected the correct faces, there will be a constant gap between the parts. Press G on your keyboard to use the magnifying glass to inspect the gap, as shown in Figure 11.19.

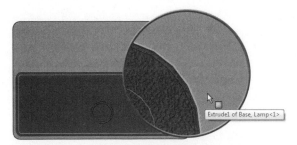

FIGURE 11.19 Inspecting the gap

Now that you have learned how to mate two parts using Width mate, you'll continue adding components to your assembly and exploring different strategies that can help you make the mating process faster and more efficient.

Use SmartMates to Mate Components

SmartMates aren't exactly a new or different kind of mate than those you could find in the Mate PropertyManager but rather a different approach to mating that can save you some time and effort. Basically, when you use SmartMates, SolidWorks will let you create the most commonly used mates automatically and without even having to open the Mate PropertyManager.

Taking advantage of the SmartMates functionality is really simple. To mate two components that are already inside an assembly, simply press and hold down the Alt key; then, in the graphics area, select an entity in one of the components and use it to drag the component onto the other, but don't drop it just yet. Instead, watch for the pointer; as you drag the component on the graphics area, whenever the pointer hovers over an entity in another component that could be a potential mate partner, it will change to indicate what type of SmartMate would be created between these two components. You can drag a component using a linear or circular edge, a planar, a cylindrical or conical face, a temporary axis, a vertex, an origin, or a coordinate system.

Types of SmartMates

The type of SmartMate that will be created depends on the type of entity used to drag the component and the type of entity found as its mate partner. The following can help you identify the SmartMates that will be created simply by observing the changes in the pointer.

This is how the pointer looks if the entity used to drag the component and the potential mate partner are both linear edges. In this case, a Coincident mate will be created.

This is how the pointer looks if the entity used to drag the component and the potential mate partner are both planar faces. In this case, a Coincident mate will be created.

This is how the pointer looks if the entity used to drag the component and the potential mate partner are both vertices. In this case, a Coincident mate will be created.

This is how the pointer looks if the entity used to drag the component and the potential mate partner are both cylindrical or conical faces or a couple of temporary axes. In this case, a Concentric mate will be created.

 This is how the pointer looks if the entity used to drag the component and the potential mate partner are both origins or both coordinate systems. In this case, a Coincident mate will be created.

 N O T E   Pressing the Tab key before you drop the component has the same effect as the Anti-Aligned button in the Mate PropertyManager; it flips the alignment of the components to be mated.

If you have a component that is not already in the assembly, you can also mate this component as you add it into the assembly using SmartMates. You will first need to open both the component and the assembly each in their own window and then, if the component is a part, select an entity and drag the part from the graphics area of its window into the assembly's graphics area. The procedure is very similar in case the component you are adding is an assembly; the only difference is that you will need to press Shift, select an entity, and then drag the component from the graphics area of its own window into the top-level assembly's graphics area. Remember, do not drop the component immediately, but follow the procedure described previously to find a suitable mate partner.

 T I P   Dragging components from one window to another is easier if you tile both windows horizontally or vertically in such a way that they are both visible at the same time. To do this, with both documents open, click Window, and select either Tile Horizontally or Tile Vertically from the menu. Both windows will be shrunk, rearranged, and displayed next to each other. You can also access Tile Horizontally and Tile Vertically from the Heads-Up Views toolbar at the top of the graphics area.

It is also possible to use SmartMates to mate components as you add them from Windows Explorer or from the Design Library, but you'll need to create mate references for these components in advance. A mate reference will specify one or more entities in the component that will be used for mating whenever you drag the component into an assembly. The creation and use of mate references, however, is beyond the scope of this book.

Mate with Peg-in-Hole SmartMate

In most cases, only one SmartMate will be created as you drag and drop a component in the assembly. However, under some special conditions, you can create multiple mates at the same time. The Peg-in-hole SmartMate is one of those multiple mates. It's actually two mates in one, a Coincident mate and a Concentric mate.

A Peg-in-hole SmartMate is usually created when the entity used to drag the component and its potential mate partner are both circular edges. These edges, however, do not need to be complete circles. Whenever this type of SmartMate is applied, a Concentric mate is added to the two circular faces and a Coincident mate is added to the two planar faces adjacent to them. Examples of components that would be mated with the Peg-in-hole SmartMate are bolts and nuts, and screws and holes. In these two cases, it's easy to see the concentric relationship between each pair of mated components, since they both have cylindrical faces, but the Peg-in-hole SmartMate can also be used to mate components that have conical faces, such as countersunk holes and screws.

This is the way the pointer will look when a Peg-in-hole SmartMate is about to be created between two components.

The following steps will demonstrate how to use the Peg in Hole SmartMate when mating components that are already in the assembly:

1. Select the Insert Components command again. After clicking the Browse button in the PropertyManager, locate and open the shade subassembly that was updated in Chapter 10. You may need to change the File Type field from Part (*.prt, *.sldprt) to Assembly (*.asm, *.sldasm) in the Open window.

2. Insert the shade subassembly into the top-level assembly by clicking and releasing the left mouse button with the mouse pointer inside the graphics area.

3. Once the shade subassembly is inserted into the assembly, you can mate it to the shaft. However, this time instead of initiating the Mate PropertyManager, you will take advantage of SmartMate's functionality. While holding the Alt key on your keyboard, select the circular edge at the bottom of the center body of the shade support, as shown in Figure 11.20, by clicking and holding the left mouse button.

4. While still holding the Alt key, as you move the mouse, the pointer will update to include a small paper clip icon next to the pointer. Move the mouse pointer to the top of the shaft. When the edge to be mated is near the top of the shaft, the shade subassembly will snap into place and the mouse pointer will once again update, but this time with the icon that signifies the Peg-in-hole SmartMate, as shown in Figure 11.21. Release the left mouse button to accept the mate.

FIGURE 11.20   Using the circular edge to drag the component

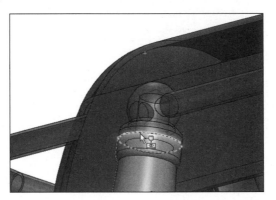

FIGURE 11.21   Icon for Peg-in-hole SmartMate

5. All that is left to do is mate the front plane of the shade subassembly and the desk lamp assembly in the same way you did earlier in this chapter. Using the Mate tool, make their two front planes parallel.

You have finished putting together all the components in the top-level assembly. The desk lamp model is now complete. Next, you'll tweak the look of the assembly by applying the appearance of brass to a few of its components.

Finish the Appearance of the Assembly

Some appearances have already been added to different components of the desk lamp assembly. Three of the components, however, remain unchanged, still in the gray plastic appearance that is applied in SolidWorks by default. In this section, you'll finish applying appearances to the assembly so it can be ready for when it's time to render it in PhotoView 360 in Chapter 17.

Not many users know this, but you can apply the same appearance to a group of preselected items at the same time simply by double-clicking the appearance of your choice in the Appearances/Scenes tab.

The following steps will guide you through the process of adding an appearance to a group of preselected items in the assembly:

1. While holding the Ctrl key down on the keyboard, select the lamp base, lamp shaft, and shade mount in the FeatureManager, as shown in Figure 11.22.

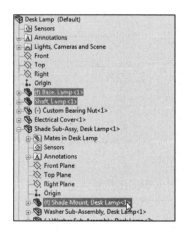

FIGURE 11.22 Selecting items for applying appearances

2. Click the Appearance/Scenes tab in the task pane. Browse to the Metal folder in the top pane of the Appearances/Scenes tab, open it, and find the Brass folder inside. Open the Brass folder.

3. In the lower pane, locate the Polished Brass material appearance. Double-click the Polished Brass material appearance to apply the material to the three selected parts in the assembly.

4. Click outside the Appearances/Scenes tab to hide the task pane.

Congratulations! The desk lamp model is now complete and even ready to be rendered. If you've followed each example presented in the previous chapters of the book carefully, by now you should be able to create your own parts and assemblies, and you should feel confident in your abilities to use basic modeling techniques.

In the next chapter, you won't be doing any more modeling, but you'll learn a few ways to control the display of your assembly, plus how to create exploded views and much more.

If You Would Like More Practice...

Even though you're done with all the modeling changes and you don't need to add any extra components to this assembly, you can still practice what you've learned in this and previous chapters.

You can try adding some or all the other components in this assembly to the Design Library by following the same procedure you used for the custom bearing nut. Going one step ahead, you could also create a new assembly of your own to have as a practice assembly, add some of those components from the Design Library to it, and try to mate them like you did in previous chapters, only this time using SmartMates. Just make sure to save this practice assembly under a different name.

Are You Experienced?

Now You Can...

- ☑ **Add components to the Design Library**

- ☑ **Add components to an assembly from the Design Library**

- ☑ **Use the Width mate**

- ☑ **Understand SmartMates**

- ☑ **Use the Peg-in-hole SmartMate**

- ☑ **Add an appearance to multiple preselected items**

CHAPTER 12

Putting It All Together: Part 2

▶ Understand Rigid and Flexible Subassemblies

▶ Insert a BOM in an Assembly Document

▶ Control the Display of the Assembly display state

▶ Understand Selection Tools for Assemblies

▶ Understand Assembly Visualization

▶ Create an Exploded View of the Assembly

In previous chapters of this book, you've focused on learning all the basic modeling techniques to build parts and then join them together in assemblies and subassemblies. You won't do any more modeling in this chapter. You finished putting together the top-level assembly in Chapter 11, "Putting It All Together: Part 1." The modeling part of your job is now completed, but you still need to learn several techniques to display, sort, and extract useful information from your assembly document, and this is precisely what this chapter is all about.

Understand Rigid and Flexible Subassemblies

In previous chapters of this book, you created all the different parts that will form your desk lamp and you joined some of them together in small assemblies that, when inserted inside the top-level assembly, will become what are usually called subassemblies.

In case you didn't notice, when you created those small assemblies, some of the parts within them were completely defined, with no degrees of freedom left, yet others, even after mating them, were still able to move or rotate around one another when dragged. However, once these small assemblies became subassemblies, moving or rotating those same parts was suddenly not possible. Why is that? Well, by default, every time an assembly is inserted inside another one, thus becoming a subassembly, SolidWorks treats this new subassembly as if it were a single unit, restricting the movement of its components. Furthermore, the mates between the subassembly's components need not be solved, but only the mates between the subassembly and its parent must be solved. This is what in SolidWorks is known as a *rigid subassembly*. By default, all subassemblies in SolidWorks are solved as rigid.

Understand Why Flexible Subassemblies Are Helpful

Sometimes, however, you may need all those individual parts inside the subassemblies to be able to move again. It may actually be necessary for them to move in order for all components to assume their correct position inside the parent assembly. Well, if that's the case, don't worry because there is something you can do about it. You can make the subassembly *flexible*, meaning that all its components will be allowed to move again, both with respect to other components inside the subassembly and also with respect to components in the parent assembly, always within the limitations imposed on them by their mates, of course. This is because when a subassembly is set as flexible, all the mates between its internal parts are solved simultaneously with all the other mates in the parent assembly. This way there is no conflict between mates and no risk of overdefining the assembly.

If you have multiple instances of the same subassembly, you can make all of them flexible or only one or a few that you choose, while leaving all other instances as rigid. You can also toggle a subassembly back and forth between being solved as rigid or flexible as needed.

Make a Subassembly Flexible

Changing the way the subassembly is solved from rigid to flexible is rather simple. All you need to do is right-click the subassembly in the FeatureManager design tree and select Component Properties. In the dialog box that will display, under Solve, select Flexible, and click OK. The subassembly will then be solved as flexible.

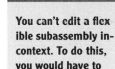

You can't edit a flexible subassembly in-context. To do this, you would have to set it back to rigid.

This icon appears near the name of the subassembly in the FeatureManager tree to indicate it is being solved as flexible.

The following steps will guide you through the process of making a subassembly flexible:

1. If you closed the assembly from the previous chapter, open the desk lamp assembly once again for further refinement.

2. Select the shade subassembly in the FeatureManager, and click the Component Properties button in the context toolbar, as shown in Figure 12.1.

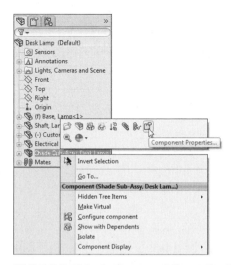

FIGURE 12.1 Component Properties button in context toolbar

3. Select the configuration named Free in the Referenced Configuration field, as shown in Figure 12.2. Click OK to accept the new configuration, and close the Properties window. Any changes you make from now on will apply only to this configuration.

FIGURE 12.2 Selecting the configuration named Free

4. Move the mouse pointer directly above the shade in the graphics area. Click and hold the left mouse button, and attempt to move the shade. You will notice that the part cannot be moved, and a tooltip will display a message stating that the component cannot be moved since it is fully defined, as shown in Figure 12.3.

5. The reason the shade's position cannot be moved is because the sub-assembly is currently set to be rigid. To make the shade subassembly flexible, select the subassembly in the FeatureManager, and click the Component Properties button in the context toolbar.

6. Near the bottom on the Component Properties window, there is a section named Solve As; in that section are two options, Rigid and Flexible. The Rigid option will be selected. Click the Flexible option, as shown in Figure 12.4, and click OK to accept the change. Making the subassembly flexible will allow its components to move.

FIGURE 12.3 Movement restricted for components in shade subassembly

FIGURE 12.4 Making the shade subassembly flexible

7. After closing the Component Properties window, try to move the lamp shade again. It should rotate freely around the thread shafts of the shade mount. If not, ensure that the Free configuration is specified in the Component Properties window. If the subassembly is set to be flexible properly, the icon next to the assembly in the FeatureManager will update to show that it is a flexible subassembly, as shown in Figure 12.5.

FIGURE 12.5 Icon showing a flexible subassembly

You have learned how to make a subassembly flexible. If you ever need to toggle it back to rigid, follow the same procedure as described earlier. Now continue reading for more interesting assembly techniques.

Insert a Bill of Materials in an Assembly Document

As you probably remember, in a previous chapter you inserted a bill of materials to a drawing document. The bill of materials, however, is not limited to drawings; you can also insert a BOM inside your assembly document. This is a relatively new functionality that was introduced in SolidWorks 2009. Notice that if you created a drawing document from an assembly, inserted a BOM in it, and then created a new BOM in the assembly document, the preexisting BOM in the drawing and the one in the assembly will not be related or linked to each other. However, starting in SolidWorks 2010, you can insert a BOM that was previously saved with an assembly into a drawing document and specify that both BOMs will be linked.

Linking the BOMs means that you can update the BOM in the drawing or the one in the assembly, and any changes made to one of them will update the other one. Only the data is linked; not the formatting. You can unlink the BOMs at any time, but if you do, you won't be able to link them again.

BOMs that you create in the assembly will appear inside the Tables folder in the FeatureManager design tree. BOMs are configuration specific. If you have several configurations in the assembly, the name of the configuration to which the BOM applies will show up next to the BOM feature.

Insert a BOM in an Assembly Document

The process of inserting a BOM into an assembly document is similar to that of inserting one into a drawing. To create a BOM in the assembly document, simply select Insert ➤ Tables ➤ Bill Of Materials, fill in all the necessary information in the PropertyManager, and select a place in the graphics area to put the BOM. Don't worry; you can always change it to a different location later.

The following steps will guide you through the process of inserting a BOM in your top-level assembly; you'll use the same template that was used for the drawing document and that you downloaded from the companion website:

1. In the menu bar, select Insert ➤ Tables ➤ Bill Of Materials.

2. The PropertyManager should look familiar by now; it is the same Bill Of Materials PropertyManager as seen in drawings. Rather than spend any time describing the options again, you'll just jump right in. In the Bill Of Materials PropertyManager, click the button next to the field in the Table Template section to open Microsoft Windows Explorer.

3. Locate the FDC BOM template you used in Chapter 7, and click Open.

4. Select the Top-Level Only option in the BOM Type section.

5. The rest of the options in the PropertyManager should be set to the default values; these selections will definitely work for what you need. If you have followed the instructions correctly, the PropertyManager should look like Figure 12.6. To accept the settings and insert the BOM into the assembly, click the green check mark.

FIGURE 12.6 BOM PropertyManager

6. The BOM will now be displayed in the graphics area, attached to the tip of your mouse pointer. As you move the pointer, the BOM

will move along with it. To place the BOM, click the left mouse button. The BOM will now be anchored to that location relative to your model, and a BOM feature will show up inside the Tables folder in the FeatureManager.

Manipulate the Bill of Materials Table

Now that you have inserted a BOM inside your assembly, let's see what else you can do with it. First, notice what happens when you zoom in and out of the model by spinning the scroll wheel on the mouse up and down. Notice how the BOM scales along with the model and always keeps its position relative to the model. Now, click and hold the scroll wheel button as you rotate the model. The BOM does not move in relation to the model; instead, it remains in the same place and always faces the viewing plane, as you can see in Figure 12.7.

FIGURE 12.7 Rotating the model

But what if what you really want is to move the BOM to a different location or resize it? You can do that easily. The following steps will show you how:

1. Move the mouse pointer to inside the bill of materials in the screen.

2. Press and hold the left mouse button with the mouse pointer directly above the cross arrows in the upper-left corner of the BOM. The pointer will display a blue icon to indicate you can move the table, as shown in Figure 12.8.

	A	B	C	D	E
1	5	Shade Sub-Assy, Desk Lamp		1	
2	4	Electrical Cover		1	
3	3	default	Shaft Bearing Nut	1	
4	2	Shaft, Lamp		1	
5	1	Base, Lamp	BASE, LAMP	1	
6	ITEM NO.	PART NUMBER	DESCRIPTION	QTY.	U/M
			BILL OF MATERIALS		

FIGURE 12.8 Pointer displaying the blue move icon

3. While still holding the left mouse button, move the table to a different place in the graphics area.

4. To resize the entire table without scaling the text, move the mouse pointer to any of the four corners of the table. When the mouse pointer turns into a diagonal arrow, click and hold the left mouse button. As you move the mouse while holding the mouse button, the table will scale, and the text will remain full size, just as shown in Figure 12.9.

5	Shade Sub-Assy, Desk Lamp		1	
4	Electrical Cover		1	
3	default	Shaft Bearing Nut	1	
2	Shaft, Lamp		1	
1	Base, Lamp	BASE, LAMP	1	
ITEM NO.	PART NUMBER	DESCRIPTION	QTY.	U/M
		BILL OF MATERIALS		

FIGURE 12.9 Resizing the table

N O T E It is possible that once you're finished either moving or resizing the BOM, you'll see the BOM PropertyManager display or a flyout toolbar appear. Click anywhere in the graphics area to close them.

Hide and Show the Bill of Materials

We could say plenty more about the BOM, but we will do that in the next chapter. For now, you will simply hide the BOM in the graphics area. Notice that you're not deleting the BOM; you're simply hiding it from view. You won't be able to see it in the graphics area, but the BOM feature will remain inside the Tables folder in the FeatureManager design tree, and you can always show the BOM again at any time. Follow these steps to learn how to hide and show the BOM:

1. Move the mouse pointer inside the boundaries of the table. Right-click with your mouse. In the menu that appears, select Hide ≻ Table. The bill of materials table will now be hidden from view.

2. To display the BOM again, click the plus (+) next to the folder labeled Tables in the FeatureManager design tree.

3. Right-click the bill of materials table in the Tables folder, and select Show Table in the menu.

You are now able to insert, modify, and hide a BOM inside an assembly document. Make sure that the BOM is very well hidden, and continue reading the next section of this chapter to learn more about how to get the best out of your assembly documents.

Control the Display of the Assembly

As you may probably remember from early chapters in this book, you can control the way in which individual components are displayed in the assembly by modifying their color, appearance, level of transparency, and display mode, or simply by hiding them. All these different display settings for the individual components in the assembly can be viewed and modified through the display pane, as you can see in Figure 12.10. Remember to click the >> at the top of the FeatureManager pane to expand the display pane. Click << to hide it.

You can also create different combinations of these display settings and store them in what's known as display states.

FIGURE 12.10 Expanded display pane

Set Display States

A display state stores information about a particular combination of display settings for the components in the assembly. Although the components remain the same from one display state to another, the way they are to be displayed in the assembly will be different. For instance, you may want to hide some components in the assembly so you can have better access to those that would otherwise be covered by them. Perhaps you want to make some component transparent so you can see those that lay underneath; for example, in the case of a large model of a car, you could make the body transparent to show the engine, the transmission, and all other internal components. You could also create several display states to show different stages in the process of assembly of a product or have a display state where all components that have been purchased from a certain manufacturer are shown in the same color.

Display states should not be confused with assembly configurations. Unlike display states, assembly configurations show different versions of a same model, but in this case the components are really not the same, or at least aren't in the same positions, from one version to the other. You can use assembly configurations to show the components of your assembly arranged in different positions or to create simplified versions of your model, where the elements are shown without cosmetic details. You can also create configurations to show how the same model would look like if you changed the size or material of some of the components. Creating a configuration where some of the components have been made light-weight is also useful, especially when working with large assemblies.

All display states available for the assembly will be shown in the bottom section of the ConfigurationManager, as you can see in Figure 12.11. Notice that Default_ Display State-1 is the only display state available for this assembly at the moment.

FIGURE 12.11 Showing existing display states

Create a Display State

Creating your own display state is easy. Simply right-click any empty area of the ConfigurationManager and select Add Display State. A new display state will be added to the list, and it will also become the active display state. Just make sure nothing is selected in the ConfigurationManager before you begin. If something is already selected, you can simply left-click anywhere in the graphics area, and that should take care of the problem.

The following steps will guide you through the process of creating a new display state and making changes to the display settings for the individual components in the assembly:

1. If you haven't already, hide the bill of materials table, and double-click the scroll wheel button to fit the assembly in the screen.

2. Click the ConfigurationManager tab in the FeatureManager.

3. Right-click anywhere in the ConfigurationManager, and select Add Display State in the menu.

4. Double-click the split bar above the FeatureManager to split the pane into two equal panes. The top pane will contain the FeatureManager, and the bottom pane will contain the ConfigurationManager.

5. Click the chevron next to the tabs at the top of the ConfigurationManager to expand the display pane. If you followed all the steps carefully up to this point, it should look like Figure 12.12. The new display state you just created appears on the list with the name Display State-1. It's highlighted in blue to indicate that it's active.

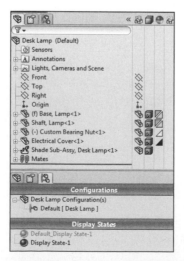

FIGURE 12.12 Showing the new display state on the list

6. Any change to a part or subassembly made in one of the four columns of the display pane will be applied to the active display state only. Click the Display Mode icon for the lamp base, and select Hidden Lines Visible in the menu.

7. Click the Hide/Show icon for the electrical cover.

If you have followed all the steps correctly, the display pane for the assembly should look like Figure 12.13.

FIGURE 12.13 Display pane after the changes to settings

Rename a Display State

So far, you've managed to create a new display state for your assembly and change the display settings for some of the components. The only problem is, the name SolidWorks gave to the display setting isn't really meaningful for you. You need to change this name to something that tells you more about the particular combination of display settings in the display state.

1. Right-click Display State-1 on the list at the bottom section of the ConfigurationManager, and select Properties from the flyout menu.

2. The Display State Properties PropertyManager will show up, just like in Figure 12.14. Under Display State Name, replace the old name with the new one, **Hidden Lines Visible**.

3. Click the green check mark to accept the name. The active display state should now appear listed under the new name in the ConfigurationManager.

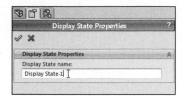

FIGURE 12.14 Renaming Display State-1

Activate a Display State

Once you start collecting multiple display states for your model, sooner or later you'll need to change from one to another. This is what is called activating a display state and can be done in a few different ways. One way to do it is by double-clicking the display state of your choice among the inactive ones in the list at the bottom section of the ConfigurationManager. Another approach is to right-click anywhere in the display pane, select Activate Display State in the flyout menu, and select a display state in the submenu. From the FeatureManager pane, you can also right-click the >> that you would usually click to show the display pane and select a display state from the list that will show up in the flyout menu.

N O T E   There's also a dedicated Display States toolbar available. To activate this toolbar, right-click anywhere in an empty area of the CommandManager, and select Display States from the list of available toolbars.

Set the Display State Mode

You may have probably noticed the option Link Display States To Configurations under the list of display states and at the very bottom of the ConfigurationManager. What exactly does this mean?

If you leave this option deselected, as you have been doing all along, then the display states are independent of the configurations in the assembly, and for this reason all display states will be available to every configuration you may have.

If, on the other hand, you select this option, then each display state you create will be assigned to only one configuration in particular, although each configuration can have more than one display state.

You are now familiar with the use of display states to control the display of the components in the assembly. Next, you'll learn about different ways in which you can select components inside the assembly.

Understand Selection Tools for Assemblies

You will now learn about several different tools for selecting components in the assembly, which can certainly come in handy from time to time. To access these tools, look for the Select button on the Standard toolbar at the top of the graphics area. You should be able to display a list of selection tools, such as the one in Figure 12.15.

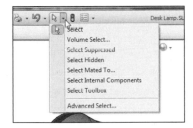

FIGURE 12.15 Selection tools for assemblies

We'll cover what each of these selection tools can do for you.

Use the Volume Select Tool

This tool allows you to visually select components in the assembly by enclosing them inside a temporary volume that you define. The way it works is best understood through an example. Follow these steps to learn how to use it:

1. If you closed the desk lamp assembly, open it again. Click the Select button, and choose Volume Select from the list.

2. For illustration purposes, you'll use this tool to select the components from the bulb subassembly. Yes, it's easier to simply select the subassembly directly from the FeatureManager, but the idea is to learn how to use this tool. Rotate the assembly so you can get a better view of the lightbulb from underneath the lamp. With the left button of your mouse, click and drag on the graphics area to define a rectangle around the components that will be selected, as shown in Figure 12.16. This rectangle is the first step in defining your volume. Note, however, that if you drag from left to right, all components inside the volume will be selected, and if you drag from right to left, then all components inside of or crossed by the volume will be selected. In this example, you are dragging a rectangle from left to right, so only components completely enclosed within the volume will be selected.

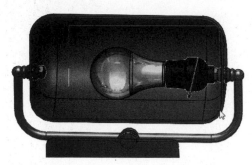

FIGURE 12.16 Defining a rectangle to select components

3. When you release the left mouse button, you should see that the rectangle has turned into a box with handles, like the one in Figure 12.17. You will probably also notice that the box doesn't seem to include all the components you wanted to select. You need to adjust this volume so it can enclose the components you want to select.

FIGURE 12.17 Volume for selection before adjustments

4. Drag the handles on the sides of the box until the volume completely encloses the lightbulb and the bulb receptacle. You may even need to rotate the model a few times to get a better view of the components. Notice that the selected components are shown in blue in the graphics area (see Figure 12.18).

FIGURE 12.18 Selected components enclosed by volume

5. Press Esc on your keyboard to finish the selection or simply initiate any other command that would be available for a multiple selection. As an example, we'll now isolate these components. Right-click anywhere in the graphics area, and select Isolate. As you may remember from Chapter 10, Isolate will hide all other nonselected components in the assembly, leaving only those you have selected visible. Make sure to click Exit Isolate to make all the components visible again before you continue.

Select Hidden

Use this tool to select all hidden components in the assembly and highlight them in the FeatureManager design tree. Follow these steps for an example of how to use this tool:

1. Make sure the Hidden Lines Visible display state that you created in a previous example is active. If it's not, activate it by double-clicking it in the list at the bottom of the ConfigurationManager.

2. Click the Select button, and choose Select Hidden from the list. You won't see any changes in the graphics area, but all the hidden components in the assembly will be highlighted in the FeatureManager design tree. In this case, the only hidden component you have is the electrical cover.

Select Suppressed

Use this tool to select all components that have been suppressed in the assembly and highlight them in the FeatureManager design tree. You don't have any suppressed components in the desk lamp assembly, but if you did, you would see that this tool works in the same way as Select Hidden. Remember, however, that unlike a hidden component, a suppressed component is not only not seen in the graphics area but is also not solved at all in the assembly.

Select Mated To

Use this tool to select all components that are mated to another component of your choice. The component itself won't be selected, however — only those that are mated to it will be. Follow these steps for an example of how to use this tool:

1. Make sure nothing is already selected in the graphics area or the FeatureManager design tree.

2. In the FeatureManager design tree, click the Shaft, Lamp component to select it; then click the Select button, and choose Select Mated To from the list of selection tools.

3. As shown in Figure 12.19, in the graphics area, three components will appear highlighted in blue: the base lamp, the custom bearing nut, and the shade mount. If needed, rotate the assembly so you can get a better view from behind. Notice that these same three components appear highlighted in the FeatureManager design tree. These are all the components that are mated to the Shaft, Lamp.

FIGURE 12.19 Components mated to the Shaft, Lamp

4. Notice that the Shaft, Lamp itself is not included in the selection. If needed, you can include it by holding down Ctrl and selecting the component from the FeatureManager design tree.

Select Internal Components

Use this tool to select all components that are enclosed by others in the assembly and out of sight. The following is an example of how this works:

1. Activate the Default_Display State-1 display state by double-clicking it from the list at the bottom section of the ConfigurationManager. Make sure that nothing is already selected in the assembly. Click the Select button, and choose Select Internal Components from the list of selection tools.

2. Although you can't quite appreciate it, the custom bearing nut has been selected, and it appears highlighted in the FeatureManager design tree.

3. Right-click anywhere in the graphics area, and select Isolate to see the custom bearing nut. Make sure to click Exit Isolate to make all other components visible again before you continue.

Select Toolbox

Use this tool to select all those components in the assembly that were inserted from the Toolbox. The components will then appear in blue in the assembly and be highlighted in the FeatureManager design tree. Since you don't have any Toolbox components in your assembly, trying to use this selection tool would only result in a message being displayed to let you know that no components met your selection criteria.

Do an Advanced Select

Use this tool to select components in the assembly based on searches for component characteristics such as mass, status, configuration name, in-context relations, display mode, and so on. The following is a quick example of how this tool works:

1. Make sure nothing is already selected in the assembly and that the display state Hidden Lines Visible is activated.

2. Click the Select button, and choose Advanced Select from the list of selection tools.

3. The Advanced Component Selection dialog box will open. From here, you'll specify your search criteria. Inside the Define Search Criteria tab, look for the Category1 column, and click the empty field below. A list of component characteristics will show. Choose Display from the list to select components based on their display mode.

4. Look for the column Condition, and click it. Display the list of options, and select =. This means that you'll define as a search criterion that the display mode of the components will have to be equal to whatever display mode of your choosing that you'll specify in just a few moments.

5. Look for the column Value, and click the empty field underneath to display the list of options. Choose HLV from the list for Hidden Lines Visible.

6. Click Apply in the dialog box. SolidWorks will then search and select all components in the assembly that have hidden lines visible as their display mode. The only component found is the Base, Lamp, and it appears highlighted in the FeatureManager design tree and selected in the graphics area.

N O T E   You can define search criteria based on more than just one characteristic by using AND or OR. For instance, you could use OR at the beginning of the next row and specify search criteria for all components that are hidden. SolidWorks would then search and select all components that are either hidden or have hidden lines visible as their display mode.

You are now familiar with all the available selection tools for assemblies and are ready to tackle your next assembly technique. Now that you know how to select the components in the assembly, let's learn how to sort them out.

Understand Assembly Visualization

Assembly visualization is part of the new functionality included in SolidWorks 2010. It provides the user with different ways to sort the components of an assembly, both in a list and in the graphics area. The components can be sorted by their properties, such as weight, mass, volume, material, and other calculated properties, or by custom noncalculated properties that you may have previously defined, such as vendor name, price, or availability. In the graphics area, the components will appear colored according to the way they've been sorted. The idea behind the color is that it helps the user visualize the relative number of components in the assembly that share the same properties.

To activate the assembly visualization tools, click the Assembly Visualization button in the Tools menu or on the Evaluate tab in the CommandManager.

The way assembly visualization works is best understood by example. In your case, you don't have any custom properties defined for any of your parts, so you'll sort them out by weight. Keeping tabs on how much the individual parts of your model weigh can come in handy when planning for costs of packaging and shipping. The following steps will guide you in the process of sorting the components in your assembly using assembly visualization:

1. Click the Evaluate tab of the CommandManager, and click the Assembly Visualization button. You will see an extra tab added to the FeatureManager pane and a list of components displayed, like the one shown in Figure 12.20. If you don't see the components being assigned different colors in the graphics area, click the colored bar on the left of the list to toggle the colors on.

FIGURE 12.20 Assembly Visualization pane

2. In the Assembly Visualization pane, the components of the desk lamp assembly will be displayed. First, ensure that the display of the value bars is turned on. Toggle the Show/Hide Value Bars by pushing the button located at the top left side of the pane. This will provide you with a graphical representation of the numeric value of the selected property.

3. Next, try toggling the Flat/Nested View button to switch between a nested view, such as the one shown in Figure 12.21, where subassemblies structures are shown as indented, to a flat view, like the one in Figure 12.22, where subassembly structure is ignored and only parts are shown. Showing the parts in the assembly is much like showing parts only in BOM tables. The double icon for some components means there's more than one instance of that component in the assembly.

FIGURE 12.21 Nested view of assembly

FIGURE 12.22 Flat view of assembly

4. If you click the File Name column header at the top of the pane, it will sort all the components in a list alphabetically.

5. Clicking the Quantity column header will sort by the number of instances for each part.

6. Click the right-pointing arrow at the head of the header bar to expand a list of available properties. As you select each property, you will see the value in the last column update to match the property displayed in the header, and, depending on the property, the value bar for each part will update. At the same time, the way the different parts in the model are colored in the graphics area will update as well.

7. Click the right arrow again to display the list of properties again. This time, select More at the bottom of the list. A new window named Custom Column will pop up to allow you to create a new column for the Assembly Visualization pane.

8. Select the field labeled Select Another Property. A list will expand to include other custom properties that are available in the parts. For instance, if materials were specified for each component, you can sort the parts by the material names. This could come in handy if you needed to order the materials used for manufacturing.

9. Below the Column Header field in the Custom Column window, you can also specify a formula that can be used for other functions. For example, you can create a column that will calculate the volume of the parts multiplied by the number of instances for each part.

10. Since you won't be creating any custom columns at this time, click the Cancel button to close the window.

11. Click the right arrow again, and this time select Total Weight in the list of available columns.

12. Click the Total Weight column header to sort the list in descending order based on the weight of the parts. The colors of each component will change to display what the weight of each part is and where it ranges in the color bar, from heaviest to lightest, as shown in Figure 12.23. Clicking the color bar will turn the display of color in the graphics area off and on.

13. Next to the color bar, there are two handles at the top and bottom of the bar. Adjusting the position of these two bars will change the color of the weight of the components. For example, if you drag the top

FIGURE 12.23 Visualization of parts sorted by weight

handle lower in the bar next to the third part in the list, the top three heaviest parts will all be the same color, red.

14. Below the parts list, you can use the rollback bar to exclude parts from the list and subsequently the graphics area. For instance, perhaps you are not concerned with parts that weigh less than 1 gram. Click and hold the left mouse button with the mouse pointer on the rollback bar. Drag the bar above the parts that weigh less than 1 gram. The components will be hidden in the graphics area (see Figure 12.24).

FIGURE 12.24 Raising the rollback bar to hide lighter components

15. So, what can you do with this information? Well, you can export the list of parts along with the values shown in the pane into an Excel spreadsheet that can be used for future calculations. Click the right arrow at the top of the pane again, and select Save As at the bottom of the list.

16. In the Save As window, browse to the location where you would like to save the Excel spreadsheet, and change the filename in the File Name field if you like. Click Save to create the spreadsheet. The spreadsheet will be saved in the specified location, and you can use it to calculate the overall weight for shipping.

17. To leave the Assembly Visualization mode, click the Assembly Visualization button in the Evaluate tab again, or simply click the exit button in the upper-right corner of the visualization pane. The Assembly Visualization tab in the FeatureManager pane will be removed.

And now that you've learned how to use assembly visualization to sort components in the assembly and extract useful information from your documents, you can continue with the next section of this chapter to learn how to create an exploded view of the model.

Create an Exploded View of the Assembly

Having an exploded view of an assembly can be extremely useful to show the relationships between all its different components, to generate instructions on how a product should be assembled, or even to make it easier to view and select components while performing stress analysis. SolidWorks allows the user to configure exploded views of assemblies, with or without explode lines included. In addition, once created, these exploded views can be edited as needed, used in drawings, or even animated.

Exploded views are configuration specific, which means that all exploded views you create will be stored in the active configuration. It's good practice to create a special configuration exclusively for the exploded view.

Create a New Exploded View

Basically, you create an exploded view by selecting and dragging the individual components of the assembly to a new location in the graphics area. This is usually done in several steps.

You use the Exploded View command to move the components, create all the necessary steps, and also edit the steps or delete them, if needed. You can find Exploded View in the Assembly toolbar or through the Insert menu. Once you are finished moving the components, you can add exploded lines to show how all these components relate to each other in the assembly. This is best understood through an example:

1. On the desk lamp assembly, make sure Default_Display State-1 is active.

2. Create a new configuration for the desk lamp assembly, and name it **Exploded**. Make that configuration active.

3. Click Exploded View in the Assembly toolbar, or select Insert ➤ Exploded View. The Explode PropertyManager will show up, and you'll be prompted to select one or more components and drag them to create an explode step.

4. Click the (+) next to the icon of the desk lamp assembly in the graphics area to display the flyout FeatureManager design tree, and select the shade subassembly by clicking it with the left button of your mouse. All components in the shade subassembly are highlighted in blue in the graphics area, and a triad or manipulator shows up, as shown in Figure 12.25. You can drag the arrows in the triad to move the component along the X, Y, or Z direction or drag the triad by its center to move it freely.

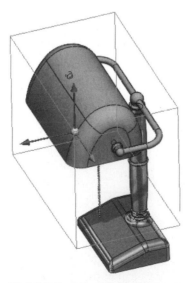

FIGURE 12.25 Triad or manipulator

5. Click the green arrow of the triad, and drag it upward. The whole subassembly will move upward, as well. If Instant3D is enabled, a ruler will appear to help you position your component, as shown in Figure 12.26.

FIGURE 12.26 Dragging the arrow of the triad

TIP You can also enter an explode distance directly from the Explode PropertyManager under Settings. To do this, you must first click one of the arrows in the triad to specify the direction and then enter the distance under Settings in the PropertyManager, click Apply, and then click Done. The component will then move the distance you entered along the axis that corresponds to the arrow you selected in the triad. A new explode step will be added to the list, and SolidWorks will get ready to accept your next selection.

6. After you place the subassembly in its new position by releasing the left button of the mouse, a new explode step appears listed in the Explode PropertyManager, and SolidWorks is ready to accept a new selection to create the next exploded step. Click the plus (+) next to the exploded step to see the list of components that were moved (see Figure 12.27).

7. Continue creating exploding steps by dragging other components. Select the shaft from the flyout FeatureManager, and drag it upward by using the green arrow in the triad, just like you did before. Place it just underneath the shade subassembly but without actually touching it; leave some

space between them. Repeat the process for Base, Lamp. As you do this, more steps appear listed in the Explode PropertyManager that by now should look like the one in Figure 12.28.

FIGURE 12.27 First explode step

FIGURE 12.28 List of explode steps so far

8. Hold down Ctrl, and select the custom bearing nut and the electrical cover from the flyout FeatureManager. By holding down Ctrl while selecting, you can drag two or more components together, if you want, even though they aren't part of a subassembly. Just one triad appears for the two of them to be moved as a unit. Use the green arrow to drag the two components downward this time. This will show up in the list of steps as Explode Step4, and both components will be listed under this step.

9. Select the electrical cover, and drag it down using the green arrow again, just like you did before. By now you should have five exploded steps on the list. Click the green check mark to close the Explode Property Manager.

Modify an Exploded View

By now you may be wondering why you didn't explode any of the components in the shade subassembly. The answer is simple. When creating an exploded view in an assembly, you can save yourself some time and effort by reusing any exploded views that have been created for the subassemblies instead of exploding their components all over again. To illustrate how this is done, we created an exploded view for the shade subassembly in advance, and you're now going to reuse it here. You may be wondering how you're going to do such a thing, when you have already closed the Explode PropertyManager. It's easy; you'll modify the exploded view you just created. Follow these steps to learn how:

1. In the FeatureManager design tree, select the shade subassembly, and click Component Properties in the flyout toolbar. Under Referenced Configuration, make sure to select the Exploded View configuration, and click OK. Now the configuration for the shade subassembly is the one that contains its exploded view.

2. In the ConfigurationManager, find the configuration named Exploded, and expand it by clicking the plus (+) next to it. You will see the exploded view you just created in the previous steps. Right-click Exploded View ExplView1, and select Edit Feature. The Explode PropertyManager will open and show all the exploded steps you had created before (see Figure 12.29).

FIGURE 12.29 Editing the exploded view

3. In the flyout FeatureManager, select the shade subassembly, and scroll down to the bottom part of the Explode PropertyManager. Click the button Reuse Subassembly Explode.

4. In the Explode PropertyManager, an extra step will be added to the list. This step contains all the explode steps for the shade subassembly (see Figure 12.30). You can always expand this step to see all the explode steps that were needed for the shade subassembly and even edit individual steps for the subassembly from here.

FIGURE 12.30 Shade subassembly explode steps added to the list

5. In the graphics area, all the components of the shade subassembly will show exploded, just as in Figure 12.31. They will be first dragged upward as one unit in Explode Step1, and then the individual components will be exploded.

6. Sometimes all you really want is to modify an individual step in the exploded view. Perhaps you would like to add a little more distance between components in the exploded view or even add or remove a component from the explode step. To edit an individual explode step from the list, right-click it, and select Edit Step. Then drag the component if needed, or click other components to add them to the step. Just for fun, right-click Explode Step5 on the list, and select Edit Step. In the graphics area, select the custom bearing nut to add it to this step. Notice under Settings that now both components are included in step 5 (see Figure 12.32). Drag the blue handle next to the electrical cover up or down to change the exploding distance in the step. Click Apply to preview the changes, and then click Done to accept them.

FIGURE 12.31 Exploded assembly

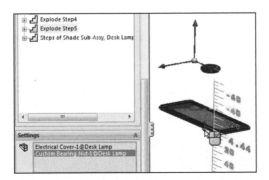

FIGURE 12.32 Including another component in the explode step

7. Undo the changes made in the previous step by clicking the circular arrow at the top of the Explode PropertyManager. Then click the green check mark to close the Explode PropertyManager.

N O T E The option Auto-Space Components After Drag in the Explode PropertyManager is really useful when exploding components that stack together in the assembly, such as screws and washers. When dragging two or more components using this option, one of the components will remain in the place where you drop it, while all the other remaining components will be equally spaced along the same axis.

Add Paths to an Exploded View

Now that you created an exploded view for your assembly, you'll also add exploded lines to it to show the relationships between the different components.

You can use the Explode Line Sketch command to add exploded lines to the view. These lines are actually 3D sketches and will always appear in phantom font. You can find the Explode Line Sketch command in the Assembly toolbar or through the Insert menu. The following steps will demonstrate how to add exploded lines or paths to the view:

1. Click the Explode Line Sketch command in the Assembly toolbar, or select Insert ≻ Explode Line Sketch. The Route Line Property Manager will appear.

2. Under Items To Connect in the Route Line PropertyManager, select the shade and the shade mount from the graphics area. The actual path created between components will depend in great part on what entity you select in the component. These entities will determine the beginning and the end of the route line. In this case, I selected a circular edge on the shade and another circular edge on the shade mount. See Figure 12.33 to make sure you are selecting the same edges.

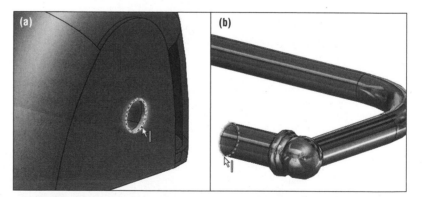

FIGURE 12.33 Circular edge selected on shade (a), circular edge selected on shade mount (b)

3. Notice the different options at the bottom of the Route Line PropertyManager (see Figure 12.34).

    When the option Along XYZ is selected, a path along the x-, y-, and z-axes is created. This option is always chosen by default. Using this option and for the two entities selected, the route line created between the two components is the one you see in Figure 12.35.

FIGURE 12.34 Options for path creation

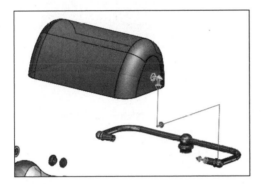

FIGURE 12.35 Path between components; XYZ option selected

If you clear the Along XYZ option, then the path will use the shortest route between components, not necessarily along the x-, y-, or z-axis, as shown in Figure 12.36.

FIGURE 12.36 Shortest route between components

The Alternate Path option simply displays an alternate route for the exploded line between components but is available only when you use the Along XYZ option. Select the Along XYZ option and the Alternate Path option to see what the alternate route would look like.

4. If you are satisfied with the route line displayed, click the green check mark in the PropertyManager to accept it. The exploded line will then show up in phantom font in the exploded view, and the PropertyManager will clear for you to select another two components and continue adding exploded lines (see Figure 12.37).

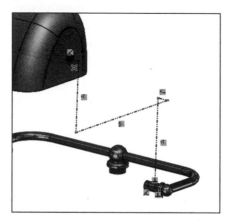

FIGURE 12.37 Exploded line between components

5. When you are done adding exploded lines to the view, click the green check mark in the PropertyManager to close it.

EDITING EXPLODED LINES

Always keep in mind that the exploded lines are, after all, 3D sketches, and as such, you can edit them later if you are not completely satisfied with the results. To edit any of the exploded lines, go to the ConfigurationManager, look for the Exploded configuration, and expand it to see the exploded view ExplView1. Expand the exploded view. The 3D sketches that correspond to the exploded lines appear listed on top of the list of exploded steps. Right-click any of these 3D sketches, select Edit Sketch to enter the Edit 3DSketch mode, and then drag the explode lines to adjust the distance between them, always based on the path options used.

Congratulations! You have worked your way through the different techniques for displaying, manipulating, sorting, and selecting in assembly documents. In the next chapters, you'll explore more about BOMs and assembly drawings. Keep on going! You are becoming experienced one chapter at a time.

If You Would Like More Practice...

If you want to continue practicing some of what you've learned in this chapter, then you could experiment creating new display states for the assembly, or finish adding explode lines to the rest of the components in the exploded view, using the same procedure that was described earlier when you added explode lines between the shade and the shade mount. Don't worry if the exploded lines are not perfect; remember that you can always edit the 3DExplode sketches later.

Watch an animation of your assembly as it collapses. To do this, right-click Explview1 in the ConfigurationManager, and select Animate Collapse from the flyout menu. All explode lines will be temporarily hidden, and you'll watch an animation of your assembly as it collapses. When you are done watching the animation, close the Animation Controller by clicking the red X button in the upper-right corner. Now watch the assembly explode again by right-clicking Explview1 in the ConfigurationManager and selecting Animate Explode.

Are You Experienced?

Now You Can...

- ☑ **Make a subassembly flexible**

- ☑ **Insert a BOM in an assembly document**

- ☑ **Use display states to control the display of the assembly**

- ☑ **Use the different selection tools available for assemblies**

- ☑ **Sort components in the assembly using assembly visualization**

- ☑ **Create and modify an exploded view of the assembly**

CHAPTER 13

Making the Top-Level Assembly Drawing

▶ Create an Exploded Assembly Drawing

▶ Link to an Assembly Bill of Materials

▶ Update the Format of the BOM

▶ Fill in the BOM

The *top-level assembly drawing* is usually one of the most important of all the drawings since it shows how the entire assembly is put together. Since the individual part drawings contain the dimensions required to make the individual components, most assembly drawings do not have dimensions unless they are required for the assembly process or are used for reference such as for the overall height and width of the assembly. It is also common to include additional information in the top-level assembly such as the process used for assembly, packaging, and storage.

In this chapter, you will be creating the last drawing for the desk lamp, which will ultimately be used for showing how the shade subassembly and the rest of the components are put together. Instead of using the top-level assembly created in the previous chapter, you should download the assembly from the companion site to ensure that the exploded view and BOM match the requirements for the steps described in this chapter. In addition to downloading the assembly, you will need to download the drawing template and save the template in the templates folder referenced by SolidWorks. If you are unsure as to which folder SolidWorks uses for templates, check the folder path by selecting Tools ➢ Options ➢ File Locations ➢ Document Templates.

Create an Exploded Assembly Drawing

In the previous chapter, you learned how to create an exploded view of an assembly. For an exploded view to be shown on a drawing, it must first be created in the assembly. After you save the assembly with the exploded view, you can then insert the model into a new drawing just like in previous chapters. Once a drawing view of the assembly is inserted into the drawing, the view must then be specified as an exploded view in the drawing view properties.

When the exploded view is shown in the drawing, usually the next couple of steps include adding the bill of materials and adding the item identifiers or balloons that are used to show which item in the BOM corresponds with the item in the exploded view. Then all that is left to do is complete the drawing and make sure all the information, including the part numbers, descriptions, and any applicable notes, is presented.

Add an Isometric View to a Drawing

After you have downloaded the desk lamp assembly and the required drawing template, you can move on with creating the assembly drawing. The only view in the drawing will be an isometric view of the exploded assembly. Many of the steps you will be using have already been described in detail in previous chapters. In fact, at this point, many of the steps in this chapter will be review and will be used to reinforce what you have already learned. For example, the following steps describe the process of adding a drawing view to the drawing:

1. Click New in the menu bar, and select the FDC Size B - No Views drawing template in the New SolidWorks Document window. Click OK to create the new drawing.

2. Press S on your keyboard, and click the Drawings button in the shortcut bar. In the Drawings flyout, select the Model View command.

3. In the Model View PropertyManager, click the Browse button. In the Open window, locate the desk lamp assembly that you downloaded from the companion site, and click Open.

4. In the Model View PropertyManager, in the Orientation section, click the Isometric button, as shown in Figure 13.1.

FIGURE 13.1 Creating an isometric drawing view

5. In the graphics area, place the isometric view of the desk lamp assembly by pressing and releasing the left mouse button. Don't worry too much about its placement at this point since you will be rearranging the view in a couple of minutes.

Adjust the Sheet Scale

After placing the isometric view of the desk lamp on the drawing sheet, you may notice that the view seems a little small when compared with how much space is available. If you were not concerned with the scale of the view in relation to the sheet format, you could have opted to change the scale of the view in the PropertyManager. However, since this will be the only view in the drawing, it should have the same scale as what is displayed in the title block. The title block reflects the scale of the sheet itself and not that of any particular view. The following steps will describe how to change the scale of the drawing, which will in turn affect the scale of the isometric drawing view:

1. Before moving on, you need to make sure that the drawing view does indeed match the sheet scale. With the mouse pointer, click the isometric view in the graphics area.

2. In the Scale section of the Drawing View PropertyManager, ensure that the Use Sheet Scale option is selected, as shown in Figure 13.2. This option will automatically update the scale of the isometric view to match the sheet scale as it is updated. Once the option is set, click the green check mark to close the PropertyManager.

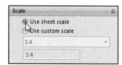

FIGURE 13.2 Specifying that the drawing view uses the sheet scale

3. To change the overall sheet scale, right-click in any blank area of the graphics area. In the right-click menu in the Sheet section, select Properties, as shown in Figure 13.3.

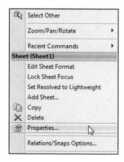

FIGURE 13.3 Accessing the sheet properties in the graphics area

 N O T E You can also access the sheet properties in the FeatureManager by right-clicking the sheet and selecting Properties in the right-click menu.

4. Near the top of the Sheet Properties window, change the sheet scale to be 1 to 3, as shown in Figure 13.4. Click OK to apply the new sheet scale. Not only will the scale in the title block update to show the new scale, but the scale of the sheet will also be displayed in the status bar.

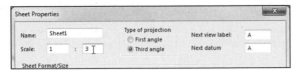

FIGURE 13.4 Specifying the sheet scale in the Sheet Properties window

Show the Drawing View in Exploded State

When the drawing view is placed in the drawing, it shows the last view that the assembly was saved as. In this case, the assembly was saved in its assembled state, not in the exploded state. To show the assembly in its exploded state, you must enable the option in the drawing view properties. The following steps describe the process to enable the option:

1. Move the mouse pointer to within the boundary of the isometric view. Click and release the right mouse button, and select Properties from the View section of the right-click menu.

 N O T E You can also access the drawing view options in the Feature Manager by right-clicking the drawing view and selecting Properties in the right-click menu.

2. In the Drawing View Properties window, select the Show In Exploded State option, as shown in Figure 13.5. Click OK to close the window.

FIGURE 13.5 Show In Exploded State option in the Drawing View Properties window

Create a Named View for the Drawing

Even though an isometric view is typically used to display exploded assemblies, sometimes the view will not properly display the components and how they are assembled. That is exactly the case in the example drawing. The isometric view of the exploded desk lamp shows all the components for this level of assembly, but it does not show how the lamp shade and shaft are put together. It may be obvious to us since we created the assembly, but it might not be clear to your target audience.

To make the assembly process of the desk lamp obvious to anybody who may look at the drawing, the drawing view needs to be rotated in such a way that all the components and how they are mated is shown. Unfortunately, because the way the shade of the desk lamp hangs, it obscures the view of where it is screwed into the shaft. In addition to an isometric view, SolidWorks has two additional views that are often helpful called *dimetric* and *trimetric*. The isometric, dimetric, and trimetric views are all forms of *axonometric projections*, which means that the model is viewed from a skewed angle to allow for better visibility of all the components.

You can access the dimetric and trimetric views in the Drawing View PropertyManager in the Orientation section. Most of the times, if the isometric view does not provide the best angle to view a model, either the dimetric or trimetric view will suffice. But in the times when even they don't work, you may find it necessary to create a custom named view. This means that in the assembly you find the viewing angle that works the best and save it with a name. Once named, the new view can be recalled in the assembly or even the referencing drawing. The next few steps will show you how to save a named view in the assembly and then use the view in the drawing:

1. Move the mouse pointer with the boundary of the isometric view again, and click and release the left mouse button.

2. In the context toolbar, select the Open Assembly button, as shown in Figure 13.6.

3. Before you can find the view that works the best for the drawing, you need to show the assembly in its exploded state. In the assembly for the desk lamp, click the ConfigurationManager tab at the top of the FeatureManager.

4. Click the plus (+) next to the Default configuration in the ConfigurationManager.

5. Double-click the ExplView1 listed below the Default configuration to activate the exploded view, as shown in Figure 13.7. You can also right-click the exploded view and select Explode or Animate Explode in the right-click menu.

> The general rule when creating drawings is that the information provided in the drawing does not leave anything for interpretation.

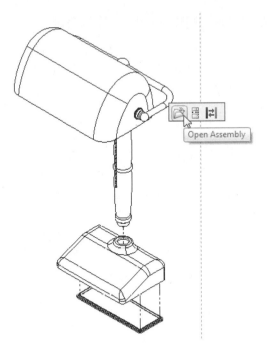

FIGURE 13.6 Opening the referenced assembly from within the drawing

FIGURE 13.7 Activating the exploded view in an assembly

6. Click and hold the middle mouse button or scroll wheel, and rotate the part around toward the front view until all the exploded components are visible and not obscured by other components.

7. Once you have settled on an orientation of the exploded assembly that would allow for the best display of all components, press the spacebar on your keyboard.

8. A new window named Orientation will pop up to display the complete list of named views for the assembly. To save the current view, click the New View button at the top of the window, as shown in Figure 13.8.

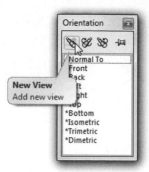

FIGURE 13.8 Creating a new named view

9. In the Named View window, name the current view **Exploded View**, and click OK to close the window.

N O T E You can recall named views in parts and assemblies from the Orientation window or in the View Orientation flyout in the Heads-Up View toolbar. Near the bottom of the View Orientation flyout, the custom named views will be listed.

10. Save the changes to the assembly, and close the assembly by clicking the X in the upper-left corner of the graphics area to return to the assembly drawing.

11. Move the mouse pointer to within the boundary of the isometric view, and click and release the left mouse button to display the Drawing View PropertyManager.

12. In the Drawing View PropertyManager in the Orientation section, you'll see a box labeled More Views. In this box, the available named views other than the primary views are listed. Click the check box next to Exploded View, as shown in Figure 13.9. Click the green check mark to close the PropertyManager.

13. Before moving on to the next section, you'll clean up the appearance of the drawing view a little by changing the display of the tangent lines. With the mouse pointer within the boundary of the view, click the right mouse button, and select Tangent Edge ➢ Tangent Edges With Font in the right-click menu.

FIGURE 13.9 Selecting Exploded View in the Drawing View PropertyManager

Link to Assembly Bill of Materials

In Chapter 7, "Creating a Simple Assembly Drawing," you inserted a bill of materials template directly into the drawing, but in the previous chapter you created a bill of materials directly in the assembly. That gives you another option to creating the BOM in the drawing. Instead of starting from scratch on the BOM, you can just insert the one that was created in the assembly. Although you can go either way and it would not have an effect on the resulting BOM in the drawing, there is an advantage to using the assembly BOM.

Using the BOM from the assembly in the drawing creates a link between the two. If either BOM is customized or items are manually added to the BOM, both will reflect this. To insert the assembly BOM into the current drawing, do the following:

1. In the assembly drawing, click S on your keyboard to view the shortcut bar. Click the Tables button, and select Bill Of Materials from the flyout, as shown in Figure 13.10.

FIGURE 13.10 Bill Of Materials button in the shortcut bar

2. The bill of materials cannot be inserted without first specifying from where the data will come. Move the mouse pointer to the drawing view, and click the left mouse button.

3. In the BOM Options section of the Bill Of Materials PropertyManager, click the Copy Existing Table option. After selecting the option, the rest of the options will disappear in the PropertyManager since the bill of materials was previously created in the assembly.

4. If there were more than one BOM available in the assembly, they would be listed in the field below the Copy Existing Table option. Since only one is available, the available BOM will be listed. Below the name of the bill of materials, ensure that the Linked option is selected. This option allows for changes made in the drawing BOM to be made to the assembly BOM, and vice versa. Since no other options are needed, click the green check mark to insert the BOM from the assembly into the drawing.

5. The BOM will be inserted, but its position in the drawing is not appropriate. Before going forward, the anchor point of the bill of material must be updated. Click the plus (+) next to the Sheet Format1 in the FeatureManager to view the anchor points for the current drawing.

6. Right-click the Bill of Materials Anchor1 listed below the sheet format in the FeatureManager. Select Set Anchor in the right-click menu. Select the upper-left corner of the title block. The BOM will snap into place.

7. Depending on the BOM template used, the BOM could be shown outside the drawing area. If your BOM does not sit directly on the title block, you may have to set the stationary corner of the bill of materials. To adjust the stationary corner, select the BOM, and then click the cross in the upper-left corner of the table to view the Bill Of Materials PropertyManager. In the Table Position section of the PropertyManager, click the Bottom Right stationary corner button, as shown in Figure 13.11. Click the green check mark to close the PropertyManager.

FIGURE 13.11 Adjusting the stationary corner of a bill of materials table

Update the Format of the BOM

When the BOM was inserted into the drawing, the format and layout are less than desirable to say the least. Before you can move on, you should make the required changes to how the BOM looks. To change the format of the bill of materials, do the following:

1. Select a cell in the bill of materials. The row and column headers of the table will be highlighted, and you'll see a cross in the upper-left corner of the table. Selecting the cross in the upper-left corner will select the entire table. After selecting the cross, the Text toolbar will be displayed next to the mouse pointer.

2. Click the Use Document Font button in the toolbar to update the font height of all text in the table to match the document properties, as shown in Figure 13.12.

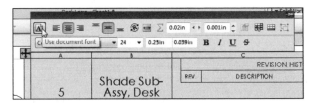

FIGURE 13.12 Use Document Font option in the Text toolbar

 N O T E The Use Document Font option means that instead of changing the font of the cells in the table individually, the font in all tables in the drawing can be changed in on the Tables tab of the Document Properties window.

3. Right-click the cross in the upper-left corner of the table again, and select Formatting ➤ Entire Table in the right-click menu.

4. Change the value of the row height in the Entire Table window to .250. Do not change the width of the columns in the window since each column will require a different value. Click OK to apply the new row height to the bill of materials.

5. After changing the height of all the rows using the Entire Table command, all the columns will update to the default value that was shown in the window. This will cause the table to become significantly bigger in width than it should be. Unfortunately, since the width of each

column requires a different value, you need to update each individually. Start by right-clicking any cell within the ITEM NO. column and selecting Formatting ≻ Column Width from the right-click menu.

6. In the Column Width window, set the width of the ITEM NO. column to be **1.019″** wide, and click OK.

7. Repeat steps 5–6 on the rest of the columns of the BOM, setting the widths of the columns to the following values: PART NUMBER = 1.843″, DESCRIPTION = 3.257″, QTY. = .844″, and U/M = .844″.

Fill in the BOM

As you have more than likely noticed, the bill of materials looks a little bare. It has a number of empty cells, and no part numbers have been assigned to any of the parts in the assembly. Many times as you are modeling a part, the last thing that may come to mind is making sure that you have added the necessary custom properties. Now that you are creating the last drawing for the project, it may be a good idea to go back and fill in those holes.

Luckily, instead of opening the parts and adding the custom properties, you can just add the required data to the cells in the BOM. Prior to 2008, changing the values in the BOM had no effect on the referenced components, but subsequent releases allowed for the BOM and referenced components to be bidirectional. As a cell in the BOM is updated, the referenced component's custom properties are updated. Also, as a component's custom properties are updated, all BOMs that reference the component are updated, as long as the link is not broken in the drawing.

As soon as you attempt to type any character into a linked cell, SolidWorks will ask if you would like to maintain the link between the component and the BOM or if you would like the new text to exist only in the drawing. In our opinion, it is usually not helpful to break the link between a BOM and its referenced component. It is probably a good idea to have the part properties reflect the drawing, but sometimes it is necessary to break the link. In those cases, it is possible to relink the BOM to the component by deleting all the text in the cell that was edited. After that, the custom properties from the part will once again be shown in the BOM.

Since you actually want the component properties to match the BOM in the assembly and drawing for this example, you will be keeping the link as you update the cells. To update the cells in the BOM and in turn update the properties of the components, do the following:

1. Select the part number cell for the lamp base, and begin typing the part number for the base as **92781-1**. As soon as you begin typing, an alert window will prompt you to keep the link of the cell to the custom properties of the part model or to break the link. Keeping the link will update the properties, which is exactly what you are trying to do. Click Keep Link in the window, and finish typing the part number.

2. Press Tab on your keyboard until the U/M cell is highlighted. When it's highlighted, update the value of the cell to **EA**, making sure to keep the link to the part.

3. Using the same techniques, populate the rest of the fields in the BOM while maintaining the links, as shown in Figure 13.13.

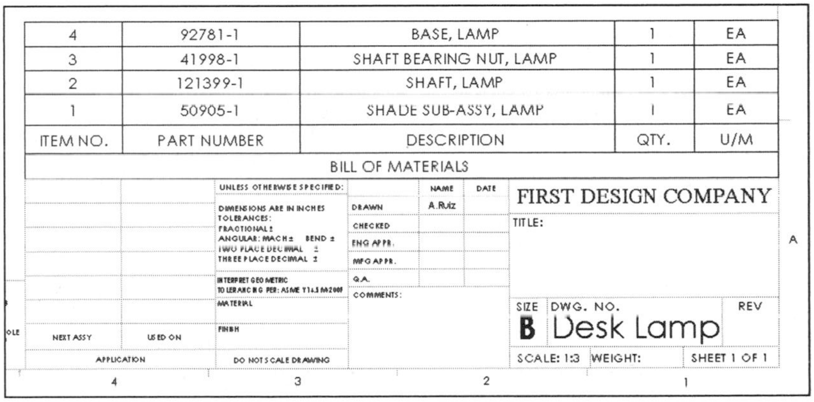

4	92781-1	BASE, LAMP	1	EA
3	41998-1	SHAFT BEARING NUT, LAMP	1	EA
2	121399-1	SHAFT, LAMP	1	EA
1	50905-1	SHADE SUB-ASSY, LAMP	1	EA
ITEM NO.	PART NUMBER	DESCRIPTION	QTY.	U/M

BILL OF MATERIALS

FIRST DESIGN COMPANY

DRAWN A.Ruiz

TITLE:

B Desk Lamp

SIZE DWG. NO. REV

SCALE: 1:3 WEIGHT: SHEET 1 OF 1

FIGURE 13.13 Completed bill of materials for the desk lamp

Add Balloons to the Assembly

You now have a filled out a bill of materials in the drawing. The reader of the drawing will eventually be able to determine the part numbers, description, and quantities of the components in the assembly. The only thing missing is for some way for the reader to know with all certainty which components are actually being shown in the drawing view. By using balloons, the item numbers in the BOM are shown attached to the various components in the drawing view. As the components are rearranged in the BOM, the value in the balloon will update. In Chapter 7, you applied balloons to the washer subassembly, and you will be doing the same process in this drawing. It doesn't hurt to cover the basics of the process again. Do the following to add balloons to the drawing by using the AutoBalloon command:

1. Press S on your keyboard, and select AutoBalloon in the Annotations flyout, as shown in Figure 13.14.

FIGURE 13.14 AutoBalloon button in shortcut bar

2. As you may remember from Chapter 7, there are a few options as to how the balloons will be arranged after they are created in the drawing. Depending on the view being annotated or the amount of allotted space in the drawing, there may be some arrangements that work better than others. But ultimately there are no rules as to which balloon arrangement is necessary in each instance. The only important factor is if the information is delineated properly.

   In our case, we believe having the balloons all in a single vertical line to one side of the model will serve best for the exploded view. In the Balloon Layout section of the AutoBalloon PropertyManager, click the Right alignment button, as shown in Figure 13.15.

FIGURE 13.15 Layout balloons in drawing to the right of the model view

3. Select the drawing view in the graphics area by clicking and releasing the left mouse button.

4. After the balloons are inserted, they will be highlighted in a blue color. As long as you do not click anything else first, you can move one balloon, and the rest will move as well. Click and hold the left mouse button while selecting one of the balloons, and move the set of balloons to the middle to have a cleaner look, as shown in Figure 13.16.

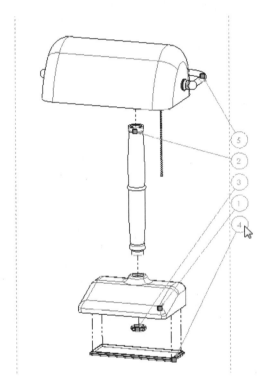

FIGURE 13.16 Arranging balloons as a group in the drawing

Reorder the Assembly Item Numbers

Last, since the balloons are shown in a straight vertical line, it might be beneficial to show the numbers in order. Not only will this give the drawing a sense of order, but it will also make it easier for the intended reader to go between the drawing view and BOM as they are trying to determine which component is which. Since the BOM in the drawing acts much like a spreadsheet, you can easily reorder the rows in the table, and the corresponding item numbers in the balloons will update as well. Using the following steps, you will reorder the components in the BOM to cause the numbers in the balloons to appear in sequential order:

1. Select any cell in the bill of materials to display the column and row headers.

2. Select the row header for the row that contains the shade subassembly by clicking and holding the left mouse button.

3. While still holding the left mouse button, drag the shade subassembly row to the bottom row of the BOM, making it Item 1. The balloon for the shade will automatically update to reflect the new item number.

4. Repeat steps 2–3 for the rest of the rows until the balloons attached to the assembly are sequentially listed with item 1 at the top, as shown in Figure 13.17.

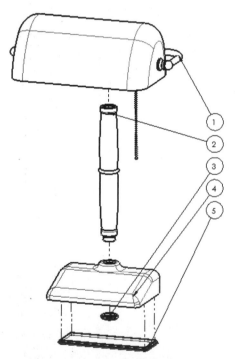

FIGURE 13.17 Balloons shown in order in the drawing

Are You Experienced?

Now You Can...

- ☑ **Insert a drawing view into a drawing**

- ☑ **Change a drawing view into an isometric view of the model**

- ☑ **Change the scale of a drawing sheet**

- ☑ **Show an assembly in a drawing view as its exploded state**

- ☑ **Create a named view in a part or assembly**

- ☑ **Display a named view in a drawing view**

- ☑ **Insert a BOM from an assembly**

- ☑ **Update component properties by modifying a BOM**

- ☑ **Reorder a BOM**

CHAPTER 14

Sharing Your Documents with Others

▶ **Create PDFs of Drawings**

▶ **Create Detached Drawings**

▶ **Save Drawings in eDrawings Format**

▶ **Export Drawings for Different Software Packages**

▶ **Use Pack and Go to Send Files**

▶ **Make Assembly Components Virtual**

▶ **Create a Part from an Assembly**

▶ **Open Files in eDrawings**

I n Chapter 5, "Creating a Revolved Part," we briefly discussed how to print a document created in SolidWorks. Hard-copy drawings are a vital tool in most organizations for use in manufacturing and document control. But what if you need to send project information outside your organization? In the past, you were often required to mail or even to have the drawing package hand-delivered to a vendor or sales team. This was often time-consuming and sometimes expensive. Luckily, with the advent of the Internet, sharing documents has become a lot more efficient.

Plenty of options are available in SolidWorks for sharing drawings, parts, and assemblies. The most common option is sending the individual files via email. However, this too can be time-consuming, if not dangerous. For example, to send a single drawing, you also need to include the referenced parts. And it is even worse for an assembly or assembly drawing because you need to also include every part and subassembly that is referenced. For extremely large assemblies, you may even need to break up the files over a couple emails since many email programs have a maximum attachment size.

Even worse than that, sending models to external vendors or sales associates can also be considered a breach in corporate security since you are sending actual model data that can be used to re-create the products. That is why many large organizations have internal regulations that prohibit sharing 3D models with outside groups. So, how can you send drawings for quotes? How can your sales team show prospective clients the exciting new designs that are being created? In this chapter, we will explore a couple of different ways you can share models and drawings with outside sources.

Many of the options we will discuss in this chapter can be used for all file formats and not just the ones used in the examples. We highly recommend playing around with each option for different SolidWorks file types to discover how each one varies.

Create PDFs of Drawings

Probably the most common way to share documents among different groups in recent years is by creating Portable Document Format (PDF) files. PDF is a file format created by Adobe Systems in 1993 for the use of sharing 2D documents. The great thing about PDF files is that they can be opened in any operating system including Windows, Mac, and Linux. The original program from which the PDF was created is not even needed to view the PDFs. In fact, the only requirement to viewing a PDF file is that you must have the most recent version of Adobe Reader, which can be downloaded for free from the Internet. That is the main reason why using the PDF file format has become so prevalent throughout nearly all organizations.

For SolidWorks users, PDF files make sharing drawings much easier for a couple of reasons. First, SolidWorks is not needed to view drawings created in PDF. There is also no need to send the actual 3D model data with the PDF. And of course, since the PDF is only a digital version of a drawing sheet with no model data, the file size is much smaller than what would be required if you were to send the model data.

Unlike many other programs, you do not need to purchase Adobe Acrobat in order to create PDF files from SolidWorks. The ability to create PDF files from drawings, parts, and assemblies is a built-in function available in all versions of SolidWorks 2010. The following steps will walk you through the process of creating a PDF file from a SolidWorks drawing; you can also apply the process to creating PDF images from parts and assemblies:

1. Open the drawing for the lamp base that you updated in Chapter 10, "Making Modifications."

2. Click the downward-pointing arrow next to the Save button on the menu bar.

3. In the flyout menu, select Save As.

4. In the Save As window, select the Save As Type field, and scroll to the entry named Adobe Portable Document Format (*.pdf).

5. Click the Options button near the bottom of the window, as shown in Figure 14.1.

FIGURE 14.1 Options button available after selecting PDF in the Save As window

6. In the Export Options window, you can select a few options that will affect how the PDF file will be created, as shown in Figure 14.2.

In the Export Options window, when creating a PDF file, there are six different options available. In most cases, there is no need to adjust any option when creating a PDF. You can often get away with the defaults, and there would be no noticeable difference. However, there may be times that small adjustments will need to be made, as in this chapter's example.

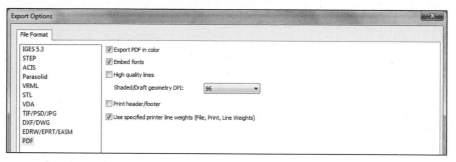

FIGURE 14.2 Export options available for PDF

Export PDF In Color   When enabled, this option creates a PDF file that matches the colors or grayscale of the document. This option is best left checked when you are creating a PDF of a part or assembly since they most often contain colors. However, we find it is often necessary to disable this option when creating PDFs of drawings. If the drawing contains both gray and black lines, text, and dimensions, then deselecting the Export PDF In Color option will create a drawing with all items shown in black, which is often better for printing.

Embed Fonts   To reduce file size, PDF files often use fonts that exist on the local PC to generate the view. This is fine as long as the fonts used to create the PDF exist on the computer opening the PDF. However, if you create a PDF from a drawing that contains nonstandard fonts, the person opening the PDF may not have the appropriate font available on their PC, and that could affect the overall look of the document. If you have any nonstandard fonts in your drawing, select this option to embed a copy of the font in the PDF, which allows the file to look the same on all systems.

High Quality Lines   This option is available only in drawings and is used to display drawing views and shaded views in high quality. If you select the option, you can also adjust the resolution of the views.

Print Header/Footer   If a header and footer are specified in the Print Options, enabling this option will include the header in the created PDF.

Use Specified Printer Line Weights   If you have line weights that are specified in the document properties, enabling this option will apply the weights to the PDF that is created. Otherwise, the default line options will be applied.

The following steps will show you how to apply any changes to the PDF options and create the file:

To adjust the thickness of the various line types, select Line Thickness in the document properties.

1. Since the drawing contains both black and gray text, you will deselect the Export PDF In Color option. This will display all text and dimensions in the drawing as black.

2. Click OK to accept the options, and click Save in the Save As window to create the PDF.

3. After clicking Save, it will take anywhere from a couple of seconds to a minute or two to create the PDF file. The time it takes to create the PDF will depend on many factors, including the complexity of the drawing and the speed of your computer. Once the file is created, you can view the PDF as long as you have Adobe Reader installed on your system. To open the PDF, simply double-click the file in Windows Explorer. The PDF is now ready to be sent to another party.

T I P   If you have an Adobe PDF printer driver installed your system, you can create the PDF by printing to the driver. The advantage of doing a Save As instead of using the print driver is that a PDF created using Save As will contain bookmarks that direct the reader to the various views in the drawing.

Create Detached Drawings

Detached drawings give you the ability to open and edit drawings without actually loading the model data into memory. Detached drawings are a great time-saver when editing drawings with complex parts or very large assemblies. The drawing loads in a fraction of the time, allowing you to edit nonmodel information in the drawing such as the title block, the notes, and the revision table. The great thing is once you have changed a drawing to a detached drawing, it doesn't have to stay that way. As long as you have the model or models used to create the drawings on your system, you can reload the model data in the drawing.

Another advantage to detached drawings is that you can send the drawing to an outside source without including the actual 3D geometry. This allows other SolidWorks users to open a drawing in the native SolidWorks format without the model or assembly. Doing it this way saves the hassle of sending each model along with the drawing, but it also prevents the release of proprietary model data.

Creating a detached drawing is easy. You don't need to create a separate drawing. You just create a drawing as you would normally, and right before you are ready to send the drawing, you save it as a detached drawing. Using the following steps, you will create a detached drawing of the lamp base that can be sent to outside vendors. Then you will reattach the model data to the drawing.

> **Sending a detached drawing is one of several ways to prevent the release of proprietary model data.**

1. If it's not already open, open the lamp base drawing that you updated in Chapter 10.

2. Click the downward-pointing arrow next to the Save button on the menu bar.

3. In the flyout, select Save As.

4. In the File Name field, give the drawing a name that will ensure that the current file will not be overwritten with the detached file you are creating. We tend to choose filenames that are a bit more descriptive to make it easier to differentiate between linked and detached drawings. So, for this case, name the new file `Base, Lamp - Detached.SLDDRW` to avoid any potential confusion.

5. Select the Save As Type field near the bottom of the Save As window.

6. In the list, select Detached Drawing.

7. Select the Save As Copy option in the window to prevent overwriting the existing drawing and losing references to the part model.

8. Click Save to create the detached drawing.

9. Close all files open in SolidWorks.

10. Click Open in the menu bar, and select the detached drawing you created. Click Open in the window.

11. Click the plus (+) in the FeatureManager next to Sheet1 to view the drawing views.

12. A new symbol will be shown next to each drawing view that looks like chain link that has been broken, as shown in Figure 14.3. This is to represent that the drawing views are no longer linked to model.

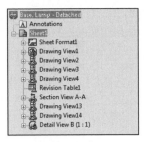

FIGURE 14.3 Drawing views shown as detached in the FeatureManager

Some users might be a little hesitant to break the link to their model data, but it is easy to reattach the model. Say, for instance, you need to make nonmodel changes to a drawing with complex model data. You can break the link long enough to make all the required changes without loading all that extra data into memory. After you make the required changes, just reattach the model, and you are ready to proceed as normal. The following steps will demonstrate how easy it is to reattach the model to a detached drawing:

1. Right-click any drawing view listed in the FeatureManager, and select Load Model in the menu, as shown in Figure 14.4.

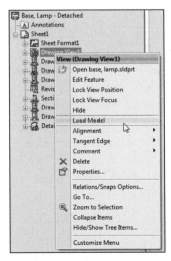

FIGURE 14.4 Loading model data in detached drawing

2. A confirmation message will be displayed asking whether you indeed want to continue loading the model data. Some users often use detached drawings as a method of viewing drawings for very complex parts and

assemblies faster than if they were attached, so keep in mind this process could take some time. However, this model is not at all complex, so the process will be very quick. Click Yes to continue loading the model.

3. If SolidWorks cannot find the file originally associated with the drawing, a window will be displayed with the message that the file cannot be located in the specified folder. If the part was moved or renamed, you can click Yes to find the file. If the part no longer resides on your system, click No to keep the drawing detached.

 N O T E   The file size for a detached drawing will be larger when compared to a regular drawing but will still be smaller than the drawing and model combined.

Save Drawings in eDrawings Format

The eDrawings software is a 2D and 3D viewer that you can download for free. The viewer can open and view SolidWorks native file formats and eDrawings formats. The advantage of using eDrawings is that you can send models and drawings to non-SolidWorks users. With eDrawings, those users can then view, section, measure, print, add comments, and even use stamps to mark the models and drawings as approved, draft, and for review.

Even though eDrawings can easily view SolidWorks native formats, saving a model or drawing in the eDrawings format will create a highly compressed file that can be much easier to send via email. If you have the eDrawings Professional software, you can also create an executable version of the document that will contain the reader program to save the recipient from downloading the viewer. The following steps will go over the process for saving a drawing from within SolidWorks to the eDrawings format. You can use the same process to export a part or assembly model to the eDrawings format as well.

1. If it's not already open, open the lamp base drawing that was updated in Chapter 10.

2. Click the downward-pointing arrow next to the Save button on the menu bar, and select Save As.

3. In the Save As Type field, select eDrawings, and click the Options button near the bottom of the window.

Before creating the eDrawings file from the active drawing, it is a good idea to take a look at the options that can be specified for the

You can download the eDrawings software for free at www.edrawings viewer.com.

file. Not all the options apply to drawings, so you will notice a couple that are grayed out and cannot be selected.

4. In the Export Options window, select the Okay To Measure This eDrawings File option to give the recipient the ability to measure various entities in the drawing by using the Measure tool in the eDrawing.

5. Deselect the Save Shaded Data in Drawings option to display the drawing views with Hidden Lines Removed.

6. Click OK to accept the options selected, and then click the Save button on the Save As window to create the file. When the file is created, it is ready to be sent to another party who has the eDrawings software installed on their system. Later in this chapter, we will briefly cover how to open eDrawings files.

Other things to keep in mind when sending SolidWorks document in the eDrawings format are that the actual data cannot be modified and that models cannot be imported into other CAD packages. That way, you can feel comfortable sending 3D models to outside sources knowing that they cannot use your feature data for tasks that you did not agree to. At most, the geometric shape can be used for 3D printing and even imported as a "dumb model" into other CAD packages.

Export Drawings for Different Software Packages

Often when dealing with vendors or other companies, you may need to import your SolidWorks data into other popular CAD packages for quoting or manufacturing purposes. When dealing with 2D drawings, the DXF file format seems to be the most common file format used for this purpose. The DXF format, Drawing Interchange Format or Drawing Exchange Format, was developed by Autodesk to allow AutoCAD drawings to be shared with other CAD packages. Because most CAD packages can interpret the DXF format, it is often used to translate 2D drawings from one non-AutoCAD software to another.

Even though this section specifically details the process for saving a drawing to the DXF file format, you can use the same steps for other file types for both 2D and 3D data. Instead of selecting the DXF file type in the Save As window, you can select from other popular file formats such as IGES, PSD, AI, ACIS, STL, and more, depending on the file type. When sharing 3D data with other CAD packages, we find that the IGES or ACIS formats work the best, but you should always check with the intended recipient to see which format they prefer.

To create a DXF file that can be imported into another CAD package from a SolidWorks drawing, do the following:

1. If it's not already open, open the lamp base drawing that was updated in Chapter 10.

2. Click the downward-pointing arrow next to the Save button on the menu bar, and select Save As.

3. In the Save As Type field, select Dxf (*.dxf), and click the Options button near the bottom of the window.

4. In the Export Options window for the DXF file, specify any additional options that you may need to set, including which version of AutoCAD the DXF should support. In most cases, you can get away with the default options unless the recipient of the file has problems opening the drawing. Once the options, if any, have been set, click OK to save them, and click the Save button in the Save As window to create the DXF file. The file is now ready to be imported into another CAD package that supports DXF files.

 T I P   There may be times that the DXF file created causes translation errors when importing the file into other CAD packages. When this happens, you can sometimes change the release level in the export options to an older version so the file will translate with no errors.

Use Pack and Go to Send Files

Imagine that your boss calls you and tells you that you need to send the assembly drawing along with the models to your manufacturing team in a different city. You quickly try to gather up all the models that are located on different parts of the network, but in the process you leave out some critical parts. The next morning you come to the office with a voice mail from an irate machinist because he was unable to complete his task. Deadlines were not met because you left out some parts from your package.

Believe it or not, this is a common scenario. It is not uncommon for different parts, including standard components, to be stored in different folders either on your local PC or on a network drive. On your PC, the assembly or drawing works great because SolidWorks is able to find all the referenced files. But another PC may not have all the same mapped drives or even access to your network. Tracking down all the referenced files, especially on very large assemblies, can be very time-consuming, and you stand the chance of missing a part or two.

Pack and Go is a handy utility built into the SolidWorks software that automatically gathers up all the parts, subassemblies, drawings, and even Design Library or Toolbox components that are necessary for the selected file to be opened. A target location can then be specified where all the files can then be copied and prepared for transmission. You can bypass the extra step of creating a single zip file since you can specify the name and location of a zip file that contains all the referenced data. That means no more calls from irate machinist, at least not for excluding models with your package.

Using the Pack and Go utility is easy, and a couple of options will help with creating a package to send to another PC. The following steps will describe the process and also cover the options available:

1. Open the desk lamp top-level assembly created in Chapters 11 and 12.

2. Click or hover over the SolidWorks logo on the left side of the menu bar.

3. In the File menu, select Pack and Go.

   A Pack And Go window will be displayed, as shown in Figure 14.5.

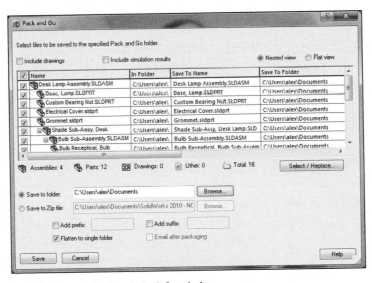

FIGURE 14.5 Pack And Go window

4. Select the Include Drawings option near the top of the window to include the associated drawings that have been created for the parts and assemblies.

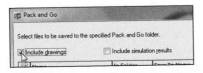

5. The list of parts and assemblies appears in a nested view to show the hierarchy of the files. If you want to show the list as a flat list without the indentions, click the Flat View option above the list, as shown in Figure 14.6.

FIGURE 14.6 Assembly structure shown in flat view

 N O T E The nested view of an assembly allows you to see how the structure of the assembly is created. It shows the relationship between parent and child documents.

6. Below the list of files a summary will provide the number of assemblies, parts, drawings, and other documents such as simulation results. Clicking the Select/Replace button will display a separate window that is used to replace the files that will be saved.

7. By default, the Save To Folder option is enabled. This option allows you to specify a new folder where a copy of each file will be placed. This option is great if you have the supporting parts, assemblies, and drawing located in different folders and you want to specify a new location for the files. To specify the new folder location, click the Browse button to navigate to the target folder, and click OK to accept the location.

8. Since this chapter is all about sharing your documents with others, you will be creating a single zip file in order to make it easier to share the models via email. Directly below the Save To Folder Option, select the option Save To Zip File, and click the Browse button.

 N O T E   A *zip file* is a single compressed file that is oftentimes much smaller in file size than the uncompressed files. Zip files can also be opened without additional software in newer versions of Windows.

9. In the Save As window, specify the location where the zip file will be saved, and specify the name of the zip file in the File Name field. Click Save to accept the location and filename.

10. The field next to the Save To Zip File option will update to include the new folder location and filename.

11. Below the Save to Zip File option, four additional options are available. The first option, Add Prefix, allows you to specify a word, letter, number, or other character that will be placed directly in front of each filename in the package. The second option, Add Suffix, does the same thing except it places the additional text at the end of the filename.

12. The Flatten To Single Folder option is used to combine files that currently reside in separate folders into one folder. Make sure this option is selected unless you want the separate folder locations to be specified in the zip file.

13. The last option, Email After Packaging, will launch your default email program and attach the created zip file automatically. Enable this option if you intend on sending the file immediately; otherwise, keep the option clear.

14. Once all the options have been set, click the OK button to create the zip file. The zip file is now ready to send to the recipient.

Make Assembly Components Virtual

We will admit that making assembly components virtual is not a very common process, but we have found it to be handy when sending small assemblies to other SolidWorks users. By making each component in the assembly virtual, there is only one file to send via email. After receiving the assembly file, the recipient can then save the virtual components externally.

1. Open the bulb subassembly that you downloaded in Chapter 9, "Modeling Parts Within an Assembly."

2. Click the downward-pointing arrow next to the Save button on the menu bar, and select Save As.

3. In the Save As window, give the assembly a new name that differs from the existing assembly. There is no need to select the Save As Copy option.

4. Right-click the first component in the FeatureManager, and select Make Virtual in the menu, as shown in Figure 14.7.

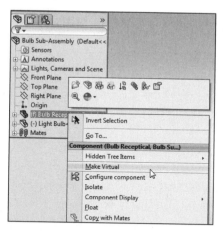

FIGURE 14.7 Making the external component virtual in assembly

5. A message will alert you that making a component virtual in the assembly will break the link to the original model. You made a new copy of the assembly exactly for that reason. Since you are fine with the outcome, click OK.

6. In the FeatureManager, the component will show that the virtual component is a copy of the original part model. This is good since you do not want to affect the original parts in any way.

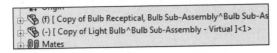

 N O T E It is not possible to make the parts of a subassembly virtual while in the higher-level assembly. You have to open the subassembly separately in order to make its components virtual.

7. After repeating the same step for the second component in the assembly, click Save on the menu bar.

8. The Save Modified Documents window will display the assembly and two parts that make up the assembly, as shown in Figure 14.8. Since each component was modified, click Save All.

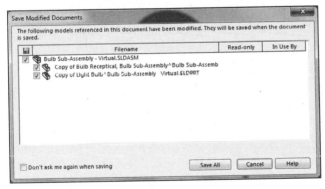

FIGURE 14.8 Save Modified Documents window

9. A second Save As window will ask whether the unsaved virtual components are meant to be saved externally or internally, as shown in Figure 14.9. Select the Save Internally option, and click OK. The assembly with the internal virtual components is now ready to be sent. The virtual components can then be saved externally on the other end.

FIGURE 14.9 Save As window with option to save internally

N O T E After making all the components internal to the assembly, the resulting file will be slightly larger than the sum of its individual files.

Create a Part from an Assembly

In the previous section, you made the components of the bulb subassembly virtual in order to send the assembly as a single file. The two drawbacks to that approach are the technique is not very useful for larger files, and the file size is slightly larger than the sum of the individual components. But the advantage is that the recipient of the file can make the components external once again and have a standard assembly with its referenced components.

Another technique that is significantly easier and works just as well for large assemblies as it does for small assemblies is creating a single part file from the assembly. Saving an assembly as a part file creates a SolidWorks part file (*.sldprt) that either contains solid bodies for each component or contains just the external surfaces as surface bodies. The resulting file is much smaller in size compared to the assembly and the parts.

When trying to decide whether this technique works for your needs, consider how the resulting part is meant to be used. If the components are meant to be used for manufacturing, then the solid bodies would need to be converted using a utility such as FeatureWorks to recognize the features, if the feature data is required. For large assemblies, this can be a painstaking process, and sending the assembly and supporting components as native SolidWorks files would probably be the best approach. However, if the feature data is not required, exporting the files as either an IGES, STEP, or Parasolid is often requested by the machinist.

We have found that using this technique works best when the part is meant solely for reference purposes or for creating renderings. We have even used this technique when we had an assembly of a vendor-supplied part and we needed to use it only as a portion of a larger assembly. By converting the parts of the assembly into solid bodies, the file size is smaller and requires less time for generation since there are no features to load into memory. The resulting part file will also not have any references to the original assembly or parts, and changes made will not update the original files.

In this instance, assume that the resulting part will be used for quoting purposes. You'll create a single part from the top-level assembly, and each component will be converted into a solid body, allowing the ability to hide and show individual components. To do this, perform the following steps:

1. Open the desk lamp assembly that was created in Chapters 11 and 12.

2. Click the downward-pointing arrow next to the Save button on the menu bar, and select Save As.

3. In the Save As Type field, select Part (*.prt, *.sldprt).
   Below the Save As Type field, you are presented with three options. Each option affects how the part will be created from the assembly.

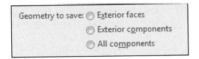

External Faces   Selecting External Faces will create a part file with no solid bodies and only the outside visible faces as surface bodies.

Exterior Components   This option will create a part file with the visible components saved as solid bodies. Any internal components that are not visible will not be saved.

All Components   This option will convert each individual component in the assembly into a solid body.

4. Select the All Components option, and click Save to create the new part file. The assembly can now be closed, and just so you can see the result, you will open the new part file.

5. Click Open in the menu bar, select the part file you just created, and click Open.

6. If prompted to proceed with feature recognition, click No.

7. The FeatureManager, instead of displaying parts and assemblies, now has a list of solid bodies, as shown in Figure 14.10. Each solid body corresponds to a component in the assembly, giving the recipient the ability to view each component individually.

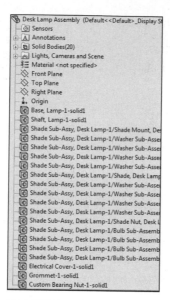

FIGURE 14.10 Components in part file converted to solid bodies

Open Files in eDrawings

Earlier in this chapter we briefly covered how eDrawings can be used as a viewer to open native SolidWorks files as well as documents saved in the eDrawings format. Before moving on to the next chapter, we'll talk about the eDrawings software. Instead of going into great detail, we will show you how to open a document in eDrawings:

1. Locate SolidWorks eDrawings 2010 in your program group, and launch the program, as shown in Figure 14.11.

FIGURE 14.11 eDrawings program

2. Select Open on the toolbar in the eDrawings window.

3. At the bottom of the Open window, you can select the file format of the file that you intend on opening, as shown in Figure 14.12. Select eDrawings Files (*.edrw).

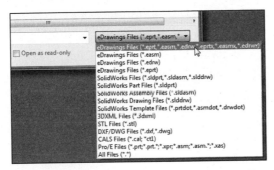

FIGURE 14.12 Selecting the eDrawings file type

4. Browse to the folder that contains the Base,Lamp.edrw file created earlier, select the file, and click Open.

5. The graphics area of the eDrawings software will now display the drawing. You will notice that it looks exactly like the drawing in SolidWorks. In fact, it is the same. The only difference is that you cannot make any changes to the drawing.

6. The user interface for eDrawings also a lot simpler from that of SolidWorks. As you can see in Figure 14.13, the tools available can be used for rotating, zooming, and measuring. That is why the program is perfect for non-SolidWorks users; it is an easy program for anybody to use.

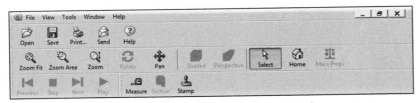

FIGURE 14.13 eDrawings toolbars

7. After you are finished exploring eDrawings, close the program.

If You Want More Practice...

Throughout the chapter we introduced you to a couple of ways to save files to make it easier to send them via email. Now would be a good time to experiment with other SolidWorks files using some of the other export formats listed in the file type field of the Save As window. Many of the file formats have their own set of options. To learn more about the options, you can click the Help button in the lower-right corner of the Export Options window.

Are You Experienced?

Now You Can...

☑ **Save a document as a PDF file**

☑ **Create a detached drawing**

☑ **Use the Pack and Go utility**

☑ **Save a document in the eDrawings format**

☑ **Save components of an assembly as virtual components**

☑ **Save an assembly as a part file**

CHAPTER 15

Creating Your Own Templates: Part 1

▶ Create Part and Assembly Templates

▶ Create a Title Block for Parts and Assemblies

▶ Create a Custom Property Tab

SolidWorks comes preinstalled with templates for drawings, parts, and assemblies as well as sheet formats for the most common drawing sheet sizes. These templates are enough to get you started when using SolidWorks, but as you become more familiar with the software, you may find yourself making changes to these templates every time you create a new document. Many companies use these templates as the starting point when creating their own standard templates, and that is exactly what you will be doing in this chapter and the next one.

Starting with the out-of-box templates that ship with SolidWorks, you will be creating a whole slew of custom templates that can be used throughout this book. In this chapter, you will be concentrating on parts and assemblies as well as some additional items that can be used in the two environments. Usually it is the duty of the CAD manager or one of the power users in an organization to create the templates that will be used, but there may be a time when that power user is you. With the skills you will learn in these two chapters, you will be able to create the most commonly used templates in SolidWorks.

Create Part and Assembly Templates

In the previous chapters, when it came time to create a new part or assembly, you were instructed to download the appropriate templates from the companion website. In the next couple of sections, you will be re-creating those templates starting with the preinstalled templates. Creating custom templates of parts and assemblies allows you to set document properties, custom properties, and other modifications for each only once.

Few organizations need to create more than one part and assembly template to be used for all modeling. But we have found that it is sometimes helpful to have multiple templates to match different part and assembly types. For instance, if your organization commonly creates models in both English and metric units, you can create separate templates for each unit type.

Create a New Part Template

The part template that comes installed with a fresh copy of SolidWorks will work for many users without any modifications. When creating the templates that ship with the software, SolidWorks did a great job of determining the combination of common document properties that works for most users. However, we have always found the need to make small changes, such as the number of decimal places on dimensions, the default display settings, and even what document properties are included by default. Custom templates can then be shared throughout your entire organization.

Making refinements to the SolidWorks templates is not only a huge time-saver in the grand scheme of things, but it is also extremely easy. Since you will be starting with the standard templates available, you will only need to make a couple of small modifications. The following steps will take you through the process of making the small changes that are required for the examples in this book:

1. Click New in the menu bar.

2. If the New SolidWorks Document window is displayed in the simplified mode that displays the three basic templates for parts, drawing, and assemblies only, click the Advanced button in the lower-left corner of the window, as shown in Figure 15.1.

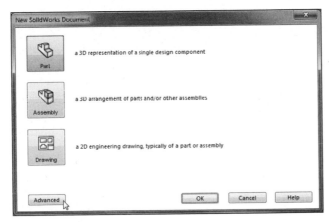

FIGURE 15.1 New SolidWorks Document default novice view

3. In the New SolidWorks Documents window, select the Part template, and click OK.

Access the Document Properties

Document properties are properties that affect the active document only. Many times there a few properties that need to be adjusted to meet your needs, and instead of remembering to do so each time you create a new part model, you can do it once in the template. All future parts created from the template will contain the properties

SolidWorks will save your preference so that each time you create a new document, the Advanced view will be the default view.

specified in the template. In this section, you will make some minor changes that will affect how you create the parts in this book.

 N O T E   Modifications made to a template will affect only future parts. Existing part models will not be updated at the same time.

1. In the menu bar, click the Options button.

2. On the top of the Options window, there are two tabs. The first tab, System Options, is where you can specify settings that will affect the entire SolidWorks environment regardless of which file is currently open. The second tab, Document Properties, is used to specify options in the currently active document only. Select the Document Properties tab to view the categories for the settings available for the current document type.

3. Since the current document is a part, the section on the left of the Document Properties window displays the option categories that apply to part documents, as shown in Figure 15.2. To view the options for each category, select the category, and the options will be displayed to the right of the section.

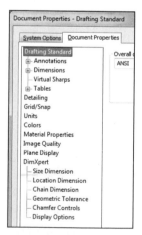

FIGURE 15.2 Document properties category list

Explore the Option Categories for Parts

Although the sections on the Document Properties tab are available in parts, assemblies, and drawings, the options available in each section relate directly to the active document. As you become more comfortable with working in SolidWorks, you may encounter the need to make fine adjustments in your document. Sometimes it could be as basic as adjusting the units in the document, but there are many more adjustments that can be made. The best way to learn about each option is to click the Help button in the lower-left corner of the window, and the description of each option in the window will be described in the Help window. Although the help file is a good start, the best way to learn is to play. We recommend opening a new document and experimenting with different settings so you can get a good feel for what can be done. The following are the main categories on the Document Properties tab along with a brief description of each:

Drafting Standard   Use this option to select a drafting standard for detailing in the active part file, as well as to rename, copy, delete, export, or load saved custom standards.

Detailing   This property contains options related to how annotations are handled in the active document including text size, importing of annotations, and the cosmetic thread display.

Grid/Snap   This property contains options on the grid display in the active document as well as the snap functionality.

Units   The Units options are used to specify the unit system used such as IPS and metric. You can also adjust the precision of dimensions, mass properties, and simulations.

Colors   In part models, you can adjust the colors for each feature type. For other color adjustments such as for the background, text, planes, and others, you should use the system colors. Sometimes it is nice to customize the colors, but if you send the file to another user, the difference may become confusing.

Material Properties   You can adjust the density of the material specified for the active part as well as how the section for the material is displayed.

Image Quality   You can adjust the display quality for the active part. You can also make further adjustments in the Performance section of the System Options section.

Plane Display   You can adjust options such as the color, transparency, and intersection of planes.

DimXpert   You can specify the default settings affecting how annotations are added to a part using DimXpert.

N O T E   DimXpert allows you to fully annotate a part model, satisfying the requirements of ASME Y14.42-2002, which eliminates the need to have separate part drawings.

Specify Options for the Part Template

The following options are the most common adjustments we usually need to make to a part file. To save time, we often make these adjustments at the template level so all our parts will be created correctly. These options are also the ones used when you created the parts and assemblies in earlier chapters. To set the document options for the template, do the following:

1. In the category list, select Units to specify the units used for dimensions, Mass Properties, and Motion Studies.

2. Ensure that the IPS unit system is selected in the Unit System section, as shown in Figure 15.3.

FIGURE 15.3   IPS unit system specified in the document properties

3. Below the Unit System section is a table that lists the type of units in the document that can be updated. For the Length row, select the downward-pointing arrow to view the number of decimals that can be specified when adding dimensions to the part model, as shown in Figure 15.4. Select the entry that shows .123; this entry will specify that dimensions in the part model and sketches will be displayed with three places after the decimal point. If you require more precision, you may specify that dimensions are displayed with up to eight numbers after the decimal points.

    After changing the number of digits that will be displayed in dimensions in the table, a bubble will display a message alerting you that since the current standard has been modified, the standard name will be changed to "ANSI-MODIFIED." At this point, you will continue making changes to the settings.

Type	Unit	Decimals	Fractions	More
Basic Units				
Length	inches	.12		...
Dual Dimension Length	millimeters	.12 / .123	2	...
Angle	degrees	.1234 / .12345		
Mass/Section Properties		.123456		
Length	inches	.1234567		
Mass	pounds	.12345678		
Per Unit Volume	inches^3			
Motion Units				
Time	second	.12		
Force	pound-force	.12		
Power	watt	.12		
Energy	BTU	.12		

FIGURE 15.4 Specifying the precision of length dimensions

4. Select Image Quality in the options tree.

5. At the top of the Shaded And Draft Quality HLR/HLV Resolution section, you can use the slider to set the image quality resolution of the part in the graphics area, as shown in Figure 15.5. By default, the slider position is in the middle of the bar. As you move the slider to the left toward the Low end, the quality of the model is of lower quality, but it does speed things up. By moving the slider toward the High end, the quality increases, but it can make some older systems run painfully slow. Move the slider to the ¾ position on the High end of the bar.

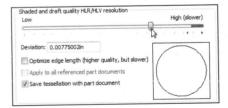

FIGURE 15.5 Adjusting the display resolution of the active part

Save the Modified Document Settings

Even though you made only a couple of adjustments to the document properties, it wouldn't hurt to save these changes for future documents. Not only will it come in handy when creating other templates that are meant to share the same options, but you can use the saved changes to update the properties of existing documents. Once a modified standard is saved, it can be recalled in another document, and the options will be applied. The following steps will save the settings that you will then use to create your assembly template with the same options.

 N O T E   You can also store standards files on a network location, giving other users in your organization the ability to update any files they may have to the current company standards.

1. In the option tree at the very top of the list, select Drafting Standard.

2. Click Save To External File.

3. In the Save As window, browse to a folder that you want to be used for storing data from SolidWorks.

4. Specify the name that you want to save the modified standard as in the File Name field, or accept the default name `ANSI-MODIFIED.sldstd`. Click Save to save the standard and to close the Save As window.

Save the New Part Template

Before you can use a new template for creating parts, you must save it in the appropriate templates folder. As soon as it is saved, it will become available in the New SolidWorks Documents window. If the template is saved in a shared network location, all SolidWorks installations that point to the template folder will also be able to use the template. Save the template as described:

1. Click OK in the lower-right corner of the Document Properties window to save the changes made to the part template.

2. Once all the options have been set per the previous sections, click Save in the menu bar.

3. In the Save As window, browse to the location where your SolidWorks templates are located. In most cases, the location for templates in SolidWorks 2010 is `C:\ProgramData\SolidWorks\SolidWorks2010\templates`.

 N O T E   If you are not sure which folder SolidWorks is using for its templates, you can find out in System Options ➢ File Locations ➢ Document Templates.

4. Click the Save As Type field, select Part Templates (*.prtdot) from the list, and change the File Name to **NER Part** to prevent overwriting your existing template. Click Save to the part template.

N O T E If you downloaded the part template in previous chapters, you can just overwrite the version downloaded or choose to skip saving the changes you made.

5. Close the part template, and it will be ready for use the next time you need to create a part file.

Create a New Assembly Template with Saved Standards

In the previous section, you created a new part template from a preinstalled template. You made adjustments to the document properties to better suit your needs, but that leaves the assembly template that you still need to create. Instead of following the same steps to create a new assembly template, you can use the modified standard template you previously saved. Since the document properties you specified in the part template correspond exactly with those you need to adjust in the assembly template, there will be no issue with importing the same options. The following steps will describe the process of importing settings previously saved.

 N O T E Not all document properties are available in all three SolidWorks file formats. There may still be additional adjustments that cannot be shared among the different formats. If you're not sure what has been imported, it is always a good idea to check how the options were applied.

1. Click New in the menu bar, and select the Assembly template in the New SolidWorks Document window. Click OK to open the new assembly file.

2. If prompted to begin the new assembly by inserting parts in the file, click the red X in the Begin Assembly PropertyManager.

3. Select the Options button in the PropertyManager, and select the Document Properties tab in the window.

4. In the Drafting Standards section, click the Load From External File button.

5. Browse to the folder in the Open window that contains the standards file you saved in the previous section. Select the file, and click Open.

6. Since all the document properties were already specified in the saved standards, all that is left to do is click OK to save the changes and close the Document Properties window.

7. Click Save in the menu bar, and browse to the folder that contains the templates that SolidWorks uses.

8. Change the file type in the Save As window to Assembly Templates (*.asmdot), and change the filename to **NER Assembly**. Click Save to save the new template. After saving the template, it is safe to close the file since there are no other options you need to set at this time.

Create a Title Block for Parts and Assemblies

In SolidWorks 2007, the ability to annotate a part or assembly was introduced. The addition of the DimXpert command gave the ability to add notes, dimensions, and even geometric tolerancing to the actual 3D model. Then in SolidWorks 2009, a bill of materials table was introduced to the 3D environment. Over the years, SolidWorks has made these enhancements to satisfy the requirements of ASME Y14.41-2003, Digital Product Definition Data Practices.

The Digital Product Definition Data Practices standard specifies how drawings can be eliminated by fully annotating a 3D model. In lieu of a 2D drawing, the design intent can be properly described to all viewing parties with a fully dimensioned part and any other manufacturing, documentation, or quality information. But there was always one bit of critical information that was very difficult to present to the recipient of the part — the information that would normally be delineated in the drawing title block. This information could always be included in notes in the model or even a separate document, but nothing beats the simplicity of a drawing title block.

Luckily, in SolidWorks 2010, the ability to add a title block to the 3D environment was finally introduced. You can insert a 2D title block table in a part or assembly that can mimic that of a drawing. No matter in what direction a 3D model is being viewed, the title block and its text will always remain normal to the viewing plane. Just like a title block in a drawing, you can link text to document or custom properties and have the text dynamically updated as the properties are updated.

You can create a title block for 3D components from scratch by modifying a table that resembles a spreadsheet. By adding rows and columns, merging cells, and adding text, you can create a floating title block that may look almost exactly like the one on your 2D drawings. Also, SolidWorks has a standard template that matches the title block in the standard drawing template. Since you will be creating your drawing template from the standard template, you can do the same with the title block template.

Insert a Title Block into a Model

Whether you are inserting the standard title block template or your own title block that matches your organization's layout, the process is the same. You launch the Title Block Table command; a title block is then placed directly into the graphics area of a part or assembly. You can then move the inserted title block anywhere in the 2D plane that is normal to the viewing plane. The following will describe the process for inserting a title block into a model.

1. Click New in the menu bar, and select the NER Part template you created earlier. Click OK to open the part.

2. In the menu bar, select Insert ➤ Tables ➤ Title Block Table, as shown in Figure 15.6.

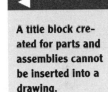

A title block created for parts and assemblies cannot be inserted into a drawing.

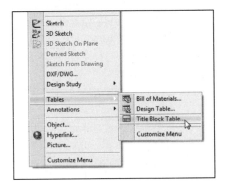

FIGURE 15.6 Title Block Table tool in menu

3. Click the Browse For Template button in the Title Block Table PropertyManager, as shown in Figure 15.7.

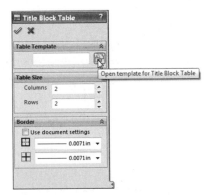

FIGURE 15.7 Opening the template for the title block table

4. Browse to the folder that contains your title block templates. By
   default the location should be C:\Program Files\SolidWorks Corp\
   SolidWorks\lang\english. Select the file named
   Title Block.sldtbt, and click Open.

T I P   You can determine the folder path for your title block templates
by referring to the Title Block Table Template path displayed in the File
Locations tab of the System Options window.

5. Click the green check mark in the Title Block Table PropertyManager
   to insert a generic title block into the part file.

6. As you move the mouse pointer in the graphics area, the title block
   table will move with the pointer. Click and release the left mouse button to place the title block in the part. Once inserted into the part
   model, as shown in Figure 15.8, you can begin to make your required
   modifications.

FIGURE 15.8 Unmodified title block table

Edit Static Text in the Title Block

The title block table that is included with SolidWorks almost perfectly matches the
title block in the drawing sheet format, but you still need to make some changes
before you can begin using it. If you required a different layout of the fields in the
title block, you would have to adjust the cells by hiding and showing cell borders
much like what is done in most spreadsheet programs. Luckily, since right out of
the box the layout matches the one that you will also use in your drawing, all you
need to do is update the text in the fields.

The first thing you will do is update the company name field and adjust its appearance. The company name field is one of the fields that is actually meant to contain
static text. This means that the text will not be linked to any outside property and

will not be dynamically updated by the system. Using skills that you have more than likely already gained in most spreadsheet programs such as Microsoft Excel, edit the text by following these steps:

1. Since this is only for practice, you will be using a fictitious company name. Select the field that currently shows the label <COMPANY NAME>, and in all capitals type **FIRST DESIGN COMPANY.**

N O T E Changes made to a title block in a part or assembly do not affect a title block in a drawing. The two types of title blocks are completely independent from each other.

2. In the floating toolbar that become visible while editing the field, you can specify the typeface of the text in the cell. Using the toolbar, set the font name to Times New Roman, set the height to 14 points, and make the text bold, as shown in Figure 15.9.

FIGURE 15.9 Adjusting the font of text in the title block table

Link Text to System Properties

Just like in a drawing, text in a title block table can be dynamically linked to properties in the active document. This means that as the value of the property is updated either manually or by another process, the text in the title block will update automatically. This helps automate many steps when using the title block table, reducing working time and eliminating the chance of forgetting to update information in the title block.

When linking a text item in the title block to a property, the property can be a custom property that already exists in the active model or a system-controlled property such as the mass of the model. If a property does not exist in the model, you can add one ahead of time or while linking properties to the text item.

System-controlled properties are read-only properties that SolidWorks uses in documents for various tasks such as controlling the filename, calculating the mass of the part, or even keeping track of who edits the document.

Linking to the system-controlled properties can save you the step of defining your own properties since the information is already generated. In the title block, you want to link to the property that returns the filename since most organizations save the file as the part number. When the filename changes, the part number field in the title block will automatically be updated. The next few steps will describe how you can connect to the filename property:

1. Double-click the cell used for the Part No. field, and click the Link To Property button.

2. Click the downward-pointing arrow in the empty field to view the available properties. In addition to the custom properties that were added previously, the available system options are also displayed. Select SW-File Name(File Name), and click OK.

3. Specify that the font of the cell is to use the document font.

Add a New Custom Property for Linking Text

In the next few steps, you will notice that the area for the description appears to be one cell, but as you click inside, you will see that it is instead a group of cells. Because the title block cannot merge cells, you will need to select one of the cells that will contain the description. As long as the description for the active document does not get too long, you will be able to maintain a link to the custom property. But if the title gets too long, the automatic height adjustment of the cell will affect the layout of the table. To avoid this, when it appears that a description will be too long, you will need to remove the linked text and instead manually break the description up into smaller parts and type each into the individual cells. As you can imagine, it would be easier to use if the description did not get too long; all the descriptions in this book should not have an issue.

In the previous section, the property that was used for linking text in the table was already available in the document. This will not always be the case when it comes time to design a new title block. In the next couple of steps, you need to link the Description field to a property that is currently not part of the document. You could go back to the Properties window discussed in earlier chapters and add the Description property prior to linking it to the title block. Luckily, you will not need to exit the title block before adding the property. You can actually call the custom properties window from the Link To Property window and add the property. Follow these steps to add a property while editing a title block table:

1. Double-click the cell in the Description field, and click the Link To Property button, as shown in Figure 15.10.

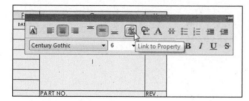

FIGURE 15.10 Link To Property button in the floating text toolbar

2. This time instead of selecting a property that is currently being used in the active part, you will be specifying a new one. Click the File Properties button in the Link To Property window. You can open the custom properties window by selecting File ➢ Properties ➢ Custom in the menu bar.

3. In the first available row of the Custom tab in the Summary Information window, select the downward-pointing arrow in the Property Name column, and select Revision from the list, as shown in Figure 15.11.

FIGURE 15.11 Selecting the description from the available property list

4. In the Value/Text Expression column of the same row, type X to be used as a placeholder. If you did not add a value to the field, once the window was closed, the new property would not be saved. Click OK to close the Summary Information window and accept the addition of the new custom property.

5. Before you can exit the Link To Property window, you need to point to the newly created Description custom property. Click the downward-pointing arrow on the empty field in the Link To Property window. In the menu, select the entry named Description, as shown in Figure 15.12. This is the new property that you just added in the previous step. Click OK to close the window.

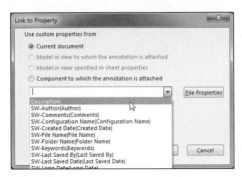

FIGURE 15.12 Selecting the Description property in the Link To Property window

6. While the description field is still selected and the toolbar available, click the Use Document Font button, as shown in Figure 15.13.

FIGURE 15.13 Specifying that the font in the title block table uses the document font

Link to a New Property with a System-Generated Value

Previously, you linked the Part Number field to the system-controlled property for the filename. When you specified the File Name property in the Link To Property window, you may have noticed that the list seemed a little short and lacked some properties. The list only displays the properties being used in the active document in other areas such as the Custom tab in the Properties window, but these are not the only system-controlled values available.

In this section, you need to add a property that will be used for the material callout on the title block. You could always link the Material field to a custom property that you will then manually edit to include the material name. But SolidWorks has a large material database included, and it only makes sense to make use of that.

You can actually link the Material field to the name of the material that is applied to the part for simulation purposes. If the material is changed, the property will update the title block.

To add the link to the title block, you still need to create a property that then displays the material applied. This is not something that is displayed as a property in the part, so it will not be shown on the pull-down list in the Link To Property window. To add the property and link it to the title block, follow these steps:

1. Double-click the cell in the Material field, and click the Link To Property button again.

2. In the Link To Property window, click the File Properties button to access the Custom tab of the Summary Information window.

3. Select the Material in the pull-down list for the property name.

4. This time, instead of typing a value, you will be selecting a predefined document property. Click the downward-pointing arrow in the Value/Text Expression field, and select Material from the list, as shown in Figure 15.14. Once selected, the value will default to Material <not specified> until one is selected in the part model. Click OK to close the Summary Information window.

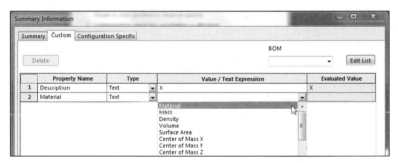

FIGURE 15.14 Linking the Custom property to a system-generated value

5. In the Link To Property window, select the entry labeled Material in the blank field, and click OK to accept the changes.

Finish the Title Block Table

There are still a number of cells that you may like to go through and link to properties, but they are not required for the exercises in this book. Instead, using the steps described in the previous sections, make some final changes to the title block:

1. Double-click the cell in the Name column that corresponds with the DrawnBy entry. Using the steps described earlier, create a new custom property named DrawnBy, and set the value to your name. Link the property to the Name Entry text box. If necessary, you can adjust the text height to fit your name completely in the space allotted.

2. Zoom into the tolerance block, and update the values per those shown in Figure 15.15. Also, add the text ASME Y14.5M-1994 in the cell used to specify the standard that interprets the tolerances.

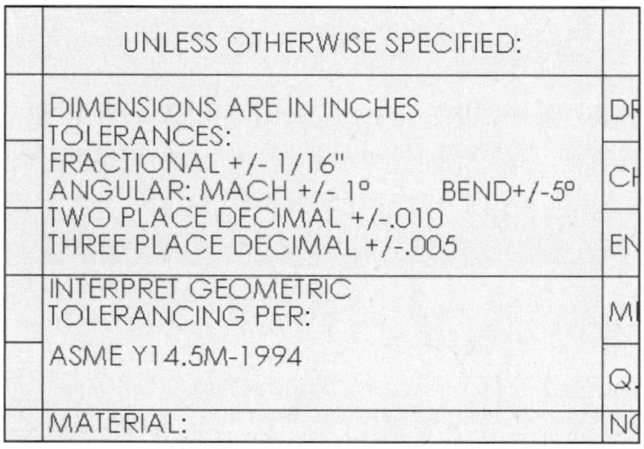

UNLESS OTHERWISE SPECIFIED:	
DIMENSIONS ARE IN INCHES TOLERANCES: FRACTIONAL +/- 1/16" ANGULAR: MACH +/-1° BEND+/-5° TWO PLACE DECIMAL +/-.010 THREE PLACE DECIMAL +/-.005	DR CH EN
INTERPRET GEOMETRIC TOLERANCING PER: ASME Y14.5M-1994	MI Q.
MATERIAL:	NC

FIGURE 15.15 Updated values for tolerance block in title block

Save the Title Block Template

The changes you made to create your own title block template are now complete, but these changes are only reflected in the current document. To keep from making these changes every time you decide to enter a title block into a model, you will need to save the title block as a template. Once saved, you can insert the title block into any SolidWorks part or assembly, and you can even place the title block on a shared drive that can be accessed by all users on the network. To create a new title block table template, do the following:

1. As you move the mouse pointer within the boundaries of the title block, the column and row headers will be displayed, and a cross will appear in the upper-left corner, as shown in Figure 15.16. Right-click anywhere within the title block, and select Save As in the menu.

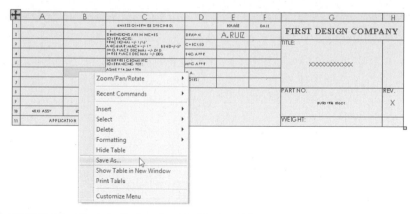

FIGURE 15.16 Saving the title block table as a template

2. Browse to the folder that contains the rest of your title block templates, and save the template as **NER Title Block**. Click Save to save the template for later use.

Create a Custom Property Tab

Throughout the various chapters in this book, we described a number of ways that properties can be updated in any given document type. Depending on your needs, you can add and edit custom properties in the Summary Information window, through the bill of materials, or even directly in the drawing title block. The information available in the custom properties is quickly becoming more and more critical.

SolidWorks 2010 introduced a new way to interface with the document custom properties that will make it easier for other users. Many organizations have some custom properties that are used in different areas such as BOMs, title blocks, Windows Explorer, and PDM programs such as SolidWorks Workgroup PDM and SolidWorks Enterprise PDM. Instead of relying on the user to know exactly what properties need to be added to a document, not only does the custom property tab give the user a clean, easy-to-use interface, but it also displays properties even if they are not part of the active document.

The custom property tab displays a custom-designed interface. The interface is normally developed by the CAD manager or power user. The property page can then be saved locally or on a network location that SolidWorks will look up every time the tab is selected. The following steps will describe the process for

> The custom property tab displays properties even if they are not part of the active document.

creating a custom properties page for the active part; you can apply the same steps to making a page for assemblies and drawings:

1. Click the Custom Properties tab in the task pane, as shown in Figure 15.17.

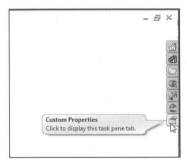

FIGURE 15.17   Custom Properties tab in task pane

2. Since no custom property page has been created for part files yet, there will be a message prompting you to create a new custom property file. Click the Create Now button. A separate program called the Property Tab Builder will launch. This program is used to create the custom property tabs for part, assemblies, and drawings.

 N O T E   You can also find the Property Tab Builder program in the SolidWorks Tools folder in the SolidWorks 2010 program group of the Windows Start menu.

Edit Group Boxes in the Property Tab Builder

Group boxes are used in the custom property tab to group similar properties together. By creating logical groups of properties, users will be able to better understand the intent of the properties and ultimately make it easier for them to decide which information needs to be entered. When creating a new custom property page, there is one group box, and before adding other controls to the page, you will change the caption to describe what the properties are that are contained in the box.

1. In the main pane of the Property Tab Builder, select the group box, as shown in Figure 15.18.

2. In the pane to the right, change the caption to say **Part Information**, and ensure that the Custom Property Attributes option is set to

Expanded. This will enable the box with its contents to be visible and readily available.

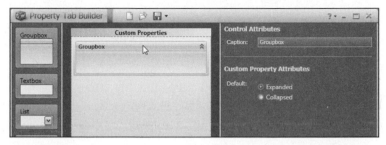

FIGURE 15.18 Selecting a group box in the Property Tab Builder

N O T E At least one group box must exist in the property page since controls can be added to group boxes only.

Add Controls to the Property Tab

Now that the group box on the new tab has a proper caption, you can start adding controls to the page. Controls are used to create the interface of the custom property tab when in use. The controls include a text box for entering in text, a list to display multiple choices for a property, a number field, and a check box and radio button for selecting options.

You must add a control to the page first and then connect it to the appropriate custom property. Each control has a different set of options available in the right pane of the Property Tab Builder. The following steps will describe the process of adding the controls and selecting their options:

1. Select a text box from the left pane by clicking and holding the left mouse button. Drag and drop the text box into the Part Information box shown in the main pane.

2. Set the caption for the new text box to say **Description**. Below the Control Attributes section, point the Name field to the Description property. The Type field should remain as a Text type, and leave the Value field empty.

3. Below the Value field there are two buttons that are used to specify how the custom property is written. The first button specifies that the value will update the custom property tab, and the next button will update the configuration-specific tab, as shown in Figure 15.19. Make sure that the Show On Custom Tab button is selected.

N O T E   Placeholder text does not need to be added to a control on the custom property tab in order for it to be available like it does in the custom property tab of the Properties window.

FIGURE 15.19   Selecting the Show On Custom Property Tab button

W A R N I N G   Two controls cannot point to the same property name even if they are used for custom properties and configuration-specific properties separately.

4. Following the same steps described, add additional text boxes for the Part Revision, Drawn By, and Material properties.

5. Make sure that the Material text box you added is selected, and in the right tab, select the downward-pointing arrow in the Value field. Select [SW-Material] from the list, as shown in Figure 15.20. This will show what material is applied to the part; if one is not already specified, it will give the user the ability to apply a SolidWorks material to the active part.

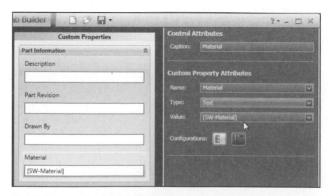

FIGURE 15.20   Additional controls added to the Custom Property tab

Save and Use the New Custom Properties Tab

The new custom property tab is complete and ready to go, but before you can use it in a part model, you need to save the new page as a template for a part file. Once the file is saved in a folder that the SolidWorks system options recognize for the storage of custom property tab files, it will instantly be available in the tab. The following steps describe the process for saving the file as a custom property tab for part files.

1. Click Save at the top of the Property Tab Builder.

2. The appropriate folder should already be displayed in the Save SolidWorks Properties Template window, but if that is not the case, browse to the folder that the File Locations tab specifies in the System Options dialog box.

N O T E   Custom property tab files can also be stored on a shared network location. The UNC path can then be added to the System Options dialog box on all computers that will use the file.

3. Keep the filename as Template.prtprp, and click Save. Click the X in the menu bar of the program to close the program.

4. Once you save the properties template, it will be automatically be ready for use in the SolidWorks part environment. Click the custom property tab in the task pane. The tab will display the properties as they were created in the Property Tab Builder, as shown in Figure 15.21.

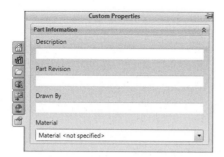

FIGURE 15.21 New Custom Properties tab

If You Would Like More Practice...

In the previous section, you created a custom property tab for a part file. Using the same steps, create a new tab for a drawing and assembly as well. After creating the new tabs, add some controls to the tabs; then go back and link the title block table to these new properties. One of the things we always tell people is that the best way to learn how to use SolidWorks is to just have fun and play. That is the only way you can learn for yourself what can and cannot be done.

Are You Experienced?

Now You Can...

- ☑ **Create a part template from an existing template**

- ☑ **Make changes to the document settings of a new part template**

- ☑ **Save modified document settings for future use**

- ☑ **Create an assembly template from a saved standards file**

- ☑ **Insert a title block table into a model**

- ☑ **Create a new title block table template**

- ☑ **Link text in a title block table to the document properties**

- ☑ **Create a new custom property tab**

CHAPTER 16

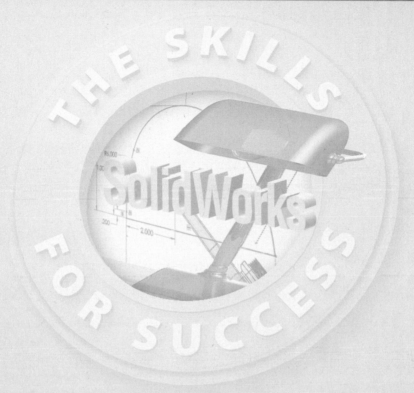

THE SKILLS
SolidWorks
FOR SUCCESS

Creating Your Own
Templates: Part 2

▷ Set the Sheet Size and Drafting Standards

▷ Start the Drawing Template

▷ Create the Drawing Title Block

▷ Learn Timesaving Features for the Drawing Template

▷ Save and Share the Sheet Format and Template

I n the previous chapter, you began the process of creating many of the templates you have used throughout this book. In this chapter, you will be concentrating on the templates and sheet formats used in the chapters related to drawings. As you have seen in the previous chapters, templates that are properly set up can save you a lot of time.

When you created the templates for parts and assemblies, you needed to make only a couple of adjustments to the document settings. However, drawing templates have more that can be included, which makes the process of creating drawings with them even easier. In addition to specifying document settings in the template, you can add the sheet format, title block, revision table, and notes. In this chapter, you will be creating a template for size B (11″ × 17″) drawings (and you can use the same process for the other drawing sizes). Creating drawing templates for each drawing size is the most common practice, since users will not need to change the sheet format for each drawing.

Set the Sheet Size and Drafting Standards

The first thing you need to do before creating a new template is to open one of the standard templates that ships with SolidWorks. The standard drawing templates offer a good starting point, allowing you to make some changes to the document settings and then add elements to finish the template. The first settings that you will adjust are the ones that specify the size of the drawing and the drafting standards that will be used when the template is put to use. To start the process, follow these steps:

1. Create a new drawing by clicking the New button on the menu bar, and select Drawing Template on the New SolidWorks Document menu. Click OK to open the drawing.

2. Since you will be using an 11″ × 17″ sheet for all the drawings in this book, you will start by creating the template for size B. Right-click anywhere in the graphics area, and select Properties in the menu.

3. In the Sheet Properties window shown in Figure 16.1, select the B size standard format, and click OK.

 N O T E   Beyond A size sheets (8½″ × 11″), drawings are drawn in the Landscape orientation.

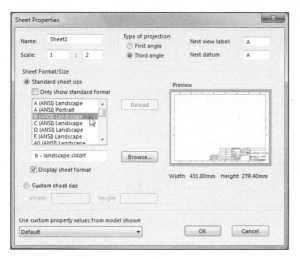

FIGURE 16.1 Sheet Properties window

Explanation of the Sheet Sizes

There are many standard sheet sizes worldwide, each controlled by the appropriate standard in each country. The two most common standards that specify paper dimensions are ANSI/ASME Y14.1 and ISO 216. The ANSI/ASME standard, the most commonly used standard in North America, refers to page sizes with a letter designation. Paper sizes in ISO are represented with the letter A, B, or C followed by a number. Since all the examples in this book are based on the ANSI/ASME standards, we will refer to page sizes as either A, B, C, D, or E. Table 16.1 describes the ANSI/ASME sheet sizes and shows the closest ISO A size.

TABLE 16.1 ANSI Sheet Sizes

Name	Inches × Inches	MM × MM	Alias	Similar ISO A Size
ANSI A	8.5 × 11	216 × 279	Letter	A4
ANSI B	11 × 17	279 × 432	Tabloid	A3
ANSI C	17 × 22	432 × 559	-	A2
ANSI D	22 × 34	559 × 864	-	A1
ANSI E	34 × 44	864 × 1118	-	A0

T I P   Instead of changing the sheet size for each drawing as you create them, save time by using the process described in this chapter to create templates for each drawing sheet size.

1. When you begin creating a new drawing, SolidWorks may prompt you, depending on your settings, to select a part or assembly from which to create a view. Since we are not going to be creating views just yet, click the red X in the PropertyManager.

2. Select the Options button in the Menu Bar.

3. Select the Document Properties tab at the top of the window to access the properties and settings that will only apply to the active document.

4. First we need to ensure that the Overall Drafting Standard displayed in the Drafting Standard field is set to ANSI. If another drafting standard is shown in the field, click the downward pointing arrow and select ANSI from the list.

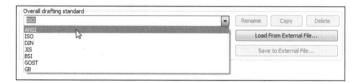

The Different Drafting Standards

Before proceeding, even if you do not use any other drafting standard, it is a good idea to be aware of each of the standards shown in the Drafting Standard section. A *standard*, when referring to drawings, is a set of guidelines and definitions that ensures drawings created meet the same minimum requirements. Without standards, drawings created by different organizations and individuals would each be created differently and would be near impossible to interpret correctly.

SolidWorks supports seven drafting standards that are used in different parts of the world. Each standard specifies how dimensions are placed, how values are represented, how arrowheads are drawn, and so on. The seven drafting standards and a brief explanation of each are as follows:

ANSI   ANSI refers to the American National Standards Institute, a nonprofit organization that maintains standards for many aspects of drawings to ensure that products produced in the United States can be used worldwide. The ANSI drafting standard in SolidWorks also includes American Society of Mechanical Engineers (ASME) standards such as ASME Y14.1, ASME Y14.5, and ASME Y14.100.

ISO   ISO refers to the International Organization of Standardization, which is comprised of representatives from standards organizations worldwide. The ISO drafting standard in SolidWorks encompasses many different standards including ISO 129:1985 and ISO 406:1987.

DIN   DIN refers to the Deutches Insitut für Normung, which translated into English is the German Institute for Standardization.

JIS   JIS refers to the Japanese Industrial Standards. Many JIS standards are derived from or are equivalent to various ISO standards. In fact, a few of the JIS standards end with a five-digit number that corresponds to an ISO standard.

BSI   BSI refers to the British Standards Institution. The BSI group was the first standards organization in the world and played a major role in the development of ISO. Many of the BIS standards are equivalent to ISO standards.

GOST   GOST refers to Gosudarstvennyy Stardart, which translated from Russian means State Standard. GOST was originally developed by the government of the Soviet Union but is now maintained by the Euro-Asian Council for Standardization, Metrology, and Certification.

GB   GB refers to Guobiao, which translated from Chinese means National Standard. GB standards are maintained by the Standardization Administrations of China. Many GB standards are based on or are equivalent to ISO standards.

All the examples and instruction in this book are based on ANSI/ASME standards.

Start the Drawing Template

Just like with part and assembly templates, a few document properties are extremely helpful to specify in the template rather than trying to remember to set them when creating a new drawing. The next couple of sections will describe the process for specifying the unit system, adjusting the line fonts, and setting the projection types. Each of these areas can easily be set when creating a new drawing, but keep in mind that it may not always be you who will be creating drawings on your system or in your organization. Specifying these and other settings in the drawing template helps ensure that each drawing created will meet the minimum requirements in your organization.

Select a Unit System

Now that you've set the sheet size and drafting standard, you must set the drawing units. In previous chapters, you set the units for the one document you were working on. That change affects that document only and does not propagate to other similar documents. Since the current drawing will become a template, there will be no need to set the units again when you create a new drawing. To set the units in the template, do the following:

1. On the Document Properties tab of the Options window, select the Units option in the menu.

2. Ensure that Unit System is set to IPS (inch, pound, second), and set the number of digits following the decimal to three for the length. Setting this option will ensure all the dimensions created on the drawing will be set to three decimal places unless they are individually changed.

 N O T E   Some organizations use more than one unit system when creating drawings. If you tend to use more than just the IPS unit system, it's a good idea to create additional templates for each unit system used.

Draw Line Fonts

Line fonts in drawings are the appearance of different types. Line types, when used on drawings, are specified in ASME Y14.2M-1992, *Line Conventions and Lettering*. The standard specifies the various types of lines as well as the thickness that they will be displayed on a drawing. How a line is represented is an important aspect of a drawing since each line type has its own meaning. For instance, a visible line is used to represent the visible edges or contours of a part. If a visible line were shown not as a solid line but as a phantom line, it would be very confusing to the reader of the drawing.

SolidWorks uses 11 available line types to represent different areas of a drawing. Each of the 11 line types has a Style setting, a Thickness setting, and an End Cap Style setting. SolidWorks has done a good job of setting the style and thickness of each line type to meet the requirements of the ASME standard. You will find that you will rarely need to adjust the line fonts unless your company has its own set of standards. For example, many companies we have worked for require the tangent edge of a part in drawings be changed to a solid line instead of a phantom line. After polling a few industry friends in other companies, we find that this is a common practice.

A *tangent edge* is the edge created when a curved surface meets the adjacent surface. By default the line type is set to be represented as a *phantom line*, as shown in Figure 16.2.

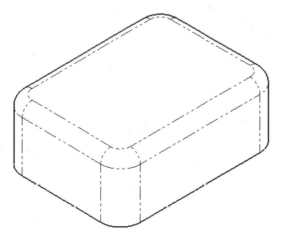

FIGURE 16.2 Drawing view shown with phantom tangent line

We're partial to showing a tangent line as a solid line because it has a cleaner look in drawings. To change the line font of tangent edges, do the following:

1. On the Document Properties tab of the System Options window, select Line Font.

2. Select Tangent Edges in the Type Of Edge section of the window.

3. In the Style drop-down menu, select the Solid line type, as shown in Figure 16.3.

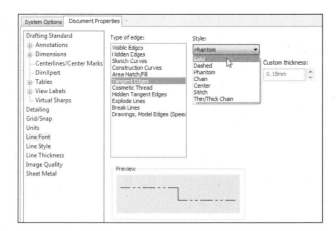

FIGURE 16.3 Selecting a solid line type

N O T E   For the specified line type to be shown in drawing views, the views' tangent edge display must be set to Tangent Edges With Font in the right-click menu for a selected view.

Set the Projection Type

To properly define a part, a drawing consists of views to show the part from different perspectives. The views are projections of the part perpendicular to the viewing plane of the drawing reader. The surfaces that are parallel to the viewing plane are represented in their true form, but surfaces that are not parallel will be foreshortened. This system of creating drawings is referred to as *orthographic projections*, and the views are referred to as *orthographic views*.

The six basic views of an orthographic drawing are Front, Back, Top, Bottom, Right Side, and Left Side. All six views are not required on every drawing; if you can fully define a part with two views, then more would be overkill. The drawing views are laid out in a standard arrangement based on the *projection type*; the projection type used depends on what part of the world you reside in. In the United States, the projected views are arranged based on the Third Angle projection type, and other parts of the world use the First Angle projection type.

Third Angle projection   Drawings created for use in the United States are usually made using the *Third Angle projection type*; however, some companies in other parts of the world have adopted the same system to prevent confusion when working with U.S.-based customers. Basically, the Third Angle projection type creates the image of a part projected onto the viewing plane that is placed between the observer and the part. Figure 16.4 shows the six basic orthographic views using the Third Angle projection type.

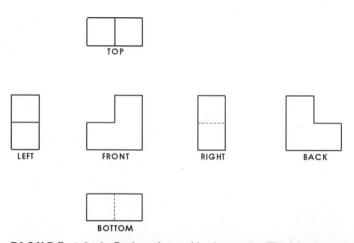

FIGURE 16.4 Basic orthographic views using Third Angle projection

First Angle projection   All the drawings in this book will be created using the Third Angle projection type, but it still would not hurt to at least understand the difference between the two projection types. *First Angle projections* have the image of the part projected onto a viewing plane with the part between the observer and the view. We know it sounds confusing, but look at Figure 16.5, and you should notice the difference between the two projection types.

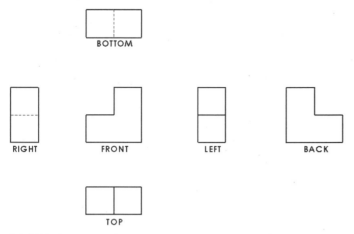

FIGURE 16.5 Basic orthographic views using First Angle projection

If your template is not set to the correct projection type, it could cause confusion. Although it should already be set properly, the following steps describe how to set up the projection type in your new drawing template:

1. Right-click in an empty area of the drawing sheet, and select Properties from the menu.

2. In the top middle of the Sheet Properties dialog box there is a section labeled Type Of Projection, as shown in Figure 16.6. Select the Third Angle option, and click OK to close the window.

You can also get to the sheet properties by right-clicking the drawing sheet in the FeatureManager and selecting Properties from the menu.

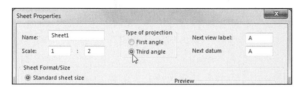

FIGURE 16.6 Selecting the type of projection in Sheet Properties

Create the Drawing Title Block

The *title block* is an important area of a drawing since it contains all the information required to allow the drawing to be properly interpreted, identified, and archived. In mechanical drawings, the title block is located in the lower-right corner of the drawing and is divided into rectangular sections that provide quality, administrative, and technical information. Although each organization has its own regulations or standards that define the content of the title block, every title block must have at least the drawing title, part number or ID number, and the legal owner of the drawing.

Custom Properties Defined

In SolidWorks, you can create drawing title blocks that link to metadata, or properties, in the drawings and models being drawn. All SolidWorks documents (parts, drawings, and assemblies) have three types of properties that can be referenced:

- ▶ System-defined properties
- ▶ Custom properties
- ▶ Configuration-specific properties

System-defined properties consist of information generated by the system such as the author, created date, filename, material, sheet scale, and so on. These properties are read-only and cannot be directly edited but are instead based on another action in the software.

Custom properties are user-defined properties that can be used for the description, vendor, company name, checked by name, drafter name, and so on.

Lastly, *configuration-specific properties* are custom properties defined by the user that apply only to specific part and assembly configurations.

File properties are used in a number of ways. Properties that are defined in parts and assemblies can be used to automatically populate fields in a drawing or bill of materials and can even be used by a PDM or ERP system. Properties in drawings can also be used to automatically update notes in different areas of a drawing in addition to being used by a PDM or ERP system. The advantage to having various locations referencing the document properties is that making changes in one location can update all the referenced areas at once. Not only is this a huge time-saver, but it also helps prevent overlooking important information that should be updated.

There is more than one way to view and change custom properties for any SolidWorks document. The first is by using the Custom Properties tab in the task pane if the Property tab was built by your system administrator or CAD manager. If the Custom Property tab is not an option, you can access the custom properties from the menu bar. Follow these steps to view, add, or edit custom properties:

1. Hover over or click the SolidWorks logo on the left side of the menu bar, and click File from the menu headings.

2. In the File menu, select Properties.

3. Ensure that the Custom tab is selected in the Summary Information window.

The *Custom tab* is where you can view, edit, or add custom properties for the active document. The *active document* refers to the part, assembly, or drawing that is currently being shown in the graphics area of SolidWorks. On the Custom tab, a table displays the currently assigned custom properties. Each custom property is shown on a numbered row, and each row is divided into four columns: Property Name, Type, Value/Text Expression, and Evaluated Value. If there are no custom properties specified for the active document, the table shown on the Custom tab will be blank. In this case, you can easily add new properties. Figure 16.7 shows the Custom tab for the Summary Information window prior to adding properties.

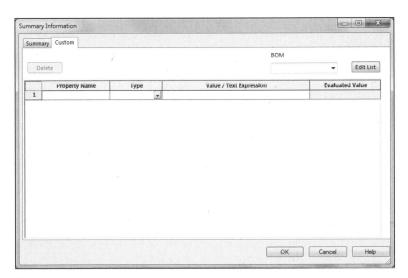

FIGURE 16.7 Custom tab for the Summary Information window

Add a New Custom Property

In the following steps, you will add a new custom property that will specify who drew the drawing:

1. In the first row, click the cell in the Property Name column.

2. After clicking the cell, a downward-pointing arrow will be shown. The arrow lets you know that there is a drop-down list available with predefined property names. Click the downward-pointing arrow, and scroll through the list until you find DrawnBy. Select the DrawnBy property name from the list, as shown in Figure 16.8. DrawnBy will now be shown in the cell.

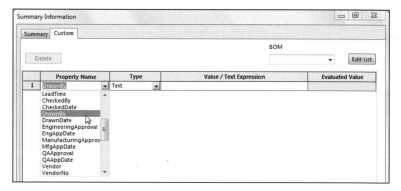

FIGURE 16.8 Adding a custom property

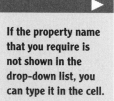

If the property name that you require is not shown in the drop-down list, you can type it in the cell.

3. The next column in the row is where you specify the value type for the property. Click the field to view the available options for the value type: Text, Date, Number, Yes, or No. The Type field specifies the value or expression that can be associated with the property. Since the DrawnBy property will require a name, select Text as the value type.

4. Click the cell for the Value/Text Expression column, and you will see another downward-pointing arrow. Click the arrow to see the SolidWorks parameters, global variables, and linked dimension names that can be associated with the named property. Selecting one of the values will automatically populate the named property with the system-generated value or a variable or linked dimension name that you specify in the document. For this property, you will instead be typing in a value to be assigned to DrawnBy. Type your first initial and last name, and hit Enter.

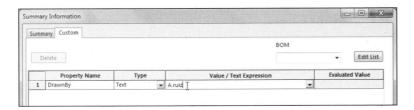

After entering your name into the Value/Text Expression field, the last cell in the Evaluated Value field will display the text you entered, and a new row will become available for the next custom property. The Evaluated Value field is used to show the actual value of the custom property. This is useful if you had selected a SolidWorks parameter, global variable, or linked dimension since it would display the actual value instead of just the name.

Manage the Drawing Title Block

Prior to SolidWorks 2009, the custom properties associated with the text items in the drawing title block had to be modified using the Properties window described earlier. In 2009, SolidWorks introduced title block management to facilitate the process of updating title block entries by allowing you to directly edit static text and text linked to properties. It used to be, prior to 2009, that when you directly edited a text item that was linked to a custom property, the link was broken, and the property was not updated. Now, when a title block is defined, the text can be directly edited, and the associated properties will be updated as well.

To take advantage of title block management, the hotspot and text items must be defined in the drawing template. The *hotspot* is the area of the drawing that will be used to initiate the Title Block Manager. When the mouse pointer lies within the boundary of the hotspot and the left mouse button is clicked, the Title Block Manager will be launched, allowing the user to edit the defined text items.

Setting up the title block in your drawing template is completely optional, but we suggest taking the extra five minutes to do it since it can be a tremendous time-saver in the long run. In this example, you will set up a template to use the Title Block Manager just to make things easier as you create drawings. Perform the following steps with the drawing that you currently are editing to make the drawing template:

1. In the FeatureManager design tree, click the plus sign next to the item labeled Sheet1 to expand it.

2. Under the Sheet1 item, when expanded, right-click the Sheet Format1 item and select Define Title Block, as shown in Figure 16.9.

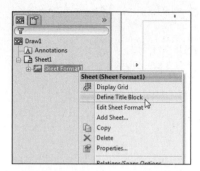

FIGURE 16.9 Creating a hotspot with the Title Block Manager

A black rectangle will be created that encompasses the entire title block area of the drawing, as shown in Figure 16.10. This will become the hotspot for the Title Block Manager. You can resize the rectangle at this point to better fit the title block, if so desired. You can move it by selecting the boundary and dragging it, and you can resize it by dragging one of the four corner handles.

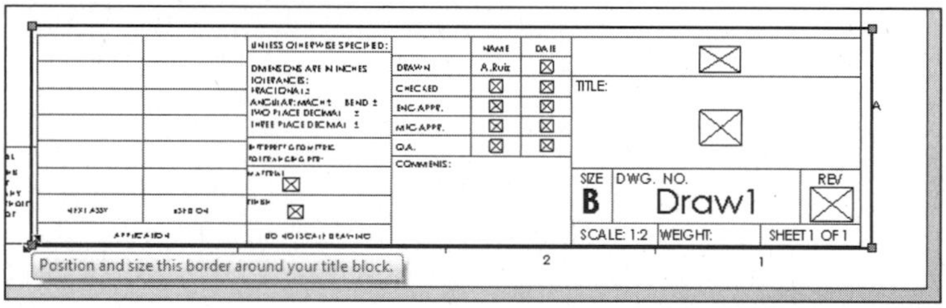

FIGURE 16.10 Border of hotspot defined with the Title Block Manager

3. With the hotspot defined, it is time to select the text items that will be used to populate the drawing title block. Zoom in closer into the title block area of the drawing to give you better access to the Company Name, Title, and Drawing Number areas.

4. Select the text box in the title block that would normally contain the drawing description. The box will turn blue indicating that the box has been designated as a title block note, as shown in Figure 16.11.

The text item will also be added to the PropertyManager in the Text Fields area, as shown in Figure 16.12. In the Text Fields area, each selected text item will be displayed with an automatically assigned number indicating the tab order. The custom property name that the text is linked to will also be shown on the same line.

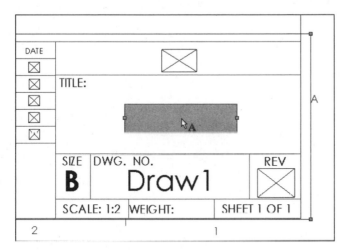

FIGURE 16.11 Specifying title block notes

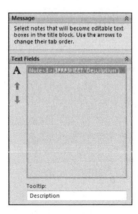

FIGURE 16.12 Text Fields area in the PropertyManager

5. Select the rest of the text items shown in Figure 16.13, which include Drawn By, Drawn Date, Checked By, Checked Date, Eng. Approval, Eng. Approval Date, Mfg. Approval, Mfg. Approval Date, QA Approval, QA Approval Date, Material, and Finish.

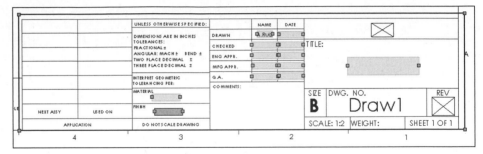

FIGURE 16.13 Selecting text items to manage a title block

You can now easily edit the title block items when you begin working on drawings in the future. Since you are making this addition to the template file, all future drawings will have the same text items selected for the title block, saving you tons of time in the long run.

Edit the Sheet Format

In the previous section, you set up the text items that are normally edited by the user in order to make them easier to change. These text items, such as the description, revision, drawn date, and material, are often different for each drawing and must be quick and easy to edit, but there are areas of the title block that should not need to be changed very often. Depending on your company standards, you may need to include confidentiality statements, general tolerances, or standard interpretation statements. Since these are often controlled by company policy, they do not need to change after they are added to the drawing template.

To add these and other similar statements to the title block, you need to edit the actual sheet format. Many people consider the terms *sheet format* and *sheet template* to be interchangeable, but they are indeed two different things, each with their own function. One way we often explain the sheet format to new users is to think of it as a sheet of clean paper with the border and title block preprinted. The only thing that needs to be done to the sheet of paper is to fill in the pertinent information and add the drawing views. A template starts with the sheet format and then additional items such as predefined drawing views, notes, and revision tables.

The next few steps will walk you through the process of editing the title block to make it ready for prime time. You'll enter into Edit Sheet Format mode and make the necessary changes.

1. Right-click anywhere on the drawing space, and select Edit Sheet Format from the menu, as shown in Figure 16.14. If the option is not

visible, it may be hidden from view on the menu. You can expand the full menu by clicking the chevron at the bottom of the menu.

FIGURE 16.14 Entering Edit Sheet Format mode

2. You are now able to edit the actual sheet format. At first glance, you may not notice any significant difference, but if you look closer, you will notice that many lines in the title block are blue and some of the text items show the custom property name. Zoom into the section of the title block that contains the proprietary and confidentiality statement.

In the current mode of the drawing, you can begin to make changes to the sheet format that will be reflected on any drawing that uses the format. The following will describe how to edit the sheet format that will be used for the drawing template.

Edit Notes

Your company may have its own confidentiality statement that it requires, but in this case you will stay with the same statement. The only thing you will need to do is add your fictitious company name where you are instructed to do so. To do this, you will need to edit the note that makes up the confidentiality statement. One of the most common tasks that you will perform in a drawing is editing notes, so let's take this opportunity to look at the process.

A *drawing note* can contain anywhere from a single character all the way up to a multiline text item much like what you would find in the general notes of a drawing. When editing notes, you can choose to overwrite the entire length of the text or edit specific words or characters. It all depends on the number of times you click the mouse button when selecting the text.

Clicking the text once will allow you to make adjustments to the entire text using the Note PropertyManager. Figure 16.15 shows the PropertyManager, which is broken up into sections for Style, Text Format, Leader, Border, Parameters, and Layer.

FIGURE 16.15 Note PropertyManager

Clicking twice highlights the text in black, which allows you to edit the entire text box, as shown in Figure 16.16. At that point, if you were to type anything, it would replace the entire text with what you type. That is great if you want to replace the entire text, but for our case, it is not what we want to do.

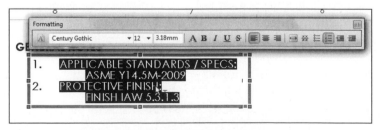

FIGURE 16.16 All text selected in text box

Clicking once again will deselect the entire text and place a cursor where you clicked. At this point, you can press Delete or Backspace to remove letters and words, or you can highlight words with the mouse pointer, as shown in Figure 16.17. If you are familiar with Windows, the process for editing text is pretty close to that of most Windows applications.

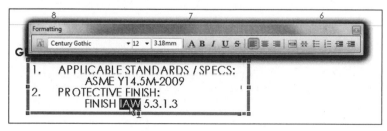

FIGURE 16.17 Selecting a word in the text box

When editing the text box, you may have noticed a new toolbar, the Formatting toolbar. This toolbar gives you quick access to the tools needed to change the format of the selected text. From the Formatting toolbar, you can change the font type, size, color, justification, and other parameters.

Edit Other Text Boxes in the Title Block

Now that you are familiar with the basics of editing text, you can make the required edits to the various text boxes in the title block:

1. Double-click the text that makes up the proprietary and confidentiality statement. The text should be all highlighted in black.

2. Click and hold the left mouse button with the pointer at the beginning of the place marker phrase <Insert Company Name Here>, and move the pointer to highlight the entire phrase, as shown in Figure 16.18.

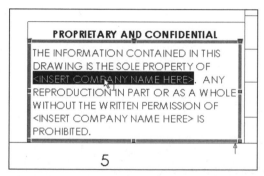

FIGURE 16.18 Editing the confidentiality statement in the title block

3. Enter the name of the company for both of the placeholder phrases. For this example, as with all drawings in this book, you will use the company name First Design Company. When you are done editing the text box, click outside the text field boundary, and it will no longer be active.

4. Pan the drawing to the right side by pressing and holding the scroll wheel on your mouse until you have unobstructed access to the tolerance block.

5. Using the same procedure as with editing the confidentiality statement, edit the tolerance block to match the values shown in Figure 16.19. You can use these values in lieu of tolerances on the some of the dimensions on the drawing.

 T I P   To enter the degree symbol with the keyboard, press and hold the Alt key on your keyboard, and type 0176. You can also insert the degree symbol with the symbols library by clicking the Add Symbol button in the PropertyManager.

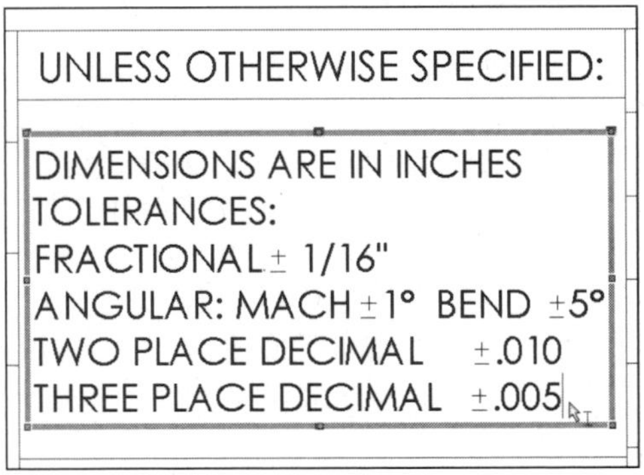

UNLESS OTHERWISE SPECIFIED:

DIMENSIONS ARE IN INCHES
TOLERANCES:
FRACTIONAL ± 1/16"
ANGULAR: MACH ± 1° BEND ± 5°
TWO PLACE DECIMAL   ±.010
THREE PLACE DECIMAL   ±.005

FIGURE 16.19 Editing the tolerance block

6. Next, the text for the geometric tolerance interpretation needs to include the line ASME Y14.5M-2009. This is the standard that all the drawings created in this book will use.

7. With the addition of the standard name, the statement is too long to fit inside of the box. There are a couple of ways to fix the overall size of the text. One approach is to change the overall height of the text, but that isn't very clean looking. So instead, you will just shrink the overall width slightly while preserving the font height. With the text selected, click the Fit Text button in the Formatting toolbar.

8. Move the mouse pointer to directly above the red handle on the text bounding box until the mouse pointer changes into a two-headed horizontal arrow. Press and hold the left mouse button, and shrink the width of the text.

9. Using the scroll wheel again, pan to the far right of the title block to give you access to the box directly above the title.

In the box above the description is an empty text box that is linked to the COMPANYNAME custom property. This is especially helpful if you are an independent contractor who needs to change the name of the owning company for each drawing. If you are already part of an organization, you should not need to change the company name for each drawing. For that reason, you are going to break the link to the custom property by typing the name of the company directly into the box.

Since the text box is now currently empty, it is not visible, but if you knew exactly where it was located, you would still be able to select it for editing. You could easily click blindly in the general area until you find the text box, but that approach can be frustrating and time-consuming. Instead, using the box selection method discussed in earlier chapters, window around the general area to select everything that falls within the selection box.

10. Click and hold the left mouse button with the mouse pointer above the left side of the box that contains the invisible text box. While still holding the left mouse button, drag a box to the lower-right side to select everything that falls within the box (see Figure 16.20).

FIGURE 16.20 Using the box selection window to find a hidden text box

11. Release the mouse button; only items that fall completely inside the box selection will be highlighted. If you didn't make the box selection too big or too small, the only item that should be selected is the hidden text box (see Figure 16.21).

FIGURE 16.21 Hidden text box revealed using a box selection window

12. With the text box now visible, you can double-click the left mouse button with the mouse pointer directly over the highlighted center point of the text. Type the name of the fictitious company into the text box, **First Design Company**. Use the Fit Text command to ensure that the company name fits entirely inside the box.

Link the Drawing Revision

We like to automate as many features on a drawing as possible. The revision letter shown in the title block is a perfect example of doing this. Later in this chapter you will be adding a revision table to track changes to the drawing. It only makes sense to link the revision letter shown in the title block to the most recent revision shown in the revision table. As revisions are added to the table, the title block will be updated. This is another perfect example of shaving off a couple of seconds that can really add up in the long run. To do this, you need to link the text box in the title block to the *Revision custom property* by doing the following:

1. While still in Edit Sheet Format mode, zoom in closer to the area that contains the Rev box.

2. Make a box selection around the Rev box, as described in the previous section, to show the text box that is currently hidden.

3. Select the text box by clicking the highlighted center point, and click the Link To Property button in the Text Format section of the Note PropertyManager.

4. In the Link To Property window, make sure Current Document is selected, and click the File Properties button, as in Figure 16.22.

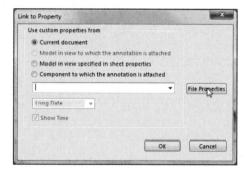

FIGURE 16.22 Link To Property window

5. The Custom tab of the Summary Information window now is shown. The active document does not have a revision level specified yet, and first you need to add the custom property. In the Property Name field, click the downward-pointing arrow to display the predefined list of properties. In the list, select Revision. The type will automatically be set to Text, which is appropriate for the property type.

6. You must enter something into the Value/Text Expression field for the Revision property, or the addition will not be saved when the window is closed. You do not want to add a revision letter just yet, so instead select the field for the property Value, and press the spacebar on the keyboard. This will act simply as a placeholder to keep the property from being removed; it will be overwritten when a revision is added to the drawing. Click OK to close the Summary Information window.

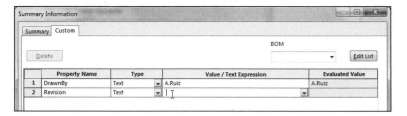

7. In the Link To Property window, there is an empty text field in the Use Custom Properties From section. This is the field that you need to specify that the Revision property is to be linked to the text in the title block. Click the downward-pointing arrow to display a list of currently available properties. Select Revision from the very top of the list, as shown in Figure 16.23. Click OK to close the window.

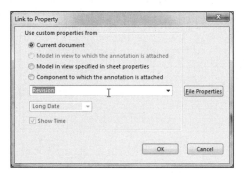

FIGURE 16.23 Linking the Revision property to the drawing title block

8. Click the green check mark in the Note PropertyManager to accept the changes.

9. With all the edits to the sheet format now complete, right-click anywhere on the drawing sheet, and select Edit Sheet from the menu, as shown in Figure 16.24.

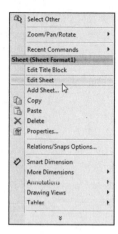

FIGURE 16.24 Entering edit sheet mode

Learn Timesaving Features for the Drawing Template

At this point in the process of creating the drawing template, you could finish up the template and move on to the next chapter. You have completed what are the minimum requirements for the drawing template, but we're always in favor of doing more up front to save time in the long run. The next few sections of this chapter are all about adding timesaving features to the drawing template.

Add Predefined Drawing Views

The first of the timesaving features for your drawing template is the addition of *predefined drawing views*. Earlier in this chapter, we covered how to use projections to create the necessary views. Many times when creating a drawing for a part or assembly, all the orthographic projections are created by the user, and then dimensions are applied. This is not really a time-consuming process, but if you are working on a large number of drawings, the few seconds per drawing can really add up. Using predefined drawing views cuts down the amount of time needed to create the primary orthographic projections for the part being documented.

When a drawing template is created with predefined views, creating a new drawing is a snap. On creation, the most commonly used projections of the part can automatically be created with dimensions in some cases — all for a couple of extra minutes during the template creation process. We'd say that is a pretty good time investment. In the following steps, you will be adding predefined views for the most common projections: Front, Top, Right, and Isometric:

1. Make sure you are in the Edit Sheet Format mode from the last step of the preceding section.

2. Hover over or click the SolidWorks logo on the menu bar to show the menus. In the menu, select Insert ➤ Drawing View ➤ Predefined.

3. A small dashed box will be shown under the mouse cursor. To place the view, click the left mouse button with the view near the middle left of the drawing sheet, as in Figure 16.25.

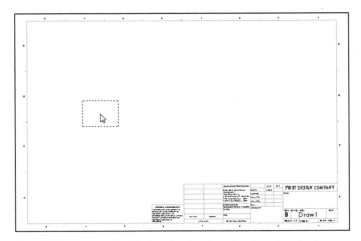

FIGURE 16.25 Placing the drawing view into the sheet

4. After placing the view, you will be able to set the view properties in the PropertyManager. You need to define what the default view will be when a part is attached to the drawing. In the Orientation section of the Drawing View PropertyManager, click the Front View button.

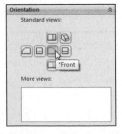

5. The other two views, Top and Right, will be projections of the Front View. This will ensure that the views always line up horizontally and

vertically with the parent view, the Front view.Instead of placing another predefined view, you will use the projection tool. First select the view added in the previous steps, and then press S on the keyboard to show the shortcut bar.

6. In the shortcut bar, click the Drawing Commands button, and select Projected View.

7. Now you can place the projected view in the drawing. Depending on what side you place the new view, SolidWorks will automatically set the view to the appropriate orthographic projection. For instance, if you place the view to the right of the Front view, the new view will be set to show the Right projection of the part. With this method, you can create eight different projections of the Front view including Top, Bottom, Left, Right, and four isometric views.

   Move the cursor to place the new view above the previously created view. This will make the view show the Top view of the part when the drawing is created.

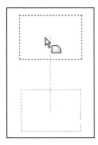

8. Select the Front view again, and select Projected View from the shortcut bar. Place the new view to the right of the Front view to create the Right projection.

9. Now all that is left to do is to predefine the isometric view of the part. Select the Front view again, and select Projected View from the shortcut bar. Drag the new view to be in line with the upper-left corner of the Front view. This will make the new view an Isometric projection of the part (see Figure 16.26).

10. With all the views created, it is important to properly spread them around on the sheet to minimize the chance of the drawing views overlapping when the part is added. To move a view, select the dashed edge of the view; the mouse pointer will change to a cross. Click and hold the left mouse button, and move the view to the desired location. Notice that when moving one view, the adjacent view(s) moves along with it.

This is the reason you used a projected view instead of inserting a new predefined view. Arrange the four views to be similar to Figure 16.27.

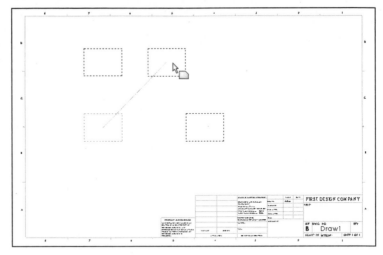

FIGURE 16.26 Placing a projected view into the drawing sheet

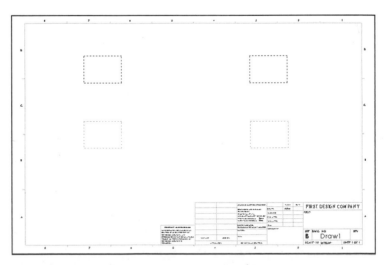

FIGURE 16.27 Arrangement of predefined views

Add a Revision Table

Revision tables are used to document the change history of a drawing. Per mechanical engineering drawing standards, such as ASME and ISO, each change made to a drawing must be documented with a revision letter, description of change, date of change, and approval at the very least. Your company or organization may have additional information that must be recorded, but you are going to use the default revision table that is already created for SolidWorks.

N O T E   For more information about revisions and revisions tables, refer to ASME Y14.35M-1997.

The advantage of placing the revision table in the template is that it will help minimize the chance of an accidental omission of the table during drawing creation. The revision table could be omitted from the drawing template, which would cause the drawing creator to manually insert the table. But, like we said, we're all about automation whenever possible.

Define the Revision Table Anchor Point

Before inserting the revision table into the drawing template, you will need to define the *anchor point*. This is the point on the drawing that the table will be attached to instead of it just floating in space.

1. In the PropertyManager, click the plus (+) sign next to Sheet1, and then click the plus next to Sheet Format1 to expand it.

2. Below Sheet Format1, there are five different *anchor types* that can be defined, as shown in Figure 16.28. These types — General Table Anchor, Bill of Materials Anchor, Hole Table Anchor, Weldment Cut List Anchor, and Revision Table Anchor — can all be set individually, but for these purposes you are concerned with only one of them. Right-click Revision Table Anchor, and select Set Anchor from the menu.

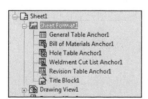

FIGURE 16.28 Selecting an anchor type for the revision table

3. Move the mouse pointer around the border and title block of the sheet format, and you will notice that any endpoint can be designated as the anchor point because a small dot highlights the point. We're always partial to placing the revision table in the upper-right corner

of the drawing area, so move the mouse to the upper-right corner of the drawing border, and click the left mouse button when the point is highlighted.

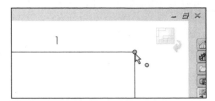

The command will automatically exit after selecting the new anchor point.

Insert the Revision Table

With the anchor point defined, it is now time to insert the revision table template that is available. As we mentioned, just to keep things simple at this point you will be using the default revision table template available, but if your company or organization has one already predefined, feel free to insert it instead.

1. Press S on the keyboard, and click the Tables button in the shortcut bar.

2. In the flyout, there are four different tables that can be inserted into the drawing: General Table, Hole Table, Bill Of Materials, and Revision Table. Select Revision Table from the flyout.

3. In the Revision Table PropertyManager, you need to select the appropriate table in the Table Template section. By default, the last revision table inserted into a drawing is shown, but if there is not one shown or you need to change the table, click the Browse For Template button.

4. In the Browse For Template window, go to the folder that contains the revisions tables. In most installations, they will be located in the `%Installation Directory%\Lang\English`. Select the file named `No Zone Column.SLDREVTBT`, and click Open.

5. In the Table Position section of the Revision Table PropertyManager, select the check box for Attach to Anchor Point. This will automatically insert the revision anchored to the point we defined earlier.

6. Ensure that the Enable Symbol When Adding New Revision option is deselected in the Options section of the PropertyManager. This is merely a personal preference of mine but if your company uses revision symbols, feel free to enable them at this point.

> **You define the location of the revision table templates in System Options ➤ File Locations ➤ Revision Table Templates.**

7. Lastly, make sure the Use Document Settings option is enabled in the Border section. This will make it easier to adjust the appearance of the table in the Document Properties if the need arises.

8. With all the appropriate options enabled, click the green check mark and the revision table will be inserted in the drawing template.

Saving Changes to the Revision Table Template

Just like with drawing templates, you can make modifications to any of the revision table templates to meet your needs and save the template for future uses. For the drawings in this book we need to make a minor change to the revision table that we will be using. Rather than just have the change reflected in the drawing template, we will also save the change to the revision table template.

The default template that we used does not have a table header designating it as Revision History. We will add this header to the table and save it in the drawing template and update the revision table template as well.

1. Select the top row of the revision table to edit the cell.

2. With Caps Lock on, type **REVISION HISTORY** into the cell.

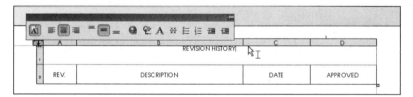

3. Select the text you just typed, and deselect the Use Document Font button on the Formatting toolbar. We always prefer to have text items in drawings use the document font because when you make a change in the document properties, all the text items will update as well. But for this case, you do not necessarily need to have the table header update.

4. After deselecting Use Document Font, an additional row will be added to the Formatting toolbar, allowing you to adjust the font for the selected text. Change the text height of the Revision Table header to 14, and click anywhere outside the table to accept the change.

The change you just made to the table will be reflected only in the drawing template and is not automatically made to the actual Revision Table template. To update the Revision Table template, you need to overwrite the existing table temple or create a new one. Here's how:

1. Right-click anywhere inside the revision table, and select Save As from the menu.

2. Browse to the folder where your revision templates are stored.

3. Select the file named `No Zone Column.sldrevtbt`, and click Save.

4. When prompted to replace the existing template, click Yes. The template has now been updated for future use.

Save and Share the Sheet Format and Template

Once you have made all the required modifications to the drawing template and sheet format, it is time to save the changes and make them available for use. You will need to save the drawing template and sheet format separately since they both have their own set of tasks. The sheet format can be saved and used in existing drawings to change sheet size or format. The drawing template will be used to create new drawings.

Save the Sheet Format

Saving the sheet format will allow you to be able to use it in existing drawings. This is helpful if you have a drawing that was created with a different template and you want to change the border and title block to meet your company standards.

You can also use saved sheet formats to change the size of a drawing sheet. For example, if you have a drawing that was originally created as a size A sheet and you decide that the sheet is too small, you can replace the sheet format with a larger size sheet without losing any other information you have already added to the drawing.

1. Once you complete all the modifications to the sheet format, hover over or click the SolidWorks logo on the menu bar.

2. Select Save Sheet Format from the File menu.

3. The Save Sheet Format window should already display the current sheet formats. If that is not the case, browse to the folder that contains the other sheet formats available for your system.

4. Instead of overwriting an existing sheet format, renaming the file will allow you to maintain different sheet formats for differing tasks. For our purposes, name the file b - landscape - FDC.slddrt, as shown in Figure 16.29.

You can refer to the Sheet Format Folder Location setting in the System Options window to determine which folder SolidWorks is using.

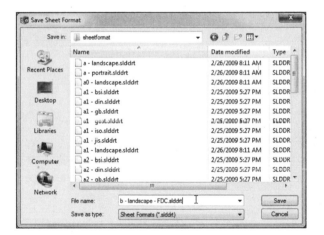

FIGURE 16.29 Renaming a sheet to incorporate another sheet format

5. Click Save.

The newly created sheet format is now available for use in existing drawings. Figure 16.30 shows the sheet format available in the Sheet Properties window. By right-clicking in an existing drawing and selecting Properties from the menu, you can change the sheet format to the one you just created.

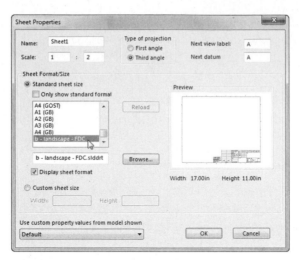

FIGURE 16.30 Selecting the sheet format in the Sheet Properties window

Save the Draw Template

It is now time to save the drawing template for later use. After the template is saved, it will be available for selection when creating a new drawing. All the changes made to the template including the options, custom properties, title block, revision table, and predefined views will be included when creating a new drawing.

1. Hover over or click the SolidWorks logo in the menu bar. Select Save As from the File menu.

2. In the Save As Type field of the Save As window, select Drawing Templates (*.drwdot). The folder location will automatically change based on the location for templates defined in the System Options window.

3. In the File Name field, enter the name for the template as FDC Size B.

4. Click Save.

5. With all the changes saved, you can now close the drawing. Click the X in the top-right corner of the graphics area.

Once the template is saved, it will become available for use and will be displayed in the Advanced view of the New SolidWorks Document window, as shown in Figure 16.31.

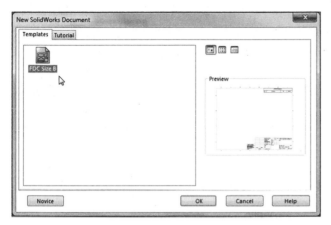

FIGURE 16.31 New template available in New SolidWorks Document window

Share Templates and Sheet Formats over a Network

Some organizations prefer to have their templates and sheet formats stored on a network drive for all the users in the organization to share. This approach saves the CAD manager time by allowing him or her to update only one template with no need to distribute it companywide. The only difference in procedure described earlier is to add the network location to the File Locations section of the System Options window.

T I P Of course, practice makes perfect, especially when making templates, since they can be a huge time-saver if set up correctly. Instead of re-creating the same template from scratch, it is a good idea to build up your library of drawing templates and sheet formats for the other sizes of drawing sheets. Using the same steps described in this chapter, create drawing templates and sheet formats for the size A, C, D, and E drawing sheets.

Are You Experienced?

Now You Can...

☑ **Create a drawing template**

☑ **Use the Title Block Manager**

☑ **Tell the difference between First Angle and Third Angle projections**

☑ **Add a revision table**

☑ **Add predefined views**

☑ **Save templates and sheet formats**

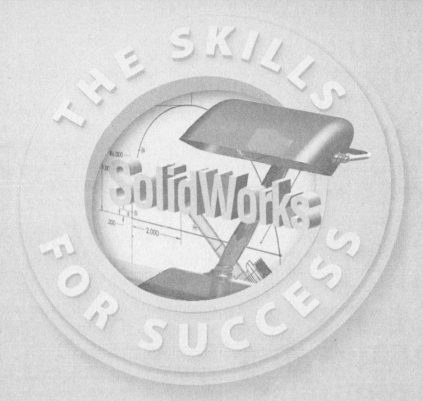

CHAPTER 17

Creating Simple, Stunning Renderings

▶ Use the PhotoView 360 User Interface

▶ Create Your First Rendering

▶ Customize Your Rendering Even More

▶ Create Renderings with Depth of Field

Throughout the preceding chapters, you have learned many new skills in SolidWorks that will ensure your success in future designs. If you were to stop reading here, you would be able to create new designs, share them with other users, and even see your designs manufactured. But, you would be missing out one other skill that was previously considered too difficult and time-consuming to be a realistic option.

Prior to SolidWorks 2008, photorealistic renderings needed to be created with software packages such as PhotoWorks, Maya, and others. PhotoWorks is a powerful rendering program that is fully integrated within the SolidWorks environment. Although very powerful, many users have found the program too complex to be usable for even the simplest of renderings.

Luckily, PhotoView 360 was introduced by SolidWorks to take the task of creating photorealistic renderings from the hands of the elite and introduce it to the rest of the SolidWorks community. *PhotoView 360* is a slicker, easier-to-use stand-alone application that is included with the SolidWorks Professional and SolidWorks Premium packages.

Even though PhotoView 360 sports a simple, easy-to-use interface, it does not skimp on the quality of images that can be created. By the end of this chapter, you will have the skills needed to create some images that can rival those created with other, more complex rendering software packages.

 N O T E   The 2011 release of PhotoView 360 will include even more tools that were previously available only in PhotoWorks. Subsequently, PhotoWorks will be discontinued after 2011.

Use the PhotoView 360 User Interface

The advantage of PhotoView 360 over PhotoWorks is its simplicity. Take one look at the user interface, as shown in Figure 17.1, and you will fall in love with its ease of use. Everything that you need in order to create stunning renderings is available in the drop-down menus at the top of the window and three separate toolbars. Without going into too much detail, we will cover what the menu and toolbars contain.

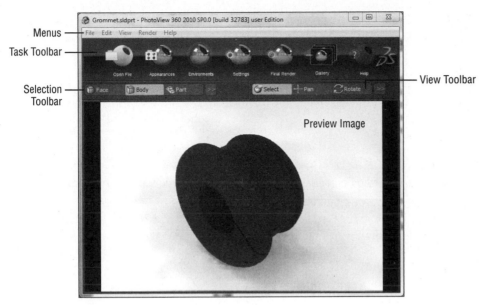

FIGURE 17.1 PhotoView 360 user interface

Menus

Just like with almost all Windows-based programs, the drop-down menus at the top of the window provide you with some basic commands, but the majority of operations you will be performing will be through the toolbars. The menu bar is broken down into the following five items:

File   The File menu contains the commands necessary for opening and closing scenes, as well as loading background images and environments.

Edit   The Edit menu contains the commands to undo the last function and redo the last undo.

View   The View menu contains the commands to stop or rest the preview in the preview image. All elements that were hidden previously in the preview image can be shown with the Unhide All command.

Render   The Settings and Render windows can be called from the Render menu. You can also recall the last rendered image and save the current preview image.

Help　In addition to the providing access to the help file and release notes, you can also view online video tutorials that will walk you through various rendering tasks in detail.

T I P　If a keyboard shortcut is available for any of the menu items, it will be displayed to the far right of the menu next to the corresponding command.

Tasks Toolbar

The Tasks toolbar contains all that is needed to create a rendering. Even if you have never used PhotoView 360 before, you will be able to quickly determine the steps that you need to follow to create a rendering since the buttons in the Tasks toolbar are shown in order that you will use in most cases. We will be covering each one of the following buttons in the process of creating the various renderings in this chapter:

Open File　The very first thing that you need to do to create a rendering is open a SolidWorks part or assembly model. The Open File button will display a standard Windows file dialog box.

Appearances　Clicking the Appearances button will open a new window that contains the entire materials database for PhotoView 360. The Appearances window is then broken down into logical sections based on the material type.

Environments   Clicking the Environments button will open a new window that contains 28 preset rendering environments that include background images, colors, flooring, and lighting.

Settings   This opens a new window that gives you access to environment, output, and camera settings.

Final Render   This begins the final rendering in a separate window based on the previously selected settings.

Gallery   This opens the default web browser and takes you to the SolidWorks website where users have previously uploaded images created in PhotoView 360.

Help   This opens the help file.

Selection Toolbar

The Selection toolbar allows you to specify how an appearance is applied to the active model in the preview image. Prior to adding an appearance, select how the appearance will be applied, using the following options:

Face   Selecting Face in the selection toolbar will only apply an appearance to the face directly under the mouse pointer once you release the left mouse button.

Body   Selecting Body in the Selection toolbar will apply an appearance to the entire solid body.

Part   Selecting Part in the Selection toolbar will apply an appearance to only one part at a time.

Assembly   Selecting Assembly in the Selection toolbar will apply one appearance to the entire assembly, overwriting any previously applied appearances at the part level.

Appearances   Selecting Appearances applies a new appearance to all items that share the same appearance. If an appearance was previously applied in SolidWorks, only the items that had their appearances applied in one operation will be selected.

View Toolbar

The View toolbar provides you with the tools necessary to manipulate the view of the model in the preview image. Even though you may ultimately be relying on your mouse for changing the view, it is sometimes helpful to be able to select the exact view tool you need.

Select   The Select tool in the View toolbar returns the selection mode. After clicking, the mouse pointer will return to the standard selection arrow.

Pan　This changes the mouse pointer to a group of four arrows pointing in the up, down, left, and right directions. To pan, click and hold the left mouse button and drag the mouse pointer. The model in the preview image will move on a plane parallel to the viewing plane.

TIP　To pan without selecting the Pan tool in the View toolbar, press and hold the Ctrl button on your keyboard, and then press and hold the mouse wheel button while moving the mouse.

Rotate　This changes the mouse pointer to a circular arrow and rotates the model in the preview image around the center point of the entire model. To rotate, click and hold the left mouse button and move the mouse in any direction.

Zoom　This changes the mouse pointer to a magnifying glass and is used to zoom in and out. The mouse pointer location in the preview image does not affect the zoom.

TIP　There are a two different ways to zoom in and out without using the Zoom tool in the View toolbar. First, spinning the mouse wheel up and down will zoom in and out. Second, holding the Shift key on the keyboard while pressing and holding the mouse wheel will zoom in and out when you move the mouse up and down.

Zoom Window　This changes the mouse pointer to a magnifying glass. Click once in the preview image to specify the center point of the zoom window, and when you move the mouse pointer out from the center, a yellow box will be displayed. When the window is the size that you desire, click and release the left mouse button once again to zoom in on the box drawn.

Fit To View　Selecting this fits the entire model into the preview image.

Create Your First Rendering

Now that you have a feel for the layout of PhotoView 360, you can dive right into the first rendering. The first image you will be creating in this section is of the top-level assembly of the desk lamp. This section will show the minimum number of steps that are required to create an amazing image.

As we mentioned earlier, the buttons in the Task toolbar are ordered in such a way to mimic the order of operation when creating a rendering. Even the most

> To rotate without selecting the Rotate tool, press and hold the mouse wheel button while moving the mouse.

> Pressing F on the keyboard will also cause the model to fit entirely within the preview image.

novice of users will have no problem creating stunning images. As you continue in the chapter, you will then explore more advanced techniques to make your renderings even more stunning.

Open a Model

Before you can create a rendering, you need to open a model. Since there are no modeling tools in PhotoView 360, the models must first be created in SolidWorks. That includes any additional parts or props that you want to include in the rendering. Since you do not need to do anything special at this time, you can open the desk lamp assembly as it is by doing the following:

1. You can open PhotoView 360 in a couple ways. First, you can locate and double-click the PhotoView desktop icon, or you can open the program through the Start menu. To open the program through the Start menu, click Start ➢ All Programs ➢ SolidWorks 2010 ➢ PhotoView 360, as shown in Figure 17.2.

FIGURE 17.2 Application icon in Start menu

2. Click the Open File button in the Task toolbar, as shown in Figure 17.3, and browse to the location where the assembly of the desk lamp is saved. Select the desk lamp assembly, and click Open.

FIGURE 17.3 Open File button on the Task toolbar

T I P   You can also open models in PhotoView 360 by dragging and dropping them onto the preview image from Windows Explorer.

Add Appearances to a Model

The term appearances in PhotoView 360 refers to the application of a material look to a face, solid body, part, or assembly. Just like how appearances are shown in RealView in SolidWorks, the appearances do not affect the model in any way other than how it is represented on the screen. PhotoView 360 comes with a fairly large database of material appearances, most of which can also be found in SolidWorks. In fact, an appearance added to a component in SolidWorks will carry over into PhotoView 360, which can be a huge time-saver.

Since you already applied some material appearances to the assembly in SolidWorks, you will not need to do it all over again at this point. However, in order to illustrate the process for applying appearances, you will change how the brass components in the assembly will appear. The following steps describe the process for applying appearances:

1. Click the Appearances button in the Task toolbar to view the complete list of appearances available.

2. In the left pane of the Appearances window, click the arrows next to the material directory names to view additional directories in order to further define the material that will be used for the appearance. Click the arrow next to the Metal directory to expand the list, as shown in Figure 17.4.

FIGURE 17.4 Metal directory in Appearances window

3. Below the parent directory for Metal, select the Brass directory. In the right pane, a variety of brass material buttons will be shown. To change the size of the icons to better fit the available space, move the slider above the material list to the right to make the buttons bigger and to the left to make them smaller, as shown in Figure 17.5.

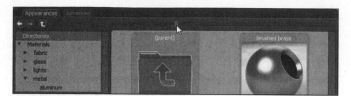

FIGURE 17.5 Slider to change the size of the Appearances icons

4. Select the Part button in the Selection toolbar to specify that the material appearance will be applied to the selected part, as shown in Figure 17.6.

FIGURE 17.6 Part button in the Selection toolbar

5. Select the Brushed Brass button in the Appearances window by clicking and holding the left mouse button with the mouse pointer directly over the material, as shown in Figure 17.7.

FIGURE 17.7 Brushed Brass icon in Appearances window

6. While continuing to hold the left mouse button, drag the material appearance into the graphics window. Move the mouse pointer to directly above one of the brass components in the assembly. Release the left mouse button, and the parts appearance will update to show the new material.

7. Continue to add the Brushed Brass material appearance to each of the brash components in the assembly.

8. You can choose to leave the Appearances window open, but to save space on the screen, you can close it by clicking the X in the upper-right corner of the window. You can also toggle the appearance of the window by clicking the Appearances button in the Task toolbar.

Change the Scene Environment

An environment applies to the background, lighting, and floor of the rendering scene. The environment spherically wraps around the model in the preview image and moves relative to the model as it is being rotated. Environments are a great way to take your rendering to the next level with minimal effort. In fact, all that needs to be done to change the scene environment is just a simple drag and drop. Once you locate an environment that you like in the Environment window, just drag and drop it into the preview image, and instantly the scene is updated.

The environments available range from a basic solid background with shadowed or reflective floors to a sunny day in a public square. Each environment has a different effect on the final appearance of the model in a rendering. With some environments, such as the sunny public square, you will also be able to see a reflection of the environment in some of the shinier components. You can use a few options to customize the scene environment, and we will cover some of them later in this chapter. For now you will just select one of the environments and leave it as is. To add an environment to the scene, do the following.

N O T E   Predefined environments are based on high dynamic range (HDR) or HDRI images.

1. Click the Environments button on the Task toolbar. A new window, much like the Appearances window, will be displayed.

2. Locate the Abstract Studio Shadow environment button. Select the environment by pressing and holding the left mouse button with the mouse pointer on the button, as shown in Figure 17.8.

3. While still holding the left mouse button, drag the environment into the preview image. Once the mouse pointer is anywhere inside the preview image, release the left mouse button.

FIGURE 17.8 Abstract Studio Shadow environment

4. The Environments window, just like with the Appearances window, can be left open and off the side of the main window. But if you do decide to close the window to save valuable desktop space, you can either click the X in the upper-right corner of the window or toggle the Environments button in the Task toolbar.

Create the Final Rendering

Now that the appearances have been applied and the environment has been set, you could make additional changes to the final output by adjusting various settings. But this time around, you will continue with the default settings and instead start the final rendering. After you see what the default rendering looks like, you can begin making fine adjustments to the settings to achieve the effect that you are looking for. Later in this chapter, we will cover how to make adjustments to the settings of the scene, but for now, the following steps will describe the process for creating the final rendering:

1. Click the Final Render button in the Task toolbar. A new window will be displayed and will immediately begin to create the final rendering. Orange squares called *buckets* will jump around the image as the final rendering is built, as shown in Figure 17.9. The number of buckets will depend on the number of cores your processor has. More cores in your CPU means more buckets, which ultimately means faster renderings.

2. To save the new rendering, click the Save Image button near the upper-right area of the Final Render window, as shown in Figure 17.10.

3. Browse to the folder where you want to save the rendered image in the Save Image window.

FIGURE 17.9 Final rendering in process

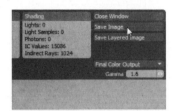

FIGURE 17.10 Save Image button in the Final Render window

4. Name the new image file Desk Lamp Rendering 1 in the File Name field. Click the Save As Type field to display the list of supported image types, as shown in Figure 17.11. In the list, select the desired file type, and click Save.

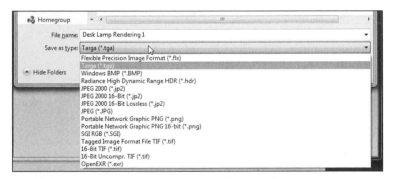

FIGURE 17.11 Supported image types for saving renderings

5. To close the Final Render window, click the X in the upper-right corner of the window, or click the Close Window button on the right side of the top pane.

 N O T E   Unlike with the Appearances and Environments windows, clicking the Final Render button in the Task toolbar will not toggle the window close. Instead, clicking the Final Render button will begin the rendering process again with the previously selected settings.

Customize Your Rendering Even More

In the previous exercise, we opted to have you generate the final rendering with the default settings. The first time we create a rendering, we always do it without making any adjustments. This allows the first rendering generated to act as a baseline, and after seeing the results, it is easier to determine what changes can be made to make the image created even more spectacular. After seeing the initial result, you can now move on to make some additional changes in the scene.

Adjust Appearance Properties

After looking at the image created in the previous section, it may be determined that the shade can be made a little bit more transparent. Unfortunately, there is no material appearance that will work for the shade without some adjustments. The following steps will describe the process for adjusting a material appearance to come closer to the final look you need to achieve in the rendering:

1. If you closed the desk lamp assembly from the previous section, click Open File in the Tasks toolbar, and select the assembly in the Load File window. Click Open.

2. Click the Appearances button in the Tasks toolbar.

3. Locate the Thick Gloss directory in the Glass material directory.

4. Click the Part button in the Selection toolbar.

5. Drag and drop the Green Thick Glass button from the Appearances window onto the shade in the preview image.

6. Click the Advanced tab at the top of the Appearances window. The window will split to show a pane at the bottom of the window with a color chart.

7. Select the shade in the preview image, and additional options will be displayed that pertain to the material appearance of the selected object, as shown in Figure 17.12.

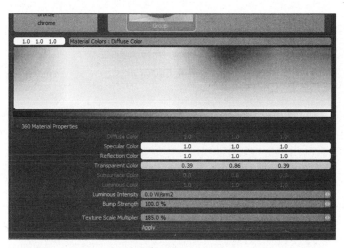

FIGURE 17.12 Material properties on the Advanced tab

8. Select the space to the left of the Specular Color property, as shown in Figure 17.13. This area is called the *item channel value* and is used to specify the color of the selected property.

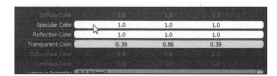

FIGURE 17.13 Specular color properties

9. Set the color in the Color window by adjusting the RGB (Red, Green, Blue) value. Changing the value in the Red, Blue, and Green fields by typing a number will change the property to a specific field. If you do

not have a specific color in mind, clicking anywhere within the color chart will change the color as well. This is a quick and easy approach, but it will be difficult to match a predetermined color. If you have the RGB or HSL (Hue, Saturation, Luminance) color, it is always better to enter in the values manually. For the shade, specify Red to be 48, Green to be 129, and Blue to be 68. Click OK.

10. Click the item channel value for the Transparent Color property.

11. Change the value of the RGB fields to be Red 16, Green 75, and Blue 16. Click OK.

Let There Be Light

In the desk lamp assembly, there is a lightbulb that is currently black since we did not previously apply a material appearance to it. It would be a nice touch to make the lightbulb light up as if in use. In the following steps, you will be adding an appearance to the lightbulb to achieve that effect:

1. Click the Appearances tab at the top of the Appearances window.

2. Browse to Area Light in the Lights material directory.

3. Click Body in the Selection toolbar, and rotate the model up until the light bulb is accessible.

4. Apply the Area Light appearance to the bulb body in the preview image.

Save Custom Camera Views

One of the new functions that was introduced in PhotoView 360 was the ability to save and recall custom camera views. As you are experimenting with different views of the model in the scene, you can save the angle of the camera pointing at the model. This is extremely handy when you are searching for that one perfect angle. To save a specific camera view, do the following:

1. Using the center wheel on your mouse, rotate the lamp until you find your desired view for the next rendering.

2. Once you have settled upon a view, you can save the view for future renderings. Click the right mouse button anywhere inside the preview image. Select Save Custom View in the menu.

3. A small window will prompt you for the name of the new custom view. In the Custom View Name window, name the view you have created, as shown in Figure 17.14, and then click OK.

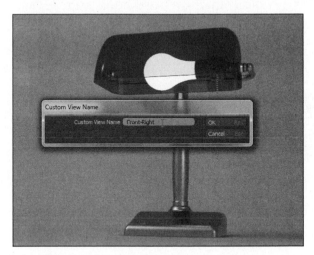

FIGURE 17.14 Naming a custom camera view

Recall a Saved Custom Camera View

Saving camera views is not very helpful if you cannot recall them when the need arises. Luckily, viewing and selecting previously saved camera views is quick and easy. To view and recall a camera view, do the following:

1. Right-click anywhere within the preview image, and select Recall Custom View.

2. A new window will display a thumbnail of the previously saved views along with the description entered when the views were saved, as shown in Figure 17.15. To recall a view, select the thumbnail in the Custom Views window, and the view will update in the preview image.

3. The Custom Views window can be left open, but to save space, click the X in the upper-right corner of the window.

FIGURE 17.15 Recalling previously saved camera views

Add a Custom Background

Another enhancement in PhotoView 360 is the ability to load custom backgrounds. Backgrounds, unlike environments, are 2D images that do not rotate relative to the model that is rotated in 3D. A background image is static since it does not move and always faces the viewing plane. That is not to say that adding a background image is not extremely helpful.

In this example, you'll add a custom multicolor background, and you can use any image. Background images can be used to add a little extra color to a scene, add a company logo, or add a realistic background for the rendering. For example, instead of adding the multicolor background, you can choose to add a background image of an office desk. You can then rotate, pan, and zoom the model until it appears to be sitting on the desk shown in the image. That is just one example, and the only limit to what you can do to the rendering with background images is your imagination.

 N O T E You can download the background image from the companion site, or you can choose to use any image file.

To add the background image download from the companion site to the current scene, do the following:

1. Click the Settings button in the Tasks toolbar.

2. Click the Environment Settings tab at the top of the Settings window, as shown in Figure 17.16.

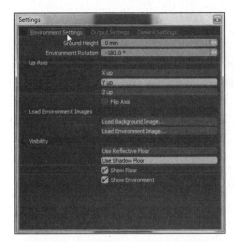

FIGURE 17.16 Environment Settings tab in Settings window

3. If the Load Environment Images section is collapsed, select the header to expand and display the options available for loading images into the rendering.

4. Under the Load Environment Images header, click the Load Background Image button.

5. In the Open Image File window, select the Tri-Color Background.jpg image that you previously downloaded from the companion site, and click Open.

Adjust the Floor Visibility

When you add a custom background, you may decide that it would look best to have the model you are rendering floating in space or even look like it is sitting on an object in the image. This is helpful if you inserted an image like a desktop for the lamp. You can turn on the shadow floor, which will make the model cast a realistic shadow on the desktop. If you have a solid-color image, like the one you inserted in the previous section, you can turn off the floor or even add a reflective floor. To adjust the floor visibility, do the following:

1. If you closed the Settings window after the previous section, open it once again by clicking the Settings button in the Task toolbar.

2. Expand the Visibility section on the Environment Settings tab if it is collapsed.

3. Clicking the Show Floor option will hide or show the floor in the preview image, as shown in Figure 17.17. If the Use Shadow Floor option is selected, only a shadow will be shown or hidden by toggling the Show Floor option. If the Use Reflective Floor option is selected, a gray reflective floor will be hidden or shown by toggling the Show Floor option. Play around with the options in the Visibility section until you have found a combination that you like.

FIGURE 17.17 Floor Visibility options on the Environments tab

4. When you are finished updating the settings for the rendering, you can close the window to save space. Click the Final Render button in the Task toolbar.

Recall Previous Renderings

When the rendering from the previous section is complete, rather than closing the window, you can compare the differences between the two versions you created. Earlier, you saved the image to a file, and you could always open that image and compare it to the one in the Final Render window. But what would you do if you did not save the image to a file?

In the Final Render window, there is a handy tool that allows you to recall previous images rendered in PhotoView 360. On the left of the window directly above the image, there are 10 numbered buttons that represent the last 10 images with the current image highlighted in orange. To switch the last image, click the button that precedes the orange one, as shown in Figure 17.18.

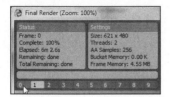

FIGURE 17.18 Viewing previously rendered images

 NOTE If the Final Render window is closed, you can open the last rendered image by clicking Render ➤ Recall Last Rendered Image In the menu.

Create Renderings with Depth of Field

For the last exercise, you'll create a new image using the Depth Of Field option made available in the 2010 release of PhotoView 360. Depth of field is a photography term that relates to how sharp an image is within a specified range of distance. Prior to 2010, images of objects separated by distance still remained sharp. In many cases, this is acceptable and even preferred by some, but it is not very realistic. If you were to use a camera to capture the same image in real life, the objects farthest from the focal point would be less clear than the objects closer. The Depth Of Field option on the Camera Settings tab of the Settings window is used to specify the focal point in the 3D environment, resulting in a more photorealistic image.

We have created the assembly you will use; you can download it from the companion site. After downloading and opening the assembly in PhotoView 360, you will need to make some additional changes to the settings before setting the camera options. To begin, do the following:

1. Click Open in the Task toolbar. Select the assembly named Depth of Field Exercise.SLDASM, and click Open.

2. If the assembly from the previous exercise is still open in PhotoView 360, you will be prompted to save or discard the changes. If you want to save the changes you have already made, click the Save button.

3. Click the Environments button on the Task toolbar.

4. Locate the 3 Point Blue environment, and add it to the preview image.

Adjust Ground Height

In the preview image, you will see that the models all look to be floating off the ground surface. Unless you are creating promotional images for a ghost-hunting TV show, you may not want the parts to just float like that. Instead of moving the parts, you need to adjust the elevation height of the ground in the Settings window. To change the ground height, do the following:

1. Click the Settings button on the Task toolbar.

2. Select the Environment Settings tab in the Settings window.

3. Type .375 in the Ground Height field. The value will be updated to be 375 µm, as shown in Figure 17.19.

FIGURE 17.19 Setting the ground height in the Environment Settings tab

Adjust the Rotation of Environment

Depending on the environment being used in a rendering, it might be better for the composition of the image to show a different part of the background behind your model. By now, you know that if you rotate the part around, the background environment will rotate along with it.

But what if you prefer to have the background move independently of the model? Luckily, there is an option for that in the Environment Settings tab. While still in the Settings window from the previous section, below the Ground Height Field, set the rotation of the environment to be 90°.

Set Camera Options

Now that you have made the rest of the necessary adjustments to the environment settings, it is time to move on to the camera options. In addition to being able to set the projection type and focal length of the camera, you can now adjust the depth of field. To set the Depth Of Field Options, follow these steps:

1. Select the Camera Settings tab in the Settings window.

2. In the Depth Of Field section, enable the Depth Of Field option, as shown in Figure 17.20.

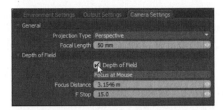

FIGURE 17.20 Depth Of Field options on the Camera Settings tab

3. You could use the Focus On Mouse button to specify the focus distance, but in this case you will specify it manually. Below the Focus At Mouse button, enter **600** to make the distance 600mm.

N O T E   The Depth Of Field settings can sometimes mean a lot of trial and error. Use the previously rendered images available in the Final Render window to try different camera configurations to find the settings that provide the best result.

4. Below the Focus Distance field, set the F Stop setting to 10mm.

5. Move the settings window off to the side, or close the window by clicking the X in the upper-right corner of the window.

6. Click the Final Render button in the Tasks toolbar.

This concludes your first step on what will probably be an amazing journey into the world of 3D modeling. In this book, we covered many aspects of SolidWorks that should allow you to be able to take and pass the Certified SolidWorks Associate (CSWA) exam and be well on the way to taking and passing the Certified SolidWorks Professional (CSWP) exam. If you take one thing from this book, we hope it is that there is more than one way to do things in SolidWorks. The best way to truly master the software is to not be afraid to try new techniques and experiment. Happy modeling!

Are You Experienced?

Now You Can...

- ☑ **Find and open PhotoView 360 in Windows**

- ☑ **Understand the PhotoView 360 user interface**

- ☑ **Add appearances to faces, bodies, parts, assemblies, and appearances**

- ☑ **Adjust appearance properties**

- ☑ **Save and recall custom camera views**

- ☑ **Add custom backgrounds to renderings**

- ☑ **Adjust floor options in rendering**

- ☑ **Use depth of field in renderings**

A

accelerator keys

A combination of keys used to initiate a menu command. Pressing Alt on the keyboard will highlight the letters next to the menu items. Then pressing the corresponding letter on the keyboard will initiate the menu item.

Aligned button

A button used in the Mate PropertyManager to set the alignment condition of standard and advanced mates. When selected, the Aligned button makes the vectors that are normal to the selected faces point in the same direction.

anchor point

1. A point in a drawing sheet format used to attach and anchor tables to prevent them from being moved. 2. The endpoint at the tip of a leader for a note, dimension, or other annotation.

Angle mate

A geometric relation between parts in an assembly used to define the angle between the components.

angle of the revolution

The angle covered by a revolved feature where a revolution is equal to or lesser than 360°.

annotations

A note or symbol used to specify the design intent of a part, assembly, or drawing. Annotations can include notes, flagnotes, geometric symbols, balloons, and hole callouts. In drawings, centerlines, center marks, hatches, and blocks are also considered annotations.

Anti-Aligned button

A button used in the Mate PropertyManager to set the alignment condition of standard and advanced mates. When selected, the Anti-Aligned button makes the vectors that are normal to the selected faces point in opposite directions.

appearances

Appearances are used to add visual properties to a model, such as color or realistic material textures, without affecting the physical properties of the model.

Appearances/Scenes tab

A tab on the task pane in which appearances and scenes can be added to the active model.

arc

A single portion of a circle equaling less than 360°.

assembly

A group of parts that when fitted together make a single unit.

assembly configuration

A single variation of an assembly with multiple versions.

autotransitioning

The ability to transition from a line to an arc, or vice versa, without selecting the Arc tool.

B

base feature

The first feature listed in the FeatureManager design tree.

bidirectionality

The ability for information to be updated in a component's custom properties when a bill of materials is updated, or vice versa.

blind hole

A hole that has its depth specified by a numerical value rather than referencing geometry in the part.

boss

A feature that protrudes from a model.

bottom-up design

A design strategy where the individual parts of an assembly are modeled and then put together to create an assembly.

box selection

A selection method used in parts, assemblies, and drawings to select entities by dragging a selection box with the mouse pointer. Dragging from left to right will select all items that fall completely within the box.

broken-out section

A section view that is not created as a separate view in a drawing. Instead, a closed profile, usually a spline, is used to specify the section on an existing drawing view, and the depth is determined by a numerical value or by selecting geometry in a drawing view.

buckets

Squares seen while rendering an image in PhotoView 360. The number of buckets seen while rendering corresponds to the number of cores in the CPU that are working on the rendering.

C

center marks

A cross in a drawing that marks the center of a circle or arc.

Center Rectangle tool

A sketch tool that sketches a rectangle with a center point.

centerlines

A type of line used to represent axes of a symmetrical part or feature in a drawing.

Centerpoint Arc tool

A sketch tool that creates an arc from a centerpoint, a start point, and an endpoint.

chamfer

A beveled edge connecting two surfaces or sketch entities.

closed loop

A selection set comprised of a set of contours that close upon themselves.

closed spline profile

A spline that has no break and closes upon itself. This is often used when creating broken-out sections in drawings.

coincident

A geometric condition where two or more entities share the same point in space.

Coincident mate

A mate tool used to make two selected entities in parts of an assembly share the same point.

collinear

A geometric condition where two or more lines share the same orientation and direction.

CommandManager

A context-sensitive toolbar that usually is docked above the graphics area and dynamically updates to the appropriate toolbar based on the modeling environment and tab selected.

concentric

A geometric condition where two or more circles or arcs share the same center point.

Concentric mate

A mate tool used to specify that two selected circular edges or cylindrical faces are to share the same centerpoint or axis.

configuration-specific properties

User-defined custom properties that are applied only to specific variations of a part or assembly (configuration) within the same model.

ConfigurationManager

A pane usually on the left side of the graphics area that is used to create, select, and view multiple configurations of a part or assembly.

confirmation corner

A way to accept or cancel features or sketches in the upper-right corner of the graphics area.

construction line

A sketch entity that aids in the creation of other geometry without actually being part of the created geometry.

context toolbar

A toolbar that appears when selecting items in the graphics area or FeatureManager that provides access to the most common set of tools for the selected items.

Corner Rectangle tool

A sketch tool that creates a rectangle by specifying the two opposite corners.

Corner Trim tool

A trim tool that is used to modify two selected sketch entities to intersect at a virtual corner.

cosmetic thread

An annotation type that is used to represent the inner diameter of a threaded boss and the other diameter of a threaded hole and can include a hole callout in a drawing.

CPU

The central processing unit or processor for a computer.

cross selection

A selection method used in parts, assemblies, and drawings to select entities by dragging a selection box with the mouse pointer. Dragging from right to left will select all items that cross the box boundary.

custom properties

User-defined information such as the description, part numbers, vendor name, and other relevant information that is added to a SolidWorks document that can be used in drawings, BOMs, and other areas of SolidWorks.

Custom Properties tab

A customizable tab in the task pane used to specify the values for a predetermined set of custom properties for the active document.

Custom tab

The tab of the Summary Information window, which you can open by selecting File ➢ Properties, that enables the user to add custom properties to the active SolidWorks document.

cut extrude

An extrusion that is used to cut away material from the 3D model.

D

degrees of freedom

The directions a part can freely move in 3D space. Three of the degrees consist of the translation in the directions of X, Y, and Z. The next three degrees consist of the rotation around the x-, y-, and z-axes.

depth of field

The distance in front of and behind the subject that appears to be in focus.

design intent

How a model reacts as parameters are updated. An improperly defined part will not react as expected and can have a negative effect on the overall functionality of the model.

Design Library

A folder structure available on the Design Library tab used for storing reusable items such as parts, blocks, and annotations.

detached drawing

A drawing that can be opened and worked in without the model files being loaded into memory. With detached drawings, the model data does not need to be present in order to be opened since the information is embedded in the drawing.

detailed view

A portion of a view that is often shown in a larger scale than its parent view. It is used to show more detail than what can be seen in the parent scale.

dimension (verb)

To apply a dimension to specify the location of a point or feature in a drawing.

dimension line

A portion of a dimension used to indicate the extent and direction of a dimension. The dimension line, in mechanical applications, is terminated at both ends with an arrowhead and contains the dimension's value.

dimensions

A numerical value used to specify the size, location, or geometric characteristic of a part or feature.

DimXpert

A set of tools available in parts that allow you to apply dimensions and tolerances to a 3D part per ASME Y14.41-2003 and ISO 16792:2006. The annotations added to the part can then be imported into drawing views.

DimXpertManager

A pane usually to the left of the graphics area that is used to list the tolerance features defined by the DimXpert for parts.

display pane

A portion of the FeatureManager design tree that can be expanded to view the various display settings in parts, assemblies, and drawings. In parts and assemblies, the settings can also be changed in the display pane.

document control

A department in many organizations whose duties include the management of all documents for a project or the entire organization. Many times, the document control department is responsible for the security, versions, visibility, and controlled audit trail of a document.

Document Properties tab

The tab in the Options window that contains the settings for the active document.

Document Recovery tab

A tab in the task pane that will list recovered files after restarting SolidWorks if the previous instance was unexpectedly terminated. For files to be recovered, the autorecover option must be enabled in the system settings.

document structure

The relationship between parts, assemblies, and drawings in SolidWorks.

document templates

A part, assembly, or drawing document that includes user-defined parameters and that is used in the creation of new documents.

document types

Documents that are used by a specific program. Types are determined by the extension following the period in the filename. In SolidWorks, supported document types include parts (*.sldprt), assemblies (*.sldasm), and drawings (*.slddrw).

Draft Analysis tool

A tool available in the Mold Tools toolbar used to check for the correct application of draft to the faces of a part.

draft angle

The degree of taper or angle on a face of a part most commonly added to parts designed for injection molding and casting to facilitate the extraction from molds.

drafting standards

Drafting presets for detailing derived from one of the supported standards including ANSI, ISO, DIN, JIS, BSI, GOST, and GB.

drag handle

A point on a sketch or feature that can be selected and dragged to create or edit an extrusion.

drawing

A 2D representation of a part or assembly often used to describe the manufacturing or assembly of components.

drawing note

Text on a drawing providing additional instructions for the manufacturing, preparation, storage, or inspection of the part or assembly in the drawing.

drawing template

A template used for the creation of new drawings. See *document templates*.

drawing views

Views on a drawing used to represent various angles of a part or assembly.

DXF

Drawing Interchange Format or Drawing Exchange Format. This is a file format developed by Autodesk to be used as a common file format between AutoCAD and other CAD programs including SolidWorks.

E

eDrawings

An application developed by SolidWorks that allows both non-CAD and CAD users to view part, assembly, and drawing data.

end condition

Options found in the PropertyManager that determine how a feature extends. It includes Blind, Through All, Up To Vertex, Up To

Surface, Offset From Surface, Up To Body, and Mid Plane.

environment

A spherical-encapsulating image that rotates in relation to a model.

extension lines

Also called *projection lines*, extension lines are the lines of a dimension that extend from a part that are used to indicate the locations on the part where the dimension applies.

extrusion

The result of a sketch that is linearly projected to create a boss or a cut on a part.

F

feature

A single shape that is used along with other features to create a part or assembly. All features are listed in the FeatureManager design tree, but not all features create geometry in the part.

FeatureManager design tree

The pane normally located to the left of the graphics area that lists the features used to create the active part, assembly, or drawing.

File Explorer tab

A tab on the task pane that duplicates the Windows Explorer functionality from the local PC and can be used to open recent documents, show files currently open in SolidWorks, and perform other common file management functions found in Windows.

Fillet

A rounded corner on a sketch or a rounded edge of a model.

FilletXpert

A utility with SolidWorks that manages, organizes, and reorders constant radius fillets.

filter bar

A field at the top of the FeatureManager design tree that enables the user to search for specific features of a part or components in an assembly.

first-angle projections

A technique for creating orthographic projections that places the object being drawn between the observer and the plane of projection.

flagnotes

A symbol used on drawing notes to call attention to a specific area of the drawing. The symbol is then used in the drawing, most often with the symbol attached to a leader or as part of the dimension being referenced in the notes.

flexible subassembly

A subassembly that allows the movement of the individual components within the limitations of its mates while in an assembly.

flip dimension

To change the direction of a dimension.

fully defined sketch

A sketch that has all the line and curve sizes and positions fully described with dimensions or relations. Once fully defined, no part of the sketch can be modified with adjusting the relations or dimension values.

G

generated view

A view, such as a detail or section view, that is based on an existing view in the drawing.

graphics area

The largest area of the SolidWorks window where parts, assemblies, and drawings are displayed.

group boxes

Boxes used the Property Builder application for grouping similar properties when designing a new tab layout.

H

Heads-up View toolbar

A transparent bar located in the upper portion of the graphics area with the most common tools available for adjusting views including Zoom, Pan, Section, Predefined view, Appearances, and so on.

helix

A 3D curve defined by its pitch, revolutions, and height. A helix is most commonly used for creating springs or threads.

Helix/Spiral tool

The tool used to create a 3D helix or a 2D spiral. The resulting entity is most commonly used as a path for creating the required feature of a part.

Help Customization option

The option to define the type of dynamic help provided while using SolidWorks. The option is most often set the first time SolidWorks is installed but can be adjusted in the Tools window.

hidden lines

A line type used in 2D drafting to represent edges that cannot normally be seen in the view because they are obscured by other geometry.

Hole Wizard

A utility in SolidWorks that aids in the creation of holes, counterbores, countersinks, tapped holes, and pipe-tapped holes.

horizontal dimension

A tool for the creation of a dimension that will be created only in the horizontal alignment in relation to the drawing.

horizontal ordinate dimension

A dimension type with only a horizontal extension line and the value.

hotspot

A rectangle encompassing a title block created for title block management that highlights when the mouse pointer enters the boundary.

hue

One of the three elements of HSL (hue, saturation, and luminance), which is a method used to define a color.

I

in-context model

A model created within an assembly with a sketch or feature related to another part in the assembly.

inferencing

A displayed relation in a sketch with visual cues such as a dotted line, icons next to the mouse pointer, and highlighted cues, such as what is seen when a midpoint is highlighted.

inferencing line

A dotted line shown while sketching between the mouse pointer and other entities in the sketch or geometry in the model. It's used to display the possible relation between the two.

injection molding

A process of manufacturing plastic components by injecting molten plastic within a mold cavity.

Instant3D

Functionality that enables the user to quickly create and modify features in parts and assemblies by dragging the geometry and using on-screen rulers.

Intersection Curve tool

A tool that creates a sketch segment where a sketch plane and a selected face intersect.

isometric view

A graphical projection of a model in a drawing that displays the model with its x-, y-, and z-axes spaced 120° apart and with the vertical z-axis.

L

leader dimension

A dimension shown with a leader and with an arrow pointing at the object being dimensioned.

line fonts

A term describing the display of a line in a drawing including its type and thickness.

line types

How a line is displayed in a drawing such as a solid line, dashed line, and so on.

luminance

One of the three elements of HSL (hue, saturation, and luminance), which is a method used to define a color.

M

mate

A geometric relationship between components in an assembly.

material

The specified substance from which a part is intended to be made when manufactured.

Mirror tool

The tool used to create a copy of a selected feature mirrored from a plane or selected face.

mirroring

The technique of creating copies of features in parts or sketch entities in sketches by mirroring from planes, faces, or centerlines.

model dimensions

Dimensions inserted into a drawing that were used in the creation of the part model. Once inserted, the dimensions remain parametric and when updated will affect the part geometry.

models

3D geometry within a part or assembly file.

N

negative draft

The display of a face when performing a draft analysis. A face that has negative draft has its angle as less than the negative reference angle in relation to the direction of pull.

neutral plane

The plane or face selected when specifying the direction of pull associated with the part draft.

Normal To command

A command that orientates a model to face the viewing plane.

O

offset

To create a copy of a selected sketch entity at a specified distance.

Offset Entities tool

A tool to offset one or more selected sketch entities, model edges, or faces at a specified distance.

on-screen ruler

A graduated measuring display used for dragging the geometry in Instant3D at a specified distance.

ordinate dimensions

A type of dimension with only extension lines marking the distance from a specified zero point.

origin

The point where the three axes intersect at the 0,0,0 coordinate of the model or sketch.

orthographic projections

Views in a drawing that are projected orthogonally from existing views meant to represent the 3D object in 2D.

orthographic view

A single view meant to represent a 3D object as a flat 2D object.

over-defined

A state in which a sketch has one or more dimensions or relations that are in conflict or redundant.

P

Parallel mate

A mate in which the selected faces, edges, or other geometry are kept parallel to each other regardless of the angle.

parallelogram

A sketched four-sided shape whose opposite sides are both parallel and equal in length.

parametric modeling

An approach to 3D modeling where the model, which is most often feature based, can be modified by adjusting its parameters such as the dimensions and relations that were used to create the model.

parent view

In a drawing, the view that was used to create a projected view.

part

A single 3D object made of features. In SolidWorks, the filename extension for a part file is .sldprt.

part configuration

A single variation of a part with multiple versions.

parting line

A line on a molded component where two or more parts of the mold meet.

path

A sketch, edge, or curve used in creating a sweep.

PDF

Portable Document Format. This is a file format created by Adobe Systems for exchanging documents across multiple platforms with a free reader.

pitch

The rate of change of a radius for each revolution of a helix.

plane

A flat construction geometry used in a part or assembly for 2D sketches, section views, and neutral planes.

positive draft

The display of a face when performing a draft analysis. A face that has positive draft has an angle greater than the reference angle in relation to the direction of pull.

Power Trim tool

A trim tool that has the ability to trim multiple, adjacent sketch entities by dragging the mouse pointer across the entities to be removed as well as extending sketch entities along their natural paths.

predefined drawing views

Empty drawing views in a drawing template that automatically create the predefined view angles when used to create a new drawing from a part.

projected view

A child view projected in an orthogonal manner from an existing view meant to represent the 3D object in 2D.

PropertyManager

A pane normally to the left of the graphics area that opens when an entity is selected or a command is initiated. Configurable parameters related to the entity or command will be displayed.

R

reference dimensions

Dimensions placed into a drawing that show the measurements of the model but are not parametric to the model. The dimensions cannot be changed but will update when the model geometry is updated separately.

reference plane

A flat construction geometry used in a part or assembly for 2D sketches, section views, neutral planes, or assembly mates.

reference triad

A symbol in the lower-left corner of the graphics area that displays the x-, y-, and z-axes and is used to orient a part or assembly as it is rotated in space.

referenced documents

In SolidWorks, files such as parts that are referenced by other files, such as assemblies and drawings.

region parameters

A set of parameters for use with variable-pitch helixes that set the revolutions or heights, diameters, and pitch rate.

relation

A geometric constraint between sketch entities and other entities or geometry that can be added automatically or manually.

renderings

Photorealistic images generated from 3D parts or assemblies.

revision custom property

A user-defined parameter that defines the revision of a part, assembly, or drawing.

revision tables

A table on a drawing used to track the changes made to the drawing.

Revolve Type parameter

A parameter in the Revolve PropertyManager that defines the revolve direction from the sketch plane.

revolved cut

A feature that was created by removing material from a part as a sketch revolves around an axis.

revolved part

A part created with single or multiple revolved features.

rigid subassembly

A subassembly that does not allow the movement of the individual components regardless of its mates while in an assembly.

rollback bar

A bar in the FeatureManager design tree that suppresses all items below when moved up the tree.

S

saturation

One of the three elements of HSL (hue, saturation, and luminance), which is a method used to define a color.

scalable

The ability to increase or decrease in size.

Search Assistant

A field located in the menu bar of SolidWorks that is used to search for filenames or text strings in all indexed documents.

sectioned views

A drawing view that provides a view of the internal features of a component by using a cutting plane.

sensors

Used in SolidWorks to monitor various properties of a part or assembly such as mass properties, dimensional values, and interference detection. A notification will alert the user when the value of the selected property deviates from the specified limits.

sheet format

The part of a drawing that includes the page size and orientation, standard text that is normally not edited in each drawing, the border, title blocks, and other standard elements of a drawing. Each separate sheet of a drawing (`*.sldasm`) can have its own sheet format allowing for different sizes and title blocks.

sheet tabs

Tabs below the graphics area of a drawing that allow the user to switch between the different pages of a single drawing.

shell

A feature that creates a hollow cavity within a part model. You can also select faces to create an opening in the part with the unselected surfaces as thin walls.

shortcut menu

A menu of tools and commands that is accessed by clicking the right mouse button with the mouse pointer directly above the model geometry, the FeatureManager design tree, and the window borders.

shortcut toolbar

A floating toolbar with a customizable set of noncontext commands that is accessed by pressing S on the keyboard while in a part, assembly, drawing, or sketch.

sketch

Lines and other 2D objects that are created on a plane or face for the purpose of creating features.

sketch entities

Lines and other 2D objects that make up a sketch.

Smart Dimension tool

A tool used for dimensioning that automatically detects the selected sketch entities and uses the appropriate dimension type.

SolidWorks Resources tab

A tab in the task pane that contains commands for getting started, community, online resources, and a tip of the day.

specular color

The highlighted color reflected off an object as light shines on it.

spiral

A 2D or flat helix.

spline

A 2D or 3D curve that is sketched using a set of control points.

status bar

The bar at the bottom of the SolidWorks window that provides information about the function being performed.

suppress

To remove entities such as features and assembly components from view as well as from calculations.

Sweep tool

The tool used to create a base feature, boss, cut, or surface feature by moving a profile along a path.

swept cut feature

A feature that removes material from a component by moving a profile along a curve.

swept feature

A feature created using the Sweep tool.

T

tangent arc

A sketched arc that is tangent to other sketch entities.

task pane

A group of tabs including SolidWorks Resources, Design Library, and File Explorer that is normally docked to the right of the graphics area.

template

A part, assembly, or drawing document that is used to create a new document. User-defined parameters, annotations, predefined views, and other geometry can be included in the new document automatically.

thin feature

A feature that is extruded or revolved with a constant wall thickness.

third-angle projection

A technique for creating orthographic projections that is created by projecting a view of the model being drawn on a plane between the object and the observer.

thread relief

A recess or undercut at the base of a thread that provides clearance for threading tools.

threaded boss

A cylindrical extrusion of a part that is threaded.

threaded hole

A cylindrical extruded cut on a part that is threaded.

3-point arc

An arc that is defined with three points (start, end, and midpoint).

3-point center rectangle

A rectangle that is sketched with a center point and a selected angle.

3-point corner rectangle

A rectangle that is sketched at a selected angle.

through hole

A hole or cutout that is extruded completely through a feature so that it breaks through the other side.

title block

A table located in the lower-right corner of a drawing that contains information related to the component being depicted such as the part number, description, material, and creator.

top-down design

A design strategy where the parts in an assembly are modeled within an assembly by referencing the geometry of other components.

transparent

The ability to view geometry through another component.

trim

To remove portions of a sketch entity that extends beyond another sketch entity that acts like the cutting plane.

Trim Away Inside

Trims open sketch entities that lie inside two bounding entities.

Trim Away Outside

Trims open sketch entities outside two bounding entities.

Trim to Closest

Trims a sketch entity to its closest intersection.

U

under-defined

A sketch that does not have enough dimensions or relations to prevent entities from being moved or changing size.

V

Vertical Dimension tool

A tool for creating a dimension that will be created only in the vertical alignment in relation to the drawing.

vertical ordinate dimension

A dimension type with only a vertical extension line and the value.

View Palette tab

A tab in the task pane that contains images of standard views, annotation views, section views, and flat patterns of the selected model for a drawing. The views can then be added to the drawing by dragging and dropping them into the drawing sheet.

virtual component

Components that are saved internally to an assembly instead of to a separate part or subassembly file.

W

workflow customization

Toggles the visibility of toolbars and menus based on the selected areas of expertise including consumer product design, machine design, and mold design.

Z

zip file

A file used for data compression and archiving that contains one or more files that have been compressed to reduce file size.

INDEX

Note to the Reader: Throughout this index **boldfaced** page numbers indicate primary discussions of a topic. *Italicized* page numbers indicate illustrations.

C

G

S